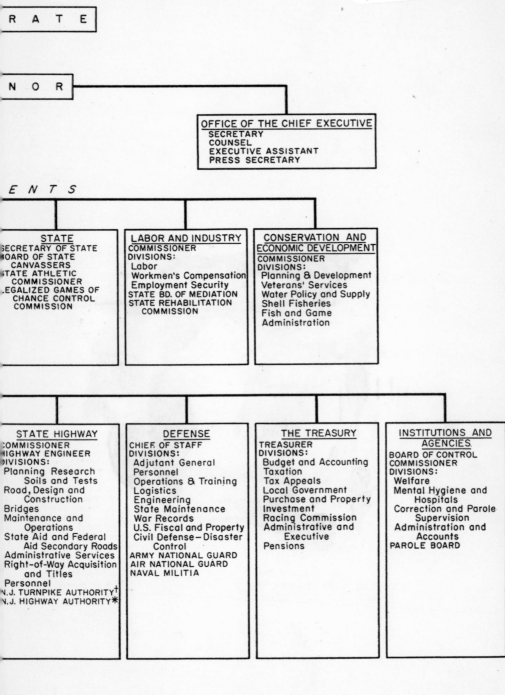

Francis A. Leigh Photograph

The Statehouse, Trenton, New Jersey

AMERICAN COMMONWEALTHS SERIES

W. Brooke Graves, *Editor*

The Government and Administration of New Jersey

AMERICAN COMMONWEALTHS SERIES

W. Brooke Graves, Edit

The
Government and
Administration of

AMERICAN COMMONWEALTHS SERIES

W. Brooke Graves, *Editor*

NEW JERSEY

BENNETT M. RICH

Director, Bureau of Government Research
Rutgers University, New Jersey

THOMAS Y. CROWELL COMPANY
New York

MANUFACTURED IN THE UNITED STATES OF AMERICA

American Commonwealths Series

THE STATES have always been, and they are today, the key units in American federalism. As Professor Charles E. Merriam has said, "The fact is that if we did not have states, it would be necessary to create them, with the same fundamental purpose that is now our goal, of maintaining the balance between liberty and authority, between central and local, and with an adequate division of functions and responsibilities. We need not apologize for our American states."

There have been books and articles in great numbers on most phases of the organization and administration of the Federal government. The number of organizations and the quality of literature relating to municipal government and administration have reached staggering proportions. For some reason not readily apparent, the states—vital though they are to our federal system—have seldom been given the attention they deserve. Students in the state field have long felt the need for more adequate information on government and administration in the individual states, on which few books have been published, and still fewer good ones.

The publication of the American Commonwealths Series represents a long-range attempt to meet this end. Students of state government everywhere will hail this effort to provide parallel studies of the governments of each of the forty-eight states and the four major territories. These studies are being written by carefully selected scholars, each particularly qualified to write on the government of his own state. Many of the authors are political scientists with nation-wide reputations. Working together as members of a team, they are attempting, in many states for the first time

in the history of the state, to present a complete description and analysis
of state governmental institutions and procedures on a sound scholarly basis.

It is believed that these volumes will have a wide variety of uses. They
will provide suitable text material for a growing number of college and
university courses, many of them required by law, dealing with the governments of the individual states. They will provide reference material and
supplementary reading for high school seniors, and for libraries of all types
—public and private, general and specialized, school and college. They
will also provide reliable information on state matters for a large number
of citizens and citizen organizations whose members are in a position to
provide civic leadership—editors, journalists, radio commentators, the
clergy, members of the bar and of the teaching profession, and others, as
well as service clubs, veterans' groups, taxpayers' organizations, chambers
of commerce, and many, many more. These volumes should also be of
use to such women's organizations as the League of Women Voters, the
American Association of University Women, and a large number of
women's literary, civic, and other clubs. Government officials in all three
branches of government, and at all levels, will find in them a wealth of information on all sorts of questions, outside of their own fields of interest
or specialization, on which they need to be informed. Most important of
all, perhaps, is the fact that, as this Series grows, it will provide for scholars
a vast storehouse of comparative information on the history, development,
and present functioning of government in the American states.

W. Brooke Graves

Editor's Introduction

NEW JERSEY has always occupied a unique place among the American states. Small in area (it is forty-fifth in size), it is one of the most populous of the states of the Union. It ranks first in farm income per acre and —in spite of rather limited natural resources—it ranks very high in the value of its manufactured products. Its extraordinary growth and development is in part attributable to its location. This factor has contributed much to the preeminent position which the state has always enjoyed in the field of transportation—first with canals, then with railways, and later with highways. Its proximity to two of the nation's major markets, New York and Philadelphia, has encouraged its great industrial and commercial development.

During the Revolutionary War nearly a hundred battles were fought upon its soil—a circumstance which led to the state being described as the "Cockpit of the Revolution." The position of New Jersey between New York and Philadelphia prompted someone during the period of the Confederation to liken it to a cask tapped at both ends. Woodrow Wilson once referred to New Jersey as "a mediating state." Thus in the past and at present—when it is largely a part of two great metropolitan areas— New Jersey's location has made possible some of its major contribution.

Important as physical factors are in the development of a state, the character of its people is even more significant. The development of New Jersey is no exception. The people of this state have from the beginning leavened conservatism with enlightened concern for the public welfare. One of the original thirteen states, New Jersey was the fourth to adopt a state constitution (July 2, 1776), and the third to ratify the United States Constitution (December 18, 1787). The combination of stability and daring characteristic of New Jersey's political history is illustrated by the fact that the state has had only three constitutions, but that when revisions were made they were far-reaching in their effects. The first constitution remained in force for sixty-eight years, the second for more than one hundred—by which time, of course, revision was more than due.

The new constitution of 1947 made significant improvements in the position of the executive branch and made possible the extensive reorganization of departments and agencies which has since taken place. The tradition of strong executive leadership, evident at least since the days of Woodrow Wilson, appears to have continued. An antiquated court system has been thoroughly reorganized and modernized under able leadership so that, in the words of Glenn R. Winters, Editor of the *Journal* of the American Judicature Society, "America's worst court system" was transformed into "America's best." Further progress was marked in the provision by the 1954 session of the legislature for the establishment of a consolidated legislative service agency. The new constitution pioneered the barring of segregation "in the militia or in the public schools, because of religious principles, race, color, ancestry or national origin." The optional charter plan, extending home rule to New Jersey municipalities, boroughs and towns, marked another significant step forward.

The constitution of New Jersey is not only the newest substantially revised state constitution, but also probably the best now in effect. A decade of hard work on behalf of revision by leading citizens preceded its adoption. This, together with a decade of enlightened government under its provisions, entitles New Jersey to a preeminent position among the states and establishes it as an example which the people and governments of other states might well emulate.

All this makes New Jersey an interesting and significant state about which to write. While, however, Professor Rich was fortunate in having a good subject, we are equally fortunate in having in him such a competent guide and interpreter. During his years as a member of the Faculty of Rutgers University, and as Director of the Bureau of Government Research, he has been continuously engaged in research and writing on problems in the field covered by this volume. As a result of his extensive experience, he has been able to give us the clear and incisive analysis of the institutions of New Jersey government which follows.

W. BROOKE GRAVES

The Library of Congress
March, 1957

Preface

THIS BOOK is intended to be a comprehensive description of the operation of the state government of New Jersey. While the functions performed at present by the state government receive primary emphasis, I have in each instance tried to place those functions in their historical setting. Furthermore, the organizational structure of the government at the various levels has been made secondary to the services performed. Therefore, the discussions of county and municipal governments are more extensive than the single chapters devoted to them may suggest. However, in the chapters relating to the constitution particular attention has been given to the historical developments culminating in the Constitutional Convention of 1947.

The comprehensive reports from their beginnings of some of the state agencies in New Jersey greatly aided the study of their development. Unfortunately, other agencies have issued statistical reports only, and others still, including some of the state's largest, have for years failed to publish any record of their operations. This lack of reports in some areas has made it difficult to present a balanced account of all agencies.

The assistance given me by literally dozens of state officials has been a great source of encouragement and stimulation. I would like to express my gratitude for their help and to note my respect for the high quality of the men and women charged with administering the public business of this state.

Most of the chapters have been reviewed in one stage or another by state officials. I am indebted to the Honorable Albert McCay, Senator from Burlington County, to Mr. Edward B. McConnell, Administrative Director of the Courts, and to Mr. Raymond F. Male, Executive Assistant to the Governor, for reading the chapters relating respectively to the legislature, the courts, and the chief executive. I am grateful also to a considerable number of department heads and staff members who reviewed the chapters relating to their specialties. Almost without exception, revisions large and small were made after the chapters of the manuscript were returned. Nevertheless, any errors of fact or interpretation remain my responsibility.

I should like to acknowledge my appreciation to the agencies and individuals at Rutgers, The State University, who contributed in one way or another to *The Government and Administration of New Jersey*. The Research Council made possible a half-time leave during the academic year 1950–51. In addition, the Council made grants to graduate students who assisted in several ways such as preparing several tables, checking bibliography, and reading proofs. In this connection, I wish to thank William Procacci, Roy Remite, and Philip H. Burch, Jr. I also want to thank the staff of the Rutgers University Library for their ever-courteous assistance in helping me to track down what seems, in retrospect, an almost endless number of state documents, reports, and other materials. I thank Mrs. Beulah H. Scheer for her exceedingly careful typing of the final manuscript. On many occasions I sought the advice of my colleagues in the Bureau of Government Research, Mr. Ernest C. Reock, Jr., and Dr. Stanley H. Friedelbaum who read a number of the chapters in manuscript form and the entire volume in galley proof. I am grateful also to Dr. W. Brooke Graves, for his many constructive suggestions.

Finally I wish to acknowledge the assistance of my wife, Jeanne Birtwhistle Rich, for her remarkable patience and understanding during the long period this project was in process and for her help in typing, proofreading, indexing, and other chores preceding publication.

BENNETT M. RICH

March, 1957

Contents

CHAPTER 1

The State and Its People

THE DAILY LIVING of the people of New Jersey depends to a considerable degree upon the functioning of hundreds upon hundreds of different governmental units. The number does not remain constant for any long period. New ones are created almost every year; occasionally a merger or a dissolution occurs. However, in every unit elected or appointed officers and employees are responsible in large or small degree for the determination and execution of public policy.

THE GOVERNMENTS OF NEW JERSEY

The government of the United States, the state government, and the twenty-one county governments taken together extend to all areas of New Jersey and to all of its people. Within the counties, in 1952, were 567 municipal governments—cities, towns, boroughs, villages, and townships. In addition, there were 548 regular school districts, and 81 special districts. All of these possessed sufficient discretion in the management of their affairs to merit classification as separate governmental units.* Table 1 lists the units by type and by county.

Each separate unit was established to provide one or more governmental services. The special district usually supplies but one service, such as fire protection or a sewerage system, for a relatively small area. The services

---

* Three attributes are essential to merit classification as a separate unit according to the Federal Bureau of the Census: (a) "existence as an organized entity," that is, the unit must have a form of organization and possess some corporate powers; (b) "governmental character," that is, whether officials are popularly elected or appointed by public officials; and (c) "substantial autonomy," that is, whether the officers control operations and revenues. U.S. Bureau of the Census, *Governments in the United States in 1952, State and Local Government Special Studies; Number 31* (Washington, 1953), pp. 6-7.

TABLE 1

GOVERNMENTAL UNITS BY TYPE AND BY COUNTY

County	Total [a]	Municipalities [b]	School Districts [c]	Special Districts [d]
Atlantic	49	23	22	3
Bergen	146	70	71	4
Burlington	94	40	40	13
Camden	80	37	37	5
Cape May	40	16	16	7
Cumberland	39	14	15	9
Essex	48	22	20	5
Gloucester	49	24	23	1
Hudson	35	12	12	10
Hunterdon	53	26	26	0
Mercer	28	13	11	3
Middlesex	55	25	25	4
Monmouth	108	52	48	7
Morris	80	39	38	2
Ocean	62	34	27	0
Passaic	37	16	17	3
Salem	29	15	13	0
Somerset	43	21	20	1
Sussex	48	24	23	0
Union	45	21	21	2
Warren	49	23	23	2
TOTAL	1,219	567	548	81

Source: U.S. Bureau of the Census, *Governments in the United States in 1952, State and Local Government Special Studies; Number 31* (Washington, 1953), p. 37.

[a] The total for each county includes the county. The final total includes the Federal government, the state government, and the twenty-one county governments.

[b] The Federal Bureau of the Census in setting up classifications for the entire United States distinguishes between municipalities and townships. It lists 334 municipalities in New Jersey and 233 townships. Under New Jersey law, the township is also a municipality.

[c] The Federal Bureau of the Census lists 481 school districts. The 67 so-called city school districts operating under Chapter VI are classified as dependent rather than independent units. The number of school districts in the table above conforms with the figures given by the New Jersey Department of Education.

[d] These figures are taken from the Bureau of the Census report. There are many agencies which are designated as districts or authorities. However, unless they have administrative or fiscal autonomy, as described in the footnote on page 1, the Bureau of the Census does not accord them a separate status.

of a school district are broader in character but they are limited also both in scope of function and in extent of jurisdiction. In contrast, the municipalities, the counties, and the state government perform a variety of services in an ever-widening area of action.

POPULATION

The services performed by the units of government are primarily in the interest of the residents of New Jersey. Since 1790, when the first census reported 184,139, the population of the state has increased twenty-six fold, to over 5,000,000. Between 1940 and 1950 the increase amounted to 16.2 per cent, a figure in excess of the 14.5 per cent increase for the country as a whole. In 1900 New Jersey was sixteenth in population rank among the states; now it is eighth, with 3.2 per cent of the nation's population (see Table 2).

TABLE 2

POPULATION GROWTH, AND RANK AMONG THE STATES

Year	Population	Rank
1900	1,883,669	16
1910	2,537,167	11
1920	3,155,900	10
1930	4,041,334	9
1940	4,160,165	9
1950	4,835,329	8

Source: U.S. Bureau of the Census. *U.S. Census of Population: 1950.* Vol. I, *Number of Inhabitants* (Washington, 1952), pp. 1-14.

The increase in population during the decade of the 1940's was not uniform among the counties. Hudson County showed a decline of 0.7 per cent. The largest relative increase was that of Ocean County, which jumped 50.2 per cent; in actual numbers its increase was 18,916. Bergen County had the largest numerical growth, 129,493. Essex, Monmouth, and Union all showed gains of more than 50,000. Essex remained the largest county with over 900,000 inhabitants. Sussex replaced Cape May as the smallest county. Selected population data on a county basis and for the state as a whole are given in Table 3.

The state has six cities of over 100,000 population: Newark, Jersey City, Paterson, Trenton, Camden, and Elizabeth. All but Elizabeth have population densities of over 10,000 per square mile. Beyond the borders of New Jersey, only nineteen cities had an equal population density. The 100 most densely populated communities in the state comprised 3.87 per cent of the area and accounted for 61.9 per cent of the total population. This seemingly intense concentration of the people in a small land area is, however, relatively less than in 1900 when the 100 most densely populated communities comprised only 3.43 per cent of the area but accounted for 71.9 per cent of the population.[1]

A projection of the population growth made by the Department of Conservation and Economic Development in 1952 indicated a possible total of

TABLE 3

SELECTED POPULATION DATA

County	Population, 1950	Per Cent Increase 1940-1950	Population Per Sq. Mile	Estimated Population, 1955
Atlantic	132,399	6.7	230	147,300
Bergen	539,139	31.6	2,314	632,800
Burlington	135,910	40.1	166	161,700
Camden	300,743	17.6	1,361	342,500
Cape May	37,131	28.4	139	42,500
Cumberland	88,597	21.1	176	98,000
Essex	905,949	8.2	7,078	970,500
Gloucester	91,727	27.0	279	106,300
Hudson	647,437	- 0.7	14,388	675,000
Hunterdon	42,736	16.2	98	46,300
Mercer	229,781	16.5	1,008	256,900
Middlesex	264,872	22.0	849	325,300
Monmouth	225,327	39.7	472	257,000
Morris	164,371	30.7	351	195,000
Ocean	56,622	50.2	89	71,000
Passaic	337,093	9.0	1,738	371,500
Salem	49,508	17.1	142	54,200
Somerset	99,052	33.2	323	115,000
Sussex	34,423	16.2	65	38,000
Union	398,138	21.3	3,865	455,000
Warren	54,374	8.4	151	59,000
THE STATE	4,835,329	16.2	643	5,420,800

Source: U.S. Bureau of the Census, *County and City Data Book 1952* (Washington, 1953), p. 282. The estimated population for 1955 was supplied by the Department of Conservation and Economic Development.

5,857,000 by 1960. The largest relative population increases were expected in South Jersey where industrial expansion has been under way for some years.[2]

New Jersey is the most highly urbanized state in the Union. The 4,186,207 persons living in urban areas constitute 86.6 per cent of the population.* Only 13.4 per cent were classified as rural. Although the state has large sparsely populated areas, the tremendous urban concentration resulted in a density of population averaging 643 inhabitants per square mile. This figure, exceeded only by Rhode Island's 749, is twelve

* In the 1950 census an urban area comprised " all persons living in (a) places of 2,500 inhabitants or more incorporated as cities, boroughs, and villages, (b) incorporated towns of 2,500 inhabitants or more except in New England, New York, and Wisconsin, where 'towns' are simply minor civil divisions of counties, (c) the densely settled urban fringe, including both incorporated and unincorporated areas, around cities of 50,000 or more, and (d) unincorporated places of 2,500 inhabitants or more outside any urban fringe." U.S. Bureau of the Census, *U.S. Census of Population: 1950*, Vol. II, *Characteristics of the Population*, Part 30, New Jersey (Washington, 1952), p. xiii.

times the national average density of 51 persons per square mile. By contrast, Nevada has 2, Wyoming 3, and Montana 4 persons per mile.

In 1950 the native-born white population amounted to 3,863,340. There were 629,775 foreign-born white, 318,100 Negroes, and 5,220 of other races.[3] Italians constituted 23.9 per cent of the foreign-born white population, Germans 12 per cent, and Poles 4 per cent. Only 3 per cent of the population twenty-one years of age and over were alien in 1950, a striking contrast to the percentage of 12.2 in 1930.[4]

The population of the state has never been homogeneous; not in colonial times, and especially not during the late nineteenth and early twentieth centuries when in decade after decade tens of thousands of immigrants swelled the census figures. New Jersey has been a genuine "melting pot."

THE ECONOMY

Manufacturing is by far the most important element in the state's economy, accounting in 1950 for 739,860 workers out of a total employed labor force of 1,962,632. The percentage of New Jersey workers employed in manufacturing—37.7—was exceeded only by Rhode Island (44.0), Connecticut (42.6), Michigan (40.9), and New Hampshire (40.4).[5] Industry groups reported by the Bureau of the Census in 1950 are shown in Table 4.

TABLE 4

EMPLOYMENT IN MAJOR INDUSTRY GROUPS 1950

Industry Group	Number Employed	Per Cent
Manufacturing	739,860	37.7
Wholesale and retail trade	350,971	17.9
Transportation, communication and other public utilities	163,332	8.3
Professional and related services	149,865	7.6
Construction	121,897	6.2
Personal services	109,426	5.6
Finance, insurance, and real estate	98,659	5.0
Public administration	80,887	4.1
Business and repair services	51,056	2.6
Agriculture	49,245	2.5
Entertainment and recreation services	16,178	0.8
Mining	4,062	0.2
Forestry and fisheries	2,534	0.1
Industry not reported	24,660	1.3
TOTAL	1,962,632	100.0

Source: U.S. Bureau of the Census, *U.S. Census of Population, 1950*, Vol. II, *Characteristics of the Population*, Part 30, New Jersey (Washington, 1952), pp. 30-52.

The importance of manufacturing may be gauged from the fact that in 1953, with 3.2 per cent of the nation's population, New Jersey's $6,451,-055,000 of manufactured goods amounted to 5.2 per cent of the nation's total. Six states exceeded New Jersey in value of manufactured products: New York, Pennsylvania, Ohio, Illinois, Michigan, and California.[6]

"Diversity" has been declared "the key to the state's industrial success." [7] The products of approximately 11,000 factories are so diverse in character that in 1953 only two groups—electrical goods and machinery, and apparel and needle products—employed as many as 10 per cent of the 854,000 workers engaged in manufacturing.[8] However, no one product dominates the economy. An analysis of the 1947 Census of Manufacturers indicates that New Jersey ranked first among the states in the number employed in the chemical industry; third in the apparel and needle trades and in electrical machinery; sixth in stone, clay, and glass and in coal and petroleum products; seventh in textiles and in transportation equipment; eighth in primary metals, in fabricated metals, and in paper products; ninth in printing and publishing; and tenth in nonelectrical machinery.[9] Manufacturing payrolls accounted for 31.8 per cent of the income payments in 1955.

The increases in manufacturing together with the growing urbanization of the state have had an important effect upon agriculture. On a relative basis agriculture has declined in importance. Notwithstanding the designation "Garden State," New Jersey agricultural income in 1955 accounted for only 1.0 per cent of income payments. This figure compares with 1.0 per cent in New York, 1.4 per cent in Pennsylvania, and 4.7 per cent for the country as a whole.[10]

The estimated New Jersey per capita income in 1955 was $2,311. This sum was exceeded by three states: Delaware, Connecticut, and Nevada.[11]

THE GEOGRAPHY

The geography of New Jersey displays a diversity that is almost unbelievable in view of the fact that New Jersey is the fourth smallest of the states. From the northernmost corner near High Point to the southernmost extremity at Cape May, the distance is 166 miles. The greatest width is 57 miles. The total area of 7,836 square miles is made up of 7,522 square miles of land, and 314 square miles of inland waters. Only three states have a smaller land area: Connecticut, Delaware, and Rhode Island. Eleven have a smaller inland water area.[12]

New Jersey is joined to the mainland of the United States at the New York border. On the west and south are the Delaware River and the Delaware Bay; the boundary to the east is formed by the Hudson River, the Newark and Raritan bays, and the Atlantic Ocean. However, the fact that the state is surrounded on three sides by water does not isolate it.

NEW JERSEY COUNTIES AND CITIES OVER 100,000 POPULATION

On the contrary, New Jersey serves as a corridor between the metropolitan centers of New York and Philadelphia, and between New England and the South and West.

Six physiographic divisions traverse the state from the northeast to the southwest. The two northernmost divisions—the Kittatinny Mountains and the Great Appalachian Valley—cut across Sussex and Warren counties. The third—the New Jersey Highlands—embraces a ten to fifteen mile wide area from the Appalachian Valley to a line running approximately from the northern corner of Bergen County to the northern corner of Hunterdon County. The Piedmont Plain, the fourth division, extends southward from the Highlands to a line bisecting the state approximately at the waist. Two thirds of the state's population live in this area. The Piedmont Plain merges in Middlesex and Mercer counties with the Inner Coastal Plain, the fifth division. The Outer Coastal Plain constitutes the sixth division, and embraces the territory south of a line roughly bisecting Monmouth and Salem counties. The shale and sand, and the relatively flat topography, which prevail in most of the three southern divisions, are in marked contrast to the more rocky surface and the rolling, hilly areas in the three northern divisions.[13]

Notwithstanding the state's high population density, about one fifth of the total land area is unoccupied. In this unoccupied area, there are no inhabitants, and the land is not used for agriculture or industry. Ownership is often unknown and—needless to add—taxes are unpaid. The northern highlands, the coastal salt marshes, and the major portion of the pine barrens have remained relatively untouched by the social and industrial development that has occurred throughout the state in recent decades.

NATURAL RESOURCES

New Jersey has few mineral resources. However, notwithstanding the lack of coal, oil, and natural gas, the state ranked thirty-third in total value of mineral production in 1953. The chief minerals were stone, clay, sand and gravel, peat, ground sand and sandstone, zinc, and iron.

The abundance of clay has made possible the development of a ceramics industry that ranks second or third among the states in dollar value. The annual output of approximately 500 plants amounts to about $300,000,000.[14]

Although New Jersey is short on mineral resources, it has one natural resource of great value—mile upon mile of sandy beach along the Atlantic Ocean. From Raritan Bay to Cape May, a distance of over 120 miles, sun, sand, and surf attract millions of vacationists annually. That the permanent residents do not rely upon nature alone to entice the vacationer is demonstrated by the more than thirty miles of boardwalks. State promotional literature modestly advertises Atlantic City, and its eight-mile boardwalk, as the greatest seashore resort in the Western world. In addition to making possible a large resort industry, the salt waters off New Jersey's shore are productive of fish and shellfish, the harvesting and processing of which serve as the leading means of livelihood in a considerable number of municipalities.

NOTES

[1] N.J. Department of Conservation and Economic Development, *Population Trends and Characteristics in New Jersey* (Trenton, 1954), unpaged.

[2] N.J. Department of Conservation and Economic Development, Research and Statistics Section, *Projection of Population in New Jersey by Counties: 1960* (1952, mimeographed), p. 2.

[3] U.S. Bureau of the Census. *U.S. Census of Population: 1950,* Vol. II, *Characteristics of the Population,* Part 30, New Jersey (Washington, 1952), pp. 30-135. The total population differs slightly from the table above.

[4] *Ibid.,* Chapter B, pp. 30-45, 30-47.

[5] U.S. Bureau of the Census, *County and City Data Book, 1952* (Washington, 1953), p. 4.

[6] U.S. Bureau of the Census, *Statistical Abstract of the United States: 1956* (Washington, 1956), p. 805.

[7] John T. Cunningham, *Made in New Jersey* (New Brunswick: Rutgers University Press, 1954), p. 5.

[8] *New Jersey Industrial Directory, 1954-55* (Union City, 1954), p. xiii.

[9] N.J. Department of Conservation and Economic Development, *An Economic Survey of the State of New Jersey,* prepared by Dr. Homer Hoyt (Trenton, 1950), pp. 26-39.

[10] U.S. Department of Commerce, *Survey of Current Business,* XXXVI (August, 1956), 10, 12.

[11] *Ibid.,* p. 10.

[12] U.S. Bureau of the Census. *U.S. Census of Population: 1950,* Vol. I, *Number of Inhabitants* (Washington, 1952), pp. 1-12.

[13] For a recent description of the physiography of New Jersey and an analysis of the state's population growth, see John E. Brush, *The Population of New Jersey* (New Brunswick: Rutgers University Press, 1956). An excellent county-by-county description may be found in John T. Cunningham, *This is New Jersey* (New Brunswick: Rutgers University Press, 1953).

[14] John H. Koenig and Edward J. Smoke, "The Ceramic Industry in New Jersey," *Review of New Jersey Business,* X (October, 1954), 10-11. See also John T. Cunningham, *Made in New Jersey* (New Brunswick: Rutgers University Press, 1954), pp. 17-23, 97-103.

CHAPTER 2

Early Constitutional Development

In 1947 the people of New Jersey adopted a new constitution, the third basic document in a period of a century and three-quarters. The first, drafted by the Provincial Congress at Burlington in 1776, served the state for sixty-eight years. The second, prepared by delegates to a constitutional convention at Trenton in 1844, was in use 103 years. The present document was approved by the people following the constitutional convention of 1947, which met at the State University in New Brunswick.

Each of these documents reflected the governmental realities of the period. But, at the same time, each was tied closely to developments of the past. The first constitution was no exception. New Jersey had been a going concern for well over a century prior to 1776.

THE COLONIAL PERIOD

The Dutch, the Swedes, and the English were the first to establish settlements in New Jersey. The Dutch settled in Gloucester County as early as 1624, and in the following decades along the Hackensack, Passaic, and Raritan rivers. The earliest Swedish community was established in 1643. Much later, toward the end of the seventeenth century, Swedes and Finns migrated from Pennsylvania into New Jersey.[1]

Early Proprietary Rule

No large-scale development of the area occurred until after 1664 when the English succeeded in wresting control from the Dutch. Almost immediately Charles II made a grant of lands, including New Jersey, to his brother James, Duke of York. In what has been described as a "casual and almost haphazard" manner, the Duke of York conveyed New Jersey to two friends, John Lord Berkeley and Sir George Carteret.[2] The two proprietors issued the "Concessions and Agreements," a document designed to establish a basis of government. There were to be a governor appointed by the proprietors, a group of councillors appointed by the governor, and an elected assembly.[3]

Within a decade Berkeley had sold his interest, and New Jersey was divided in half. By the Quintipartite Deed of 1676, a formal division of the territory was effected along a line drawn from Little Egg Harbor to the northernmost branch of the Delaware River. Subsequently, East New Jersey came to be controlled by twenty-four proprietors and West New Jersey by a much larger number including William Penn. The "Laws, Concessions and Agreements" of 1677 established a form of government for West New Jersey that, from the standpoint of providing representative government and guaranteeing personal liberties, was more liberal than the original Concessions and Agreements.

After 1664 various groups of dissenters, some from England and many from New England, established homes in the state. The New England group objected strenuously to the assumption that governmental authority resided in the proprietors. Some resisted the requirement of an oath of fidelity; others objected to the payment of a quitrent since they had purchased land from Governor Richard Nicolls of New York. Eventually, the proprietors were forced to relinquish their governing power, although they retained their rights in the land. In 1702, after thirty-eight years of proprietary rule, New Jersey became a royal colony united with New York under New York's governor.

Eighteenth-Century Developments

After 1702 there were no longer separate legislative bodies for East Jersey and West Jersey. But the strong feeling of division continued, as evidenced by the legislature's insistence upon meeting alternately in Perth Amboy and in Burlington.[4] The legislative history of the period reflects the continuing struggle between the proprietors, who managed to control the council, and the increasing body of small landowners who controlled the assembly. Both groups, however, were able to unite upon one issue, the desirability of a governor whose principal responsibilities were concerned with New Jersey alone.[5] This unity bore fruit in 1738 when the Crown recognized New Jersey as an independent colony.

Independence from New York did not result in a single-minded and harmonious government. Rivalries had developed among the proprietors, among various religious sects, and between the Scots—who had moved in considerable numbers into the area around Perth Amboy—and the English. West Jersey was more homogeneous, but the stand of its large

Quaker population against bearing arms was a source of frustration to governors charged by the royal officials with defending the province. The militia problem was acute until after the beginning of the wars with France when the necessities of self-defense resulted in a unity of action on matters previously the subject of prolonged dispute.

After the defeat of the French, Great Britain initiated new financial and military policies. Revenues were to be raised from, and troops were to be stationed permanently in, the colonies. New Jersey did not react as quickly as some of the other colonies to the passage of the Stamp Act in 1765. Nevertheless, the assembly in a meeting, which Governor William Franklin declared "illegal, irregular and unconstitutional," sent delegates to the Stamp Act Congress. Later the assembly adopted a series of resolutions identical with those of the Stamp Act Congress. When the act was repealed, both the council and the assembly sent letters of thanks to the king. However, the passage of the Townsend Acts, imposing duties upon a number of products including tea, again set off a series of protests in which New Jersey joined.

The New Jersey legislature also expressed its disapproval over the British decision to quarter troops in the colonies. The assembly declared that this was "as much an Act for laying Taxes on the Inhabitants as the Stamp Act." [6]   Grudgingly, however, funds were voted by the assembly for quarters and supplies.

Over the opposition of Governor Franklin, the assembly followed the example of Virginia in establishing a Committee of Correspondence. Early in 1774 a standing committee was appointed to keep in touch with the other colonies. But events were moving too rapidly for the legislature. A movement was started in Essex for a convention of delegates from all the counties. In July, 1774, seventy-two delegates met in New Brunswick. The first provincial congress, as it was later called, elected representatives to the first Continental Congress. In May, 1775, after the outbreak of hostilities at Lexington and Concord, delegates to a second provincial congress were elected at a series of meetings. Regulations were adopted concerning the organization of the militia, and steps were taken to raise money for defense. A third congress in August set up plans to elect delegates yearly in order that a regularized and continuing body might be available. A fourth provincial congress met in October. A committee of safety was set up to act in the interim prior to the next scheduled meeting in April, 1776.

The provincial assembly was called into session in November, 1775, by Governor Franklin. Resolutions were passed declaring that reports of any movement for independence were groundless. Thus, for a short time, there were two legislative bodies. However, the royal government had lost all influence. Governor Franklin endeavored to call a meeting of the legislature for June 20, 1776. The provincial congress resolved that his summons should be disregarded. On June 21, one day after the royal legislature was supposed to meet, the provincial congress resolved "that a government be formed for regulating the internal police of the Colony . . . . " [7] A new government was about to be born.

THE CONSTITUTION OF 1776

Two days before the adoption of the Declaration of Independence, the members of the New Jersey provincial congress completed the draft of a new constitution. The new charter was drawn up in a period of forty-eight hours.[8] Speed seemed essential since the British fleet had anchored off Sandy Hook. The members of the congress were fully aware of their precarious position. They knew that their efforts might fail. But they had already decided to form a new government and had authorized delegates to the Continental Congress to vote for independence. The constitution that they hastily put together was simple and brief. In large measure it was based upon the documents that had served as the framework of government during the colonial period. The new charter was never ratified by popular referendum. Instead, "by tacit acquiescence and open approbation" it received "the assent and concurrence of the good people of this state . . . . " [9]

Legislative and Executive Branches

The Constitution of 1776 provided for an all-powerful legislature consisting of a Legislative Council and a General Assembly. Representation in both houses was based on locality.* The extraordinary amount of authority lodged with the legislature was the result of a widespread and deep-seated distrust of colonial governors. The governor's complete dependence upon the legislature was obtained by the provision that he be elected annually in joint meeting. The technique of election by the legislature also was used for the selection of the entire judiciary and of the principal administrative officials.[10] The Council was the Court of Pardons as well as the Court of Appeals, the highest court of the state.

The duties imposed upon the governor were more judicial than executive in character. Although he was given the "supreme executive power," the constitution gave no indication as to what was included in this grant. For example, he had no appointive powers whatever, nor did he have the veto power. He was commander-in-chief of the militia. As presiding officer

* Each county was authorized to select one person for the Council and three for the Assembly. However, the legislature could "add to or diminish" the number of members in the Assembly in order to obtain "more equal representation." *N.J. Constitution of 1776*, Art. III.

of the council, the governor was the state's highest judicial officer. The constitution also made him chancellor and surrogate general, both judicial offices.

Deficiencies of the First Constitution

A significant defect of the constitution was its failure to recognize a new development in political theory that was soon to be accepted in every one of the United States, namely, the doctrine of the separation of powers. There was no clear-cut distinction concerning the functions properly performed by the legislative, executive, and judicial organs of the government. Instead, the legislature either performed or controlled the functions of all three branches.[11]

A second defect of the constitution was the lack of an amending clause. For a time the argument was advanced that none was necessary since the legislature could make any changes it desired. Supporters of this position cited the fact that the constitution placed so few restrictions on the legislature; the only limitations were contained in the oath which each legislator took, to preserve annual elections, trial by jury, and freedom of religion.* Those who favored "legislative omnipotence" argued that the New Jersey legislature was a copy of the British Parliament. This theory came to have less and less significance as the practices of other states and the influence of the new Federal Constitution were brought to bear on New Jersey. Instead, there arose an insistent demand that the acts passed by the legislature be statutory rather than constitutional and that a procedure be established whereby the people themselves could be heard on fundamental questions. The theory that a constitution was superior to ordinary law was rather generally accepted by 1800 and was asserted by the chief justice of the New Jersey Supreme Court in 1804.†

The Constitution of 1776 contained no separate bill of rights, and this omission was used as an argument for revision. Objections also were made to the qualifications for voting and for membership in the legislature, to the character of legislative appointments, and to the dependence of the judiciary upon the legislature.[12] One especially practical reason for a new constitution was cited by Governor William Pennington in his messages of 1840 and 1841. He called for the separation of the offices of governor and chancellor on the ground that the increase in judicial business made desirable "a distinct, permanent officer wholly withdrawn from political

---

* The articles on freedom of religion did not guarantee complete freedom. Article XIX implied that only Protestants were eligible for office.

† "Now to say that the legislature can alter or change such a constitution, that they can do away that very principle which at the same time gives and limits their power, is in my view a perfect absurdity. It is making the creature greater than the creator. It is establishing despotism without limitation and without control." Opinion of Chief Justice Andrew Kirkpatrick, *State* v *Parkhurst*, 9 N.J.L. (IV Halsted), 427, 433 (1802).

influences." * Popular demand for a convention continued to grow until finally in 1844, at the request of Governor Daniel Haines, long an advocate of revision, a bill was passed calling for the election of delegates to a constitutional convention.†

THE CONSTITUTION OF 1844

The Convention

The act calling for the constitutional convention left no time for lost motion. Passed on February 23, 1844, the law set March 18 as the date for electing delegates, and August 13 as the date for submitting the revised constitution to popular vote.[13] The number of delegates was to equal the membership of, and to represent the constituency of, the General Assembly. Delegates were paid two dollars per day plus a travel allowance.‡

Once the decision was made to hold a convention, party bickering was laid aside and an agreement was worked out by the central committees of the Democratic and Whig parties whereby the delegates would be divided equally between the two parties. The plan worked well except in Monmouth County, which sent five Democrats instead of four Democrats and one Whig. Of a total of fifty-eight delegates thirty were Democrats and twenty-eight were Whigs.

The delegates were able and experienced. Almost 60 per cent had had legislative service. There were three former governors and three Supreme Court justices. Seven delegates had served in Congress.

The convention was in session from May 14 through June 29.§ General

---

* Pennington, however, did not favor a constitutional convention. ". . . I believe it safer to submit to the inconveniences of our present charter, rather than incur the hazards of a radical change." N.J. *Minutes of Assembly*, 1842, p. 18.

† Efforts to change the Constitution of 1776 were fruitless. A proposal by the legislature for a convention was defeated by popular vote in 1800, and a proposed amendment changing the date of convening the legislature was similarly defeated in 1819. Charles R. Erdman, Jr., *The New Jersey Constitution of 1776* (Princeton: Princeton University Press, 1929), ch. IV.

‡ The state treasurer reported that $8,059.99 was "paid for convention to prepare constitution." N.J. *Minutes of Assembly*, 1845, p. 274.

§ No official record of the convention was maintained. Shortly after the delegates assembled the question of employing a reporter to record the debates was argued for five hours and defeated. A reporter for *The Trenton State Gazette* gave an amusing account of the vacillations on the question by the Chief Justice of the New Jersey Supreme Court, Joseph C. Hornblower: "Judge Hornblower, who voted against it in the morning, moved a reconsideration, but as the rules required two thirds to reconsider, he withdrew his motion. His unsteadiness called forth some animadversions, to which he replied in a curious, and, as I understand, a characteristic speech. He said he was originally against it—that on conversing with the mover, he had changed his mind, and come to the conclusion that the course was a proper one—that on listening to the first part of the debate, he recurred to his original opinion against it—that the eloquent speech of the gentleman from Mercer (Mr. Green) had again unsettled his mind, and he had moved to lay it on the table acceptance of the weaknesses of the Constitution of 1776 was reflected in the formation of the eight committees to draft the new document. The first three committees were to consider the legislative, executive, and judicial branches. The others considered appointment and tenure, suffrage and the time of meeting of the legislature, amendments, miscellaneous questions, and a bill of rights.

Major Provisions of the Constitution

Although there was general agreement that the structure of the new constitution should recognize the theory of the separation of powers, there was much debate over the degree to which the legislature should surrender its prerogatives. For example, the governor was given a veto, but a majority of the membership, the same number required to pass a bill initially, could override his veto. The people, rather than the upper house, were to elect the governor, and his term of office was increased threefold. But he was not permitted to succeed himself. The appointing power was divided between the governor and the legislature. The joint meeting device was retained. By this means the legislature selected the treasurer, prison officials, and common pleas judges.

There was no recognition of the need for a governor who would be the state's chief administrator. Indeed, fear was expressed that, with the separation of the governor's executive and judicial duties and the setting up of a permanent chancellor, the governorship would be of so little importance as to be unattractive.* This view is understandable after an examination of the executive functions performed. In his annual message to the legislature in 1843 Governor Pennington reported on the inconveniences suffered by New Jersey shippers as the result of a quarrel between New York and Virginia, the presentation of public documents to the American Atheneum at Paris, and resolutions from several states such as one from Massachusetts protesting the annexation of Texas.[14] He presented also the reports of the trustees of the school fund, the quartermaster, the commissioners of pilotage, and the keeper of the state prison. The ordinary operating expenses of the government were $62,736.37.[15] With so few of the service and regulatory functions which the state later was to assume, there

---

till he could bestow on it further consideration—that this motion failing, he came to the conclusion to vote against it, and that he moved a reconsideration out of respect for the large minority who had voted for it. What a catalogue of changes! If ever I am tried for my life before his honor, I shall be very careful to procure counsel who are able to make the 'worse appear the better reason.' " Proceedings, op. cit., p. 49.

* "We must presume the Governor to be a respectable man. He may not be a Lawyer, and I don't think the Governor ever will be a Lawyer again. I mean a practicing Lawyer, for the office will not be worth the acceptance of a man with a good practice." Speech of delegate Peter Clark, ibid., p. 185.

seemed to be no urgent reason for strengthening the governor's administrative hand. Nor was the convention ready to do so. The only operating problem of any size was the supervision of the state prison, and this was placed in the hands of a keeper selected by the legislature in joint meeting.

The separation of the governor from judicial duties was a subject needing little debate. Implementation of the theory of the separation of powers also meant taking away from the upper house its judicial function as the court of last resort. This separation proved a more difficult problem. The Court of Appeals (the Legislative Council) was "not the Court for the correction of Errors but the Court of high errors!" [16] The Committee on the Judiciary Department proposed that the members of the Council (Senate) no longer sit as judges but that the Supreme Court sit with six lay judges selected "for their integrity, their experience, and their plain, practical, sterling common sense." [17] This novel plan was accepted. The governor, with the Senate's consent, was authorized to appoint the chancellor, the justices of the Supreme Court and the judges of the Court of Errors and Appeals. The legislature was permitted to retain its control over appointments to the common pleas courts. Existing statute law was drawn upon heavily to complete the court structure.

Existing law was the source of much that went into the constitution. The suffrage article, the clause prohibiting imprisonment for debt, and the article concerning the election of militia officers had their origins in statute law. Neighboring state constitutions were utilized to some degree, the best example being the amending article, which was taken in large part from the Pennsylvania constitution. Of course, the basic source was the original New Jersey constitution.

The convention produced a document that met the major objections to the old constitution. But, in spite of the emphasis upon the theory of the separation of powers, the delegates failed to make a clear-cut break in many areas. For example, the governor retained judicial power as a member of the Court of Pardons. The legislature retained the executive power of appointment over many offices. Although the authority of the legislature was curbed to some degree, that body remained by far the most powerful of the three branches of government.

On June 28, after seven weeks of debate, during which the convention was in session thirty-seven days, the delegates adopted the constitution by a vote of fifty-five to one.* The following day the document was presented to Governor Daniel Haines. The constitution was published once each

---

* The delegate voting "no" objected to the retention of the system of county representation in the Senate. One member asked to be excused from voting. Isaac H. Williamson, the first president of the convention, was forced by illness to leave a few days before adjournment. The vice-president, Alexander Wurts, succeeded to the presidency. *Ibid.*, pp. 603-11.

week for six weeks in the newspapers. On August 13 it was ratified by almost a six to one margin; the popular vote was 20,276 to 3,526.

AMENDMENTS TO THE 1844 CONSTITUTION

Although 103 years elapsed before New Jersey witnessed another constitutional convention, less than a decade passed before the governor and the legislature agreed to the creation of two special commissions designed to propose amendments. In his annual message to the legislature in January, 1852, Governor George F. Fort recommended "preliminary steps . . . to effect a reform in the practice and proceedings of the courts of justice in this state." [18] The following month, an act was passed creating the first of New Jersey's seven constitutional commissions. It was a limited commission of "three discreet" members confined by law to the consideration of amendments relating to the courts and to increasing the number of elective officials.[19] However, the commission's proposals were unacceptable to the legislature. A similar body was created in 1854. It met a similar fate.[20]

The next two decades saw a growing dissatisfaction with the means adopted by the legislature to meet the increasing demands of a rapidly growing state. As early as 1853 Governor Fort had called attention to the evils arising out of requests by private groups for special legislation. "Attention to the *public business* should be of paramount consideration," he observed, "and special legislation avoided where it is possible to embrace measures, proper in themselves, within the scope of a general act . . . . " *

Amendments of 1873

By 1873 special legislation accounted for nine tenths of the business of the legislature. In calling for an end to the system, Governor Joel Parker pointed out the great disparity between public and private legislation: "The general public laws passed at the last session are contained in about one hundred pages of the printed volume, while the special and private laws occupy over twelve hundred and fifty pages of the same book." [21] Again a constitutional commission was created to propose a remedy.[22] This time no limitation was placed upon the deliberations of the fourteen commissioners. Their recommendations were accepted in large part by the two succeeding legislatures and twenty-eight amendments were placed before the people.[23] All were adopted at a special election in 1875.

---

* N.J. *Minutes of Assembly*, 1853, Appendix, p. 15. Governor Fort pointed out that in nine years 356 special charters of incorporation had been passed together with eighty supplemental acts. The number of special acts of incorporation was thirty-five in 1845. In 1851 and again in 1852 the number was seventy. *Ibid.*. p. 16.

The more significant changes made by the amendments were as follows: *

1. Absentee voting authorized for persons in the armed services.

2. Appointive powers of the governor increased to include the common pleas judges and the keeper of the prison.

3. Property assessed "under general laws, and by uniform rules, according to its true value."

4. Free public schools authorized.

5. Legislative salaries increased from $3 per day for forty days and $1.50 thereafter to $500 per annum.

6. Restrictions placed upon the passage of private, local, and special laws.

Amendments, 1875-1947

From 1875 to 1947 the constitution was amended on but three occasions.† The first of these occurred as a result of the evil influence that racing interests exerted over the legislature. A political revolution occurred in 1893 and a new legislature was elected pledged to effect reform. By a close popular vote, an amendment forbidding gambling was adopted in 1897.[24] At the same time, an amendment was passed prohibiting recess appointments to persons who previously had failed of confirmation by the Senate. Thirty years later, in 1927, an amendment was adopted authorizing the legislature to pass general laws that would permit municipalities to enact zoning ordinances. The last amendment, adopted in 1939, permitted pari-mutuel betting at race tracks.

THE DRIVE FOR REVISION IN THE 1940'S

The signal for what was to become a seven-year battle for constitutional revision was given by Governor Charles Edison in his inaugural address of January 21, 1941. He called for a convention to consider the "fundamental troubles with New Jersey's governmental system."

You legislators are aware of the reasons why revamping of the State Constitution is needed.

---

* Not included in the amendments proposed by the legislature were a number of recommendations by the commission such as (1) debt limits for county and city governments, (2) publication of all bills one day before passage, and (3) a legislative oath renouncing the acceptance of bribes.

† During the period from 1875 to 1939 several efforts were made to change the constitution either by amendment or by general revision. Constitutional commissions were appointed in 1881, 1894, and 1905. The latter two were limited to judicial reform. On five occasions between 1881 and 1913 the Assembly passed bills calling for a constitutional convention. They were blocked in the Senate because of fear that the convention would change the system of representation in the upper house. John E. Bebout, "New Task for a Legislature," *National Municipal Review*, XXXIII (1944), 18. For a list of amendments approved by at least one house see Erdman, The New Jersey Constitution, *op. cit.* pp. 31-36.

We have more than four-score independent, or semi-independent State agencies, some with their own incomes and budgets, some which are little governments on their own.

No one, therefore, can say just what the government of New Jersey costs. No one can get a complete picture of what is going on.

The Governor should be given effective control over this administrative conglomeration. The eighty agencies should be consolidated into no more than twenty and a Governor's cabinet drawn from their executives.

A veto power that amounts to something should be given to the Governor. He is the one State official elected by all of the citizens and should have power to stop faulty, partisan or sectional legislation.

The Governor's term should be changed to four years and the elections should be held in years other than Presidential election ones to avoid confusion of National and State issues.

The existing representative inequality that permits a majority of the Senate to be formed from the representatives of fifteen per cent of the people should be eradicated. If the two-house Legislature be retained, which is a debatable question, the term of Senators should be lengthened to four years. The term of Assemblymen should be two years.

A new Constitution should be more amendable.

The needlessly confusing system of courts should be altered to produce an arrangement that would be simple, responsible and less costly.[25]

Constitutional Commission of 1941

The influence of the new governor coupled with pressure from civic groups and individual legislators interested in revision caused the legislature to create New Jersey's seventh constitutional commission.* The commission was composed of seven persons. Two were appointed by the House, two by the Senate, and two by the governor. The seventh was selected by the six appointed commissioners.†

In certain areas the commission recommended sweeping changes. An entirely new court system was suggested designed to obtain unification and centralized administration. The governor was given greatly increased control over the administrative structure. He was authorized to allocate, by executive order, all executive agencies among nine named departments. His appointive power was increased, his term extended, and in many other respects his position was considerably enhanced.

---

* A large number of civic, business, and labor groups coordinated their efforts through the New Jersey Committee for Constitutional Convention. The name was later changed to Committee for Constitutional Revision.

† L., 1941, Joint Resolution No. 2, p. 1084. The members of the Commission were: Robert C. Hendrickson, Chairman (later United States Senator); Walter S. Freund; Crawford Jamieson; James Kerney, Jr., editor, *Trenton Times;* John F. Sly, Director, Princeton Surveys; Walter D. Van Riper (later Attorney-General); Authur T. Vanderbilt (later Chief Justice of the New Jersey Supreme Court); Charles R. Erdman, Jr. (later Commissioner of Conservation and Economic Development), Secretary.

The commission failed to touch upon a number of basic problems, such as the question of rural versus urban representation in the legislature, the troublesome "true value" tax clause, or the clause on gambling that permitted big-time betting at race tracks while forbidding a church's or firemen's bingo game. Nor was the commission representing the best thinking of the times when it carried over the prohibition on a second term for the executive and required limited biennial sessions of the legislature.[26]

The commission contributed to its own failure by an undiplomatic display of political bias. No member of the commission represented the large body of Democrats who recognized the leadership of Mayor Frank Hague of Jersey City. This group's natural suspicion of the commission was reinforced by certain recommendations that seemed designed especially to harass the Hague forces. One of these, the requirement of ten years experience as a member of the bar before appointment to the superior court, would have resulted in Hague's son being removed from the top court of the state. Thus the recommendations of the commission met with mixed reactions. The legislature blocked a unique recommendation of the commission that would have authorized that body to submit a revised constitution to the people in November, 1942. Instead, lengthy hearings were held by a joint legislative committee in the summer of 1942, and a decision was made to abandon revision efforts while so many men were away at war.[27]

The Legislature in the Role of a Convention (1944)

This decision did not sit well with many citizen groups actively promoting revision. A bill was introduced in the next session calling for a referendum at the general election of 1943 on the question of authorizing the legislature to sit as a convention. The bill was passed in both houses but only after Walter E. Edge, who was about to become the Republican nominee for governor, exerted pressure on the Senate.[28] Even then, the Senate's acceptance was obtained only after the passage of amendments forbidding changes either in the bill of rights or in the system of legislative representation.[29] By a decisive majority of 154,000, the people voted to set the revision machinery in motion.

The constitution produced by the legislature was essentially the draft of the commission of 1941-42. Adoption of the constitution by the legislature was brought about in large part by Governor Edge who held up all patronage until the work on the proposed constitution was completed. The vote in the legislature was on a strictly partisan basis.[30]

The campaign for revision in 1944 proved to be one of the most bitter in the state's history. The presidential duel between Roosevelt and Dewey was a matter of secondary importance. Every alleged weakness in the proposed constitution was exploited by Mayor Frank Hague who led the forces fighting revision.

Certain clauses that seemed to be aimed directly at Hague were used by him with good effect to arouse opposition all over the state. One of these, which gave the governor broad investigative powers, was cited as a threat to every municipal official.[31]   The State Grange advertised against any change because of the concern of farmers over the future of the Board of Agriculture.   Both the Congress of Industrial Organizations and the American Federation of Labor came out in opposition because of the failure to spell out sufficiently the rights of labor.   Uncertainty was expressed also over the status of women's rights.   One by one, other interest groups sided with the opposition.

In addition to traditional arguments against the added executive powers given the governor, there was much concern expressed over his power to control court personnel.   Edge denied that he would abandon the tradition of bipartisan appointments, but the charge was made that he intended to appoint an all-Republican court, which would hold office for life.[32]   In full-page newspaper advertisements, Hague argued that the revision was the work of the railroad lobby and that taxes on railroads would be eliminated if it were not defeated.   This would come about, he argued, as the result of the elimination of the "true value" tax clause and the substitution of the phrase "standards of value" for the assessment of property.

In the closing hours of the campaign, Catholics were importuned to vote against revision.   They were told that the exemption of Church property from taxation would be eliminated, that the divorce laws would be relaxed, and that the sanctity of the confessional would be endangered.[33]

On this disturbing note the campaign ended.   The revision forces suffered a decisive defeat.   Out of 1,453,391 persons voting on the referendum, 789,956 favored retention of the old constitution while 663,435 voted for revision.[34]

NOTES

[1] New Jersey History Committee, *Outline History of New Jersey* (New Brunswick: Rutgers University Press, 1950), pp. 9-11.

[2] Charles M. Andrews, *The Colonial Period of American History, The Settlements III* (New Haven: Yale University Press, 1937), pp. 179-180.

[3] *New Jersey Archives,* 1st Series, I, 28.

[4] Edgar Jacob Fisher, *New Jersey as a Royal Province 1738 to 1776* (New York: Columbia University, 1911), p. 103.

[5] See Edwin P. Tanner, *The Province of New Jersey 1664-1738* (New York: Columbia University, 1908), pp. 232-42.

[6] Fisher, *op. cit.,* p. 432.

[7] *Ibid.,* p. 492.

[8] Charles R. Erdman, Jr., *The New Jersey Constitution of 1776* (Princeton: Princeton University Press, 1929), pp. 25-42.   This book covers thoroughly constitutional developments from the period of the Revolution to the Constitution of 1844.

[9] Inaugural address of Governor William Livingston, Sept. 11, 1776, *New Jersey Archives,* 2nd Series, I, 201.

10 N.J. *Constitution of 1776*, art. XII. See Richard P. McCormick, *Experiment in Independence* (New Brunswick: Rutgers University Press, 1950), pp. 69-102.

11 For an excellent treatment of the political theories underlying the Constitution of 1776 and the Constitution of 1844, see John Bebout, *The Making of the New Jersey Constitution, Reprint of Introduction to the Proceedings of the New Jersey State Constitutional Convention of 1844 Together with a New Foreword* (Trenton: MacCrellish and Quigley Co., 1945).

12 For an extended statement of the faults of the constitution see William Griffith, *Eumenes: Being a Collection of Papers Written for the Purpose of Exhibiting Some of the More Prominent Errors and Omissions of the Constitution of New Jersey, as Established on the Second Day of July, One Thousand Seven Hundred and Seventy-Six; and to Prove the Necessity of Calling a Convention for Revision and Amendment* (Trenton: G. Craft, 1799).

13 *Proceedings of the New Jersey State Constitutional Convention of 1844, Compiled and Edited by the New Jersey Writers' Project of the Work Projects Administration with an Introduction by John Bebout.* Sponsored by the New Jersey State House Commission, 1942, p. 8.

14 N.J. *Minutes of the Assembly*, 1843, pp. 14-18.

15 *Ibid.*, p. 78.

16 Statement of Chief Justice Hornblower, *Proceedings . . . , op. cit.*, p. 230.

17 *Ibid.*, p. 232.

18 N.J. *Minutes of Assembly*, 1852, Appendix, p. 17.

19 Laws of New Jersey (hereinafter cited as L.), 1852, p. 546.

20 L., 1854, pp. 544-45.

21 N.J. *Documents of the Ninety-seventh Legislature of the State of New Jersey and the Twenty-ninth under the New Constitution* (Jersey City, 1873), p. 31.

22 L., 1873, p. 844.

23 For the report of the commission, see N.J. *Senate Journal*, 1874, pp. 49-59. For the amendments, see *ibid.*, pp. 782-87.

24 William Edgar Sackett, *Modern Battles of Trenton*, Vol. II (New York: The Neale Publishing Co., 1914), p. 44.

25 N.J. *Minutes of Assembly*, 1941, pp. 49-50.

26 For an analysis of the commission's proposals, see Bennett M. Rich, "Convention or Commission?" *National Municipal Review*, XXXVII (1948), 133-39.

27 N.J. *Record of Proceedings Before the Joint Committee of the New Jersey Legislature to Ascertain the Sentiment of the People as to Change in the New Jersey Constitution.* 1942. For the majority and minority reports of the Joint Legislative Committee, see pp. 868-83. For the Report of the Commission on Revision, see pp. 909-58.

28 Walter Evans Edge, *A Jerseyman's Journal* (Princeton: Princeton University Press, 1948), p. 258.

29 L., 1943, ch. 217, p. 575.

30 See notes by John E. Bebout in the *National Municipal Review*, XXXIII (1944), 88, 200.

31 *The New York Times*, November 4, 1944, p. 12.

32 *Ibid.*, Nov. 3, 1944, p. 17.

33 *Ibid.*, Nov. 4, 1944, p. 12; Nov. 8, p. 9; Edge, *op. cit.*, pp. 283-84. See also the files of the *New Jersey Law Journal* for October and November, 1944.

34 *Manual of the Legislature of New Jersey*, 1945, p. 679.

CHAPTER 3

The Constitution of 1947

FOR TWO YEARS following the bitter struggle of 1944, constitutional revision seemed a dead issue. But the corpse sprang suddenly to life when Governor Alfred E. Driscoll, in January, 1947, devoted a portion of his inaugural address to the necessity for a new constitution. He proposed a popularly elected convention.

THE CONSTITUTIONAL CONVENTION

Before any bill calling for a convention was introduced in the legislature, conferences were held between the Governor and party leaders to work out such matters as a time schedule, the place of meeting, and the number of delegates. A tight schedule was arranged: nomination papers were to be filed by April 14, the vote on the question of calling a convention and the election of the convention delegates to take place on June 3, the convention to be convened on June 12 and to be adjourned by September 12, and the convention's proposals to be ratified or rejected by the voters on November 4.

To remove the convention as far as possible from a political atmosphere, the New Brunswick campus of Rutgers, The State University, was selected as the site.* An early agreement to elect sixty delegates on the same basis as the sixty representatives in the General Assembly met with opposition from representatives of the rural counties. To appease their fear of urban

* A sincere effort was made to keep partisan politics at a minimum; nevertheless, decisions of this kind had their political implications. The support of the Democrats, so lacking in 1944, was needed to assure revision. One means to obtain needed cooperation was to hold the convention in Middlesex County, a Democratic stronghold.

domination, an extra delegate from each county was added making a total of eighty-one.

Convention Call

The bill calling for the convention followed the general pattern of the law passed in 1944, which excluded certain subjects from consideration. But in 1944 there had been no fear that anyone would contemplate violating the law. The legislators themselves were drafting the constitution. They were the ones most interested in preserving their status. On the other hand, in 1947, once the legislature passed the bill calling for the convention, it had nothing further to say. If the rural counties were to maintain their advantage in the system of representation, it was necessary to tie the hands of the delegates as tightly as possible.

Doubt existed concerning the constitutionality of an act placing limits upon a constitutional convention, since the proposals of a convention were declared to be the expression of a sovereign people. Thus, the law providing for the referendum was worded so that when the people cast a vote in favor of a constitutional convention, they were also binding the delegates to take no action on the problems of (1) the territorial boundaries of the counties and (2) the basis of representation in the General Assembly and in the Senate. The ballot was as follows:

> For such a constitutional convention, in-
> structed to retain the present territorial
> limits of the respective counties and the
> present basis of representation in the
> Legislature.
> Against such a constitutional convention.

In order further to assure that the forbidden subject would not be acted upon, each delegate was required to take an oath that he would "abide by the instructions of the people as contained in the referendum . . . . " [1] As a final measure of protection, designed to satisfy the most suspicious legislators, the convention was prohibited from arranging for the submission of the constitution to the people until the secretary of state had certified that the document complied "with the instructions of the people." With these safeguards the bill sailed through the legislature by a vote of 20-0 in the Senate and 59-0 in the House.

Election of the Delegates

Taking a leaf from the record of the convention of 1844, Governor Driscoll suggested that, in order to keep party politics at a minimum, delegates be selected on a bipartisan basis. This was done in thirteen of the twenty-one counties. Party leaders agreed on a slate of candidates. For example, in Democratic Middlesex County, which was entitled to four delegates, the Democratic organization selected two candidates and the Republican organization selected two. A fifth candidate who ran as an independent was snowed under. In Hudson County, seven Democrats and three Republicans were selected. However, in Essex County thirteen Republicans were selected since the county organization refused to divide the honors with the minority party. But the net result over the state as a whole was a gain for the Democrats. This gesture on the part of the party in power, the Republican Party, had its effect in the convention's initial operations, which were remarkably free from party strife.

Indeed, the solicitude for the interests of the minority party paid immediate dividends. Almost no opposition developed to the calling of a convention. Mayor Hague, speaking as the state's Democratic leader, declared in favor of the convention—a gesture that was not meaningless as later evidenced by his own county's fifteen to one affirmative vote. Civic groups were almost unanimous in their endorsement of the project. Convinced that they had everything to gain and nothing to lose, the voters approved the holding of the convention by a ratio of five to one.* At the same time they elected the required eighty-one delegates.† The party distribution was Republicans fifty-four, Democrats twenty-three, and Independents four.

The high level of ability of most of the delegates reflected the general desire for an able group to undertake so important a task. The delegates by no means represented a cross section of the state in terms of education, economic status, or occupation. Of the eighty-one delegates, fifty were lawyers, twenty-one of whom were either active or retired judges. Twenty-five delegates were serving or had served in the state legislature. One had been a United States Senator. Sixteen had teaching experience. Eight were women, one of whom was the wartime commander of the women marines. There were one doctor, one labor leader, an engineer, a university president, two bankers, two stockbrokers, and the president of Johnson and Johnson. Other delegates represented a variety of interests.

Preparatory Work

In order to expedite the opening of the convention, a considerable amount of preparatory work was necessary. Constitutional materials to which the delegates could refer had to be obtained, and the physical arrangements needed to keep the convention going had to be set up. It

* The vote was 275,209 to 53,280. *Manual of the Legislature of New Jersey,* 1948, p. 658. To set apart the act of calling a constitutional convention from the primary election, which was held the same day, the law forbade the use of voting machines on the constitutional issue. Instead, specially colored paper ballots were required. L., 1947, ch. 8, p. 24.

† The thoroughness of party control in New Jersey is evidenced by the fact that for 81 positions there were only 118 candidates. *The New York Times,* June 1, 1947, p. 40.

seemed advisable also to work out a preliminary plan of organization. Research materials were prepared by a group of professors, attorneys, and state officials.

The physical arrangements for the convention were under the general supervision of the director of finance and taxation. The desks of the legislators were moved from the State House to the convention hall for the use of the delegates. A public address system enabled the delegates to be heard without moving more than a few feet from their desks. To supplement and to assist the stenographic staff, all of whom were state employees on loan from various agencies, a sound-recording device was installed. The proceedings in all general sessions and committee hearings were recorded and mimeographed.*

Organization of the Convention

Governor Driscoll called together a representative group of delegates on June 9 to make preliminary plans for the charter meeting. Rules, which had been previously prepared, were discussed and agreement was reached on the number and scope of committees.

The delegates met in the gymnasium of the State University on June 12 at 10 A.M. After a pageant depicting scenes representative of eras from 1776 to the present, the convention got down to work. The value of the organizational planning on the part of the Governor and his staff was soon evident. Within three hours working time the formalities incident to the certification and swearing in of the delegates were concluded; the Governor, who presided, had presented his views of the convention's task; a president, two vice-presidents, and a secretary had been elected; rules had been adopted for the governance of the convention; and a time table had been agreed upon for the meetings. This procedure was in sharp contrast to the opening of the 1844 convention when several hours were consumed in a debate over the question of opening the meeting with prayer.

The convention recessed for one week in order to permit Dr. Robert C.

* The decision to record hearings as well as the full convention meetings was made at the last minute, and there was little time to select and test a battery of stenographers. Instead, several department heads were given instructions from the Governor's office to furnish stenographic and clerical personnel. Some of those ordered to report were inexperienced in taking continuous dictation at the normal speaking rate and, as a consequence, some of the earliest hearings were incomplete. The number of stenographers at first was insufficient to cope with five or six simultaneous hearings all of which lasted several hours per day. This meant that each stenographer had to take continuous dictation for sometimes as much as four or five hours, leaving little time to transcribe the take. The editing, stencil cutting, and mimeographing operations were consequently delayed. However, by the time the convention was ready to begin general debate, August 11, all hearings had been mimeographed, indexed, and bound, and a copy of each committee's proceedings placed on every delegate's desk. The hearings ranged in size from 330 double-spaced legal-sized pages for the Committee on Taxation and Finance to 762 for the Committee on the Judiciary. The deliberations of the committees were not recorded.

Clothier, President of Rutgers University and President of the Convention, to appoint nine standing committees. Eleven delegates were appointed to each one of the following committees: Rights, Privileges, Amendments and Miscellaneous Provisions; Judiciary; Legislative; Taxation and Finance; Executive, Militia and Civil Officers. Seven were appointed to each of the remainder: Submission and Address to the People; Arrangement and Form; Rules, Organization, and Business Affairs; Credentials, Printing, and Authentication of Documents.

The practice of meeting in full session every Tuesday morning was adopted in order to take up any problems affecting the convention as a whole. Committee meetings were held Tuesdays, Wednesdays, and Thursdays. Every person who wanted to testify had an opportunity to do so at the public hearings that began on June 23.

After the hearings were completed, the committees drew up tentative proposals. These were distributed in order to obtain public reaction. Additional hearings were held before final revision and submission to the convention.* The period from August 11 to August 28 was one of general debate on the floor of the convention. On September 10, two days before the deadline specified by law, the proposed constitution was signed by the delegates and presented to the Governor.

Obtaining Popular Support

The delegates were acutely conscious of the fact that their summer's labor would be in vain unless the people were convinced of the worth of the new document. As early as July 15, the convention had acted to create a Committee on Public Relations and Information "to furnish to the citizens of New Jersey information on the discussions, debates, and conclusions of this Convention through the medium of the press, radio and such other facilities as may be available." [2] The committee was empowered to function, through a paid staff, after the close of the convention. A special information service was set up to prepare materials. The daily newspapers had their own representatives in attendance at the convention so that the work of the information service was chiefly for the benefit of the weekly newspapers. Special recorded programs were made for the use of radio stations.

One of the minor problems of the convention was the distribution of funds between the newspapers and the radio. About $150,000 had been used in 1944 on newspaper advertising. Mindful of the adverse vote at that time, the convention decided to spend no large sum on this medium.

---

* Two of the committees failed to follow this commendable procedure. The Committee on Taxation and Finance and the Committee on Rights, Privileges, Amendments, and Miscellaneous Provisions held additional hearings only after their proposals were printed and ready for submission to the convention. Neither committee made any last-minute change.

However, the newspapers obtained a reversal of the decision and $80,000 was appropriated for newspaper and radio advertising.

After the convention was concluded, the newspapers carried a series of six one-quarter-page advertisements outlining in simple language the major changes in the constitution. An unusual feature of the radio broadcasts was a series of spot announcements. Nine stations carried six one-minute comments per day. During the period October 8 to November 3, about 1,650 of these announcements were broadcast.

Many of the delegates participated vigorously in the campaign for ratification. The subject was a natural one for service clubs and for civic organizations of all kinds. But this time there was no organized opposition. On November 3, the constitution was adopted by a vote of 653,096 to 184,632.[3]

Cost of the Convention

The legislature appropriated $350,000 for the expenses of the convention and an additional $125,000 for the costs incurred by the counties incident to the special election in June. The law authorizing the convention provided that the delegates were to be reimbursed for their expenses up to $10 per day but they were to receive no compensation. Over forty state employees served the convention in an administrative, secretarial, and clerical capacity.

Major Controversial Issues

The five committees concerned with the substance of the constitution varied their methods of approach from adding a new clause or smoothing out ambiguous language to creating an entirely new article. Specific changes in the major articles of the constitution will be reserved for appropriate chapters. However, two rather unusual subjects will be considered since they were of such fundamental importance to the convention. Strange though it may seem, the success or failure of the convention hinged upon the solution of these two problems, neither of which would have been of especial importance in any state except New Jersey. Both problems— gambling and municipal taxes on railroad properties—have had a long history, each one causing an almost unbelievable amount of bitterness.

Gambling

What to do with the clause on gambling generated the greatest amount of heat both in and out of the convention. This "offensively detailed and internally inconsistent provision" prohibited all gambling except pari-mutuel betting at race tracks.[4]

Of forty-seven witnesses before the Committee on the Legislative, twenty-seven discussed the gambling issue exclusively.[5] Representatives of some veteran and fraternal groups and the Holy Name Society wanted a provision that would legalize various "games of chance," such as bingo, so long as the profits were used for charitable purposes. Opposing this view were representatives of Protestant church organizations who argued for the elimination of all gambling.

The committee had a number of alternatives from which to choose. It could (1) omit any reference to gambling, (2) prohibit all gambling, (3) liberalize the clause to permit gambling for charitable purposes, (4) retain the provision then in force, or (5) evade the issue by referring the question to the people.[6] Each of the first four alternatives was sure to provoke an emotional outburst. The committee chose the fifth alternative. Unfortunately, the method selected also aroused opposition. The committee decided to place two proposals before the people. One was simply the existing provision. The second legalized gambling for charitable purposes. Opponents of all gambling were thus placed in the unhappy position of being forced to vote for some gambling. An immediate howl of protest arose. The committee quickly modified the second alternative to provide for local option before any municipality could authorize a game of chance.

The plan for alternative proposals was abandoned when Attorney General Walter Van Riper ruled that the solution recommended by the committee violated the law setting up the convention. Rather than endanger the work of the convention by possible court action over the legality of alternative proposals, a search began for another way out. A clever proposal by Senator Arthur Lewis was attractive to all groups and was quickly adopted. His proposal prohibited the legislature from legalizing any form of gambling unless the people "heretofore" had given, or "hereafter" gave, the authorization.[7] In effect, this solution maintained the *status quo*. The people had "heretofore" authorized betting at race tracks. Therefore, this form of gambling would be continued. The proposal did not increase legalized gambling. On the other hand, an opportunity was presented for future action:

Thus it was that the delegates accepted neither the moral arguments of the Protestant ministers, the logical arguments of the realists who decried the hypocrisy of the present gambling situation, nor the economic arguments of the fraternal and church organizations, and instead resorted to the old political technique known as "passing the buck." [8]

The convention concluded debate on this thorny issue by passing a resolution memorializing the legislature to take up the problem and submit specified games of chance to the people at the election in 1948. However, the issue was not resolved until 1953 when bingo games and raffles were authorized by constitutional amendment.

The Tax Clause

The fate of the new constitution hung by an exceedingly slender thread as late as August 26, only one convention day before general debate was concluded. The machinery of the convention almost came to a dead stop while efforts were being made to resolve the deadlock over the wording of the clause on taxation. The settlement finally reached was not made as a result of arguments in open debate nor even by the action of the Committee on Taxation and Finance. The settlement was achieved through last-minute private conferences of the Governor and key delegates. Their final proposal, though little understood, was enthusiastically received by the delegates and was passed with almost no debate.

The immediate issue was one of increased tax money for cities in which were located large amounts of railroad property. Specifically, the issue was one of more railroad tax money for the cities in Hudson County. Former United States Senator John Milton, a delegate from Hudson County and a legal adviser to Mayor Hague, frankly said he desired "to get more money for Jersey City." [9]

For six years, Mayor Hague had led the fight to revoke legislation passed in 1941 giving the railroads preferential tax treatment. By this law, railroads paid a tax to the municipality of three dollars per 100 dollars assessed valuation on second-class property—that is, stations, yards, and terminals.* This was considerably below the average tax rate and resulted in a loss to the cities in Hudson County in which 78 per cent of such property was located. Jersey City alone had 60 per cent of all second-class railroad property in the state. As tax rates on homes and businesses increased to five, six, and seven dollars per hundred, the inequity of the fixed tax on railroad property also increased. Hence the determination of the Hudson County delegation to seek relief.

The problem was complicated by the wording of the tax clause. One of the amendments to the former constitution passed in 1875 provided that "property shall be assessed for taxes under general laws, and by uniform rules, according to its true value." [10] The words "according to its true value" had always provoked controversy and much litigation.† As a consequence, there was a considerable movement for the elimination of the "true value" clause.

One proposal, supported by the New Jersey State League of Municipalities, would have provided for an equal burden of taxation on all real property. This would have made unconstitutional the legislation of 1941. The suggestion was voted down by the Committee on Taxation and Finance, whereupon Mayor Hague announced that he might be compelled to

* See page 133.
† In testifying before the Committee on Taxation and Finance, Dr. John F. Sly, Director of the Princeton Surveys, said: ". . . I think I can say advisedly that I know of no state that raises so much money so inequitably as New Jersey, and that this is due in part, to the restrictions of these constitutional provisions." N.J. *Constitutional Convention of 1947*, V, 621.

fight the new constitution: "because of the attitude of the committee in favoring the railroads, there is great danger that this issue will influence the people to reject the constitution in its entirety, as they will never permit railroad influences to dominate the preparation of a new constitution." [11]

The Committee for Constitutional Revision, an interest group of private citizens, had proposed substituting for "true value" the words "according to classifications and standards of value to be established by law." [12] Representatives of the Governor added their support to the proposal. This sounded too much like the clause in the proposed constitution of 1944 which Mayor Hague had charged could permit discrimination. The proposal was voted down on July 29 by the committee, notwithstanding a special appearance by Governor Driscoll who told the committee that "with the proper constitutional foundation, I will make it my business, as soon as economic conditions permit, to recommend to the Legislature that type of a tax system that will, generally speaking, insure equality of treatment for all the citizens and adequate support for the State and its political subdivisions." [13]

The action of the Committee on Taxation and Finance in first voting down a proposal agreeable to the Hudson County delegation and then refusing to accept the proposal backed by Governor Driscoll signalled the end of its deliberations on the issue. From then on the question was fought out on the highest political level with representatives of the Governor meeting with Mayor Frank Hague Eggers and other top Hudson County delegates. The convention itself knew of developments only when compromise proposals were introduced, though not debated, on the floor. On the night of August 25, Democratic and Republican leaders reached a compromise. This was presented the next morning to the Committee on Taxation and Finance, which refused to do more than introduce the compromise on the floor. The delegates were delighted that the leaders of both parties were satisfied. Bipartisan support for the constitution was thus assured. With only a few minutes of debate, the tax clause was adopted by a vote of seventy to four. The clause as finally adopted follows:

Property shall be assessed for taxation under general laws and by uniform rules. All real property assessed and taxed locally or by the State for allotment and payment to taxing districts shall be assessed according to the same standard of value; and such real property shall be taxed at the general tax rate of the taxing district in which the property is situated, for the use of such taxing district.[14]

The words "true value" were eliminated. The taxing power was left in the legislature's hands but so long as there was a tax on second-class railroad property, one rate only could be applied. The adoption of the new tax clause meant an estimated $5,000,000 annually for Jersey City, which would now be able to collect the full rate (then approximately seven dollars) rather than the three dollar rate fixed by the legislature in 1941. Mayor Hague was elated over the turn of events. He pronounced the new constitution "one of the greatest documents ever offered the people in the state's history . . . . I cannot too strongly urge all of you to support it on Election Day . . . . With this new constitution, we forgive everyone— because we won." [15]

There were those who were skeptical of the new tax clause. Some, such as former Governor Edge, felt that the administration's zeal to obtain bipartisan support for the constitution had resulted in giving too much to the Democrats.* Others thought that the Democrats had bought a pig in a poke for $5,000,000. For most people, including the delegates, the subject was so complex that the less said about it the better. Time and the courts would supply the answer.

The Amending Clause

The delegates to the convention of 1844 had been careful to provide a means of amending the constitution. By so doing, they formalized the accepted theory that a constitution could be altered only if the electorate concurred. They were just as careful to make the process a difficult one, for they were convinced that the fundamental law should not be changed in haste. In the 1844 constitution a majority of the members of each house in two successive legislatures had to agree upon an amendment before a special referendum could be held. Furthermore, an amendment once defeated could not be brought up again for five years.

The fact that the amending machinery had been used successfully on only four occasions seemed to many people an evidence of the need for a more liberal provision. A particular object of attack was the requirement of a special election. Designed to isolate all partisan issues from the amending process, the special elections in actual practice had failed to fulfill their original purpose. They were costly (about $800,000 each) and because they were poorly attended, were more easily susceptible of boss control.[16]

The Committee on Rights, Privileges, Amendments, and Miscellaneous Provisions heard a number of suggested changes from organizations including the League of Women Voters, the Congress of Industrial Organizations, and the Committee for Constitutional Revision. Other organizations, such as the New Jersey Farm Bureau, opposed any change. Minutes of the committee reveal the lack of enthusiasm of most of its members for any liberalization. However, they did agree in principle to a suggestion of the Committee for Constitutional Revision that the governor be a check

---

* "All support is welcome if the future price is not too high. The unanimity is almost embarrassing." A speech of Governor Edge as reported in the *Newark Evening News,* October 30, 1947, p. 6.

against ill-advised legislative action. As finally adopted by the committee, the clause specified that amendments could be submitted to the people if passed by a three-fifths vote in both houses and approved by the governor or by a two-thirds vote in both houses if the governor disapproved. Suggestions for the initiative and referendum and for periodic revision were unacceptable to the committee.

The rural counties feared that periodic revision might be used to curb their advantage in the legislature. This was revealed vividly on the floor of the convention. The proposal was made to include a periodic revision clause whereby the people could signify their desire, every twenty-five years, for a constitutional convention. The convention was to be of a limited character in that there was to be no change in the basis of representation in the legislature. An amendment was adopted stating that the number of delegates to any convention twenty-five years hence should be eighty-one, each county to have the same number as it had representatives in the General Assembly.* This plan to bind a convention twenty-five years hence so irritated the sponsor of the original proposal, Senator Van Alstyne of Bergen County, that he dropped all effort to obtain periodic revision.

The proposal of the committee that the governor participate in the amending process was then modified by the convention. The plan finally adopted provided that if three fifths of the total membership of each house approve, an amendment may be submitted to the people in a general election. If only a majority approve, the proposed amendment must be acceptable to the legislature in the following legislative year before submission to popular referendum.† An interesting feature of the new amending clause is the requirement of a public hearing twenty days prior to a legislative vote on a proposed amendment.

The new amending process was first used in 1953. Two proposals

---

* Mr. Richard Baisden's analysis of the vote on the amendment is revealing. The delegates from the small counties obtained the support of Hudson County on this issue. The vote follows:

	Yes	No
Small counties (2-3 delegates)	25	2
Medium-sized counties (4 delegates)	4	7
Large counties (except Hudson)	3	26
Hudson County	9	1
TOTAL	41	36

Richard N. Baidsen, *Charter for New Jersey, The New Jersey Constitutional Convention of 1947* (Trenton: New Jersey Department of Education, Division of the State Library, Archives and History, 1952), p. 76.

† Under the new plan for biennial election of the General Assembly, the same group of legislators might be involved. This may result in a larger number of submissions to the people.

received the necessary three-fifths vote in each house. One authorized bingo games and raffles subject to legislative controls; the other extended the tax exemption of veterans' widows.

IMPORTANT FEATURES

The success or failure of the constitutional convention depended upon a solution of highly explosive issues. However, features of the new document that were fundamental to changed governmental practices were adopted without undue controversy.

The Constitution of 1947 strengthened markedly the position of the governor. His term was lengthened, and he was permitted to succeed himself once. The terms of the only officers recognized by the new constitution—the secretary of state and the attorney general—were limited to the governor's term, thus eliminating the danger of constitutional officers who owed no responsibility to the governor. The legislature was forbidden to elect or appoint any executive, administrative, or judicial officer except the state auditor.

The requirement that existing agencies be allocated among not more than twenty principal departments set the stage for a major reorganization of the administrative structure. This feature enabled the governor to supply a degree of managerial leadership and control that was impossible under the old constitution. His position as a legislative leader was also strengthened. The number necessary to override a veto was increased; the device of the conditional veto was introduced; and the time for consideration of bills was increased. The legislature, in turn, gained from the almost complete elimination of the pocket veto, thus forcing the governor to declare himself on every piece of legislation.

The constitutional provisions governing the judiciary were completely rewritten. A small Supreme Court was established in place of the unwieldy Court of Errors and Appeals. The new body was given extensive administrative powers over a greatly simplified court system. However, complete integration was not achieved since the county court was accorded constitutional status.

Additions to the bill of rights were designed to prevent discrimination because of religion, race, color, ancestry, or national origin. The right of persons in private employment to organize and bargain collectively was recognized. An effort was made to provide increased home rule by means of a constitutional direction to the courts to construe liberally measures favoring municipalities and counties.

The new constitution achieves to a considerable degree an effective separation of powers among the three branches of government. The document is reasonably short and contains a minimum of nonconstitutional material.

It is much more flexible than its predecessors. As a consequence, the will of the people regarding the form, functions, and philosophy of government should more easily prevail.

NOTES

[1] L., 1947, ch. 8, p. 36.

[2] New Jersey, *Constitutional Convention of 1947,* I, 100.

[3] *Manual of the Legislature of New Jersey,* 1948, p. 661.

[4] John E. Bebout, *Some Reflections upon the Draft Constitution Approved by the New Jersey Constitutional Convention* (New Jersey Committee for Constitutional Revision, September 24, 1947, mimeographed).

[5] *Convention of 1947, op. cit.,* III, 517 ff.

[6] Richard N. Baisden, *Charter for New Jersey, The New Jersey Constitutional Convention of 1947* (Trenton: New Jersey Department of Education, Division of the State Library, Archives and History, 1952), p. 34.

[7] *Convention of 1947, op. cit.,* I, 427-28.

[8] Baisden, *op. cit.,* p. 39.

[9] *The Daily Home News,* New Brunswick, July 30, 1947, p. 21.

[10] Constitution of 1844, art. IV, sec. VII, par. 12.

[11] *The New York Times,* July 26, 1947, p. 2.

[12] *Convention of 1947, op. cit.,* V, 544.

[13] *Ibid.,* p. 771.

[14] Constitution of 1947, art. VIII, sec. I, par. 1.

[15] *Newark Evening News,* October 21, 1947, p. 9.

[16] Charles R. Erdman, Jr., *The New Jersey Constitution—A Barrier to Governmental Efficiency and Economy* (Princeton: Princeton University, School of Public and International Affairs, 1934), p. 19 n.

CHAPTER 4

Popular Control of Government

THE VAST MACHINERY of state government is responsible ultimately to the electorate. The bill of rights of the New Jersey constitution declares that "all political power is inherent in the people." However, the process of determining the popular will is in itself complicated. It involves not only the final mechanical act of tallying individual votes but all of the steps taken by the party organizations, and often by an array of citizen organizations, in persuading the potential voter to cast his ballot for a particular candidate or for a particular issue.

POLITICAL ORGANIZATION

Party organization in New Jersey is established through a combination of state law and the rules of the parties themselves. The law effectively prohibits the development of third parties by the requirement that, in order to be designated on a ballot, a party must have obtained 10 per cent of the votes in the preceding election for members of the General Assembly.

Party committees, both Republican and Democratic, function on all levels. The most important cog in the party machinery is the county committee. It consists of one man and one woman from each "unit of representation" in the county. They must be residents of the unit. A unit of representation may be either one election district within a municipality or a combination of districts depending upon the county committee's bylaws. Members of the county committee are elected annually at the primary. Following the primary, the committee members meet to elect a county chairman and a vice-chairlady.

The municipal committee is made up of elected members of the county committee who reside in the municipality. The members elect one of their number as chairman.

The state committee consists of one man and one woman elected from each county every four years at the time of the gubernatorial primary. The state committee also meets annually. A chairman is elected from among the members, to serve for four years. Members of the national committee are selected by the state committee.

A state convention of each party is held annually. The qualification requirements for membership are exceedingly complicated. In general, the convention consists of the party candidate for governor, or, if in a year in which no governor is to be elected the governor himself is a member of his party convention; the party candidates for the state legislature and for Congress; the party's state senators and members of Congress holding office whose successors are not to be chosen at the ensuing general election; and the state committee. For example, after the spring primary in 1953, the 134 delegates invited to the Republican convention by the call of the state chairman included the nominee for governor, the ten candidates for the state Senate, the ten holdover senators, the sixty candidates for the Assembly, the two United States Senators, the nine members of Congress, and the forty-two members of the state committee.

The convention is held in Trenton on the second Thursday following the primary election. A major item of business is the adoption of a party platform. The convention appoints a five-member committee on resolutions to receive all proposed planks submitted to the convention and to prepare a tentative platform for consideration at a second meeting two weeks later.

VOTING

Every qualified voter may cast a ballot for all elective offices. In addition, he may vote upon all questions submitted to the people.

Qualifications

The qualifications for voting are set forth in the state constitution.[1] They are four in number: citizenship in the United States, age of twenty-one years, residence in the state for one year preceding the election, and residence in a county for five months preceding the election.* In addition to meeting these qualifications, a person must be registered. On the negative side, the constitution states that an idiot or an insane person may not vote. Further, the legislature is authorized to deprive of the right of suf-

* In second-class cities having a population of less than 100,000 a thirty-day residence qualification prevails. In fourth-class cities not exceeding 20,000 the residence qualification is fifteen days.

frage persons who have been convicted of certain crimes. Blasphemy, treason, murder, rape, conspiracy, forgery, and larceny of above the value of six dollars are among the designated crimes. The person convicted may have his suffrage restored by pardon or by law.*

Registration

New Jersey has had since 1943 a system of permanent registration applicable for all elections.[2] Although there is no specific constitutional authorization for registration, the courts have long held that in order to obtain honest elections, the legislature had power to prevent from voting those who had not registered:

> From an examination of the election law relating to registration it is difficult to perceive how a duly qualified voter is deprived from voting in any case where he has complied with the regulations prescribed by the legislature concerning the exercise of that right. Of course, if a qualified voter, under the constitution, neglects to obey the prescribed legislative requirements necessary to qualify him as a voter, he has no one to blame but himself if he loses his right to vote. It is his own act which deprives him from exercising the voting privilege. It is quite clear from the decisions of the courts of this state that though an individual falls within the class of those entitled to vote by virtue of the constitutional declaration, nevertheless, the manner in which and how he shall become entitled to exercise the right extended to him or her, is left to the sound discretion and wisdom of the lawmaking power of this state.[3]

Registration, then, is a condition that must be met prior to the voter's exercise of his right of suffrage.[4] The registration of voters is a function of the county board of elections. In counties having a superintendent of elections, the responsibility falls upon a commissioner of registration.

Permanent registration forms require the following information from applicants: name, place of residence, statement concerning age, citizenship, and residence, whether a native-born citizen or a naturalized citizen, place of preceding registration, signature, and oath or affirmation. The forms also contain space for a twenty-year voting record showing the ballot number and the political party voted for in the primary election and the ballot number cast in the general election. In actual practice, a check mark rather than the ballot number is used to indicate that a vote has been cast. At each election the voter is required to sign a signature-comparison record.

Signature copy registers are held by the county throughout the year. They are turned over to the municipal clerk on the second Monday pre-

* L., 1948, ch. 438, p. 1695. The clause "restored by law" was interpreted by Chancellor Walker to mean action by the Court of Pardons rather than action by the legislature. He held that to restore the right of suffrage was, in effect, to remit a penalty, an executive function, and not a prerogative of the legislature. *In re N.J. Court of Pardons,* 97 N.J. Eq. 555 (1924-25). The new constitution appears designed to invalidate this interpretation by the clause ". . . when pardoned or otherwise restored by law to the right of suffrage. . . ." Art. II, par. 7.

ceding the primary or general election.   He transfers the register to the district election boards for use in mailing sample ballots and during the election.*

The voter's registration is permanent unless he fails to vote at least once during four consecutive years.   Failure to vote in the prescribed period results in the transfer of his form to an inactive file.   Reregistration is then necessary.   As a means of keeping the lists up to date, a government reply postal card is sent after each national election to every registered person who did not vote asking whether he is still residing at the address indicated on his registration form.   If a registrant has moved within the county, he may, by executing a change of address notice, have his registration form transferred to the appropriate register.   Removal from the county or state results in the transfer of the form to the inactive file.   Public notice of the transfer must normally be given.   If the registrant failed to vote during four consecutive years, or if his name was ordered stricken from the list by the courts, no published notice is necessary.

As a further means of keeping the registration lists in order, municipal officials, charged with issuing moving permits and recording deaths, are required to notify the county election board.   The county prosecutor is required to report those disfranchised as a result of court convictions. Reregistration is necessary in order to vote following restoration of citizenship rights.

Complaints against the action of registration officials may be taken to the county court.   If satisfied that the complainant is entitled to vote, the judge may issue an order directing the local board of elections to permit the person to cast his ballot.

Permanent registration is simply one phase of the election process.   It is a device that depends heavily upon effective administration.   Lacking careful supervision, the evils often prevalent in the old system of annual registration may be continued.

Ballots and Voting Machines

A cross ($\times$), plus ($+$), or check ($\checkmark$), in black ink or black lead pencil, may be used to mark a ballot.   The voter must make a mark opposite the name of each candidate he favors.   In New Jersey it is not possible to mark a cross under the party designation and thereby vote for all candidates of the party.   Write-in votes are legal although the law requires that the voter, in addition to writing or posting the name, must also place a mark opposite the name.

In presidential elections, the names of the candidates for President and Vice President are placed on the ballot.   The names of the electors are

* In counties having a superintendent of elections, the registers are turned over directly to the boards of election.   Sample ballots are sent out by the county.

omitted. To vote for the party electors, it is necessary only to mark the ballot opposite the names of the candidates for President and Vice President.

Titles of offices are arranged on the ballot according to law. For example, in counties having more than twelve freeholders, the following arrangement is prescribed for the columns of each of the political parties:

electors of President and Vice President of the United States; member of the United States Senate; Governor; member of the House of Representatives; member of the State Senate; members of the General Assembly; sheriff; county clerk; surrogate; register of deeds and mortgages; county supervisor; members of the board of chosen freeholders; coroners; mayor and members of the municipal governing bodies, and any other titles of office.[5]

The place on the ballot of each party column is determined by lot. For example, in a county election the county clerk is responsible for drawing lots and for awarding to the party first drawn the favored column at the left of the ballot. Where there are several persons running for one office, as in a primary, the position of each individual is determined by lot. Paper cards, alike as to size, substance, and thickness are placed in a box; the box is required to be shaken thoroughly before any card is withdrawn. Voters may witness the drawing.

Public questions are placed at the foot of the ballot. However, any question that concerns the people of the entire state, such as a constitutional amendment, is placed at the head of the ballot.

Preparation of the ballots to be used in a general election is the responsibility of the county clerk. He is required to deliver them to the clerk of each municipality three days before the election. Sample ballots are prepared by the county clerk for distribution to the voters. In counties having a superintendent of elections, and in counties where the board of elections chooses to do so, the ballots are mailed on a county-wide basis. Elsewhere, the ballots are furnished to the municipal clerk who turns them over to the district boards for distribution by mail.

Prior to casting his ballot, the voter is required to sign his name in the district poll book. If the signature does not compare with that in the signature copy register, then it is the duty of each member of the district board to challenge the individual's right to vote.* He may be challenged on other grounds also either by a member of the board or by an authorized challenger. When a prospective voter has been challenged, he may be permitted to vote after taking an oath or affirmation that he is qualified. However, the board may by majority vote decide against giving a ballot to any prospective voter.† The voter is required to cast his ballot in secret.

* Failure to do so has been held not to invalidate the result of an election. *In re Clee,* 119 N.J.L. 310 (1938).

† A candidate may act as a challenger or he may appoint two challengers for each election district. The chairman of the party municipal committee in local

Voting machines are required in first- and second-class counties and may be adopted elsewhere by action of the governing body of the county or of the municipality or by popular referendum. The machines are constructed to meet detailed requirements established by law. For example, they must assure secrecy in the act of voting and must contain protective devices to prevent tampering. The machines must provide facilities for a minimum of forty office columns, and a maximum of nine parties and thirty public questions.[6] In addition, space must be provided for write-in votes. To insure that the machines comply with the law, the secretary of state is required to approve each type before it may be used.

Custody and care of the machines is the responsibility of the county board of elections or, in first-class counties, the superintendent of elections. In some municipalities, where the machines were purchased by the governing body, the municipal clerk is custodian. Before the machines are prepared for an election, representatives of the parties must be afforded an opportunity to examine them in order to determine whether they are in proper working condition. After this examination, the machines are sealed. The party representatives are required to certify that the counters were set at zero. After the machines are transferred to the polling places, the municipal governing body is responsible for supplying police protection against tampering or damage.

Absentee Voting

The Constitution of 1947 states that in wartime a member of the armed forces may not be "deprived of his vote by reason of absence from his election district." An almost identical provision was included in the Constitution of 1844. However, a new clause was inserted in the 1947 Constitution: "the Legislature may provide for absentee voting by members of the armed forces of the United States in time of peace." [7] The prevailing interpretation placed upon this clause was that the constitution prohibited the legislature from any action which would permit other absentees to vote. Enabling legislation in 1948 applied only to veterans. A storm of protest arose in the presidential election of 1952 when many thousands of people were disfranchised. For example, the wives of veterans who were living at army posts outside the state were unable to vote.

Public pressure to extend the absentee voting privilege resulted in new legislation in 1953. Persons physically unable to go to the polls as well as those absent from the state were made eligible to vote.[8] Whether this legislation is constitutional remains for the courts to determine. Certainly, extension of the absentee voting privilege, under adequate safeguards,

---

elections, or the chairman of the county committee in primary elections and in elections involving more than one municipality, may appoint two challengers for each district.

would seem to be in the public interest. Should the courts determine that in view of the constitutional language the legislature had exceeded its authority, an amendment would be necessary to accomplish the objective of the 1953 legislation.

NOMINATIONS

Candidates for public office are nominated by petition. The only exceptions, aside from an occasional write-in nomination, are electors for President and Vice President of the United States, who are nominated at state conventions of the political parties.* Presidential and vice presidential electors nominated by state party conventions must be certified to the secretary of state by the presiding officer and secretary of the convention. The convention may appoint a committee to fill vacancies.

Petition

The nominating petition sets forth the name, place of residence, and post office address of the candidate and the title of the office. Each person signing the petition must be legally qualified to vote. In signing, the individual pledges that he will support the candidate named. It is unlawful to sign more than one petition for the same office.

A candidate is placed in nomination in the political unit concerned providing qualified voters equal to 2 per cent of the vote cast for the General Assembly at the preceding election sign the petition. The percentage figure is modified by a provision that an aggregate of 800 signatures will qualify a candidate for a state-wide office and 100 signatures for any other office. The candidate is required to accept the nomination in writing. A 1949 law requiring that a candidate take an oath of allegiance was declared unconstitutional.[9] Complaints concerning an invasion of the candidate's rights may be taken to the courts.

Although the petition is used to nominate candidates, a vacancy after the primary may be filled by action of the party committee. This provision of the law has been subjected to grave abuse. For example, in a county that is dominated by a party organization, a dummy slate of candidates is sometimes placed in nomination. Following the primary, the party organization may order the entire slate to resign. Vacancies may then be filled by the party committee. If the office to be filled is of a state-wide character or involves the voters of more than one county, the selection of a candidate to fill a vacancy is made by the state committee, otherwise by the county committee or that portion of it representing the area concerned.

* The petition may be used to nominate electors other than those nominated by the party conventions. L., 1930, ch. 187, p. 671.

Direct Primary

The direct primary took the place of the old convention system at which party members conducted a caucus and selected a candidate. The convention was the primary. Over the years the convention system was denounced as being unrepresentative of the party membership and simply a tool of private interests. New Jersey's first law regulating primaries, enacted in 1878, was designed to eliminate voting by persons not resident in the area in which the caucus was held.[10] During the same year an act was passed making the giving of a bribe to a delegate, or the acceptance of a bribe, a high misdemeanor.[11]

The direct primary was introduced in 1903 and was applicable to the nomination of ward and township officers only.[12] The Republican election officers supervised the Republican ballot box; the Democrats, the Democratic ballot box. The law also provided that the ballot was to be printed at public expense. In 1907 the law was extended to cover municipal and county officials and members of the state Senate and the General Assembly.[13] Two years later county and city committees were included. In 1911 the Geran act, a measure sponsored by Woodrow Wilson, extended and improved the direct primary and provided for personal registration in municipalities of over 5,000 population.[14] Numerous changes have since been made in the law, the last major revision taking place in 1930.[15]

The purpose of the direct primary is twofold. The first is to provide a method for the members of one party to select one of their own number as the nominee of the party in the general election. The second purpose is to provide a means of electing party officials.

A candidate for the party nomination may have his name placed on the ballot by a petition signed by qualified voters of his party. The number of signers required varies from 10, if the election is confined to a single election district, to 1,000 for state-wide elections. By endorsement of the petition, the candidate may have printed opposite his name on the ballot a statement of up to six words distinguishing his candidacy.

No statement or slogan is permitted for presidential candidates. Nor is the consent of the candidate required to place his name on the ballot. However, he may avoid the primary by filing a written declination with the secretary of state.[16] The popular vote in the presidential primary is not binding upon the delegates to the national convention.

A sample primary ballot of each party is mailed to every registered voter. The procedure for voting in the primary election and in the general election is substantially the same. For example, write-ins are permitted in the primary as well as in the general election. In both, the votes must be canvassed and certified.

New Jersey has a closed primary system; only qualified voters who are registered as members of a party may vote.* The voter has an opportunity to cast his ballot only for members of his own party. The closed primary is designed to develop party responsibility. If those owing no allegiance to the party control party nominations, then, it may be argued, the development of party responsibility is impossible. The closed system also prevents party raiding, that is, participation by the members of other parties in order to defeat the foremost candidate. However, party raiding is not impossible in New Jersey. Failure to vote in two succeeding annual primary elections enables one to cast a ballot for members of the opposite party. He is required simply to sign and file a declaration indicating the political party in whose primary he wishes to vote.

Many people avoid the primary since they are forced to declare their party preference. Some fear having any party label attached to them on the ground that for business or other reasons they may suffer. This attitude plays into the hands of the political boss. He has less opposition in winning the primary for the candidate of his choice. The voter who shies away from the primary often finds that in the general election he has no choice. He is limited to voting for one of two candidates each of whom was selected by a small group in charge of the party's machinery.

Perhaps the major criticism of the primary in New Jersey is that it does not work as originally intended. In most areas of the state the primary is not used as a means of selecting the party candidate; rather it simply confirms officially the choice of the professional politicians. Often there is no candidate for the party nomination except the individual selected by the party leaders. There may be some virtue to the pre-primary selection of a candidate providing the leaders represent adequately the party membership. How often this is true is difficult to determine. To run against the organization choice is normally a futile undertaking. In most instances, the primary is no more effective in representing the great body of voters than was the old convention system.[17]

The primary's great virtue becomes evident in those rare instances when the people become thoroughly aroused. The primary then affords an opportunity for the selection of a candidate who represents the party membership as a whole. A committee of the American Political Science Association recently declared that no workable substitute had been found for the direct primary and that in spite of its imperfections it should be retained.[18]

As indicated previously, the primary serves as a means of electing party officers. Delegates and alternates to the national conventions of the political parties, held each four years, are elected at the April primary. The

* About three fourths of the states have the closed system. In the open system, the voter need not disclose his party affiliation. See American Political Science Association, *Toward a More Responsible Two-Party System, A Report of the Committee on Political Parties* (New York: Rinehart, 1950).

chairman of the state committee is responsible for notifying the secretary of state of the number to be chosen.* Members of the county and state committees are also elected at the primary.

ELECTION ADMINISTRATION

Election administration is primarily the responsibility of the counties. However, both the state and municipalities perform limited functions.† At the community level is the election district headed by a district board of registry and election. The districts are small, from a few hundred voters to a maximum of 1,500 where three voting machines are to be used. In 1955, there were 4,071 districts among the state's 567 municipalities.[19] The adjustment of district boundaries is the responsibility of the municipal governing body except in first-class counties where the county board of elections serves as the districting body. Tallying the vote, whether cast by paper ballots or by machine, is a decisive step. With the machine the process is simple, the results can be quickly determined, and the opportunity to commit fraud is greatly reduced.

The district board consists of four members appointed annually by the county board and apportioned equally between the two largest political parties. Any legal voter who has voted for three consecutive years in the same political party may apply for a position as a member of a district board. The applicant is required to swear that he possesses the needed qualifications, such as good moral character, reasonable knowledge of the duties to be performed, and ability to add and subtract. Actually, the appointments are made almost entirely through political channels.

The board is required to organize on the second Tuesday preceding the primary election and to elect one of its members as judge and chairman. An inspector, of different political faith, is also elected. As a means of preserving order at the polls, each member is invested with the power and duties of a constable.

Certified statements of the result of the election must be sent by the district board to both the municipal and the county clerks. The superinten-

---

* The number is determined by the National Committee for each party. See Richard D. Hupman and Samuel H. Still, Jr., *Manner of Selecting Delegates to National Political Conventions and the Nomination and Election of Presidential Electors* (Washington: U.S. Government Printing Office, 1956).

† For example, the secretary of state receives certain petitions and election returns, and prepares and transmits certificates of election in some instances. A state board of canvassers examines district and county board returns. The municipal clerk has a number of functions, especially in connection with local elections, such as receiving nominating petitions for primary elections, printing ballots, and making the election equipment available. Except in municipal elections, the printing of ballots is a function of the county clerk.

dent of elections, in counties having that officer, is also entitled to a certified statement. Where the election involves a congressional district or the people of more than one county, a certified statement must be sent to the secretary of state. On the Monday following an election, the board of county canvassers is required to meet and examine the statements submitted by the district boards. Four statements of canvass are prepared, one for submission to the county clerk, one to the secretary of state, and one to each of the chairmen of the Republican and Democrat state committees. The board of state canvassers, consisting of the governor and four members of the Senate, is required to meet on the fourth Tuesday after the election and determine the votes cast in congressional districts or where the election concerned the people of more than one county.* Upon receipt of their statement of determination, the secretary of state prepares a certificate for the candidates. Certificates of election for members of the United States Senate, the House of Representatives, and the members of the Electoral College are signed by the governor.

Above the district boards are the county boards of election. They also consist of four members, two from each of the major parties. They are commissioned for terms of two years by the governor upon nomination by a party committee consisting of the chairman and vice-chairlady of the county committee, the state chairman, and the state committeeman and committeewoman.† The method of appointment of the county boards has been criticized as making inevitable partisan political control of every aspect of election machinery. The fact that the constituency of the board at both the municipal and county levels is bipartisan does not guarantee an honest and efficiently run election. Two observers of New Jersey election procedures contend that "bipartisanship encourages corrupt bargains. This development is the more insidious, because the appearance of adverse interest makes the fact of alliance more difficult to expose." [20]

The county board is required to organize each year early in March. A chairman and a secretary, of different political parties, are elected from the membership. Offices and equipment are supplied by the Board of Chosen Freeholders. The county board of elections is also the board of canvassers for the county. In this capacity, the county clerk is the clerk of the board.‡

* For example, in December, 1956, the board of state canvassers certified the presidential election. Votes were cast by 2,493,774 persons out of a total registration of 2,846,794. Thus 87 per cent of those eligible voted. President Dwight D. Eisenhower received 1,606,942 votes and Governor Adlai E. Stevenson 850,337. N.J. Result of the General Election Held November 6, 1956 (Compiled under Direction of the Secretary of State).

† In 1938 the court issued an ouster judgment when the governor issued a commission in disregard of the statutory procedure. Driscoll v. Sakin, 121 N.J.L. 225 (1938).

‡ The board of canvassers is legally a separate body. There may be no mingling of duties. In 1937 the Essex County board of elections adopted a resolution to tabulate the election results on election night directly from the returns of the district election boards. The law requires the board of canvassers to meet at Monday

There is no state board of elections or other agency to supervise and coordinate the work of the various boards. This decentralized responsibility for administering elections has been declared to result in increased expense, impaired efficiency, and ineffective enforcement of the election laws.[21] Critics of the present system—or of the lack of system—favor the creation of a department of elections at the state level. Functions now being performed by various state, county, and municipal officers would be concentrated in the department. The head of the department together with the operating staff would be prohibited from engaging in direct or indirect political activity. Bills designed to effect reforms in the administration of elections have made little progress.

CAMPAIGN EXPENDITURES

The law establishes limits to campaign expenditures, the amount varying with the office to be filled. Fifteen cents per voter may be expended for a municipal office. For a county office with a fixed annual salary, the limit is one half of the annual salary. A candidate for governor or United States Senator may spend up to $100,000. These sums are exclusive of travel expenses.

Before receiving any contribution or making any campaign expenditure, candidates for the United States Senate, the House of Representatives, and governor are required to appoint a campaign manager and to file a certificate of the appointment with a bank or trust company. A second certificate must be filed with the secretary of state designating the campaign manager and the depository. Deposits and withdrawals are regulated by law. Candidates for other offices, where the amount authorized by law to be spent exceeds $500, are also required to appoint a manager and to file a certificate in the office in which the petition for nomination was filed. A candidate may appoint himself as campaign manager.

On the Friday or Saturday preceding the election, the campaign manager must file an itemized statement of all money contributed. The statement must be accompanied by affidavits both by the manager and the candidate. Within twenty days after the election, a supplementary report is required showing the amount originally filed and the total expenses incurred. Banks having campaign fund accounts must file the deposit slips and the withdrawal vouchers.

Notwithstanding the detailed legislation concerning individual campaign expenditures, the laws have little real meaning. Actually, there is no

---

noon following the election to check the canvass made by the county clerk from the statements of the district boards. The court set aside the resolution on the ground that the county board of elections could not decide what the board of canvassers should do nor could the canvassers as such proceed "at a time and in a manner different from the mandate of the statute." *Young* v. *Essex County Board of Elections*, 120 N.J.L. 529, 531 (1938).

effective limitation. The restrictions on the amount the candidate himself may spend do not apply to the state, county, or municipal committees. Thus the party organization is free to receive contributions and to disburse funds on behalf of the party candidates.

CITIZEN PARTICIPATION

Interest in Voting

The degree of citizen interest in elections varies. Normally, the greatest interest occurs during presidential election years. For example, in 1952, 88 per cent of those registered in New Jersey voted. However, during the gubernatorial election of 1953 only 69 per cent of those registered cast their ballots. The new constitution was adopted in 1947 by only 52 per cent of the registered voters. In many municipal and school districts, candidates are often elected, and important issues decided, by a small fraction—perhaps as few as 10 per cent of the registered voters.

Not all of those who are eligible to vote are registered to do so. The Political Action Committee of the Congress of Industrial Organizations conducted a study in 1950 that revealed that 31.7 per cent of the adult population throughout the state were not registered. The highest percentages of nonregistered citizens occurred in the industrialized areas; 38.8 per cent were not registered in Essex in contrast with 7.1 per cent in Cape May.[22]

Voting Patterns

New Jersey's political allegiance is difficult to analyze. Party alignments have shifted back and forth with first the Democrats and then the Republicans exercising control. Out of eleven presidential elections in the second half of the nineteenth century, from 1856 through 1896, the Republicans carried the popular vote of the state on only two occasions. Of the fifteen presidential elections from 1900 through 1956 the Republicans have won ten, the Democrats five.[23] In fifteen gubernatorial campaigns from 1856 through 1898 the Republicans won five elections, the Democrats ten. In the eighteen campaigns from 1900 through 1953 each party was victorious nine times.[24]

In contrast to the relative balance between the parties in elections covering the state as a whole, elections covering counties or congressional districts have been dominated by the Republicans. Since 1900 the state Senate has been in the hands of the Democrats only twice, in 1913 and in 1914. The closest approach to Democratic control since that time was in 1937 when, because of a vacancy, each party had ten seats. Democratic control of the assembly also has been infrequent, occurring only in 1907, 1911, 1913, 1914, 1932, and 1937; the lower house delegations were tied once, in 1919. During most of the twentieth century the Republican majority was in a ratio of from two to one to four to one in the Senate and frequently two to one or more in the General Assembly.[25]

The principal reason why the Republicans have controlled the legislature so often lies in the geographical distribution of the strength of the two parties. Democratic strength has been concentrated, chiefly in Hudson County, whereas the Republican strength has been more widely distributed. For example, in the presidential election of 1948, which the Republicans won by a vote of 981,124 to 895,455, Hudson County went Democratic by 182,979 to 111,113—a majority of 71,866. Middlesex County has also been regarded as overwhelmingly Democratic, although in the election of 1956 President Eisenhower carried all but one of the twenty-five municipalities. This heavy concentration of Democratic votes in a few areas accounts for the relatively even total state vote although a county by county tabulation favors the Republicans.

The rapid economic development of the state that has taken place since World War II may alter markedly the political alignment within the counties. The post-World War II industrialization of the area from below Camden along the line of the Pennsylvania Railroad to Newark has resulted in a greater diffusion of Democratic strength, with the result that elections in a number of the counties are now much closer. From the point of view of a healthy two-party system a less consistently one-sided division in the legislature would seem desirable.

NOTES

[1] See also Richard P. McCormick, "Suffrage and the Constitution," *N.J. Constitutional Convention of 1947* (Trenton, 1951), II, 1360-72. For an excellent account of early developments see Richard P. McCormick, *The History of Voting in New Jersey, A Study of the Development of Election Machinery, 1664-1918* (New Brunswick: Rutgers University Press, 1953).

[2] L., 1943, ch. 218, p. 580.

[3] *In re Freeholders of Hudson County,* 105 N.J.L. 57, 61-62 (1928).

[4] *In re Ray,* 26 N.J. Misc. 56 (1947).

[5] L., 1951, ch. 315, p. 1120.

[6] L., 1941, ch. 166, p. 526.

[7] Art. II, par. 4.

[8] L., 1953, ch. 211, p. 1577.

[9] *Imbrie* v. *Marsh,* 3 N.J. 578 (1950).

[10] L., 1878, ch. 113, p. 178.

[11] L., 1878, ch. 204, p. 318.

[12] L., 1903, ch. 248, p. 603.

[13] L., 1907, ch. 278, p. 697.

[14] L., 1911, ch. 183, p. 276.

[15] L., 1930, ch. 187, p. 671.

[16] L., 1952, ch. 2, p. 12.

[17] For an early and excellent study see Ralph Simpson Boots, *The Direct Primary in New Jersey* (New York: published doctoral dissertation, Columbia University, 1917).

[18] American Political Science Association, *Toward a More Responsible Two-Party System, A Report of the Committee on Political Parties* (New York: Rinehart, 1950), p. 71.

[19] *Manual of the Legislature of New Jersey,* 1956, p. 698.

[20] Nathan L. Jacobs and Morris M. Schnitzer, "Report on the Proposed Revision of the New Jersey Election Law," *University of Newark Law Review,* V (June, 1940), 190.

[21] *Ibid.,* p. 187. The last revision of the election laws occurred in 1930. N.J. *Minutes of Assembly, 1930,* "Election Law Revision Commission, Report," pp. 443-57.

[22] Congress of Industrial Organizations, Political Action Committee, *The Effectiveness of PAC in New Jersey* (Newark, 1951, mimeographed), pp. 1-3.

[23] *Manual of the Legislature of New Jersey,* 1953, pp. 648-49.

[24] *Ibid.,* 1954, pp. 643-44.

[25] *Ibid.,* pp. 218-21.

CHAPTER 5

The Legislature:

COMPOSITION and ORGANIZATION

THROUGHOUT THE COUNTRY, "the tendency is toward the reduction of the total number of legislators." [1] However, the total of eighty-one New Jersey legislators does not reflect a reduction made to keep in line with the national trend. On the contrary, the state has always had a small legislative body. The size of the Assembly has remained unchanged since the Constitution of 1844, that of the Senate since the creation of Union County in 1857.

STRUCTURE AND COMPOSITION

The upper house in New Jersey is composed of 21 senators, one from each county. Only Delaware and Nevada, each with 17, have a smaller number. The lower house is composed of 60 members apportioned among the counties according to population. Five states have a smaller representation—Delaware 35, Idaho 59, Nevada 47, New Mexico 55, and Wyoming 56. However, taking both houses together, the legislature of New Jersey is the fourth smallest. Nebraska, with a unicameral legislature, has 43, Delaware has 52, and Nevada 64. New Jersey's 81 is in sharp contrast with that of the largest legislature, New Hampshire, which in 1957 has 424 members.

Senatorial Districts

When the Constitution of 1776 was adopted, each county was permitted one member in the upper house. This was a natural development. During the period when New Jersey was a royal colony, the council had consisted of twelve members, six from East Jersey and six from West Jersey. There was little reason to suspect that representation based upon geography would result in serious inequality based upon numbers. At the time of the first Federal census in 1790, there was a remarkable similarity in population distribution among the New Jersey counties. Hunterdon was the only county with a population greater than 20,000, and that by a margin of only 253. Sussex with 19,500 and Burlington with 18,095 were close behind. Cumberland and Cape May were the only counties under 10,000, the latter having but 2,571.

The lone dissenting vote in the constitutional convention of 1844 was in protest against the principle of equality of representation in the upper house. However, marked disparities in representation had only begun to appear. Essex with a population of 44,512 in 1840, Monmouth with 32,912, and Burlington with 32,809 were the leaders in population growth. But during six of the eight decades from 1840 to 1910 the state increased in population over 30 per cent for each ten-year period. By 1910 Hudson had become the leading county with 537,231. Essex followed with 512,-886. These two giants with over a half million people each had now far outstripped all other counties, the nearest being Passaic with 215,902. Inequality of representation had become an accomplished fact.

No serious effort has been made to change the basis of representation.* To have done so would have been futile. Although Governor Edison in 1941 called for an end to the "existing representative inequality," little attention was given to his recommendation.[2] The constitutional commission of 1941-42 ignored the subject completely. The members of the commission recognized that the rural counties would not part with their control of the legislature, and that any suggestion to change the system of representation would nullify other phases of the commission's report. In 1943 the bill providing for a public referendum on the question of authorizing the legislature to sit as a constitutional convention specifically excluded the system of representation from discussion in the convention. This pattern was followed again in 1947.

The prospect of any constitutional change affecting representation in the upper house is, for all practical purposes, nonexistent. However, over the next decades, it is not improbable that the development of the state will result automatically in lessening the impact of urban-rural differences. The 1950 census evidences this transition (see map on page 54). Counties which were formerly largely rural in character are becoming industrialized. Others are being peopled by those who work in the cities and who are thus keenly aware of urban problems. Essex and Hudson are no

* In 1954 the county served as the basis for representation in the upper house in six states: New Jersey, Idaho, Montana, Nevada, New Mexico, and South Carolina. *The Book of the States, 1954-55* (Chicago: The Council of State Governments, 1954), pp. 114-18.

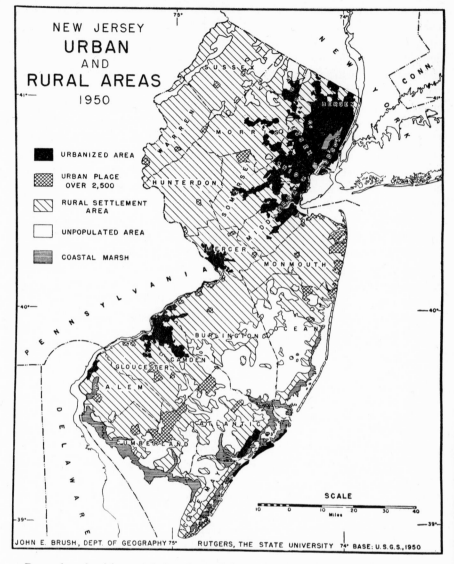

NEW JERSEY
URBAN
AND
RURAL AREAS
1950

URBANIZED AREA

URBAN PLACE
OVER 2,500

RURAL SETTLEMENT
AREA

UNPOPULATED AREA

COASTAL MARSH

SCALE

JOHN E. BRUSH, DEPT. OF GEOGRAPHY   RUTGERS, THE STATE UNIVERSITY   BASE: U.S.G.S.,1950

Reproduced with permission from John E. Brush, *The Population of New Jersey* (New Brunswick: Rutgers University Press, 1956), p. 2.

longer the only big counties. In 1950 there were twelve counties having a population of over 100,000, with Somerset, Gloucester, and Cumberland not far behind.

Urban problems are now pressing for solution. For example, school finance and water supply are subjects that plague the people of many counties; they are not questions for the big cities alone. Urban-rural differences will tend to diminish as the solution of urban problems becomes a matter of state-wide rather than local concern.

Assembly Districts

Members of the General Assembly are elected on an at-large basis in each county. The county is no longer divided into districts. The lower house was elected on an at-large basis until 1852 when assembly districts were created. The legislative reapportionment following the census of 1870 created districts with little regard for the principle of equality of representation. For the next two decades, gerrymandering—that is, the creation of voting areas favorable to the party in power—was practiced by whichever party had a majority.

The act of 1891 set up districts grossly unequal in size. For example, in one district in Camden County there were 10,500 inhabitants; in another, 60,000. In Monmouth County part of one district was an island in the middle of another district. The eleventh district in Essex County was described as a rainbow, the fourth district as a cross, and the second as a panhandle. The total result was characterized as "an artificial anatomy of a living county hewn into *disjecta membra*." [3]

The division of the counties into Assembly districts was declared unconstitutional in 1893. The Supreme Court declared:

And it is inconceivable that the distinguished body of men who composed the constitutional convention should have contemplated an apportionment of members within the several counties by means of assembly districts, not in proportion to population or under any other restriction, which should give to one qualified voter a voice in the election of members of the assembly equal to that of three or any indefinite number of voters who exercise their elective franchise at another voting place within the same county. [4]

Notwithstanding this decision, the legislature again set up Assembly districts in 1906. The action was immediately challenged with the result that the Court of Errors and Appeals upheld the 1893 decision of the state Supreme Court. Once again the legislative act was declared unconstitutional.

Although gerrymandering has been eliminated, the present system is not without its faults. The election of a number of assemblymen places a considerable burden upon the voter, especially in the more populous counties. For example, in Essex in 1953 each voter had to select twelve. The system also operates greatly to overrepresent the majority party. In Essex County, in 1953, the Republican candidates for the General Assembly averaged about 125,000 votes, the Democratic candidates about 117,000. [5] Notwithstanding the large minority vote, no one of the twelve assemblymen was Democratic. A system of election by district rather than at-large would have resulted in a more equitable distribution of seats.

In the primary election, particularly, the existing method of election at-large operates to the advantage of the organization as opposed to the independent candidate. Normally, organization candidates are grouped on the ballot and some slogan is used to identify them. This is an indication to regular party supporters throughout the county that these are the select candidates. All others fight hopeless odds.

Party practice in the primary varies considerably. For example, in Essex, Hudson, and Middlesex candidates are selected through party machinery. In Union County, on the other hand, the primary is usually open, the organization making no effort to dictate the selection of candidates for the lower house.

Apportionment

The apportionment problem arises only in the General Assembly since the constitution requires that each county have one senator. The Constitution of 1776 provided that each county should have three members in the General Assembly. The principle of representation according to population was recognized by the provision that in order to assure "more equal representation" the legislature could increase or diminish the number of representatives from any one county so long as the total did not fall below the minimum of thirty-nine for the thirteen counties then in existence.[6] In 1830 an act was passed linking the apportionment of seats to the Federal census.[7] The Constitution of 1844—and there was no change in 1947— limited the size of the house to sixty, with each county having at least one member, and provided for an apportionment "among the said counties as nearly as may be according to the number of their inhabitants."[8] The apportionment was to be made by the legislature at the first session following the census.

After the adoption of the 1844 constitution, the first apportionment of seats was based on a fixed ratio of "one member for every eight thousand two hundred and fifty inhabitants, and one for any residue, being a fraction of that number, exceeding one half thereof . . . ."[9] Succeeding acts prescribed no system but merely alloted a certain number of seats to each county.[10] The question of the timing of the apportionment arose after the census of 1920. The first legislature failed to take any action. A suit was brought to disallow the reapportionment act of 1922 on the ground that it had been passed subsequent to the constitutionally prescribed session for apportionment. The state Supreme Court held that failure to perform a duty did not cancel the obligation; "the duty is a continuous one, and is cast in turn upon each legislature succeeding that which has defaulted. . . ."[11]

Failure to establish an equitable method of distribution results in apportionment legislation based to a considerable extent upon the political strength that each party can muster at the moment. On the national level this problem was solved in 1941.[12] Congress provided for apportioning the House of Representatives according to the mathematical system of "equal proportions." This system reduces to a minimum the relative difference in the two basic criteria for an equitable apportionment, the population per representative and the individual's share in a representative. The New Jersey General Assembly differs from the national House of Representatives in size, but the principle of apportioning the membership is precisely the same.[13] Legislation to effect the apportionment by the method of equal proportions was adopted in the Senate. However, the house did not approve this proposal, or any other. As a consequence, the apportionment made after the 1940 census remains in effect as of 1956.

THE LEGISLATOR

Qualifications

The constitutional qualifications for membership in the legislature have remained the same since 1844.* The first requirement is that of age— twenty-one for the General Assembly, thirty for the Senate. The second requirement is citizenship. The third is residence in the state, four years for the Senate, two for the General Assembly. The fourth is residence in the county for one year. Finally, a person must be entitled to vote.

These requirements are similar to those of other states. Obviously, the constitutional requirements are a mere beginning; the real qualifications are those of an individual's standing with his party and with the voters.

Term of Office

Members of the General Assembly are elected for two years, members of the Senate for four. Until the recent constitutional convention established these terms New Jersey had the unenviable record of being the only state in the entire country to retain the one-year term for the Assembly. Members of the Senate under the old constitution served three years.

The theory underlying the distinction in tenure was based on the premise that the lower house was made up of members who were intimately related to small constituencies. More frequent elections, it was argued, assured an assembly more truly representative of popular sentiment. This theory actually had little relevancy in New Jersey since members of the Assembly represented precisely the same constituency as members of the Senate.

The new constitution adjusted the time of elections of members so that there would be no conflict with the Federal elections. The legislature is elected in odd-numbered years.

* The new constitution uses the word "resident" rather than "inhabitant."

Compensation and Allowances

Compared with most states, New Jersey's legislators are well paid. However, this condition is of relatively recent origin. From 1875 until the new constitution was adopted the annual legislative stipend was fixed in the constitution at $500.

The new constitution properly omits any mention of specific salaries. Instead, the legislature is authorized to determine by law what compensation shall be paid its members. In 1954 the salary was increased to $5,000 per year effective in 1956.[14] Members receive no traveling allowance or maintenance expense. They do receive passes entitling them to free transportation on the railroads within the state.

The quaint custom developed of paying legislators the full year's salary on the opening day of the legislative session. This custom was legalized in 1948. The law provides that as soon as a member is sworn into office, his full compensation shall be paid.[15]

Background of Legislators

Attorneys constitute the principal occupational classification in the New Jersey legislature. A recent study covering the nation as a whole indicated

TABLE 5

OCCUPATIONS OF NEW JERSEY STATE LEGISLATORS

Profession	1925		1935		1945		1955	
	Senate	Assembly	Senate	Assembly	Senate	Assembly	Senate	Assembly
Attorney	9	23	14	32	10	25	15	27
Advertising and publishing	0	2	1	1	1	0	2	0
Real estate and insurance broker	1	7	2	4	1	5	0	4
Banker	2	3	0	0	1	1	0	2
Industrial executive	0	3	1	1	0	3	2	5
Entrepreneur	1	6	1	3	4	4	1	0
Farmer	4	5	0	2	0	0	0	2
Union representative	0	0	0	0	1	2	0	2
Education	0	1	0	4	0	3	0	3
Physician	1	0	2	3	0	1	0	0
Engineer	0	3	0	0	1	3	1	3
Newspaperman	0	1	0	0	1	0	0	0
Accountant	0	2	0	0	0	2	0	0
Other	3	4	0	10	1	11	0	11
TOTAL	21	60	21	60	21	60	21	59*

Source: *Manual of the Legislature of New Jersey*, 1925, 1935, 1945, 1955.
a One vacancy.

TABLE 6

YEARS OF LEGISLATIVE EXPERIENCE, 1954

Years Experience	Assembly	Senate
1	22	4
2	1	1
3	15	2
4	2	0
5	7	0
6	1	1
7	7	2
8	1	1
9	0	1
10 or more	3	8
TOTAL	59 [a]	20 [a]

Source: *Manual of the Legislature of New Jersey,* 1954.
[a] There was one vacancy in each house.

that of 7,475 legislators, 1,674, or 22 per cent, were lawyers.[16]   This percentage is almost reversed in the New Jersey Senate.   As indicated in Table 5, out of 21 senators in 1955, fifteen were attorneys.   All other occupations combined amounted to only 29 per cent of the total.   Only two other occupations had as many as two members.   The four members of the minority party were attorneys.   In the Assembly, there were 27 lawyers out of the total membership of 60.   Industrial executives were the second most numerous classification with five members.

No woman has ever been elected to the state Senate.   However, women in surprisingly large numbers have served in the Assembly.   There were seven women members in 1955.

The youngest member of the Senate in 1955 was thirty-six, the oldest sixty-four.   The median age was fifty.   In the Assembly, the youngest member was thirty-two, the oldest fifty-nine, and the median, forty-four.

Turnover in the legislature is high, especially in the Assembly.   Appointments to administrative and judicial positions, advancement from the Assembly to the Senate, defeat at the primary or general election, and a tradition in some counties of a limit on the number of sessions any person is entitled to serve—all play a part in bringing about constant change.   In Hudson and Essex counties, the members of the Assembly are rotated at the will of the party leaders.   For example, in 1954, no one of the twelve members in the Essex delegation had served more than three years.   In Hudson, three of nine members had served longer than three years, one having had continuous service since 1939.

Table 6 shows the number of years of legislative experience in each house for 1954.   Over one third of the members of the Assembly were in their first year.   Only 20 per cent had more than five years.   On the other hand, the Senate was composed of old legislative hands. Almost two thirds had more than five years experience either in the Assembly or in the Senate. Forty per cent had served ten or more years.

LEGISLATIVE ORGANIZATION

Initial Organization

The initial meeting of the legislature occurs on the second Tuesday in January. It is accompanied by a considerable amount of pomp and cere-mony. Senators are usually dressed in formal afternoon attire. A large crowd is ordinarily in attendance.

Each house meets separately to organize. The preceding Senate presi-dent calls that body to order and after the election of a president pro tempore, who swears in new members, a president is elected. Custom in New Jersey dictates that the majority leader of the preceding year shall succeed to the office of president. By another custom, adopted in recent years, the retiring president is elected president pro tempore for the entire year. A secretary is also elected, and the rules of the preceding year are adopted. Then a delegation is sent to the governor to advise him that the Senate is organized.

A similar procedure is followed in the Assembly. At the first meeting of a newly elected Assembly, the clerk of the preceding year calls the house to order. One assemblyman is selected to swear in the other members. Each legislator then signs the roll, the official record of membership. As in the Senate, the presiding officer is changed each year, last year's ma-jority leader succeeding to the office of speaker. Representatives of large and small counties annually rotate these positions, the actual selection ordinarily being made weeks before in a pre-session party caucus. The Assembly also adopts rules and notifies the governor that it is organized. In addition, each house notifies the other that it is sitting. All this is done before the houses meet jointly to hear the governor's annual message.

Officers

The president of the Senate ordinarily wields considerable power. Obvi-ously, much depends upon the individual who holds the position. By Senate rules, the president recognizes a member who desires to speak. He decides parliamentary questions subject to an appeal to the whole body. All committees are appointed by the president. He has much to say about the order in which bills, resolutions, and reports are brought to the floor. In recognition of his extra responsibilities, the constitution authorizes the president an additional salary equal to one third his com-pensation as a senator.

The speaker of the Assembly is also in position to exercise great influence. He recognizes members, a potent weapon in silencing debate or in cutting off the minority. He decides parliamentary questions, subject to appeal, and has general direction of matters in the Assembly. This includes the determination of the committee to which a bill shall be referred, the preparation of a calendar of bills and resolutions, the presentation to the house of memorials and papers of various kinds, and the preservation of order on the floor and in the galleries. He appoints all committees although this power is circumscribed to a considerable degree by action of the party caucus. The speaker receives the same salary as the president of the Senate.

Employees

The election of other officers and employees to assist the legislature is controlled by the majority party. Unlike the Congress where both Republicans and Democrats nominate slates, even though the result may be a foregone conclusion, the party in power in New Jersey grants limited patronage to the minority. Usually the vote is unanimous for legislative employees such as supervisors of bills, journal clerks, committee clerks, doorkeepers, gallery keepers, file clerks, messengers, pages, and stenographers. The number of employees is determined by law, but neither house feels any compulsion either to abide by or to change the law. For example, twelve clerks to Assembly committees are authorized by law; there were forty-four in 1953. In the Senate four are authorized; nineteen were appointed in 1953. The law provides for a secretary to the Senate president only; yet in recent years each senator has had a secretary. The law also sets the salaries of legislative employees. However, each house follows the practice of granting a bonus of from 50 to 100 per cent.

These departures from the law are defended on the ground that one legislature cannot bind a succeeding body in the regulation of its own affairs. As a matter of courtesy, one house will not object to additional employees for the other house and by the same token the chief executive will not interfere with the legislature's desires concerning its own housekeeping.

In 1954 the total number of Senate employees, exclusive of senatorial secretaries, was sixty-three. In the Assembly the number was sixty-six. However, the real work of the houses was done by a small fraction of this number. Many positions, such as committee clerks, doorkeepers, gallery keepers, and pages, were filled as a reward for political effort and without any expectation of substantial service to the legislature. A few vital positions were filled by employees of long experience.

Sessions

All sessions of the legislature are required by law to be held at Trenton. Regular sessions ordinarily last about three months until the latter part of

April. If the legislature is fearful of the actions of the governor, it may take an extended recess. Thus the session is not officially ended until late in the year or until the next session convenes. This practice was followed by the Republican legislature during the administrations of Democratic governors A. Harry Moore and Charles Edison and again during the incumbency of Governor Robert Meyner.

During a regular session the legislature usually meets one day a week, on Monday afternoon. In the early weeks, while bills are being introduced, meetings may be quite short. Later, they are more extended and may be held two or three times a week. The practice of meeting but once a week is made possible by the small size of the state since Trenton can be reached by automobile from the farthest corner of the state in less than three hours. The practice also enables a legislator to hold a full-time job in his home community.

In addition to regular sessions of the legislature, there are several other categories of meetings. Joint sessions are used for ceremonial occasions, such as hearing a message from the governor. A joint session may also be used to hear arguments concerning alleged contempt of the legislature. The state auditor is appointed in joint meeting.

Special sessions may be called by the governor "whenever in his opinion the public interest shall require." Although the governor may ask that a particular subject be considered, the legislature is not limited in its discussions to that subject.* The constitution requires the governor to call a special session "upon petition of a majority of all the members of each house." However, short of a threat of impeachment or by obtaining the support of public opinion, the legislature has no effective means of enforcing this provision.

Special sessions of the legislature, usually referred to as constitutional sessions, meet forty-five days after final adjournment to reconsider bills vetoed by the governor. Special sessions of the Senate are called occasionally to confirm nominations. The term executive session refers to deliberations behind closed doors. The Senate follows this practice in considering nominations.

The split session—that is, a period for the organization of the legislature and the introduction of bills followed by a recess and then by deliberation on the bills—has no constitutional basis in New Jersey. Nevertheless, by means of legislative rules requiring the introduction of bills within a period of six weeks, combined with recess periods of varying lengths, the legislature in effect achieves a split session. This device was first used in New Jersey

---

* In twenty nine-states there are restrictions on the agenda of special sessions. For example, in Pennsylvania only those subjects may be considered which are included in the governor's call. See *Our State Legislatures* (rev. ed.), Chicago: The Council of State Governments, 1948), p. 5. Students of legislative practice look upon these restrictions with disfavor.

in 1930.   Its object was to curtail the last-minute passage of bills hastily introduced.   However, in actual practice in New Jersey and elsewhere, the split session has not had the beneficial effect originally anticipated.

Leadership

The source of leadership in the legislature varies with the political climate.   Rarely does the legislature itself have exclusive control of its destiny.   This is not unnatural, for the whole democratic process depends upon the operation of political parties, the leadership of which is often outside the legislature.   However, outside control of legislative action may easily become insidious and evil if the individuals wielding power are not themselves responsible in some rather direct way to the popular will.

One element of authority consists of the presiding officer and majority leader of each house, together with a few key members.   If the governor is of the same political faith as the majority representation in the legislature, he constitutes a second element.   He may be, and frequently is, the most important single power in determining the course of legislation since he is the recognized representative of the whole people and in addition may be the accepted leader of his party.   Nor is his patronage power to be discounted as a factor affecting the course of legislation.   The governor is also the head of a large administrative organization whose various departments themselves constitute important pressure agencies for the passage of legislation.

Powerful business interests or party leaders may at times dominate legislative action.   Under such circumstances there is always the danger that the interests of the people will be made secondary.   Periods when the legislature was influenced to an unhealthy degree by persons outside the state government have not been infrequent.   At various times in the latter part of the nineteenth century and in the early twentieth century, railroad, racing, and public utility interests dominated the actions of many legislators.   In more recent times political bosses have played important roles.

Legislative leadership is not static.   There are many centers of power, each vying against the others.   The governor, the county chairmen, the majority legislators from the small counties, and those from the large counties—all are influential in determining legislative direction.   In the 1950's both the majority and the minority membership of the legislature have been more free from outside domination than at any time in recent history.

THE COMMITTEE SYSTEM

The committee system in state legislatures is not so highly developed as in the Congress of the United States, and New Jersey is no exception.   The purpose of committees is to divide the work of preparing legislation among small groups.   No legislator can expect to be equally well informed on all

TABLE 7

COMMITTEES OF THE SENATE AND ASSEMBLY, 1956

Senate	Assembly
STANDING COMMITTEES	
Agriculture, Conservation and Economic Development	Agriculture, Conservation and Economic Development
	Subcommittee on Commerce and Navigation
	Subcommittee on Fish and Game
Appropriations	Appropriations
	Subcommittee on Anticipated Revenue
	Subcommittee on Claims and Pensions
Business Affairs	Business Affairs
	Subcommittee on Banking
	Subcommittee on Insurance
Education	Education
	Subcommittee on Elementary Education
	Subcommittee on Higher Education
Federal and Interstate Relations	Federal and Interstate Relations
	Subcommittee on Interstate Cooperation
Highways, Transportation and Public Utilities	Highways, Transportation and Public Utilities
	Subcommittee on Public Utilities
	Subcommittee on Transportation
Institutions, Public Health and Welfare	Institutions, Public Health and Welfare
	Subcommittee on Institutions and Agencies
	Subcommittee on Health and Welfare

subjects, but by means of a system of committees each member has an opportunity to obtain a special competence in a few fields. However, in New Jersey, except in a few instances, the committee system has failed to develop expert legislators. This failure stems from the fact that few committees have had any real function to perform.

Number and Size of Committees

One of the reasons for the failure of the committee system has been the number of committees and the number of committee assignments per member. Up to 1954 there were thirty-four standing committees in the Senate consisting of from five to seven members each. In addition, there were seven joint committees and three special committees. Obviously each of the twenty-one senators had to serve on several committees. Two Republican senators served on twelve committees each. In the Assembly, there

TABLE 7

(*Continued*)

Senate	Assembly
STANDING COMMITTEES—*continued*	
Judiciary	Judiciary
Labor and Industrial Relations	Labor and Industrial Relations
	Subcommittee on Labor
	Subcommittee on Industrial Relations
Public Safety, Defense and Veterans Affairs	Public Safety, Defense and Veterans Affairs
	Subcommittee on Veterans Affairs
Revision and Amendment of Laws	Revision and Amendment of Laws
State, County and Municipal Government	State, County and Municipal Government
ADMINISTRATIVE COMMITTEES	
Introduction of Bills	Introduction of Bills
Printed Bills	Printed Bills
Rules and Order	Rules and Order
Ways and Means	Ways and Means
	Subcommittee on Incidental Expenses
JOINT COMMITTEES	
Financial Reports	Financial Reports
Passed Bills	Passed Bills
Printing	Printing
State Library	State Library
SPECIAL COMMITTEES	
Investigating Committee	Conference Committee
COMMISSION	
Law Revision and Legislative Services	

were forty-three standing committees of from five to seven members, nine joint committees, and five special committees.

In 1954 the number of committees was greatly reduced. The committees of each house now cover the same areas of legislation. Formerly, not only did the standing committees differ in title and jurisdiction, but one house would have a joint committee on a subject that was not recognized by the other house. This change constitutes a substantial forward step in legislative reorganization.

The Senate now has twelve standing committees, ten of which consist of five members each. Two, appropriations and judiciary, have seven members each. There are four administrative committees, four joint committees, one special committee, and one commission.

The Assembly also established twelve standing committees. Each consists of seven members. However, there are also seventeen three-member subcommittees. For example, the standing committee on Agriculture, Conservation and Economic Development had two subcommittees, one on commerce and navigation and one on fish and game. The Assembly has four administrative committees and four joint committees to match those of the Senate. There are one special committee and one commission. Table 7 gives the titles of Senate and Assembly committees as of 1956.

Normally, a Senate committee of five would have one minority member. An Assembly committee of seven would have one or two minority members.

Committee Procedures

Assembly rules call for meetings of standing committees each week; notice of the meeting must be posted in the Assembly chamber and in the State House. In past years this rule was honored more in the breach than in the observance; many of the committees had no bills referred to them. No official record of committee meetings was maintained, nor was there a record of committee discussions.

Senate rules require that every bill be reported in writing, whether favorably or not, and that the report indicate how each member voted. In the past an unfavorable report was a rarity; bills were allowed to die in committee instead. In the Assembly, a bill may be reported by a majority of a standing committee. If the report is adverse, the introducer must be notified. The Assembly may not take action on an adverse report unless the sponsor of the measure is in his seat.

Each house has procedures for relieving a committee of any measure. In the Assembly twenty-four hours notice must be given before a motion may be entertained to relieve a standing committee of a bill. The written petition of eleven senators is required to force a bill out of a Senate committee.

The constitutional convention of 1947 and the administrative reorganization that followed seemed to have little effect upon the operations of the legislature. However, in recent years changes of considerable magnitude have occurred. For example, whereas public hearings formerly were a rarity, committees are now making increasing use of this device to sound out public sentiment. The sizable reduction in the number of committees, effected in 1954, should be of help also in giving meaning and importance to committee functions.

LEGISLATIVE COSTS

Legislative costs in the fiscal year 1956 (exclusive of the costs of legislative study commissions) amounted to 0.31 per cent of the total state budget. Of $937,563 appropriated by the legislature for its own housekeeping, 54 per cent went for salaries of the members themselves, their officers and employees, and the staff of the Law Revision and Legislative Services Commission. The largest single item was the $408,333 for the salaries of the eighty-one members. The remaining 46 per cent of the 1956 legislative budget was principally for use in connection with the preparation and printing of public documents, such as the *Minutes* of the Assembly and the *Journal* of the Senate.

Legislative expenses in the fiscal year 1956 amounted to seventeen cents per capita (based upon the estimated 1955 population). A study made in 1943 placed New Jersey thirty-ninth among the states in legislative expenditures per capita.* It is significant that the seventeen-cent per capita expenditure of New Jersey in 1956 was exceeded in 1943 by fifteen states.

Legislative expenditures in New Jersey could no doubt be reduced by the elimination of personnel who admittedly perform no services. In 1954 savings were made by eliminating some of the separate printings of the same bills, particularly where the new printing involved technical amendments. But economies of this kind should be balanced off by expenditures designed to make the legislator's role as effective as possible. For example, the members of the legislature have no office facilities in Trenton. Facilities are inadequate for conducting public hearings and for holding meetings of committees. In recent years an increasing emphasis has been placed upon the need for research into legislative problems, an area in which New Jersey has been notably lacking. Improvements along these lines would cost money. But adequate facilities and technical assistance are just as essential for the legislature as for any governmental agency or private business.

NOTES

[1] Belle Zeller (ed.), *American State Legislatures,* Report of the Committee on American Legislatures, American Political Science Association (New York: Crowell, 1954), p. 62.

[2] New Jersey *Minutes of Assembly,* 1941, p. 50.

[3] *State* v *Wrightson,* 56 N.J.L. 126, 154 (1893).

[4] *Ibid.,* p. 197.

[5] *Manual of the Legislature of New Jersey,* 1954, pp. 595-98.

[6] Constitution of 1776, art. III.

[7] L., 1830, pp. 57-58. This principle was extended in 1838 by a law requiring a reapportionment after each Federal census. L., 1838, p. 57.

[8] Constitution of 1844, art. IV.

[9] L., 1851, pp. 289-90.

[10] For a review of early apportionment legislation see Stanley H. Friedelbaum,

* *Interim Report of the New York State Joint Legislative Committee on Legislative Methods, Practices, Procedures, and Expenditures* (Legislative Document No. 35, Albany, 1945), p. 23. The figure used in the interim report was the amount budgeted for the legislature in 1944—$119,800. A more accurate figure would have been the amount expended the preceding year—$209,800. The use of the latter figure would have placed New Jersey twenty-sixth among the states.

"Apportionment Legislation in New Jersey," *Proceedings of the New Jersey Historical Society,* LXX (October, 1952), 262-77.

[11] *Botti* v *McGovern,* 97 N.J.L. 353, 356 (1922).

[12] 55 U.S. Statutes-at-Large 761.

[13] Rutgers University, Bureau of Government Research, *Legislative Apportionment in New Jersey, A Survey of Modern Methods Available* (New Brunswick, 1952), p. 7.

[14] L., 1954, ch. 204, p. 763.

[15] L., 1948, ch. 16, p. 64.

[16] Zeller, *op. cit.,* p. 71.

CHAPTER 6

The Legislature:

POWERS and PROCEDURE

ONE OF THE STRIKING FEATURES of the constitutional development of New Jersey has been the changing concept of the legislature's authority. Under the first constitution the legislature was all-powerful. The doctrine of the separation of powers among three coordinate branches had not become accepted. But in the Constitution of 1844, in the amendments of 1875, and again in the new constitution, not only were legislative prohibitions made a part of the constitution, but authority formerly exercised by the legislature was transferred to the governor and to the judiciary. As a consequence, the executive and the judicial branches have been raised to a position approaching in importance that of the legislative branch.

GENERAL LEGISLATIVE POWERS

The principal function of the legislative branch is to determine state policy. As the social and economic life of New Jersey increases in complexity, the areas in which legislation is desirable and necessary increase in number. However, the scope of legislative authority is not all-embracing. Legislative action is limited both by the Constitution of the United States and the Constitution of New Jersey.

In brief, the Federal Constitution authorizes the national government to exercise certain enumerated and implied powers and prohibits the states from exercising such functions as entering into treaties or agreements with foreign powers, engaging in war, coining money, or levying tariff duties. Governmental powers that do not belong exclusively to the national government and that are not prohibited to the states—or to the national government—are, according to Article X of the Federal Constitution, "reserved to the States respectively, or to the people." Thus, the residuary powers of the states are exceedingly large. However, in exercising these powers, the states are subject to the limitations of the Fourteenth Amendment:

No State shall make or enforce a law which shall abridge the privileges or immunities of citizens of the United States. Nor shall any State deprive any person of life, liberty or property without due process of law, nor deny to any person within its jurisdiction the equal protection of the laws.

In drafting the 1844 and 1947 constitutions, there was no necessity for enumerating those powers which the legislature might exercise, but rather those which it might not. As a consequence, a major portion of the legislative article is concerned with limitations upon legislative action. For example, the legislature may not "appoint any executive, administrative or judicial officer except the State Auditor"; it may not grant a divorce, authorize gambling except under certain restrictions, or pass general laws containing provisions that are private or local in character. The powers of the legislature are limited also by the judicial systems of the state and national governments. The constitutionality of any legislative act may be challenged in the courts.

The authority of the legislature is not restricted simply to the passage of bills. It shares in the executive power of appointment. For example, the advice and consent of the Senate are required in connection with the appointment of the principal administrative officers and the judiciary. The legislature also exercises the judicial functions related to an impeachment proceeding. The Senate acts as the trial court in cases where the Assembly has impeached an official.

Special and Local Legislation

Many of the constitutional limitations on legislative action resulted from efforts to bring an end to legislative abuses. For example, in the 1870's it was not uncommon for the legislature to pass acts removing individual municipal officials or changing the internal organization of a municipality. Private and local legislation consumed the greater portion of the energies of the legislature. Governor Joel Parker called for corrective action in his annual message of 1873:

The constitution should require general laws, and forbid the enactment of all special or private laws embracing subjects where general laws can be made applicable. This would dispense with at least nine-tenths of the business brought before the Legislature under the present system.[1]

Public pressure for reform was sufficiently strong to force the legislature's acceptance of the recommendations of the constitutional commission of 1873. Amendments were proposed and subsequently ratified by popular vote completely prohibiting certain kinds of private, local, or special laws and placing procedural limitations on others. For example, the legislature was prohibited from "regulating the internal affairs of towns and counties," granting to corporations exclusive privileges or franchises, altering highways, or vacating any public grounds. Any legislation covering these and other subjects was required to be general in nature. In other subject areas the amendments required public notice prior to the enactment of special legislation. The problem of establishing procedures for giving notice was left to the legislature. The law now requires that the notice to apply for passage of a special bill shall state the object of the bill. It must be signed by at least one person applying for passage, and be published, one week prior to introduction, in a newspaper in each county affected by the measure.* Proof of publication must be presented at the time the bill is introduced.[2]

With the adoption of the Constitution of 1947, separate provision was made for local laws. The constitution declared that upon petition of the governing body and by a two-thirds vote of all the members of each house, special legislation could be enacted regulating the internal affairs of municipalities and counties. The constitution left to the legislature the task of spelling out the details of the petition and adoption process. An enabling statute was passed in 1948, but it has been little used.[3]

In 1952 the Law Revision and Bill Drafting Commission prepared a listing of the private and local acts passed in the fifteen-year period 1938-1952. Of 186 private and local acts—an average of 12 per year—50 were for pensions to state or municipal employees or to veterans, 69 concerned the vesting of titles to properties that had escheated to the state, and 35 concerned municipal annexations or changes in boundaries.[4]

The absolute prohibitions in the 1875 amendments proved to be of limited value, especially in the local government field. The legislature quickly adopted the practice of classifying cities and counties. General laws were then passed applying to all cities of a given class. When the principle of classification was upheld by the courts, the legislature divided the classes by using language designed to qualify a particular class. For example,

This act shall be inoperative except in cities bordering on the Atlantic Ocean in counties of the fifth class having a population of less than one hundred fifty thousand according to the last Federal census.[5]

In 1945, when the above act was passed, there were two fifth-class counties. Monmouth County had a population of 161,238; Atlantic County had 124,066. Four cities in Atlantic County border on the ocean,

---

* Unless the special act concerns "benevolent, religious, charitable or educational institutions," the person interested in the act is required to pay into the state treasury an assessment of $25.

namely, Atlantic City, Brigantine, Margate, and Ventnor City. The act was designed to remove these cities from the rent control provisions of the Office of Price Administration. In holding the law unconstitutional the court declared that the demand for housing in these four cities "which have no war industries, is no greater than the demand for housing in various metropolitan districts throughout the state in which defense plants and factories are working on two and three shifts a day." The court declared that the legislation was just as appropriate to other areas as to those in Atlantic County. It continued:

> The distinctions are not substantial but illusory. The test of the generality of a law that it shall embrace all and exclude none whose conditions and wants render such legislation equally appropriate to them has not been met and by this test, the act is a special and local one and is discriminatory and unconstitutional.[6]

In the illustration above, the effort of the legislature to divide a class failed. However, in other instances, the efforts were successful. As a consequence of this type of language, the legislature remains relatively free to pass local legislation. However, over the years there has been less and less concentration of attention on purely local matters. Perhaps the most frequent use of special legislation in the last decade has been in the field of public employee pensions. Governor Meyner has vetoed pension measures couched in general language, but applying to one person, on the ground that the legislation was special in nature. The governor's attitude, together with the broadening of Federal social security to include state and local employees, should relieve much of the pressure on the legislature.

In summary, special and local legislation is no longer a particularly troublesome problem. The change has perhaps been due in some degree to preventive constitutional and statutory devices, but these devices were circumvented whenever the legislature wished to do so. Special legislation has not been eliminated, but it has been reduced in importance. The people have more and more demanded that legislation be general in character, applying to all on an equal basis. Then, too, the legislature itself has assumed a greater degree of responsibility than was prevalent in the latter part of the nineteenth century.

Investigatory Powers

In many states the power of the legislature to enact laws includes also the power to obtain, through investigation, pertinent information upon which to base legislative action. This has not always been the case in New Jersey.

In the exercise of the investigatory function, compulsory process may be used either directly by the legislature or through its committees to obtain the attendance of witnesses and the production of relevant books and papers.[7]   Both the speaker of the Assembly and the president of the Senate have power to issue a warrant ordering the sergeant at arms of the house concerned to arrest anyone failing to obey the summons of a committee. Willful disregard of a committee's summons, refusal to be sworn, or refusal to answer proper questions constitutes a misdemeanor.   A witness may not be excused from answering questions on the ground that to do so might incriminate him.   On the other hand, his answers may not be used in evidence against him except in a criminal prosecution for perjury.

In past years legislative investigations have been made of a variety of subjects in New Jersey including elections, law enforcement, the civil service, insurance companies, and the jury system.[8]   One of the most famous investigations was initiated in 1929 when a joint committee was authorized to investigate violations of law in any state, county, or local government.   Legislation was enacted providing for a joint session to arrest, try, and imprison up to six months anyone judged to be guilty of contempt of the two houses.[9]

The investigation was aimed at Mayor Frank Hague of Jersey City who was suspected of having profited from the sales of property in condemnation proceedings.   The committee also examined witnesses about alleged irregularities with respect to bus franchises and about payments made by motion picture proprietors to keep the city from enforcing ordinances on Sunday closings.   The investigating committee subpoenaed Mayor Hague and asked him ten questions, each of which he refused to answer.   Most of the questions centered around the source of funds for the purchase of expensive properties in Jersey City and in Deal.

After Mayor Hague had refused to answer the questions of the committee, he was subpoenaed before a joint session of the legislature and the questions were repeated.   Again he refused to answer.   He was adjudged in contempt by the joint session and arrested.   In a habeas corpus proceeding he was released whereupon the legislature through the sergeant at arms appealed to the Court of Errors and Appeals.   The state's top court declared that the legislature had invaded the judicial department:

. . . investigations of alleged violations of the criminal law are strictly judicial in their nature, and, under the constitution the legislature has no more power to conduct such investigations than has the governor, who constitutes the third branch of our governmental system . . . .   In refusing, therefore, to answer these questions, relating as they did to matters, inquiry into which was outside of the jurisdiction of the legislature, Hague was exercising a legal right, and, this being so, the legislature was without power to punish him for such refusal . . . .[10]

A more recent legislative investigation concerned the administration of the attorney general's office and the dismissal by the attorney general of a crime investigator.   In 1953 a committee composed of four members from each house conducted protracted hearings on the manner in which the state had endeavored to suppress crime. Sensational statements made by the dismissed investigator were later retracted. In the meantime, however, much damage had been done to the reputations of a number of individuals, including the Governor of the state.

The inquiry pointed up the necessity for the exercise of great care by a legislative investigating body. In commenting on the investigation the *New Jersey Law Journal* declared:

> The Committee's procedure and the course of examination under the resolution gave the guise of official sponsorship to many unsubstantiated and inexcusable defamatory statements . . . it is only in the long run that spectacular fictions can be overcome by humdrum facts. The immediate harm to individuals and the damage to confidence in government is beyond question.[11]

As the consequence of a supreme court decision in 1954, the narrow investigative limits within which the state had operated for a quarter of a century were greatly broadened.[12] The court's action followed a lengthy public controversy in Jersey City. City Commissioner Frank Hague Eggers, a nephew of the former city leader, endeavored to quash a subpoena issued by a committee of the governing body. Basing his argument upon the 1930 decision involving his uncle, Commissioner Eggers argued that the investigation concerned the possible violation of the criminal law. This, he declared, was a judicial matter within the power of the grand jury and the courts. The court specifically overruled the Hague case. It held that the investigation had a legitimate public purpose, that of obtaining information as a basis for remedial or corrective legislation. In commenting on the decision, the *New Jersey Law Journal* declared that New Jersey had been returned to "the ranks of the great majority of jurisdictions which recognize and enforce broad investigatory powers in the legislature." [13]

QUANTITY OF LEGISLATION

As Table 8 indicates, the quantity of legislation has increased slightly over the last quarter century. From the standpoint of the numbers of laws enacted, the period of the 1870's was the most productive. For example, in 1873 a total of 723 laws was enacted. In 1953 the total was 391. However, much of the early legislation was of a private and local nature.

The quantity of legislation is one indicator of the burden placed upon the conscientious legislator. A great many bills are of relatively minor importance. Some are merely minor modifications of existing law. The good or bad features of others can be determined with little effort. However, as the demands increase for the state to assume new functions, legis-

TABLE 8

LEGISLATIVE WORKLOAD

Year	Bills Introduced [a]			Laws Enacted [b]	
	Senate	Assembly	Total	Number	Per Cent
1925	217	489	706	247	35
1930	313	391	704	279	39
1935	385	419	804	330	41
1940	349	519	868	263	30
1945	279	356	635	309	48
1950	373	473	846	344	40

Source: For bills introduced, N.J. *Minutes of Assembly* and *Senate Journal.* For laws enacted, *Manual of The Legislature of New Jersey.*

[a] Duplicate bills are seldom introduced in the Senate and Assembly.

[b] Joint resolutions excluded. The number of joint resolutions enacted amounted, on the average, to about 5 per cent of the laws enacted.

lators are faced with policy decisions of great moment. In the past New Jersey's lawmakers have been handicapped by the lack of adequate staff assistance regularly providing them with factual, objective analyses of the implications and significance of proposed legislation.

LEGISLATIVE SERVICES

Hearings by Standing Committees

The committee system is important as a sounding board for public opinion, and, within limitations, as a source of information for members of the legislature. It is always the practice in the national government, and is becoming somewhat more frequent in the states, for committees to hold public hearings before referring major bills to the floor of the legislature. In the past legislative committees in New Jersey have held hearings to gauge public opinion only in unusual circumstances.

The lack of hearings on many important measures has brought considerable criticism of the legislature in recent years. Aside from the hearings of the appropriations committee, this device has been used usually only when there was a considerable public clamor.* Hearings are not popular with legislators since they involve extra trips to Trenton and more time away from their regular businesses. Rules require notice of commit-

* The appropriations committee does not hold hearings on the expenditures of many departments. If the department voices no objection to the amount requested by the governor, hearings are not held. The force of public opinion upon a legislative committee was demonstrated on March 7, 1950. The governor's budget message provided for the curtailment of the State Library and the elimination of the State Museum. Pressure on the legislature to restore these cuts was so great that at the beginning of a public hearing on the proposed reductions, the appropriations committee told the large audience crowded into the Assembly chamber that the appropriations for the library and the museum would be restored.

tee hearings, but the meeting may be changed at the convenience of the committee. Unless an alert newspaperman reports the change, persons desiring to attend hearings may find the legislative chamber empty.

The failure of the committee system in New Jersey has been due principally to the dependence of the legislators upon party leadership. If the leadership approved a bill, it would pass. If not, it would die. Under either circumstance, committee action seemed unnecessary. As a consequence, legislators came to regard all but a few committees as unimportant. Perhaps the 1954 reduction in the number of committees, together with the vigorous efforts on the part of some legislators to increase the prestige of the committees, will result in a much more responsible system.

Special and Interim Committees

During a legislative session, and frequently at the end of a session, the legislature establishes special committees. Some consist of members of the legislature only. Others consist of legislators and lay representatives. The expenses of some are financed by appropriations. Others receive no assistance in any form. The special committees are usually of a temporary nature and are created to study and recommend legislation on one subject. During 1953 at least fifteen special committees were in operation. An indication of the varied subjects of study may be obtained from the following titles: [14]

Joint Commission to Study the Methods, Practices and Procedures of the Legislature
Joint Commission on Law Enforcement
Commission on State Tax Policy
Election Laws Study Commission
Commission on Educational Television
Commission to Study the Non-Contributory Retirement Benefits to State and Local Government Employees
Legislative Commission on Statute Revision
Joint Committee to Study the Subject of Public Accounting
Joint Commission to Study the Use of Flammable Fabrics in Wearing Apparel and Other Articles
Traffic Safety Legislation Study Commission
Commission to Study the Problems and Needs of Mentally Deficient Persons
Assembly Commission to Investigate the Proposed Increase in Toll on the Camden-Philadelphia Bridge
Assembly Committee to Investigate the Construction of a Third Tube for the Lincoln Tunnel
Senate Committee to Study Legislation Regulating the Right of Uniformed, Paid Firemen to Engage in Effective Collective Bargaining
Joint Commission to Study the Problems of Drainage and Stream Clearance.

Law Revision and Bill Drafting

Drafting legislation is a task for the specialist. An individual legislator may have an idea that he wishes translated into a bill. But he often needs assistance in translating the idea into appropriate legal language and proper form. Then, too, the hundreds of statutes passed each year must be classified and consolidated in order to be usable. Occasionally conflicting and overlapping provisions are found in the permanent statute law. Confusing and redundant expressions are not uncommon.

In order to obtain technical assistance in the difficult task of consolidating and simplifying the statutes, the legislature in 1939 created a Commission on Statutes. This body was replaced by a Law Revision and Bill Drafting Commission in 1944.[15] Following the recommendations of a legislative study commission, a new and considerably enlarged body was established in 1954.[16] A Law Revision and Legislative Services Commission is now charged with supervision over an agency known as the Law Revision and Legislative Services.

The commission consists of four members from each house appointed by the presiding officer of that house. Each member continues in office so long as he is a member of the house from which he was appointed. A chairman and a vice-chairman are elected annually by the members. An executive director and chief counsel, appointed at the pleasure of the commission, serves as the principal executive officer in charge of the three operating units of the agency—a Division of Counsel to the Legislature, a Division of Law Revision and Bill Drafting, and a Division of Legislative Information and Research.

By legislative rule, all bills proposed for introduction in either house must be examined and approved as to form prior to introduction. For example, new material proposed for insertion in an existing law must be italicized. The examination is limited to the form of the bill and does not cover the substance. To aid persons preparing bills, the commission publishes annually a *Manual for Use in Drafting Legislation for Introduction in the New Jersey Legislature*.[17]

The last revision of the statutes was completed in 1937. Since then, substantive revision of the statutes has been accomplished both by the staff of the commission and by groups of experts in particular fields whose efforts were guided by the commission. However, the substantive revision of the criminal statutes accepted by the legislature in 1953 was accomplished by a special Legislative Commission on Statutory Revision that operated outside the framework of the permanent law revision agency.

Legislative Fiscal Analysis

One of the newest agencies of the lawmaking branch operates in the field of fiscal analysis and control. Late in 1954 the office of legislative budget and finance director was authorized. The enabling act provided for the appointment of a director by the Law Revision and Legislative Services Commission for a term not to exceed six years.

One of the principal functions of the director is to prepare data for the use of the Joint Appropriations Committee. In this connection he is required to examine the requests for appropriations made by the administrative agencies. He is authorized to attend the budget hearings normally held by the director of the Division of Budget and Accounting. The approval of the legislative budget and finance director is required before the state treasurer may transfer any item of an appropriation. The director is responsible also for the fiscal affairs of the legislature itself, including the certification to the governor of requests for appropriations by its committees and agencies, and the maintenance of accounting records.

Legislative Reference Services

In 1911 the state librarian was directed by the legislature to collect information pertaining to proposed legislation, and to prepare digests of materials upon the request of members of the legislative body. However, neither personnel nor funds were made available. When the State Library was made a part of the Department of Education in 1945, a Legislative Reference Bureau was created as a unit of the Bureau of the Law Library. In recent years a considerable effort has been made to recruit professionally trained research personnel to function as legislative reference specialists. The work of the staff ranges from the spot check to the completion of lengthy formal studies.

The Legislative Reference Bureau does no bill drafting. However, staff members supply secretarial services to some legislative committees. The bureau also maintains complete records on legislative measures and acts as a distributing agency on legislative materials.[18]

PASSAGE OF A BILL

The constitution sets up a number of guideposts that the legislative body is required to observe with respect to the lawmaking process:

1. Bills must be read three times in each house before final passage.
2. A full calendar day must separate the second and third readings in either house unless a bill is declared to be an emergency measure—an action requiring a three-fourths vote of the house membership.
3. A majority of the members must approve passage of a bill.
4. On final passage the yeas and nays must be recorded.
5. Each law must concern one object only, to be expressed in the title.
6. Any law revised or amended must be set forth at length and not by title only.

7. General laws must not embrace any provision of a private, special, or local law.

8. Public notice must be given of the intention to pass private, special, or local laws.

9. Laws shall begin "Be it enacted by the Senate and General Assembly of the State of New Jersey."

10. Revenue bills must originate in the general assembly.[19]

Rules of Procedure

In accordance with the constitutional authorization to "determine the rules of its proceedings," each house has an elaborate set of regulations governing the introduction, consideration, and passage of bills. In the Assembly four copies of a bill must be presented to the secretary of the speaker. After the bill is numbered and listed, one copy is made available to legislative correspondents, the others sent to the Committee on Revision and Amendment of the Laws. After examination as to form, one copy is held for the files of the Law Revision and Bill Drafting Commission. The two remaining copies go to the speaker, who notes upon the original the committee to which the bill is to be sent. When the clerk reads the number, title, and committee reference of each bill given to him by the speaker, the bill is then said to have been introduced and to have gone through its first reading. Bills are virtually never read in their entirety.

All bills are supposed to be introduced during the first six weeks of the legislative session. The written consent of a majority of the Committee on Introduction of Bills is necessary to authorize an exception.

After first reading, a bill is printed and referred to the appropriate committee. The bill may be reported out by a majority of the members of the committee. A minority of the committee may also submit a report. The committee may report the bill as originally presented, revise or substitute another proposal, or kill the bill by inaction.

When a bill is reported favorably, it is placed on the house calendar and at the appropriate time is advanced to a second reading. Amendments, if any, to be introduced from the floor, are made at this time. After second reading, one day must elapse before a bill can be ordered to a third reading and final passage. The time lapse may be disregarded providing three fourths of the membership declare the bill an emergency measure.

The Senate also has a detailed body of rules. If the two houses do not agree on a bill, Senate rules provide that "the Senate may either recede, insist and ask a conference, or adhere, and motions for such purposes shall take precedence in that order."[20] Normally when the houses do not agree, a compromise is worked out by the majority leadership.

Final enactment of a measure requires thirty-one votes in the Assembly and eleven in the Senate. The tabulation of votes in the Assembly is speeded by means of electrical roll call machinery.

Action by the Governor

Once a bill has passed both houses, two members from each house who are members of the Joint Committee on Passed Bills present the measure to the governor "for his approbation." The role of the governor in connection with the lawmaking process is considered in some detail in Chapter 7. Suffice it to say here that after the governor receives a bill he may give it his formal approval; he may permit the bill to become a law without formal approval in accordance with time limitations prescribed in the constitution; he may veto the bill on a conditional basis, that is, return the measure with his suggestions for modification; finally, he may return the measure with his veto. The terms "conditional veto" and "absolute veto" are commonly applied in New Jersey to the last two actions. A bill returned with a conditional veto may be passed a second time by a majority of the membership in each house. A two-thirds vote is required to override the absolute veto.

The Conference (caucus)'

Unwritten rules may be of greater importance than those spelled out in writing. The caucus system in the New Jersey legislature does not appear in the published rules of either house. Yet it operates in both.

In the Senate every bill is subject to approval by the majority party meeting secretly in caucus before any discussion may take place on the floor. Prior to 1952, the affirmative vote of eleven of the fourteen Republicans was required in order to release a bill or an appointment for floor action. Eleven votes were necessary even though one or two members were absent. The seven Democratic senators could not possibly block the passage of a bill since a majority of the entire Senate was already pledged to vote for it. In the event a bill did not have a sufficient number of Republican votes there was no way of obtaining the help of the Democratic members since there was no effective means of getting the bill before the entire Senate.

The constitutionality of the caucus was challenged in 1950 by the Democratic members of the Senate on the ground that it violated one clause of Article IV: "The yeas and nays of the members of either house on any question shall, on demand of one fifth of those present, be entered on the journal." [21] The attorney general held that the constitutional provision was not operative until a bill was actually before the Senate. An attack was directed also at Rule 18, which required a committee to report a bill upon the written petition of eleven senators. The attorney general held that Rule 18 did not violate the constitution "in the absence of constitutional specifications for, or restraint upon, legislative committees as regards the treatment of measures committed to them. . . ." [22] This pronouncement left the minority party with no means, aside from public opinion, of forcing a change.

Perhaps the most striking illustration of caucus rule in recent years was the Senate's refusal in 1948 to confirm the reappointment of Spencer Miller, Jr., to the position of state highway commissioner. A public official of the highest integrity, Miller had incurred the wrath of a few senators whose road construction plans he had not approved. Miller was favored by the six Democratic members and by eight or perhaps nine of the fifteen Republicans. No discussion of the issue was possible on the floor nor was any vote taken since the caucus system prevented the release from committee of the Governor's nomination.

Prior to the election of 1951 the caucus system came in for a rather severe public attack. As a consequence of the election of four Republican senators pledged to alter the caucus, a modification was adopted in the spring of 1952. "A majority of the members of the majority" is now required. In 1956 bills were released to the floor providing seven of the thirteen Republican senators gave their approval.

Opposition to the old system stemmed as much from choking off discussion as from blocking the passage of bills or appointments. In past years, it was impossible to bring out in public debate on the floor of the Senate the merits and demerits of a particular bill until the last minute when the measure was already assured of passage.

The Assembly also operates according to caucus rule. Ordinary bills require approval of a majority of the majority membership before they may be brought on the floor. However, the practices of the Assembly are less strict than those of the Senate regarding release of a bill from committee. As indicated previously, any member may, upon twenty-four hours notice, move to release a bill. Debate on this motion may actually become a debate on the merits of the bill itself. Thus public debate is not stifled.

LOBBIES AND PRESSURE GROUPS

The legislature has been called "a sort of battleground for the various interests of the state." [23] These interests are sometimes of a broad character devoted to the welfare of all the people, but, unhappily, organizations of this type are few in number. Sometimes groups of people are associated for the purpose of promoting one field of interest dedicated to the public good. In general, those who are bound together for the purpose of improving the whole society or even one phase of society are not to be feared. On the contrary, they constitute a perfectly legitimate means by which citizens express themselves: "Group representation through the lobby has obviously become as much a part of the democratic process as the political party." [24]

Occasionally, the zeal of a group interested in improving one function of government tends to cause them to lose their proper perspective. As a consequence, in their effort to obtain funds or personnel or a particular form of organization to promote that function, they may ride roughshod over the claims of those promoting other equally necessary functions.

Unfortunately, there are many pressure groups whose interests are narrow and selfish. Representatives of these groups are responsible for the sinister connotations of the word "lobbying." The regulation of lobbyists is aimed at curbing or at least bringing into public view the operations of paid agents of those representing relatively narrow fields of interest.[25]

The Lobby as a Source of Information

An increasing number of organized groups have become aware of the need for obtaining and disseminating factual information concerning their particular interests. Several organizations, such as the New Jersey Education Association, the New Jersey State Chamber of Commerce, and the New Jersey Taxpayers Association, maintain research agencies staffed by highly qualified professional personnel. The information collected is distributed to legislators and to the public.

Often, because of the large volume of proposed legislation and the limited resources of the state agencies serving the legislature, the information presented to a legislator by a pressure group constitutes the only data available to him in considering proposed legislation. On occasion, the information supplied by some of the dozens of pressure groups is lacking in objectivity. Some groups are extremely clever in their ability to present data that at first glance appear to be completely objective but actually are distorted to suit the purposes of the lobbying group.

Registration of Lobbyists

In 1951 lobbyists were required to register in twenty-nine states. Nineteen states required the filing of expense accounts, and twenty-two prohibited "contingent payments"—that is, payments to a person only if the legislation was passed or defeated in accordance with the interests of the employer. The most stringent law was that of California, enacted in 1950, which authorized committees of the legislature to exercise wide control over legislative advocates.[26]

Lobbying has proved exceedingly difficult to regulate. Increased efforts among the states in recent years to establish controls have not been reflected in New Jersey. Aside from the prohibition of bribery, there is no legislation whatever concerning lobbying in this state.*

---

* The bribery of legislators is classified as a high misdemeanor punishable by a fine or imprisonment or both. So also is the acceptance of a bribe. L., 1898, ch. 235, p. 791. For an early effort to regulate lobbying, see N.J. *Minutes of Assembly,* 1906, "Report of Committee to Investigate Rules and Regulations Affecting the Privileges of Lobbyists," pp. 156-69.

IMPROVING LEGISLATIVE PERFORMANCE

Following the adoption of the new constitution in the fall of 1947, the executive and judicial branches of the government were caught up in a reorganization movement of great magnitude. The participation of the legislative branch was limited to the passage of enabling laws. The members of the legislature seemed relatively unconcerned about extending the reorganization movement to their own branch. However, public dissatisfaction—particularly with the caucus—in the early 1950's was responsible for a number of new legislators and a much more receptive attitude toward suggestions for procedural reform.

Procedural Reform

In 1953 a Commission to Study Methods, Practices, and Procedures Employed by the Legislature was created. Consisting of four members from each house, the commission was instrumental in effecting a number of changes. The caucus system was modified in the Senate, and a major reorganization was effected in the organizational structure of the committee system. In late 1954 the commission recommended a substantial enlargement of the research and technical services available to members of the legislature.

The Role of the Public

Members of the legislature are easy targets of criticism. In the public mind there is a tendency to attribute the shortcomings of one legislator to all of his colleagues. The honest, conscientious member who does his utmost to study pending legislation and to vote in the interest of all the people of the state gets little credit for his efforts. Yet the success of the democratic process depends upon the election of a preponderance of legislators who are responsive to their public trust.

There is no easy answer to the problem of improving public confidence in the action of the legislature. Procedural reforms would help. A greater use of public hearings, an expanded research program, open discussion of issues, increased minority participation, controls on lobbying activities— these are within the competence of the legislature. But the ultimate responsibility for a legislative body of the highest quality depends upon the people themselves.

So long as the people of any area are willing to submit to boss rule, or so long as they are satisfied to be represented by a legislator who in reality represents someone else, the people of that area are doing a disservice to the people of the whole state. Public confidence in the legislature will rise and fall as public participation in the election process rises and falls. Intelligent and active participation by the public generally—particularly in the pre-primary and primary phases—will provide the best guarantee of a legislative body all of whose members place their public obligations above all others.

NOTES

1 N.J. *Documents of the 97th Legislature* (1873), p. 31.

2 L., 1897, ch. 2, p. 12.

3 L., 1948, ch. 199, p. 995.

4 L., 1952, *Schedule 7, Appendix,* pp. 527-31.

5 L., 1945, ch. 84, p. 423.

6 *Sbrolla* v *Hess,* 23 N.J. Misc. 229, 239 (1945).

7 See statement of Justice Case in *McRell* v *Kelly,* 124 N.J. Eq. 350 (1938).

8 For an index of investigations, see Dorothy F. Lucas, *Bibliography of New Jersey Official Reports 1925-1945* (Trenton: Department of Education, Division of State Library, Archives, and History, 1947), pp. 243-44.

9 L., 1929, ch. 1, p. 11.

10 *Court of Errors and Appeals—In re Hague,* 9 N.J. Misc. 89, 93-94 (1930).

11 Editorial, "The Truth and Nothing But the Truth," *New Jersey Law Journal,* LXXVI (July 2, 1953), 228.

12 *Eggers* v *Kenny,* 15 N.J. 107 (1954).

13 *New Jersey Law Journal,* LXVII (August 19, 1954), 4.

14 *Legislative Assistance for New Jersey* (Trenton: The Law and Legislative Reference Bureau, Division of the State Library, Archives and History, New Jersey Department of Education, 1953), pp. 10-13.

15 L., 1939, ch. 91, p. 182, and L., 1944, ch. 105, p. 274.

16 L., 1954, ch. 254, p. 921.

17 See also N. J. Law Revision and Bill Drafting Commission, *Ten Years of Continuous Revision of Statutes in New Jersey, a Report on the Work of the New Jersey Law Revision and Bill Drafting Commission, January 9, 1940 to January 9, 1950, by Charles DeF. Besore.*

18 *Legislative Assistance for New Jersey op. cit.,* p. 9.

19 Art. IV, secs. IV, VI, and VII.

20 Senate Rule No. 56 (1954). The rules of each house are printed in the legislative manual.

21 Sec. IV, par. 4.

22 "Attorney General's Opinions," *New Jersey Law Journal,* LXXIII (1950), 19.

23 Dayton David McKean, *Pressures on the Legislature of New Jersey* (New York: Columbia University Press, 1938), p. 9.

24 William Miller, "The Legislature: Lobbying," N.J. *Constitutional Convention of 1947,* II, 1577.

25 For the methods used by pressure groups, see McKean, *op. cit.,* pp. 188-217.

26 Belle Zeller, "State Regulation of Lobbying," *The Book of the States, 1952-53,* (Chicago: The Council of State Governments, 1952), p. 110.

CHAPTER 7

The Governor

THE GOVERNOR of New Jersey is the only publicly elected member of the state administration. The constitution grants him the executive power and places upon him the responsibility for taking "care that the laws be faithfully executed." [1] He is charged with supervising the administrative machinery of the state government including the appointment of key officials and the control of an involved fiscal apparatus. He is given a part in legislation through his messages, his approval or rejection of bills, and his rule-making power. He shares judicial responsibilities by virtue of his appointment of judges and his power of pardon. He is commander-in-chief of the militia.

But the gubernatorial powers recognized by the constitution are of no greater importance than other, extra-constitutional, powers, which stem from the office but depend for their effective use upon the character of the individual holding the position. Included in this category are the powers the governor may exercise as the representative of the whole people and as the leader of his party.

EVOLUTION OF THE OFFICE

As a result of the reaction to the extensive and often arbitrary powers exercised by governors representing the British Crown, the Constitution of 1776 gave the governor almost no authority. Although he was the "supreme executive power," the constitution failed to spell out the meaning of this phrase. He had no power of appointment, almost no voice in legislation, and the method of his selection left him at the complete mercy of the legislature.* He had, it is true, a number of judicial functions to perform and was commander-in-chief of the militia.

* He was elected annually by the Council and Assembly in joint meeting.

The reaction that produced so weak an office had its own reaction. The large amount of authority granted to the legislature in 1776 proved to have been misplaced. As a consequence, the convention of 1844 curbed to some degree the power of the legislature and strengthened, in a mild sort of way, the executive office:

The men of 1844 had learned to trust the legislature less than did their forebears of 1776, but they were not disposed to trust the governor much more. The constitution of 1844 departs therefore from the principle of legislative responsibility for the general conduct of the government, which was implicit in the constitution of 1776, without making provision for any other system of responsibility.[2]

As the population increased from 372,859 in 1840 to 1,444,933 in 1890 and to 4,835,329 in 1950, a greater and greater number of functions was thrust upon the state. Administrative machinery, employing several thousand persons to perform these functions, was created. The people tended to hold the governor responsible for supervising this machinery in spite of the legislature's insistence upon its responsibility for the selection of many heads of major departments. It was not until the convention of 1947 that the way was opened for the chief executive to assume a constitutional position in keeping with the tremendous governmental responsibilities forced upon him by a rapidly expanding and increasingly complex society.

Since 1844 the constitution has recognized the theory of the separation of powers, and the Constitution of 1947 contains the statement "the powers of the government shall be divided among three distinct branches, the legislative, executive, and judicial." [3] Although each branch is forbidden to encroach upon the powers of any other, the legislature is not confined to legislative powers exclusively nor the governor to executive powers. The constitution provides specifically for certain exceptions. For example, the governor participates in lawmaking when he approves or rejects a bill.[4]

The courts have not been disposed to usurp the prerogatives of the governor. Indeed they have exercised extraordinary care in decisions involving the office of the chief executive. A disputed election in 1856 resulted in a statement of the supreme court emphasizing the necessity for avoiding judicial encroachment upon the executive. The question involved the court's power, by *mandamus,* to compel the governor to issue a commission certifying the election of a surrogate in Passaic County:

. . . we are of the opinion that the *mandamus* must be denied, upon the broad ground that this court has no power to award a *mandamus,* either to compel the execution of any duty enjoined on the executive by the constitution, or to direct the manner of its performance. The exercise of such power would be an unwarrantable interference with the action of the executive within his appropriate sphere of duty . . . .

While it is the acknowledged duty of courts of justice to exert all their appropriate powers for the redress of private wrongs, it is no less a duty sedulously to guard against any encroachment upon the right, or usurpation of the powers, of the co-ordinate departments of government. In the delicate and complicated machinery of our republican system, it is of the utmost importance that each department of the government should confine itself strictly within the limits prescribed by the constitution.[5]

Only since the convention of 1947 has there been any measure of equality among the three branches.* Under the 1776 and 1844 constitutions, the legislature was by far the most powerful. It remains the dominant body, but from the standpoint of constitutional power the governor is now in a vastly improved position to perform the increased functions of his office.

THE CHARACTER OF THE OFFICE

Qualifications

In common with most states, New Jersey has three constitutional qualifications for the office of governor—minimum age, United States citizenship, and residence in the state for a number of years. The Constitutional Convention of 1844 set the minimum age at thirty, required United States citizenship for a period of twenty years, and residence in the state for seven years. The convention of 1947 made no change in these requirements. It is rather interesting to note that the only qualification in the Constitution of 1776 was for "some fit persone, within the colony, to be governor. . . ." This qualification is similar to the requirement in the *Model State Constitution* of the National Municipal League for "any qualified voter of the state." †

Nomination and Election

Officially, the direct primary is the means of selecting the party nominee

* "For the first time in New Jersey history, and almost for the first time in the history of the American states, there will be a state government of three departments relatively equal in power, each of which should be able, with reasonable singleness of purpose, to devote adequate attention to its main job." John E. Bebout, *Some Reflections upon the Draft Constitution approved by the 1947 New Jersey Constitutional Convention* (Mimeographed, September 24, 1947), p. 1.

† (5th ed., New York: National Municipal League, 1948), art. V, sec. 501. In general, the more simple the qualifications, the less the controversy. North Dakota was much upset in 1935 because of the clause requiring the governor to have five years residence within the state. The eligibility for office of the winning candidate was challenged on the ground that he had lived and voted in another state within the prescribed period. The state supreme court upheld this contention and the lieutenant governor succeeded to the office. Roy L. Miller, "The Gubernatorial Controversy in North Dakota," *American Political Science Review*, XXIX (1935), 418-32.

for governor.   Actually, in most instances, the voters in the primary election merely confirm the choice of the party leaders.

So long as the governor was elected for a three-year term, election conditions varied greatly.   For example, in every twelfth year the election of governor was concurrent with that of the President.   For that election national questions overshadowed state issues.   To a lesser degree, national issues also outweighed state issues in years when congressional elections concurred with a gubernatorial contest.   Now the gubernatorial election is held in the odd-numbered years.   This plan is much to be preferred for it enables the people to concentrate their attention upon state issues and state personalities.*

Term of Office

The governor's term of office is four years.   He is eligible to succeed himself once only.

At the time of the Constitutional Convention of 1947, New Jersey was the only state in the Union with a three-year term for governor, and the 1844 constitution made the governor ineligible to succeed himself.   This dual handicap played havoc with long-term planning.   A governor was too new to get much done his first year, and he was ineffective his third year because interest was concentrated on the election of his successor.   "Politicians," said Woodrow Wilson in discussing the question of ineligibility to re-election, "smile at the coming and going of governors as some men in Washington have smiled at the coming and going of Presidents, as upon things ephemeral, which passed and were soon enough got rid of if you but sat tight and waited. . . ." [6]

In 1927 an effort was made to extend, by amendment, the term to four years although the prohibition on succession was retained.   Because the wording of the amendment placed the gubernatorial election in the same year as the presidential election, the Democrats objected on the ground that the amendment worked to their disadvantage since the Republican party was strongest in national elections.[7]   The amendment was defeated.

In the Constitutional Convention of 1947, extension of the governor's term and his eligibility to succeed himself were the first proposals considered by the Committee on the Executive, Militia and Civil Officers. All those who had held the office of governor were asked to testify.   Governor Driscoll and former governors Hoffman, Larsen, and Moore appeared before the committee; Edison and Edge filed written statements with the committee.   There was virtually unanimous agreement on lengthening the term to four years.   However, there was sharp division over the

---

* ". . . the problems of government in any one of the states are large and significant enough to the well-being of citizens to warrant a decision based upon their own merits."   W. Brooke Graves, *American State Government* (4th ed., Boston: Heath, 1953), p. 323.

question of succession. The extreme points of view were represented by
A. Harry Moore, three times the state's chief executive, who advocated unlimited succession, and Walter E. Edge, who recommended retention of
the existing limitation. The committee's proposal of a four-year term with
a maximum of two terms in succession was adopted by the convention.
The new provision represents a substantial advance over the old. However, it answers only in part the penetrating questions raised in the committee by former Governor Moore, who asked, ". . . why should anyone
deny the people the right to elect their own representatives? . . . Why
should we eliminate from the prospective field of candidates from whom
the people can make a choice, the one individual whose qualifications they
are best able to judge—the then current governor?" [8]

Compensation

The governor's annual salary is $30,000. In addition, the legislature
appropriates funds for the maintenance of the executive mansion, known
as Morven, in Princeton. In 1951 the legislature accepted the mansion as
a gift from former Governor Walter E. Edge and Mrs. Edge. Governor
Meyner was the first chief executive to make his official residence at
Morven.

Vacancies and Succession

New Jersey has never had a lieutenant governor. Under the Constitution of 1776, the vice president of the council was given the "supreme
executive power" in the absence of the governor. This precedent was continued by the Constitutional Convention of 1844. However, the title
was changed to president of the Senate.

There was some consideration given to establishing the office of lieutenant governor in the convention of 1947. The Committee on the Executive, Militia, and Civil Officers was opposed to the idea of a lieutenant
governor presiding over the Senate. Unsure of other functions to be performed by a lieutenant governor, the committee defeated a proposal to
establish the office. Instead, the existing line of succession was continued
—that is, the president of the Senate followed by the speaker of the General Assembly—with the additional provision that a further line of succession be established by law.*

Disability. The 1844 Constitution provided no means of determining
whether the governor was physically capable of performing his official
duties.† With the experience of other states in mind the Committee on

* New Jersey is one of eleven states having no lieutenant governor. *The Book of
the States, 1954-55* (Chicago: The Council of State Governments, 1954), p. 501.
Seven states, including New Jersey, name the presiding officer of the Senate as the
immediate successor to the governor; three name the secretary of state.

† This deficiency provoked a serious controversy in Illinois during the two-year

the Executive, Militia and Civil Officers evolved a plan to determine the existence of a vacancy. They proposed, and the new constitution provides, that if a governor-elect fails to qualify for office within six months, or whenever the governor is absent or "unable to discharge the duties of his office by reason of mental or physical disability, the office shall be deemed vacant." [9] The determination of the vacancy is to be made by the supreme court. However, the action of the court is contingent upon receiving from the legislature a resolution "declaring the ground of the vacancy." To be valid, the resolution must be adopted by a two-thirds vote of the entire membership of each house. After the resolution is received, the court is required to give notice of the vacancy, conduct a hearing, and obtain proof before it may declare the existence of the vacancy.

The purpose of this clause of the constitution is laudable; the procedure is too involved. Further, it has the grave defect of making a political issue out of a simple question of fact. Is the governor able to perform his duties, or is he not? * To require a two-thirds vote of the entire membership of each house may result in the introduction of all sorts of irrelevant political considerations.

Resignation. On four occasions since 1844, the resignation of the governor resulted in the president of the Senate exercising the powers and duties of the chief executive.† Twice, in 1899 and 1913, because there was neither a governor nor a president of the Senate, the powers and duties of the governor's office devolved upon the speaker of the General Assembly. Twice, in 1920 and in 1935 when there was no governor, the presidency of the Senate changed hands when the new legislature organized on the second Tuesday in January. This meant that for a period of one week, until the newly elected governor was inaugurated, the new president of the Senate exercised the governor's powers.

The question whether a person who had served as acting governor could run for the governorship was presented to the courts in 1899. Edward Clifford was ordered to be executed by the Hudson County Court of Oyer

---

illness of Governor Horner, 1938-1940. There were long periods when he was not able to go to the State House, and the charge was made that the duties of the office were being performed in his name by a "bedside cabinet." See Clyde F. Snider, "Gubernatorial Disability," *The University of Chicago Law Review,* VIII (1941), 521-29. Wisconsin in 1942 and Georgia in 1946 had serious disputes arising out of the deaths of governors-elect.

* For example, in Mississippi the secretary of state is empowered to submit the question of disability to the judges of the supreme court who investigate and make a determination. *Constitution of Mississippi,* art. V, sec. 131. In Alabama, any two of seven officials may ask the supreme court to determine the governor's mental condition. *Constitution of Alabama,* art. V, sec. 128.

† On January 31, 1898, John W. Griggs resigned to become United States Attorney General; on March 1, 1913, Woodrow Wilson resigned to become President of the United States; on May 16, 1919, Walter E. Edge resigned to become United States Senator; on January 3, 1935, A. Harry Moore resigned to become United States Senator.

and Terminer. A stay of execution was granted by Foster M. Voorhees, president of the Senate, who was acting governor after the resignation of Governor John W. Griggs. Some months later Voorhees resigned from the Senate, and David O. Watkins, speaker of the General Assembly, became acting governor. He granted Clifford a further stay but ordered the execution to take place at the termination of the reprieve. Clifford's counsel then argued that when Voorhees became governor, he was no longer senator. Therefore, his resignation as senator was not valid and he was, in fact, still governor when Watkins ordered the execution. The supreme court said:

> The provision is that in case of the resignation of the governor, the powers, duties and emoluments of the office shall devolve upon the president of the senate, and not that the president of the senate shall thereby become governor, and hold the title and the office until another governor is elected . . . .
> He [Voorhees] is still president of the senate, with the added duties required of the chief executive of the state imposed upon him.
> There is no language in the constitution from which it can reasonably be inferred that his office of president of the senate was to be vacated. He retains his office of senator and as president of the senate, and not as governor. He exercises the added powers and performs the superimposed duties.[10]

This decision was not without its political implications. Voorhees had resigned from the Senate in order to run for governor. The court's decision on January 4, 1899, meant that Voorhees, who had been elected governor, was eligible for the office.[11]

Absence. By custom, the governor deliberately leaves the state for a short period each year in order that the president of the Senate, and in a few instances, the speaker of the General Assembly may have the honor of presiding as acting-governor. From 1900 through 1951 there were forty-one acting governors. In the period from 1947 through 1953, New Jersey had one governor and thirteen acting governors.[12] One departure from the state on business resulted in court action over the powers of the acting governor. On June 20, 1942, President of the Senate I. Grant Scott assumed the duties of acting governor while Governor Charles Edison was attending a governors' conference in North Carolina and for the next two weeks exercised the powers of the office. Edison returned from his trip, the train arriving in Newark at about 9:15 A.M., June 25. Shortly afterward he talked with Scott by phone. Apparently he did not give Scott any notice that he was assuming the duties of the office. Instead, he left the state three days later and did not return until early in July. During this entire time Edison's staff continued to recognize Scott as acting governor. At 11:30 A.M. on June 25, shortly after Edison had telephoned, Scott signed an alcoholic beverage bill, the legality of which was subsequently challenged on the ground that the president of the Senate was exceeding his authority. The state supreme court held otherwise. The court observed that the people have a fundamental right "never to be without a Governor" and that the right is meaningful "only when the people know that the Governor is in the state. . . ."

Implicit, therefore, in the arrangements for the President of the Senate to exercise the executive powers and duties of the Governor during the latter's absence is the correlative duty of the Governor to give notice to the acting-Governor that he has returned to assume his duties. We, therefore, hold that the word "return," in these circumstances, contemplates that the Governor comes back to the state and advises his pro-temporary successor that he is ready to resume his executive powers and duties.[13]

Filling a Vacancy. The new constitution is somewhat more specific than the old about filling a vacancy. An election to fill the unexpired term is called for unless the vacancy was not determined until so near the general election day (sixty days) that it would be impossible to conduct a bona fide election. In this event, the vacancy would not be filled until the next general election. No election to fill a vacancy may be held in the year of the regular gubernatorial contest.

EXECUTIVE POWERS *

The Appointive Power

One of the most significant features of the people's increasing reliance upon the governor has been the added authority given him in connection with appointments. Popular feeling in this respect has turned almost full circle since 1776.

The first constitution gave the governor no appointive power whatsoever. The legislature alone had the authority, in joint meeting, to appoint state officials and most county officials. It was the abuse of that authority, especially in connection with county appointments, that resulted in a demand for modification of the legislature's powers. As a consequence, in the Constitutional Convention of 1844, the selection of militia officers, the attorney general, the secretary of state, the judges of the higher courts, and all county prosecutors was placed in the hands of the governor. A further development occurred in 1875 when, by amendment, the legislature lost to the governor the power to appoint judges of the courts of common pleas and the keeper of the state prison. However, the governor was not a free agent, since in each instance the consent of the Senate was required.

Appointments by the legislature in joint meeting were not eliminated completely. As administrative functions increased and new departments were established, the legislature used the joint meeting device for the selec-

* For the governor's military and other powers, see the appropriate chapters.

tion of department heads. This practice furnished one of the major talking points for those favoring revision of the constitution since it made difficult, if not impossible, any effective control of administration by the governor.[14]

The Constitution of 1947 eliminated the legislature as a competitor of the governor in making appointments by the specific prohibition that " neither the Legislature nor either house thereof shall elect or appoint any executive, administrative or judicial officer except the state auditor." [15] However, the new constitution does not eliminate legislative influence altogether, for the clause requiring confirmation by the Senate is retained.

The requirement of Senate confirmation raises the question of the governor's authority to make appointments after the legislature has adjourned.* The authority of the governor to make appointments during a period of adjournment was first interpreted by the courts in 1802. Notwithstanding the language of the Constitution of 1776, which gave the appointive power to the legislative body, Governor Joseph Bloomfield filled a vacancy in the office of clerk of Essex County while the legislature was not in session. Chief Justice Kirkpatrick dissented from the supreme court's denial of the governor's authority, and his position was later affirmed by the court of errors. He argued that since the governor had the supreme executive power, he had an "indispensable duty" to cause "the laws to be executed when the ordinary provisions for that purpose fail." [16] This principle was incorporated in the Constitution of 1844:

> When a vacancy happens, during the recess of the legislature in any office which is to be filled by the Governor and Senate, or by the Legislature in joint meeting, the Governor shall fill such vacancy, and the commission shall expire at the end of the next session of the Legislature, unless a successor shall be sooner appointed . . . .[17]

After 1850 the recess appointment came to be used by governors as a device to escape Senate control. Governors Haines, Bedle, McClellan, Ludlow, and Abbett resorted to this practice. The supreme court held that if an abuse existed, it was the privilege of the legislature to institute impeachment proceedings. In an opinion in 1888, Justice Van Syckel wrote:

> Even though the governor should be guilty of a breach of duty in refusing to send any nomination at all to the senate, during its session, it would be none the less within his power, and his duty after the adjournment, to fill the vacancy . . . .
>
> This court has no right to instruct the governor as to matters which involve his duty only and not his power. We cannot know the circumstances which influenced his action, and must presume that he acted rightly.[18]

* It is the established practice in New Jersey to construe the word "recess" as the period following the final adjournment sine die of the Legislature. See opinion of Attorney General Theodore D. Parsons, *New Jersey Law Journal*, LXXII (1949), 133.

The practice of using the recess appointment to circumvent Senate control was limited in 1897 by a constitutional amendment forbidding the appointment of any person who had been refused confirmation by the Senate. The Constitutional Convention of 1947 changed the language slightly, but the intent was to prevent the governor from appointing *ad interim* anyone whose confirmation had been refused.

Removal

Prior to the adoption of the new constitution, the governor had no constitutional power of removal. State Supreme Court Chief Justice Mercer Beasley wrote in 1873:

I have not been able to perceive any intimation, not even the least, either in the constitution of this state, its system of laws, or legal observances, that this right of superintendency over, or power of removal from public office, except in instances of statutory specification, has been delegated to the executive head of the government.[19]

The only means of removing an official was by impeachment until the legislature began the practice of authorizing the governor, under certain conditions, such as neglect of duty, to remove the head of a specified office. For example, when the Department of Banking and Insurance was created in 1891, the governor was empowered to remove the commissioner "for cause." [20]

The constitutionality of the legislature's action in authorizing the governor to remove an official was challenged on the ground that the removal power was a judicial function and could not be conferred upon the governor. However, the supreme court refused to accept this view. Gradually the practice grew of specifying by law the grounds for removal. But there was no general law. In 1911 Governor John Franklin Fort indicated to the legislature his feeling of frustration:

It is humiliating to demand that wrongs be righted and that extravagance, illegality or incompetency cease, and have a subordinate (it may be an underling in some department or institution) treat your suggestion with contempt or possibly criticise you for making it, and be powerless to deal effectively with the contumacious, corrupt or incompetent officials.[21]

Governor George S. Silzer, in 1925, told the legislature that an increase in the governor's power of removal would "provide a speedy method of improving the public service." [22]

The Convention of 1947 gave the governor, for the first time in New Jersey history, a constitutional removal power. But it is by no means unlimited. There are varying means of removal for the several categories of officials. Individual heads of principal departments, except the secretary of state and the attorney general, who have a definite term of office, are removable at the governor's pleasure. Other officers and employees who receive their compensation from New Jersey, except members of the legislature, the judiciary, or officers elected by the legislature in joint meeting, are removable for cause and then only "after notice, the service of charges and an opportunity to be heard at public hearing . . . . " [23] Executive officers of boards that head principal departments may be removed by the governor upon notice and opportunity to be heard.

In effect, then, the governor's power of removal is limited to several of the individual heads of departments. Other officials are protected by the words "for cause." This phrase has a definite legal meaning—formal charges sustained in a court of record.

Power of Pardon

The governor's power of pardon is an executive, not a judicial, power.* It is "founded on considerations of the public good, and is to be exercised on the ground that the public welfare, which is the legitimate object of all punishment, will be as well promoted by a suspension as by an execution of the sentence." [24]   Under the first constitution the governor and the Council possessed the power. Under the Constitution of 1844, pardons were granted by the Court of Pardons consisting of the governor, the chancellor, and the judges of the Court of Errors and Appeals. The governor had but one vote.

The constitution now makes clear the governor's sole responsibility for granting pardons. He and he alone takes action. A commission may be established to assist him, but its function is limited to aiding and advising. The courts have held that the general power of pardon includes the power also to remit fines and to commute a sentence. However, a person pardoned is not entitled to the return of a fine already paid.[25]

The constitution recognizes the distinction between a pardon and a parole.† The Constitution of 1844 made no mention of parole. This omission led to a controversy as to whether a parole was or was not a pardon. Attorney General Edmund Wilson gave an opinion in 1912 concerning the validity of legislation passed the preceding year that established maximum and minimum terms for prisoners. Wilson argued that a parole was a prison regulation and that the legislature was in no sense delegating any part of the power of the court of pardons.[26] The new constitution resolves any possible question by the simple statement that "a system for the granting of parole shall be provided by law." [27]

* "In this state and country the pardoning power is, and always has been, a prerogative of the executive department. In this state it is expressly bestowed in Article 5 of the constitution relating to the executive department." *In re N.J. Court of Pardons,* 97 N.J.Eq. 555, 558 (1925).

† For a description of the existing parole system see page 244.

THE LEGISLATIVE POWER

The governor is in position to exercise a strong influence upon legislation. There are many avenues along which he may act. Some, such as his right to send messages to the legislature, to call special sessions, to approve or to veto bills, and to promulgate rules, are recognized specifically by the constitution.

Messages

The constitution gives the governor a free hand in sending communications to the legislature. He is required to send a message at the opening of each regular session. He may send messages "at such other times as he may deem necessary. . . ."

The degree to which governors accept this constitutional invitation depends chiefly upon their personalities. For example, the annual message may be simply a report, or it may be a call to action. It may urge specific legislation, or it may recommend a commission to study and report later, or it may call for a cautious "do nothing" approach.

In commenting upon the right to send messages, Governor Woodrow Wilson defended the practice of preparing accompanying bills:

It seems perfectly clear that it is the explicit prerogative of practically every American executive to recommend measures if he pleases in the form of bills. It is no presumption on his part, therefore, and no invasion of the rights of any other branch of government, if he presses his views in any form that he pleases, upon the law-making body.[28]

In the early years, the inaugural address and the annual message were normally the major official communications to the legislature from the governor. Then, after 1844, came the veto message and after 1916 the budget message. The special message is used also to emphasize the necessity for quick action on legislation. Formerly, all messages were delivered to each house by the governor's secretary, but in recent years personal appearances before a joint meeting have become frequent.

Special Sessions

The governor may call a special session either of both houses or of the Senate alone. Normally, the principal reason for convening the Senate would be to act on appointments. The constitution contains a provision, by which the legislature may petition the governor to call a special session. The constitution states that he "shall" call the legislature. However, the value of this provision is doubtful since neither the legislature nor the courts could force him to act.

Approving Legislation

Prior to 1947, governors largely ignored the provision establishing a time limit for the consideration of bills passed at the close of a legislative session. The 1844 constitution provided that any bill presented to the governor and not signed within five days after adjournment was dead.* As the mass of last-minute legislation increased, it became physically impossible for the chief executive to pass intelligently upon hundreds of bills within five days. In order to avail themselves of a longer period, governors reinterpreted the clause "after it shall have been presented to him." The clerk of a friendly legislature was asked to present the governor with the bills only as rapidly as they could easily be considered. In this way, bills became law two months or more after the period intended by the constitution.

On one occasion the constitutionality of a law was challenged on the ground that an act delivered to the governor on April 13, 1906, the day the legislature adjourned, was not approved until June 12. Relying upon earlier decisions that "an enrolled statute of this state is conclusive proof of its enactment," the court refused to receive the evidence.[29] It observed also that to rule against the legality of such a measure might introduce a condition of chaos since 1,359 bills had been approved after the legislature adjourned during the period 1884-1905.

The above practice could also work in reverse. An unfriendly legislature might cause much embarrassment by passing all its bills at the close of the session and then immediately dumping them in the lap of the governor. At the Constitutional Convention of 1947, Governor Moore testified that the attitude of the legislature was occasionally, "Send them over to that So-and-So and let's see what he is going to do." [30]

The members of the 1947 convention recognized the governor's need for a period in which to study new legislation before giving it his approval. At the same time they wished to eliminate the questionable practice of ignoring the five-day limit. Therefore a new approach was adopted.

Now, the governor is given forty-five days after adjournment in which to approve or disapprove a bill. It becomes law *unless* he returns it with his objections to the legislature, which automatically reconvenes on the forty-fifth day. The only exception to this procedure is in the event final adjournment of the legislature is within forty-five days of the end of the

* Art. V, par. 7. Holding bills for longer than the constitutional five days was authorized by the legislature in 1880 (*L.*, 1880, ch. 173, p. 259). The act was repealed in 1895 (*L.*, 1895, ch. 426, p. 817). Governor Werts said the law had been regarded as unconstitutional. The editors of the *New Jersey Law Journal* state that "prior to the administration of Governor Abbett, in 1884, no bills appear as approved more than five days after the adjournment, and only forty out of more than ten thousand appear as approved after the close of the session." In 1891 only five of the 285 general bills were approved within the five days after adjournment. *New Jersey Law Journal*, XXVIII (1905), 290-91.

legislative year, in which case, bills not signed by the governor within forty-five days of final adjournment are dead.

Veto Power

Under the Constitution of 1776, the governor was a member of the Legislative Council. His was but one voice—he voted only in case of a tie.

The question of giving the governor a veto was the subject of a long and spirited debate in the Convention of 1844. To some delegates, the veto was a means of protecting the people from rash acts of the legislature; to others, it was simply a holdover from colonial days when it was used to protect the crown against the people. The convention voted against a strong veto and adopted a clause that was the object of gubernatorial denunciation for the next hundred years.

As adopted in 1844, the veto power was exceedingly weak since a majority of the members, the same number necessary to pass the bill in the first place, could override the veto. One change was made after 1844. Among the amendments passed in 1875 was a provision authorizing the governor to veto individual items in an appropriation bill.

At the Constitutional Convention of 1947, the veto clause was subjected to severe attack. Testimony uniformly favored strengthening the governor's position. So general, indeed, was the sentiment for a strengthened veto clause that the recommendations of the committee calling for a two-thirds vote to override provoked little public comment. An effort was made on the floor of the convention to retain the existing provision, but the attempt failed by a vote of sixty-four to eight. An amendment requiring a three-fifths vote to override the governor's veto was also defeated —forty-eight to twenty-five.[31]

A feature introduced in the Constitution of 1947 permits the governor to veto a bill conditionally. This means that he may return a bill to the legislature with his recommendations for amendment. If the legislature agrees with his suggested changes, the bill may be repassed by a majority of the members and submitted to the governor a second time. He then has ten days in which to sign or reject the revised bill. He may not return a bill to the legislature a second time.

During the six-year period from 1948 through 1953 Governor Driscoll sent 516 veto messages to the legislature. The number ranged from 51 in 1948 to 123 in 1952. At no time did the legislature pass a bill over Governor Driscoll's absolute veto. However, 151 measures included in the total of 516 were subsequently approved by the governor after suggested revisions had been accepted by the legislature.[32]

Extraconstitutional Means of Influencing Legislation

The legislative powers of the governor are not limited to the formal procedures established by the constitution. He has a number of additional avenues, extraconstitutional in character, for accomplishing his program.

These powers are large or small depending to a considerable degree upon the personality of the governor himself.

The first stems from the office. The governor has one tremendous advantage over any individual member of the Senate or the General Assembly; he is the representative of the whole people. Particularly in recent years, all over the United States, the people have come to look to their governors for leadership. As a consequence, when a governor asks the legislature for specific action, he is to a very real degree speaking for every citizen of the state. The legislature is less and less disposed to turn a deaf ear to his desires.

As the representative of the whole people, the governor may appeal for public support when his requests are denied or when he sees something amiss that cannot be corrected by virtue of his constitutional powers. By releases to the press or speeches before various groups, he may be able to persuade the legislature to do his bidding.

As leader of his party the governor also wields a considerable amount of authority. This power is recognized in every state, but it is especially important in New Jersey where organized party politics reaches into the most remote corner. Needless to add, the influence of some governors has been dimmed by their allegiance to the party boss.

One of the most frequently used and in many ways the most effective means by which the governor influences legislation is through conferences with key legislators. Governor Wilson went so far as to attend the caucus of his party. Opponents immediately criticized him for undue interference with the legislature. Governor Meyner has followed the practice of meeting with a group called the Legislative Conference prior to each day's proceedings. The conference consists of the governor and his counsel, the president of the Senate, the speaker of the Assembly, and the majority and minority leaders of each house.

A final means by which the governor exercises a measure of control over legislation is through his patronage powers. For example, Governor Edge made perfectly clear that he would not make any appointments in 1945, pending a favorable vote upon his legislative program. Some years later he observed:

I do not wish to seem cynical, but it is difficult for a modern governor to be a great administrator and a great legislator at the same time. The appointing power, for better or for worse, is an important factor in his legislative program.[33]

THE FUNCTIONING OF THE OFFICE

The Functioning of the Office

The people of New Jersey expect their chief executive to manage the state government. This involves making budgetary decisions and making appointments to hundreds of positions. Frequent conferences are necessary with state, Federal, and local officials on a host of matters relating to day-to-day operations as well as to longer range policy matters. But the people expect the governor to do much more than just manage the government. He must assume the leadership in formulating state policies. This involves the presentation to the legislature of a carefully worked out legislative program. Through press conferences, and by means of the radio, television, and a multitude of personal appearances, the governor must also report to the people on what the state is doing. He is New Jersey's highest ceremonial functionary and as such is expected to participate in events of various kinds. He is the leader of his political party as well and must somehow meet the demands upon his time made by municipal, county, state, and national party officials.

In order to perform all of these functions, the governor requires an office staff. Throughout the United States, no two governors organize their offices in precisely the same manner.[34] In New Jersey the tendency has been to operate with a small staff—too small, indeed, for the governor's own personal welfare, and that of the staff, and for the most effective disposition of state business. As a consequence, governors have been handicapped in supplying a degree of supervisory control over administration commensurate with the additional authority granted the office in the new constitution.

The governor's principal assistant is his executive secretary. The executive secretary is in charge of the professional and clerical staff. One of the principal functions of the executive secretary is to act as a buffer. An amazing number of people want to talk personally with the governor—departmental officials, legislators, party functionaries, not to mention a considerable number of citizens. The executive secretary must choose among those who should talk with the governor and those whose needs can best be met by referring them to the administrative agencies. Mail addressed to the governor and invitations to speak or to attend ceremonial functions must be put through a similar screening process. The secretary plays a considerable role also in the selection of prospective appointees for positions in the state government.

Relations with the press, and public relations generally, are the responsibility of the secretary and a few executive assistants. The burden of preparing news releases, arranging for radio and television appearances, answering a heavy load of correspondence, conducting research, and serving as an extension of the eyes and ears of the governor falls upon this small group.

The counsel to the governor is also a part of the chief executive's immediate staff. His principal function, and that of his assistants, is to serve as legal adviser on matters of interest to the governor. This may include actual bill drafting or a review of bills prepared at the governor's request. Bills passed by the legislature are reviewed by the counsel, who recommends to the governor that he approve or reject a particular measure. Suggested amendments to legislation, and the preparation of veto messages fall within the area of the counsel's responsibility. Other aspects of his work include the investigation of cases involving executive clemency, the extradition of fugitives from other states, and the review of sales of riparian rights.

NOTES

[1] Art. V, sec. I, par. 11.

[2] John Bebout, *The Making of the New Jersey Constitution, Reprint of Introduction to the Proceedings of the New Jersey State Constitutional Convention of 1844 Together with a New Foreword* (Trenton: MacCrellish and Quigley Co., 1945), p. ciii.

[3] Art. III. The language of the 1844 constitution was similar.

[4] *Ross* v *Freeholders of Essex,* 69 N.J.L. 291 (1903).

[5] *The State* v *The Governor,* 25 N.J.L. 331, 349, 351 (1856).

[6] Letter of Wilson to A. Mitchell Palmer, February 5, 1913, from *Congressional Record,* 64th Cong., 1st sess., LIII, 12620, quoted in John E. Bebout, *Documents and Readings in New Jersey Government* (Ann Arbor: Edwards Brothers, Inc., 1931), p. 167.

[7] Bebout, *Documents, op. cit.,* p. 75.

[8] N.J. *Constitutional Convention of 1947,* V, 64.

[9] Art. V, sec. I, par. 8.

[10] *Clifford* v *Heller,* 63 N.J.L. 105, 110, 111 (1899). On other grounds the order of Watkins was set aside. *Ibid.,* p. 119.

[11] William E. Sackett, *Modern Battles of Trenton* (New York: The Neale Publishing Co., 1914), II, 73.

[12] *Manual of the Legislature of New Jersey,* 1954, p. 21.

[13] *In Re An Act concerning Alcoholic Beverages,* 130 N.J.L. 123, 131 (1943).

[14] The lack of uniformity concerning the conditions of appointment and tenure is well illustrated by Amos Tilton in his "The Appointive Power—Tenure, Removal and Confirmation of Officers," N.J. *Constitutional Convention of 1947,* II, 1383-1409.

[15] Art. IV, sec. v, par. 5.

[16] *State* v *Parkhurst,* 9 N.J.L. 427, 441-42 (1802).

[17] Art. V, par. 12.

[18] *Fritts* v *Kuhl,* 51 N.J.L. 191, 206, 208 (1888).

[19] *State* v *Pritchard,* 36 N.J.L. 101, 111 (1873).

[20] *McCran* v *Gaul,* 95 N.J.L. 393, 396 (1920).

[21] N.J. *Senate Journal,* 1911, p. 16.

[22] N.J. *Minutes of Assembly,* 1925, p. 29.

[23] *Constitution of 1947,* art. V, sec. IV, par. 5.

[24] *Cook* v *Freeholders of Middlesex,* 26 N.J.L. 326, 333 (1857).

[25] *Cook* v *Freeholders of Middlesex,* 27 N.J.L. 637 (1858).

[26] *In re N.J. Court of Pardons,* 97 N.J.Eq. 569 (1925).

[27] Art. V, sec. II, par. 2.

[28] Hestor E. Hosford, *Woodrow Wilson and New Jersey Made Over* (New York: Putnam, 1912), p. 73.

[29] *Bloomfield* v *Freeholders of Middlesex,* 74 N.J.L. 261, 265 (1907).

[30] N.J. *Constitutional Convention of 1947,* V, 69.

[31] *Ibid.,* I, 216-20.

[32] *Newark Evening News,* August 17, 1953.

[33] Walter Evans Edge, *A Jerseyman's Journal* (Princeton: Princeton University Press, 1948), p. 271.

[34] Homer E. Scace, *The Organization of the Executive Office of the Governor* (New York: Institute of Public Administration, 1950, mimeographed), pp. 54-60.

CHAPTER 8

Administrative Reorganization

SEVERAL EFFORTS have been made over the last forty years to improve the administrative organization of the New Jersey state government. Changing philosophies as to just what constitutes a proper organization are reflected in the reports made from time to time by various groups selected to examine the administrative structure.

EARLY EFFORTS AT REORGANIZATION

The Wilson Era

The impetus to administrative reorganization in New Jersey was given by Governor Woodrow Wilson. Questions of "efficiency and economy" received first place in his 1912 message to the legislature:

The government of New Jersey, like the governments of most of the older States, has developed on its administrative side, not systematically, but by patchwork, and mere accretion: by the multiplication of boards and commissions, by the addition of first this piece and then that piece to existing departments. There has been constant addition, no subtraction, no elimination, no coordination. It has grown very much as the State House itself has grown, but without the necessity of at least some semblance of architectural unity, without the connecting corridors and the common roof which the State House must of mere physical necessity be given.[1]

At Wilson's suggestion, a seven-member commission was created by law to study the consolidation of different departments "whose separate duties are now intimately related." The commission urged that reforms be effected, otherwise "the number of departments, boards, commissions and officials will continue to grow, expenses will multiply, and a state tax will necessarily result." [2]

In recommending consolidation, the Wilson commission criticized the practice of organizing a separate agency for each function. The commission urged that government agencies be operated on the same lines as a business corporation, "with a Board of Directors and a chief, corresponding to the President of a corporation." [3] Although the boards of directors were to be appointed by the governor with the consent of the Senate, the commission gave no consideration whatever to the governor as the actual operating head of the state government. The report continued:

We have conferred with many who have given special study to the reorganization of governmental bodies, and, without exception, we believe that the conclusion which they have reached is that the most effective system consists in a board and a Commissioner, the former to define policies—in short, to be, as it were, a legislative body; and the latter to be an executive to carry into effect the policies of the State as set forth in the laws and in the rules enacted by his board.[4]

During the period 1915-1920, a considerable number of the Wilson commission's recommendations for consolidation were adopted.*

The Bright Committee (1925)

The state's reliance upon boards and commissions was severely criticized in 1925 by the Bright Committee. This legislative investigating body obtained the services of a Chicago group to study the operations of the state government. Emphasis again was placed upon the adoption of modern business practices. However, this time the commission form of organization was declared to have been "overdone" and any success of the agency was "in spite of rather than because of that type of organization." The committee averred that a single administrator responsible directly to the governor could "accomplish greater results and eliminate a great deal of red-tape and delay." [5]

In order that the governor might exercise "the authority expected of him," the committee proposed that the ninety-six permanent and temporary departments and commissions be consolidated into fourteen departments and an independent comptroller's office. The legislature took no action on any of the Bright Committee's proposals.

* Departments of Health, Conservation and Development, Commerce and Navigation, and Shell Fisheries were created in 1915; also the State Board of Taxes and Assessments. The Bureau of Industrial Statistics was merged with the Department of Labor. In 1916 the Department of Labor was reorganized, and the Department of Agriculture created. Departments of Architecture and Municipal Accounts were created in 1917. Charitable and penal institutions were consolidated under the Department of Charities and Corrections in 1918, renamed the Department of Institutions and Agencies in 1919.

The Institute of Public Administration Survey (1929)

An extensive survey was made in 1929 by the National Institute of Public Administration. The legislature empowered Governor Morgan F. Larson to employ experts, and appropriated $100,000 to cover the cost of the study. An exceptionally competent staff was assembled under the general direction of Mr. A. E. Buck. This group condemned the lax administrative practices in a number of state agencies and listed almost 150 specific constitutional, statutory, and administrative recommendations. A general reorganization, beginning with the governor's office, was proposed. The group observed that the increasing number of functions performed by the state required leadership that could not be supplied by a governor and top officials who came to Trenton only one day a week.[6] The institute suggested the consolidation of the various agencies into thirteen major departments responsible to the governor, and the creation of a Department of Audit responsible to the legislature.

The institute's critical analysis was resented by Governor Larson who advised the legislature to proceed with care before adopting any recommendations "many of which are radical and experimental, and all of which are more or less involved and complicated . . . ."[7] The institute report was not shelved immediately, however. Governor A. Harry Moore, upon taking office in 1932, used it as a basis of action, recommending that all state administrative agencies be consolidated into twelve departments. Once the reorganization was effected, he proposed that "these changes in the administration of the State's business . . . be walled up in the constitution, proof against tinkering and ill-considered change and modification."[8] Thus, as new functions were required, they would be incorporated within existing departments.

When his proposals failed to obtain the support of the Republican Senate, Governor Moore invited the School of Public and International Affairs of Princeton University to survey the state's administration and finances. The university study recommended a Department of Fiscal Control with accounting, budgeting, and purchasing divisions.[9] A single head was recommended for the State Highway Department in place of the four-member highway commission. The report sought a number of economies in the state government that would have reduced expenditures approximately 8 per cent. Subsequently, the legislature created the offices of state commissioner of finance and state auditor. It also established a single head for the highway department.

Changes in the Forties

Reorganization was much discussed in succeeding gubernatorial campaigns, but little was accomplished. The constitutional revision movement of the early 1940's also focused attention on the state's sprawling administrative structure. The Constitutional Commission of 1941-42 referred to the governor as an executive in name only, who was "hampered by whimsical laws and inadequate constitutional authority." [10] The commission recommended the allocation of all executive functions within nine departments, which were named in the proposed constitution. Thus, in their anxiety to reduce the number of agencies, the commission attempted to freeze not only the number of departments to be created, but also the specific names of those departments. The commission sought a flexible constitution, yet its recommendations with respect to some phases of administrative organization were the exact opposite.

Several of the commission's suggestions were carried over into a constitution proposed by the legislature in 1944. The number of departments was changed to a number not to exceed twenty. The governor was authorized to allocate by executive order all agencies among these departments so as to group them "according to major purposes." A resolution of each house of the legislature was necessary to disapprove any executive order. The defeat of the proposed constitution by public referendum put an end temporarily to any discussion of administrative reorganization through constitutional revision.

Meanwhile, Governor Edge set about to achieve administrative integration as far as was possible through legislative action. With both a Republican Senate and General Assembly, his chances of success were much greater than those of his two Democratic predecessors, each of whom had to contend with a Senate controlled by the opposition party. A Commission on State Administrative Reorganization, representing each house of the legislature and the governor, was appointed to recommend changes in the administrative structure. The commission considered first a number of questionable administrative practices that had developed in the office of the attorney general. Their proposal for a new Department of Law was adopted, following modification by the legislature early in 1944.[11] A reorganization plan was then submitted consolidating a number of semi-independent fiscal agencies into a new Department of Taxation and Finance. This proposal, designed to provide an integrated fiscal system, was also approved.[12]

Other plans proposed by the commission and adopted between 1944 and 1947 related to changes in the structural framework of the Department of Education,[13] the formation of a new Department of Conservation,[14] and the abolition of board control over the Department of Health in favor of a single administrator with full power to prescribe internal organizational procedures.[15] As a result of the recommendations of the commission, twenty-four agencies were consolidated within five major departments.[16]

REORGANIZATION AND THE NEW CONSTITUTION

Obstacles

Fundamental reforms were impossible without substantial changes in the state constitution. Although the governor was theoretically the chief executive officer, the constitution effectively kept from him the authority necessary to direct the affairs of the state. Several factors accounted for the governor's inability to supply effective direction. These may be summarized as follows:

1. The constitution provided for the election of two principal officials, the state treasurer and the comptroller, by the legislature, meeting in joint session.[17] This device was used by the legislature as a means of selecting other administrative officers. The director of the Office of Milk Industry and the commissioner of the Department of Alcoholic Beverage Control were elected in this manner. Thus the governor, the only popularly elected official, had to work with major administrative officers not of his choosing.

2. The three-year term of the governor plus the constitutional prohibition of a second successive term made impossible any continuing leadership or control on the part of the chief executive.

3. The long terms of some constitutional officers served to destroy any feeling of personal responsibility to the governor. The attorney general and the keeper of the prison had constitutional terms of five years. The terms of other agency heads were fixed by law, many for periods longer than that of the governor. As a consequence, each incoming governor inherited literally dozens of top officials in whose appointments he had exercised no voice. His limited removal power extended to a relatively small percentage of this group.

4. The governor's role as commander-in-chief was severely compromised by the lack of harmony between two constitutional officers, the adjutant general and the quartermaster general, each of whom had built up a separate department.

These constitutional disabilities made impossible the development of a fully integrated administration. A further disability had assumed serious proportions over the years. The long-standing practice of growth, "by patchwork and mere accretion" condemned by Wilson, had resulted in a host of boards, commissions and independent agencies. A study made in 1943 revealed 42 boards, 47 commissions, 3 councils, 4 authorities, and 6 miscellaneous agencies.[18] Although one quarter of these were consolidated between 1944 and 1947, at least seventy administrative agencies were in existence at the time of the 1947 constitutional convention. Sheer weight of numbers prevented adequate executive supervision.

Small wonder, then, that executive reorganization was a major problem facing the convention. Notwithstanding extensive testimony setting forth the evils of the existing system, a majority of the Committee on the Executive, Militia and Civil Officers was not disposed to accept in full the recommendations of reform groups. Strong pressure from the friends of agencies headed by boards, such as the Department of Institutions and Agencies and the Department of Agriculture, made it politically inexpedient to give the chief executive full administrative control. These departments had achieved a status that virtually defied executive tampering.

Convention Accomplishments

Nevertheless, far-reaching constitutional changes were introduced. The governor's term was lengthened, he was permitted to succeed himself once, and the overlapping terms of other constitutional officers in the executive branch were eliminated. The governor was granted specific authority to investigate any state administrative official and to obtain information under oath concerning the official's conduct of his office. The commander-in-chief's authority over the military was enhanced by the elimination of the constitutional offices of adjutant general and quartermaster general. The legislature was forbidden to elect or appoint any executive, administrative, or judicial officer except the state auditor.

Perhaps the most important provision in connection with the governor's administrative control was that requiring the allocation of existing agencies among not more than twenty principal departments. This clause set the stage for a major reorganization of the administrative structure.

Following the adoption of the new constitution in November, 1947, a commission representing the legislature and the administration prepared plans for the allocation of all executive agencies among fourteen departments. Individual reorganization bills were drawn up for each department. Thirteen of these were passed, the fourteenth failing because of a controversy over the procedure for selecting the commissioner of education. An act was passed, however, designating the Department of Education as one of the principal departments.

All the new provisions, taken in their entirety, strengthened immeasurably the governor's constitutional position and gave him an opportunity to furnish a degree of leadership, direction, and control over the operating agencies probably unequalled in any of the states.[19] However, the governor's constitutional authority over the principal departments is not complete. The constitution states that "the head of each principal department shall be a single executive unless otherwise provided by law."[20] In each of nine departments headed by an individual, the appointing power is shared with the Senate. Five departments are headed by a board or commission. In four of these, the members are appointed by the governor with the consent of the Senate. In the fifth, the Department of Agriculture, the board members, although formally appointed by the governor with Senate consent, are in fact selected by delegates of farmers' associations meeting in an annual agricultural convention. In three of the five departments headed by boards or commissions—civil service, public utilities, and education—the governor designates the president or the chief executive officer. Executive officers appointed by the Board of Agriculture and the Board of Institutions and Agencies must, in accordance with the constitution, have the governor's approval. Thus, although the chief executive has a considerable measure of control over the selection of twelve of the heads of the fourteen principal administrative departments and some control over the remaining two, he does not have full selective authority in any case.

The governor's removal power is also limited, although to a lesser degree than his appointive power. The new constitution divides into three categories the governor's authority to remove his department heads: single executives serve at the governor's pleasure; the secretary of state and the attorney general serve during the term of office of the governor; executive officers of boards may be removed upon notice and opportunity to be heard. The net result is to give the governor complete freedom in the removal of seven of the nine single department heads, a somewhat restricted authority in the case of departments headed by boards, and no authority with respect to the attorney general and the secretary of state unless charges are preferred.

An Appraisal of the Reorganization

An analysis of the laws establishing the fourteen principal departments reveals an achievement falling somewhat short of complete administrative integration. The reorganization acts are considerably more restrictive than the constitution requires. They hamper control by the department head, first by freezing the internal structure and second by compromising him with respect to the appointment of his divisional directors. In health, civil service, defense, and highways the department head has wide discretion; he can create, consolidate, or eliminate divisions almost at will. In treasury, law and public safety, and others, the divisional structure is fixed. Whenever the department head desires to effect a change, he must seek enabling legislation. These variations stem in part from the nature of the functions performed and in part from the pre-1947 status of the agencies concerned. The more technical and specialized the function, the greater was the tendency to free the department head from statutory restrictions. However, where an agency of considerable importance was brought into a department, the reorganization acts nearly always accorded the unit divisional status.

Undoubtedly, there were also political reasons for the variations in the discretion given department heads by the reorganization acts. The specialized nature of the operations in some departments offered few opportunities for political appointments. As a consequence, the department head was permitted wide latitude. In agencies requiring administrators with less technical training, the department head was relieved of responsibility—or at least required to share his responsibility with the governor and the Senate. Approximately twenty division heads are appointed by the governor with Senate consent.

Inattention to the chain-of-command theory is evidenced further by the statutory term of many division heads. In some instances department heads who serve at the pleasure of the governor have, as subordinates, division heads who are appointed by the governor and serve during the governor's term. Removal power is also vested in the governor, not in the department head. The department head may initiate each appointment or removal, but his freedom of selection and his ultimate control of the agency may be severely prejudiced.

In effect, many of the reorganization acts performed a twofold disservice to the department chief. His control over the department was appreciably reduced by the fact that he could not alter the fundamental structure without legislation. In the long run this may tend to discourage organizational developments in keeping with changes in function. His control was lessened also by the provision for gubernatorial appointment of division heads. Much depends upon the attitude of the governor and the political pressures of the moment. In the past, members of the legislature have often looked upon the top-level positions in a number of agencies as avenues either for personal advancement or for discharging political obligations. Senate consent meant political selection. The reorganization acts do not alter the pattern. Since the initial allocation of all agencies to fourteen principal departments, no new departments have been created.

Rigid adherence to the number fourteen has resulted in a legal structure that sometimes does not reflect actual conditions. The New Jersey Turnpike Authority is the best, although by no means the only, illustration of an organizational fiction. By law, the Turnpike Authority was placed in the State Highway Department.[21] Actually, it operates as an independent entity. The New Jersey Supreme Court has declared that the authority is "in but not of" the State Highway Department.[22] The state highway commissioner is not a member of the Turnpike Authority. His staff does not participate in its operations.

There are still many agencies that do not function as integral parts of the departments to which they have been allocated.[23] However, two powerful factors tend to support the continuing drive for integration. One is the problem of obtaining operating funds. Regardless of its former status, each unit's asking budget must have the approval of the department head. A second formidable budgetary hurdle is the hearing and determination by the Treasury Department's division of budget and accounting. Finally, on the executive side, there remains the problem of obtaining the governor's approval. Financial control is a powerful means of inducing cooperation. The second unifying factor is personnel turnover. Retirements, deaths, and resignations create opportunities for new minds unfettered by previous practices. Time can be an able ally of a determined department head.

Although the reorganization acts do not measure up fully to the standards established by the constitution, and although the integration of many formerly independent agencies has not been completed, these failures should not obscure the substantial accomplishments of the last several years. Since the initial allocation of agencies to the principal departments, scores of less spectacular forward steps have been taken. The most meaningful feature of the revision-reorganization movement has been the continuing nature of the efforts to improve the state's administrative structure and the efficiency of its operations.[24]

NOTES

[1] Document No. 1, "First Annual Message of Woodrow Wilson, Governor of New Jersey, to the Legislature of New Jersey, January 9, 1912," N.J. *Legislative Documents,* 1911, I, 4.

[2] *Message of James F. Fielder, Governor of New Jersey Transmitting to the Legislature the Second Report of the Commission upon the Reorganization and Consolidation of Different Departments of the State Government Whose Functions are Interrelated* (Trenton: MacCrellish and Quigley, 1914), p. 7.

[3] *Ibid.,* p. 16.

[4] *Ibid.,* pp. 17-18. The study commission was in touch with similar groups in a number of states and with the National Economy and Efficiency Commission appointed by President Taft.

[5] *Reports of the Joint Legislative Survey Committee of New Jersey* (Trenton: 1925), p. 36.

[6] National Institute of Public Administration, *Report on a Survey of the Organization and Administration of the State Government of New Jersey* (Trenton, 1930), p. 12.

[7] Message of March 29, 1930. See also, A. E. Buck, *The Reorganization of State Governments in the United States* (New York: Columbia University Press, 1938), pp. 162-63.

[8] N.J. *Minutes of Assembly,* 1932, p. 92.

[9] *Report on a Survey of Administration and Expenditures of the State Government of New Jersey with Recommendations of Economies for the Fiscal Year 1933-34* (Princeton: The School of Public and International Affairs of Princeton University, 1932), p. 35.

[10] N.J. *Report of the Commission on Revision of the New Jersey Constitution* (Trenton, 1942), p. 19.

[11] L., 1944, ch. 20, p. 50.

[12] L., 1944, ch. 112, p. 287.

[13] L., 1945, ch. 51, p. 138.

[14] L., 1945, ch. 22, p. 62.

[15] L., 1947, ch. 177, p. 792.

[16] Leon S. Milmed, "State Administrative Organization and Reorganization," N.J. *Constitutional Convention of 1947,* II, 1446.

[17] Constitution of 1844, art. VII, sec. II, par. 2.

[18] Milmed, *loc. cit.*

[19] See Tables 5 and 6 in *Reorganizing State Government, A Report on Administrative Management in the States and a Review of Recent Trends in Reorganization* (Chicago: The Council of State Governments, 1950), pp. 22-25.

[20] Art. V, sec. IV, par. 2.

[21] L., 1948, ch. 454, p. 1856.

[22] *New Jersey Turnpike Authority* v *Parsons*, 3 N.J. 235 (1949).

[23] *Report of the Commission to Study Organization and Operation of the Executive Branch of the State Government, Submitted to the Legislature January 10, 1956*, p. 8.

[24] Bennett M. Rich, "Administrative Reorganization in New Jersey," *Public Administration Review*, XII (Autumn, 1952), 251-57. Excerpts from the article are included with the permission of the *Public Administration Review*.

CHAPTER 9

Defense

THE STATE'S ORGANIZATION for defense has undergone drastic changes in recent years. The constitutional, statutory, and administrative revision that has taken place since 1947 was designed to effect an integration of the armed services under a unified command. This objective was virtually impossible prior to the adoption of the new constitution.

The Constitution of 1844 required two officers—the adjutant general and the quartermaster general—to be appointed by the governor with the advice and consent of the Senate. No limit was set upon their terms of office. As a consequence, there developed the unmilitary practice of life tenure for these staff positions. From 1837 to 1948 only five men held the office of quartermaster general.

EARLY MILITARY ORGANIZATION

The military functions of the state were divided between separate departments built up around the two constitutional officers. The Adjutant General's Department became responsible for recruiting, organizing, mobilizing, commanding, disciplining, training, and administering all units of the organized militia. The Quartermaster General's Department was responsible for supply and maintenance functions. Although the governor was the constitutional commander-in-chief, his command effectiveness was limited by the life tenure of the two generals. Conflict between the departments was not uncommon especially when divergent personalities occupied the two offices.*

* A bitter controversy developed during 1942. Governor Edison charged the quartermaster general with "laxity of supervision" in connection with expenditures for food at the chief executive's summer cottage in Sea Girt. The adjutant general conducted an investigation and substantiated the governor's charge. A Senate in-

Reorganization of the military departments was often recommended in the past. In 1930 the National Institute of Public Administration advised the assignment of all military functions to an adjutant general who would serve at the governor's pleasure.[1] The same basic idea was included in the report of the 1941-42 constitutional commission.[2]

The first positive step toward reorganization was taken in 1947 when, upon the recommendation of Governor Driscoll, a law was passed placing the adjutant general and the quartermaster general under the governor and his chief of staff.[3] The position of chief of staff was a new office to be filled by the governor, the incumbent to serve at his pleasure. By executive order, based on a 1937 law, the two departments were combined into a Department of Defense, and the chief of staff was directed to redefine the duties of the constitutional officers to conform as closely as possible to the staff structure of the United States Armed Forces.[4]

The status of the constitutional military officers was the subject of considerable discussion during the Constitutional Convention of 1947. Former Governors A. Harry Moore and Morgan F. Larson claimed that the traditional organization was adequate. Governor Driscoll favored the appointment of all officers on a merit basis and in accordance with Federal standards. This point of view was accepted by the convention. As a consequence, neither the adjutant general nor the quartermaster general is mentioned in the new constitution. This omission effectively eliminated the life tenure tradition.

DEPARTMENT OF DEFENSE

In May, 1948, as a part of the state reorganization, the legislature ratified the reforms already initiated by executive order.[5] All functions of the two old departments were transferred to the new Department of Defense.

Organization

The chief of staff is head of the department. He is appointed by the governor, with the advice and consent of the Senate, from among "qualified active officers in the [United States] military service." He serves at the governor's pleasure on a full or part time basis and under his direction. With one exception, that of the civilian defense director, who is appointed by the governor, the chief of staff is completely free to organize the department. Both functions and personnel may be assigned as he directs.

The internal organization of the department follows the staff structure of the United States Armed Forces as closely as possible. The following

---

vestigating committee declared the quartermaster general was not responsible for the procurement of food at the cottage. See the *New York Times*, Feb. 21, 1942, p. 21, Feb. 22, p. 20, Aug. 13, p. 20; N.J. *Senate Journal*, 1942, pp. 842-69.

officers and administrative units report directly to a deputy chief of staff who is on a full-time basis and acts for the chief of staff:

> Adjutant General *
> Personnel Division
> War Records Division
> Operations and Training Division
> Logistics Division
> Fiscal and Finance Division
> Construction and Property Management Division
> Public Information Division
> United States Property and Disbursing Officer
> Division of Civil Defense

With the exception of the civilian defense director, the head of each staff division is a member of the New Jersey National Guard or the Naval Militia.

Function

The principal military function of the department is to perform the staff work incident to the recruitment, training, operations, and administrative and logistical support of the Army National Guard, the Air National Guard, and the Naval Militia. The officer commanding each of these components is responsible to the governor through the chief of staff. The total strength of the National Guard, including both army and air commands, was 14,815 on October 31, 1955.[6]

Finances

The cost of financing the state's armed services is shared by the state and Federal governments. The state is responsible for a portion of the headquarters administrative costs and most of the expense of caring for armories. State military expenditures in 1955 amounted to approximately $1,400,000.

Federal aid is received for the construction of facilities and target ranges, payment of civilian employees, field training expenses, and other items. During the fiscal year ending June 30, 1955, apportioned funds to New Jersey amounted to $6,398,511 for the Army National Guard and $2,755,-867 for the Air National Guard. In addition, the state received armament, vehicles, and other equipment paid for from funds not apportioned to the states.[7]

---

* The present adjutant general, though bearing the same title as the former constitutional officer, fills an entirely new position. He is now a coordinating staff officer and is responsible for certain administrative duties within the department such as processing official correspondence, and recording, authenticating, and communicating orders and regulations to troops and individuals in the militia. Department of Defense, *Staff Functions*, General Order No. 2, 4 January, 1952.

THE NATIONAL GUARD

All able-bodied male citizens between the ages of seventeen and forty-five are members of the state militia. With certain exceptions, each militia member is subject to the call of the governor in the event of insurrection, riot, or danger to the public safety. However, in practice, only that part of the militia which is organized is subject to the governor's call. The Army and Air National Guard and the Naval Militia fall in this category. They are organized forces recognized by Congress. The creation of any military force without congressional authorization would be contrary to the Constitution of the United States.[8]

There are in reality two national guards—one a state organization, the other a Federal body. The National Guard of the state is under the command of the governor. Its basic purpose is to preserve peace and order and to protect life and property within the state. However, all Federally recognized units (in New Jersey there are no others) are also a part of the National Guard of the United States. As such they are included in the ready reserve and are liable for active duty in time of war or in the event of a national emergency declared by the Congress or proclaimed by the President. Each member of the National Guard of the several States, Territories and the District of Columbia, as the collective state units are called, is also a member of the National Guard of the United States. His oath of office requires that he obey orders both of the President of the United States and the governor of his state.

Armament, uniforms, and equipment of the National Guard of New Jersey are supplied by the Federal government. The particular units the state has are decided upon by the Department of the Army in consultation with state officials. This is done in order that the National Guard of all the states will, in conjunction with the Army, make a balanced force. New Jersey is the home of the 50th Armored Division and a number of non-divisional units.

Training is a function of the state. However, in order to obtain Federal recognition, the state force must meet the minimum standards established by the National Guard Bureau of the Departments of the Army and the Air Force. These standards apply to strength, training, equipment maintenance, operational readiness, and others. Regular Army and Air Force officers are assigned to instruct in the latest approved tactical doctrines. They have no command status over National Guard units. On the other hand, neither are they subject to orders of the state officials.

Recruitment is largely a problem of the individual units of the National Guard. So long as Federal and state qualifications concerning age, physical condition, and other standards are met, the members of each unit—for example, the 114th Tank Battalion, with headquarters at Vineland—

are responsible for keeping that unit at the approved strength. Those persons already in a unit invite their friends to join with them. The state constitution prohibits segregation in the National Guard. Thus any official action to create separate white and Negro units would be illegal. However, the policy of selective recruitment may have much the same end result.

Armories are provided by the state. Counties and municipalities desiring local units of the guard are encouraged by the state to provide land. Armory construction costs are met from state and Federal appropriations.

There is little restriction on the governor's use of the National Guard. Throughout the United States, in recent years, the guard has been called upon to cope with a variety of emergency duties such as quelling mob violence, protecting courts, and aiding in search and rescue operations. Perhaps the most frequent emergency duty has been in connection with public disasters such as fires, floods, and tornadoes. For example, two battalions of the National Guard of New Jersey were called out in May, 1950, to protect property and to maintain order in South Amboy at the scene of a munitions explosion. Guardsmen patrolled the streets for three days.[9]

AIR NATIONAL GUARD

Following World War II, air units of the National Guard were accorded separate status as the Air National Guard. Fighter-bomber squadrons are now organized into combat wings paralleling the Regular Air Force. Motor vehicle, maintenance, supply, medical, and other supporting elements are included in each wing.

THE NAVAL MILITIA

New Jersey's Naval Militia consists of the units and personnel of the United States Naval Reserve located within the state. As a consequence, supervision of the activities of the naval arm is considered to be more of a Federal than a state problem. This is evidenced by the small number of naval personnel attached to the Department of Defense and by the budget for naval activities, which for the fiscal year 1954 was only $4,500.

NEW JERSEY STATE GUARD

In the past, whenever the National Guard was called into active Federal service, the states had no organized forces for their own protection. In 1940 Congress approved the organization and maintenance by the states of military units subject to Federal regulations. As units these forces were not subject to call into Federal service. However, they were eligible to receive Federal arms and equipment.[10]

The New Jersey State Guard was organized in 1941. At the end of 1945, the aggregate strength of officers and enlisted men was 2,076. Turnover in the organization was exceptionally high, over 10,000 men being processed in five years. Over 2,200 of this number were, as individuals, inducted into the Federal service.

The major use of the State Guard was in the protection of vital installations, such as bridges, reservoirs, and power plants. In some states, the State Guard was called upon to aid in preventing civil disturbances and in assisting during catastrophes. During World War II, there was no incident in New Jersey necessitating the mobilization of the State Guard by the governor for any purpose other than the guarding of vital installations.

The authority of the states to set up military forces other than the National Guard was rescinded by Congress in 1947.[11] However, in 1950, when it became evident that the units of the National Guard would be needed on active service for indefinite periods, Congress again authorized the establishment of other state military organizations, subject to regulation by the Secretary of the Army.[12] In 1955 the states were again authorized—this time on an indefinite basis—to maintain military forces other than the National Guard.[13] No action had been taken either by the Federal or state government to reactivate the New Jersey State Guard as of late 1956.

VETERANS' SERVICES

During World War II a special agency was created to assist New Jersey's war veterans—the Division of Veterans' Services in the Department of Economic Development. It was charged with helping the veteran to obtain the state and Federal benefits to which he was entitled. The division was made responsible also for coordinating the various services intended to aid the veteran and with circulating information of special interest to him.[14]

A New Jersey Veterans' Employment Plan was originated in 1945 to aid those returning veterans, about 70 per cent, who had no job security under the provisions of the Selective Service Act. The plan—accepted by over 1,800 employers—called for employment preference to handicapped veterans, surveys to determine suitable positions for the handicapped, and a voluntary pledge from industrial concerns to employ one able-bodied veteran for every able-bodied nonveteran.

A Veterans' Loan Authority was created in 1944 to enable veterans to establish small businesses or to purchase household furnishings.[15] Loans were arranged through regular banking institutions with the authority acting in the capacity of a guarantor. As initially organized the authority had a $5,000,000 capitalization; the amount was raised to $11,000,000 in 1946. Total loans guaranteed by the authority as of June 30, 1955, were

$46,582,796. Of this amount the state had purchased from the banks loans in default amounting to $4,059,501. Cases involving veterans who had not shown good faith were referred to the attorney general for collection. By June 30, 1955, the attorney general had collected $1,152,894, or 28.4 per cent of the amount in default.[16]

Other veterans' services administered by the Department of Conservation and Economic Development include the Veterans' Emergency Housing Program, the War Orphans Education Act, the Blind Veterans Pension Law, and the Paraplegic Pension Law.* In assisting veterans with claims for pensions for educational benefits, and in connection with employment rights, the department works closely with other state agencies as well as with Federal agencies, such as the Department of Labor, the Civil Service Commission, and the Veterans' Administration. A *New Jersey Division of Veterans Services Bulletin* is published weekly and distributed to service groups. In 1954 there were approximately 800,000 veterans in the state.

CIVIL DEFENSE AND DISASTER CONTROL

Civil defense had its origin in World War II, when legislation was enacted giving the governor broad powers in time of an emergency caused by enemy attack or sabotage. He was authorized to employ all available state resources and those of the counties, municipalities, and other political subdivisions and to "commandeer and utilize any personal services and any privately owned property necessary to avoid or protect against such disaster or threatened disaster. . . ."[17] Local governing agencies were forbidden to adopt any regulations at variance with those of the governor. The governor's rule-making authority was declared to extend to "any matter that may be necessary to protect the health, safety and welfare of the people. . . ."[18] This broad grant did not long go untested. The authority of the governor to make regulations concerning blackouts, air raids, and other matters was challenged as an unconstitutional delegation of legislative power. In upholding the act, the Essex County Court declared:

We must take judicial notice of the fact that the acts of war are as unpredictable and uncertain as the future unknown acts of God; and therefore if the people are to be protected against them or be trained to meet them, the power of prescribing the conditions under which they are to be met must be so flexible as to permit them to be changed or regulated upon practically a moment's notice. The person entrusted with the regulating of the administrative functions, in this case the Governor of the State, must, if he is to be effective, be clothed with authority to act as situations occur from time to

* Veterans who are blind or paraplegic or who are victims of multiple sclerosis are eligible to receive annual state pensions of $500. For the veterans' housing program, see Chapter 19, page 279.

time. Otherwise the policy of the legislature, namely, to provide the people of the state with every possible protection, becomes a nullity.[19]

The need for a well-organized and coordinated plan to protect the civilian population in time of peace as well as in time of war was brought sharply into focus in 1950 and again in 1951. The detonation of 600 tons of explosives at South Amboy on May 20, 1950, killed thirty-one persons and caused injury to 350. A call for physicians and ambulances was broadcast. However, the roads were so clogged with sightseers that those able to help had great difficulty reaching the scene. The hospitals were quickly overcrowded. No one was in charge of rescue and first aid operations with the result that for many hours the scene was one of chaos. A similar condition prevailed in February of 1951 when a train wreck at Woodbridge killed eighty-three persons and injured over 300. A number of persons are reported to have died who might have been saved had the rescue operations been coordinated. For example, a first aid squad would load an ambulance and dispatch it to the nearest hospital. When the ambulance arrived, the hospital was already filled to capacity. The hunt for a hospital that was not already filled in some cases took hours. Proper organization at the scene of the accident would have resulted in lower loss of life.[20]

In order to provide an organizational structure designed to be of assistance in any emergency, a civilian defense and disaster control law was enacted late in 1953. A disaster is defined as:

. . . any unusual incident resulting from natural or unnatural causes which endangers the health, safety or resources of the residents of one or more municipalities of the State, and which is or may become too large in scope or unusual in type to be handled in its entirety by regular municipal operating services.[21]

Determination of the existence of a disaster, whether actual, imminent, or threatened is the responsibility of the governor. When he determines that the disaster is beyond the control of local authorities, he is authorized to assume command. He may or may not proclaim an emergency.

Office of Civilian Defense

To enable the governor to carry out these emergency powers, the office of civilian defense director was created by legislative act in 1942. The office was transferred to the Department of Defense in 1949.[22] The director of civil defense is by law also the state disaster control director. The director is appointed by the governor and serves at his pleasure, with or without compensation as the governor may desire. Deputies are also appointed by the governor. The normal functions of the director include planning, organization, training, mobilization, and direction of the personnel and facilities engaged in civil defense and disaster control activities.

However, all the powers placed in the hands of the governor with respect to civil defense may be delegated to the director. Any action he takes must be in the name of the governor.

Although the director's official chain of command is through the chief of staff of the Department of Defense, civil defense and disaster control are considered to be primarily civilian in nature. As a consequence, the military plays a relatively small part in the planning and execution of the state's civilian defense operations. The director is assisted by technical advisory committees consisting of specialists in fields such as transportation, communications, public health, and public welfare.

The organizational structure for civil defense and disaster operations consists of a state headquarters, and regions, counties, and municipalities. There are three regions. For example, Disaster Control Region 1 embraces Bergen, Essex, Hudson, Morris, Passaic, Sussex, and Union counties. Regional offices are maintained at centrally located State Police facilities.

Local Organization

The new act places important responsibilities upon the counties. The Board of Chosen Freeholders is required to appoint a county disaster control coordinator and a deputy. Each appointment is subject to the approval of the state director who is responsible for the supervision and control of the county officers. The county coordinator's function is to organize the resources of the county government and to assist the municipalities through the development of mutual aid plans. Staff officers are assigned the following functions: police, fire, medical, welfare, communications, transportation, engineering, and public relations. For example, the *State Disaster Control Plan* calls for the county director of welfare to serve as county welfare coordinator.[23] However, the county police coordinator is required to be an active chief of police or other law enforcement officer. He is selected by the municipal police chiefs within the county. The county fire coordinator is selected in the same manner, that is, from and by the municipal fire chiefs.

The municipality is the basic governmental unit for disaster control. The mayor of each municipality is required to appoint a disaster control director, and a defense council of not more than fifteen members. The director, with the approval of the mayor, appoints a deputy who, if possible, is a salaried employee of the municipality. The actual conduct of disaster control operations is the responsibility of the director. He may proclaim an emergency whenever in his opinion a disaster is imminent or has already occurred.

The establishment of a disaster control center and the recruitment and training of personnel are the responsibility of the director. As in the county, staff officers administer police, fire, medical, welfare, communications, transportation, engineering, and public relations functions. Appointments are made by the director. Whenever possible, the regular head of a comparable function in the municipal government serves as a staff officer to the director.

The operating problems at the municipal level include the organization and training of police reserves, fire reserves, and rescue and first aid squads. Emergency hospitalization facilities must be provided as well as emergency fire-fighting equipment, water supply, and communications.

Federal funds are allocated among the states on a population basis. The Federal contribution may not exceed 50 per cent of the cost of procuring supplies and equipment. Nor may Federal funds be used for state or local administrative expenses.

Mutual Aid Compacts

In the event of war or of large-scale disaster, mutual aid among the states would be of great importance. New Jersey acted in 1951 to make mutual aid possible by the passage of legislation authorizing the governor and the director of civil defense to enter into civil defense and disaster compacts with other states or political subdivisions.[24] Mutual military aid compacts were also authorized.[25] Previously, an official would have been acting illegally if he had sent fire equipment, for example, across the state boundary. Or a doctor, licensed in Pennsylvania and living in Philadelphia, would have been practicing illegally if he had endeavored to assist in Camden during an emergency. Problems such as these may be eliminated by the terms of the compact.

New Jersey and New York were the first states to enter into a civil defense compact. The document was sent to Congress and to the Federal Civil Defense Administration in April, 1951. During the same year New Jersey, New York, and Pennsylvania entered into a compact to provide mutual military aid in an emergency.[26]

Mutual aid agreements between two or more political subdivisions of this state were also authorized. Such an agreement would give the civil defense services going into another community the "same powers, duties, rights, immunities and privileges they would ordinarily possess" in their own community.[27]

NOTES

[1] *Report on a Survey of the Organization and Administration of the State of New Jersey* (Trenton, 1930), p. 14.

[2] *Report of the Commission on Revision of the New Jersey Constitution* (Trenton, 1942), p. 19.

[3] L., 1947, ch. 105, p. 529.

[4] L., 1937, ch. 49, p. 101. The executive order was dated July 3, 1947.

[5] L., 1948, ch. 82, p. 473.

6 N.J. *Annual Report of the Chief of Staff, 1955* (Trenton: Department of Defense, 1955), pp. 7, 26.

7 U.S. *Annual Report of the Chief National Guard Bureau, Fiscal Year Ending 30 June 1955* (Washington, 1956), Appendix D.

8 Art. I, sec. x. See *Smith* v *Wanser*, 68 N.J.L. 249 (1902).

9 *Annual Report of the Chief National Guard Bureau*, 1950, p. 43.

10 54 U.S. Statutes-at-Large 1206.

11 61 U.S. Statutes-at-Large 449.

12 64 U.S. Statutes-at-Large 1072.

13 69 U.S. Statutes-at-Large 686.

14 L., 1944, ch. 85, p. 168. In the reorganization of 1948, veterans' services was given divisional status in the Department of Conservation and Economic Development. See also L., 1952, ch. 347, p. 1128.

15 L., 1944, ch. 126, p. 345.

16 N.J. *Annual Report of the Commission of Conservation and Economic Development 1954-1955* (Trenton, undated), p. 73.

17 L., 1942, ch. 251, pp. 680-81.

18 *Ibid.*, p. 685.

19 *State* v *Natelson Brothers*, 21 N.J. Misc. 186, 190 (1943).

20 See Glendon A. Schubert, Jr., "For Defense or Disaster," *National Municipal Review*, XLI (1952), 294-99.

21 L., 1953, ch. 438, p. 2404.

22 *Ibid.*, p. 397. The title of the head of the office was changed to director of civil defense in 1951. L., 1951, ch. 72, p. 461.

23 N.J. *State Disaster Control Plan* (1954), p. 12.

24 L., 1951, ch. 8, p. 28.

25 L., 1951, ch. 2, p. 13.

26 *The Book of the States, 1952-53* (Chicago: The Council of State Governments, 1952), pp. 24, 360.

27 L., 1951, ch. 72, p. 462.

CHAPTER 10

The Revenue System

NEW JERSEY has the distinction of having the lowest state tax collections per capita among the forty-eight states. According to *The Book of the States,* tax collections at the state level in 1955 were $45.35 per capita. New Jersey was also the lowest in state taxes expressed as a per cent of state and local taxes; state taxes constituted 25.9 per cent of all state and local taxes. In Pennsylvania the percentage was 49.4, in New York 39.2, in Michigan 58.1, and in New Mexico, at the opposite extreme, 78.9.[1]

One conclusion that might be drawn from New Jersey's low per capita

TABLE 9

NEW JERSEY STATE TAX COLLECTIONS, FISCAL YEAR 1956

Source	Amount
Beverage taxes	$ 18,828,082
Boxing-Wrestling taxes	20,077
Cigarette taxes and licenses	23,844,263
Corporation taxes	38,742,618
Inheritance-estate taxes	16,533,950
Motor fuel taxes	69,432,317
Motor vehicle fees	53,886,917
Outdoor advertising taxes	89,360
Pari-mutuel taxes	22,912,721
Railroad taxes	18,450,500
Total Major State Tax Collections	$263,268,253
Collections for State Use	247,071,105 [a]

Source: N.J. Department of the Treasury, *Summary of Annual Fiscal Report* (Trenton, August 31, 1956, mimeographed).

[a] State collections for local use amounted to $14,795,182. Of this sum railroad property taxes accounted for $14,138,601. Taxes dedicated for specific purposes and not included in the collections for state use amounted to $1,401,966.

state tax is that a prudent administration had managed the state's operations in an exceptionally economical manner. A second conclusion might be that the people of New Jersey received fewer services from their state government than the people of other states. A third might be that an inordinate share of the cost of all services performed by government had been placed on the local units. A considerable amount of evidence could be obtained to support each of these conclusions.

The over-all per capita state and local tax burden in New Jersey—that is, the amount paid in taxes at both state and local levels—does not depart markedly from the amounts paid on a per capita basis in adjacent states. In 1948-49, non-payroll taxes amounted to $106 per capita. This sum compared with $132 in New York, $116 in Massachusetts, $102 in Connecticut, and $80 in Pennsylvania.[2] Based on individual income, these payments amounted to 7 per cent in New Jersey and New York, 8 per cent in Massachusetts, and 6 per cent in Pennsylvania and in Connecticut.

A more recent study, for the fiscal year 1953, showed that the burden of state and local taxes in New Jersey was 7 per cent of state income payments. The percentage in New York was 8.9, in Massachusetts 9.2, in Connecticut 6.5, and in Pennsylvania 6.4. The 7.0 per cent figure placed New Jersey thirty-eighth among the states in terms of state and local taxes as a percentage of income payments. The total tax burden—Federal, state, and local—amounted to 33.10 per cent of income payments. Twenty-seven states had a higher tax burden.[3]

Closely related to the question of the total tax burden is the question of tax distribution or tax equity. The Commission on State Tax Policy has stated that in comparison with the practices of adjacent states, property owners and public utilities in New Jersey pay a disproportionately large share, while individuals and businesses pay a disproportionately small share.

Direct taxation is principally in the form of inheritance and estate taxes. Individuals pay indirect taxes on cigarettes, alcoholic beverages, and on parimutuel bets at the racetracks. Automobile owners pay license and gasoline taxes. Property owners pay a general property tax. Owing to the relatively specialized bases of these taxes, the observation has been made that "individuals pay taxes in New Jersey only when they own property, die, drink, smoke cigarettes, bet on horses or drive an automobile."[4]

Businesses owning real property pay the general property tax. In addition, all corporate enterprises pay a state franchise tax based on allocated net worth. There is no similar tax on unincorporated business. Selected enterprises pay special taxes—railroads, public utilities, insurance companies, banks and financial businesses.

THE PROPERTY TAX

The general property tax is the principal source of revenue in New

Jersey. Of the approximately $828,850,000 in state and local tax reve-nues in 1956, $579,800,000 came from the general property tax at the local level. This amounted to 70 per cent of all state and local taxes. All of the property tax was used for the support of local government, except approximately $4,300,000 of railroad taxes, which was used for state pur-poses.* Table 10 shows the amount of the general property tax assessed in 1956 according to types of property.

TABLE 10

AMOUNT AND DISTRIBUTION OF GENERAL PROPERTY TAX, 1946-1956

Tax	Amount (millions of dollars) 1946	1956	Per Cent Change, 1946-1956
Real property (land and buildings)	227.2	489.3	115.4
Railroad property	7.4	14.4	94.6
Tangible personal property			
Household goods	5.4	13.6	142.9
Farm stock and machinery	0.5	1.0	100.0
Business inventories	17.0	29.3	72.4
Other business tangibles	11.6	32.2	177.6
TOTAL	269.4	579.8	119.3

Source: James A. Arnold, Jr., "New Jersey Property Tax in 1956," *New Jersey Municipalities*, XXXIII (November, 1956), 19.

On a basis of $100 of valuation taxable, the average rate in 1956 was $7.89. In 1939, the average rate was $4.61. However, the rate of the tax means little without reference to the basis of assessment, a problem of long standing in New Jersey.

Assessment Practices

Assessment ratios vary widely, ranging in 1951 from 16 per cent of actual appraisal value in Ocean County to 56 per cent in Hudson County. Among the municipalities, the ratios ranged from under 10 per cent in seven to over 60 per cent in two. The state-wide average was 34 per cent.[5] As the pressure on municipalities for revenues increases, the ten-dency is to push up assessments. Another factor affecting the net valua-tion taxable is the number of church, educational, and other properties that are exempt from taxation. In 1955 over 23 per cent of the total property valuation was exempt.

Tangible Personal Property

Assessment practices differ widely also with reference to various types of personal property. For example, household goods are by law liable

* The property tax on main stem railroad property is retained for state use; the tax on second-class railroad property is for local use.

for taxation at the local rate. In some communities, notably Essex County, a considerable revenue is derived from this source. In most municipalities, however, a nominal value is placed on furniture and other household personalty. In Hudson County such property is not assessed at all. Farm stock and machinery throughout the state are assessed, for the most part, at nominal values.

Tangible personal property, whether business or individual, is legally subject to tax at the local rate and at full value. The difference between the true value and the assessed value represents the difference between the potential tax and the actual tax. A source of worry for business is that "tax lightning"—that is, a sudden increase in assessed values—may close the gap.

The major portion of tangible business personalty is in inventories. Because of the varying types of inventories—raw materials, finished goods, semifinished goods, and work in process—assessment is difficult. The rate of turnover of various types of inventories further complicates the problem. The Commission on State Tax Policy has said that:

the inherent economic characteristics of machinery and equipment and of business inventories are so different from each other and even more so far from those of land, that any tax system which assumes to treat them alike is destined to produce at its best severe inequalities and inequities.[6]

In determining the assessed valuation of business tangibles, negotiation has often been substituted for taxation.[7] After analyzing the experience of individual taxpayers, the Commission on State Tax Policy reported a "disgraceful degree of inequality and inequity in the application of the tax not only among municipalities but even within the same municipality." [8] As a first step toward a solution of the business personalty tax, the commission recommended that a classified property tax be substituted for the general property tax; in this way recognition could be given "to the differences between personal property and real property and between the various kinds of personal property." [9] In an earlier report the commission declared that, in the final analysis, equal treatment of individual taxpayers could best be achieved by a net income tax. However, this solution was not recommended by the commission on the grounds that the Federal government had pre-empted the field of income taxation and that such a recommendation would be "otherwise unacceptable." [10]

Steps Toward Reform

In recent years the state government has taken an increased interest in the elimination of property tax inequities. Early in 1952 the state treasurer urged county boards of taxation to begin the compilation of data indicating the ratio of assessed values to sales values. The purpose of gathering these data was to enable the county board to equalize assessment ratios among the municipalities of the county. In July, 1953, a local property tax bureau was established within the Division of Taxation in the Department of the Treasury, and a staff was recruited to act as a service agency in stimulating improved assessment administration.

TAXES ON BUSINESS

Corporation Business Tax

Corporations pay a state franchise tax for the privilege of doing business. The tax is levied upon that portion of the net worth of the corporation which may be allocated to New Jersey. In determining net worth, the corporation is authorized to deduct its liabilities from its assets.* The allocation is made by one of two formulae, the one producing the greater percentage being used: [11]

Formula 1

$$\frac{\text{Total assets in New Jersey}}{\text{Total assets everywhere}} = \text{per cent}$$

Formula 2

$$\frac{\text{Real and tangible property in New Jersey}}{\text{Real and tangible personal property everywhere}} = \text{per cent}$$

$$+$$

$$\frac{\text{Receipts in New Jersey}}{\text{Receipts everywhere}} = \text{per cent}$$

$$+$$

$$\frac{\text{Wages and salaries in New Jersey}}{\text{Wages and salaries everywhere}} = \text{per cent}$$

$$\|$$

$$\text{per cent} \div 3 = \text{per cent}$$

The tax is levied at the rate of two mills per dollar or twenty cents per $100 of allocated net worth. The minimum for domestic (state) corporations is $25, for foreign (out-of-state) corporations $50, and for investment companies $100.

The corporation business tax was enacted in 1945 as a replacement for two taxes: the general property tax upon intangible personal property and the capital stock tax. The law was designed to end one opportunity for "tax lightning"—that is, the sudden application of a much heavier tax. The law authorizing the taxation of intangible personal property by local assessors at the local rate had been on the statute books since 1851. However, the law was not enforced because to have done so would have meant confiscation. For example, the average state rate in 1944, before the passage

* Corporations whose total assets are under $100,000 are permitted to compute their tax by means of a short rate tax table.

of the Corporation Business Tax Act, was $4.74 per $100 of valuation. There were few items of intangible personal property—stocks, bonds, bank deposits, and so forth—which earned 4.74 per cent. As a consequence, taxing authorities tended "to ignore or compromise rather than to confiscate." [12] After 1938 a number of municipalities pounced upon the intangible tax base as a fruitful source of income. Increased assessments in Jersey City, Paterson, Camden, and Newark were reported to amount to hundreds of millions of dollars.

Business interests became apprehensive and a number of corporations took steps to protect themselves. From 1938 to 1944, 170 corporations migrated to the Borough of Flemington where they established a business situs. This practice was known as colonization. Each corporation that moved its statutory office to Flemington added to the ratables of the borough, thereby making possible a smaller rate of taxation. The $3.91 rate in 1937 fell to 28 cents in 1943. The before and after statistics of Flemington's net valuations taxable are as follows: [13]

Year	Net Valuation Taxable	Tax Rate per $100 of Valuation
1937	2,742,000	3.91
1938	47,696,000	.67
1944	268,367,000	.43
1951	3,620,761	5.59

In 1945 a State Commission on Taxation of Intangible Personal Property declared that "the present intangible property tax law, both in its substantive provisions and in its administration, is indefensible—a detriment to the economic development of the State and a travesty on equitable treatment as among taxpayers." [14] The commission recommended that the tax be abandoned. It recommended also that a corporation franchise tax law enacted in 1884 and known as the capital stock tax be eliminated. This was a small tax on the par value of capital stock. It was graduated downward from one mill to one twentieth of a mill depending upon the amount of stock issued. A part of the capital stock tax also was a levy per share of three cents for companies issuing up to 20,000 shares. The rate was graduated downward for larger issues. Domestic corporations employing 50 per cent of their capital stock in four industries—manufacturing, mining, horticulture, and agriculture—were exempt from paying the tax. Thus in 1944, 2,637 out of 29,844 domestic corporations paid no capital stock tax.

Closely allied with the franchise tax on domestic corporations was a capital stock tax on foreign corporations. Enacted in 1937, this tax was simply "a charge for the privilege of doing business without reference to the value of the privilege." [15] By splitting their capital accounts between capital and surplus, and by other devices, corporations were able to reduce their tax liability.

The Corporation Business Tax Act of 1945 based on net worth was designed to reduce the inequalities among corporation taxpayers. The rate was established to produce an income roughly equivalent to the capital stock tax and the tax commission's estimate of "a reasonable tax upon intangible personal property held by corporations." [16] The tax was designed as a measure of the "employment of capital." It had no relationship to sales or income. The act relieved unincorporated businesses from all worries about payment on intangible personal property. The replacement tax did not apply to individual businesses or to partnerships. They pay nothing toward the support of the state government.[17]

The Financial Business Tax

The exemption of intangible personal property by the Corporation Business Tax Act of 1945 raised questions concerning the constitutionality of the state tax on the stock of national banks. Federal statutes required that any tax on national bank stock "shall not be at a greater rate than is assessed upon other moneyed capital in the hands of individual citizens of such state coming into competition with the business of national banks." [18] However, national and state banks in New Jersey were taxed at a 7.5 mill rate per dollar on the value of their shares of stock.

In order to satisfy Federal statutory requirements, the Commission on State Tax Policy recommended the imposition of a tax on business enterprises employing moneyed capital in competition with the national banks.[19] The tax was to apply to such businesses as industrial banks and personal and sales finance companies.

The Financial Business Tax Law was enacted in 1946.[20] It is an excise tax for the privilege of doing a financial business. The rate is 7.5 mills per dollar on the taxable net worth. For businesses operating in more than one state an allocation percentage is derived, based on the ratio between gross business in New Jersey and total gross business. Proceeds of the financial business tax are distributed in equal shares to the county and to the municipality in which the business is located.

Insurance Premium Tax

Insurance companies pay a tax based on gross premiums. However, the premiums taxable may not exceed 12.5 per cent of the total premiums. Life insurance companies pay 2 per cent of the taxable premium on all life policies and 1 per cent on annuity contracts. The rate for other kinds of insurance is 2 per cent of the taxable premiums. All insurance companies, whether organized in New Jersey or elsewhere, pay the tax on premiums collected for insurance risks in this state.

As a result of legislation adopted in 1945, insurance companies are permitted to deduct, from the amount due the state under the gross premiums tax, sums paid to municipalities as local taxes on capital and surplus. The practice of assessing the capital and surplus of insurance companies was first adopted in 1903. As the insurance companies grew, they became an important source of local tax ratables—14 per cent in Newark. Certain provisions relating to the taxation of intangibles were declared unconstitutional by the United States Supreme Court in the spring of 1950. Faced with a tremendous tax loss, an agreement was worked out involving a franchise levy on taxable premiums. The agreement prevented Newark from sustaining a disastrous revenue reduction.[21]

Tax on Public Utilities

Utilities, other than railroads, pay a franchise tax and a gross receipts tax. Although assessments of taxes are made by the state, collection is a local responsibility. Funds from these taxes do not enter into the state budget.

The franchise tax is levied against all utilities on the basis of the lines or mains—water, sewer, telephone, telegraph, gas, electric, and street railway—along public streets, highways and other public places. The tax is at the rate of 5 per cent of such proportion of the gross receipts of the utility as the length of the lines or mains in New Jersey bears to the whole length of the company's lines or mains. Where gross receipts do not exceed $50,000 the rate is 2 per cent. The number of companies and the amount of tax paid in 1955 are shown in Table 11.

TABLE 11

PUBLIC UTILITY FRANCHISE TAXES, 1955

Classification	Number of Companies	Franchise Tax
Street Railway	2	$ 34,560
Gas and Electric	16	14,875,283
Water	108	979,155
Telephone and Telegraph	10	5,496,057
District Telegraph	1	970
Sewer	8	33,758
Municipal Electric Corporations	2	25,637
TOTAL	147	$21,445,423

Source: N.J. *Annual Report of the Division of Taxation, 1955* (Trenton, 1955), p. 32.

The franchise tax is apportioned by the state to the municipalities. The ratio used is the value of the utility's property along the streets and highways of a given municipality to the value of the utility's total property along the streets and highways of the state.

The gross receipts tax is levied in lieu of the local personal property tax against street railway, sewerage, gas, and electric companies using public streets, highways, and other public places. The tax rate is the same as the average rate of taxation in the state. It is levied against that portion of the utility's gross receipts allocated to New Jersey. Thus in 1955, two street railways, sixteen gas and electric companies, seven sewer, and two municipal electric corporations paid $26,258,206.[22] The gross receipts tax is apportioned to the municipalities on the basis of the proportion of a utility's property in a given municipality to the utility's total property in the state.

RAILROAD TAXES

Railroad taxation has been at the root of much political and economic strife in New Jersey. Questions pertaining to the amount of taxation and to the distribution of tax revenues have produced almost endless controversy. Therefore, it seems desirable to give a brief account of the changes in railroad tax policy before describing the present system.

Early History

Early taxes on railroads were in the form of transit duties. The Camden and Amboy Railroad and Transportation Company, chartered to operate between New York and Philadelphia in 1830, paid a tax of ten cents per passenger and fifteen cents per ton of merchandise. The tax was supplemented by dividends from stock given the state in return for a monopoly of the New York–Philadelphia traffic. Some railroad companies were taxed a fraction of 1 per cent on their capital stock; others on the cost of the roads. Many escaped taxation altogether. Often the tax did not become operative unless a net income of 6 or 7 per cent was obtained.[23]

Nevertheless, railroad taxes and dividends played a substantial part in the state's revenues, accounting for an average of 69 per cent of the money needed for normal state operations during the period from 1834 to 1850.[24] By 1861 railroad taxes and dividends totaled over $223,000 while the ordinary expenses of the state were $145,000.[25]

Because of the increasing need of local governing units for revenue and also because of dissatisfaction over the uneven application of the tax laws, there was a considerable demand for uniform legislation applying to the railroads. Such a law was passed in 1873. A state tax of 0.5 per cent was to be levied on the "cost, equipment and appendages" of railroads.[26] Local governments were authorized to tax the real property, excluding the main roadbed, at 1 per cent. This meant a total tax of 1.5 per cent on real property outside the main track and roadbed. A commissioner of railroad taxation was to make the assessments. True value was substituted for cost as the assessment standard following the constitutional amendment of 1875.[27]

The system of classifying railroad property dates back to 1884. Four classes of property were established:

Class I: The main stem—the roadbed not to exceed 100 feet in width.

Class II: Other real property used for railroad purposes, such as tracks (other than main stem) buildings, water tanks, riparian rights, docks, etc.

Class III: Tangible personal property including rolling stock.

Class IV: The remainder of the property including the franchise.

All four classes were taxed at the 0.5 per cent rate but Class II property was, in addition, to be taxed at a rate of 1 per cent for local purposes.[28] As railroad terminal facilities increased, municipal officials resented the fact that property formerly taxable at normal rates could be taxed at only 1.5 per cent when it was purchased by the railroads. Furthermore, the one-half per cent went to the state. In 1897 the state relinquished its 0.5 per cent to the municipalities.[29] A special commission in 1905 recommended that Class II property be taxed at local rates. The legislature adopted this proposal at once.[30] Then, in 1906, it changed the tax on Classes I, III, and IV from the 0.5 per cent to an average state rate of taxation, computed by dividing total property taxes to be raised by the total value of all property.[31] State revenues over and above the amount received in the past from the 0.5 per cent tax were to be used for the benefit of the schools. However, gradually the legislature diverted the railroad revenues from the support of local education to the support of a number of state institutions. As a consequence, the original plan to assist local education failed to materialize.

Withholding of Taxes

Thus a pattern of taxation was established: classification of railroad property, assessment by the state, and distribution of tax revenues between state and municipal governments. This pattern continued until 1941. A basic change occurred at that time as the result of the economic strain of the depression years which brought the whole system of railroad taxation to a state of virtual collapse. A number of the railroads had withheld a portion of the taxes levied while they took to the courts the validity of the assessments made on railroad property. The railroads favored capitalized earnings as the proper basis of valuation. During the depression period this would have meant the complete elimination of railroad taxes. The assessment practice of the state was based almost exclusively upon a judgment of the physical value of individual items of tangible property. It took no account whatever of the earning power of the railroads.

From 1932 to 1940 the major railroads, with the exception of the Pennsylvania, withheld payment of over $34,000,000 in taxes. Interest on the delinquent principal, determined on the basis of "one per centum for each month until paid," amounted to over $24,000,000.[32]

In order to afford relief to the railroads, the legislature in 1941 enacted a law providing for installment payments of the principal and for remission of the interest.[33]   The attorney general brought action in the Court of Chancery to restrain the state treasurer from executing the law, alleging the statute's unconstitutionality on the ground that it contravened Article I, paragraph 20, which prohibited the appropriation of public funds to private corporations.   The attorney general was upheld both in the chancery court and later in the Court of Errors and Appeals.[34]   As a consequence, the railroads were forced to pay the entire amount of approximately $60,-000,000 principal and interest.[35]

A New Plan

The new formula adopted by the legislature in 1941 placed a flat rate of three dollars per $100 valuation on "all property used for railroad purposes upon the true value thereof." [36]   In addition, a franchise tax based on earnings was introduced.   The base of the tax was obtained by capitalizing at 3 per cent the net railway operating income allocated to New Jersey, deducting the assessed valuation, and levying a tax of 3 per cent on the remainder.   As amended in 1942, the franchise tax provided a minimum payment of $4,000 or 30 per cent of the net railway operating income, whichever was greater.   The law also provided a maximum of 120 per cent of the railroad's property tax.   The tax on Class I, III, and IV property, plus one half of the franchise tax, was to be for state use; the tax on Class II property, plus one half of the franchise tax, was to be used locally.

As a consequence of this change in the formula, railroad taxes were reduced.*   During the period 1941-1947 the railroads would have been assessed $151,400,000 under the old formula.   Under the new tax, they were assessed $131,400,000.[37]

The franchise tax operated unevenly upon individual railroads.   Also the amount of revenue provided decreased from more than $11,000,000 in 1943 to $1,800,000 in 1947.   Dissatisfaction with the railroad tax structure was especially notable in Hudson County, which had 78 per cent of all Class II property in the state.   The property tax rate in Jersey City climbed from $5.21 in 1941 to $7.73 in 1947.   Yet railroad property could be taxed only at the three-dollar rate.†

---

* Litigation developed over the method of assessment.   Under the old method taxes for 1941 would have amounted to $18,100,000.   Under the legislation adopted in 1941, as amended in 1942, the assessment amounted to $15,000,000.   The supreme court held that the law was unconstitutional as applied to taxes for 1941. *Jersey City* v *State Board of Tax Appeals* 133 N.J.L. 202 (1945).   This decision was reversed by the Court of Errors and Appeals.   *Jersey City* v *Kelly* 134 N.J.L. 239 (1946).

† The Weehawken Class II railroad property accounted for 38.73 per cent of the total net valuation.   In Jersey City the percentage was 24.31.   *Third Report of the*

The Constitutional Convention

The question of railroad taxation was at the heart of the discussion of the tax clause in the Constitutional Convention of 1947. After a tense struggle Hudson County's plea was heeded and a tax clause adopted which, in effect, outlawed the 1941 railroad tax legislation and provided for the taxing of all real property at the "general tax rate of the taxing district in which the property is situated, for the use of such taxing district." [38]

The action of the convention made new legislation essential. The 1948 session of the legislature adopted a plan suggested by the Commission on State Tax Policy designed to bring in approximately the same annual revenue. The property tax and the franchise tax were retained. Class II property was to be taxed at the local rate, and the tax was to be used for local purposes. But part of the tax on Class II property was credited against the state tax assessed on Class I and Class III property.* The credit was to cease at the end of 1951. This was designed to lessen the burden on those railroads with large holdings of Class II property.

The ad valorem tax on Class I and Class III property was set on a sliding scale ranging from $2.05 in 1948 to a fixed tax of $1.20 per $100 of valuation after 1951, when the Class II credit would cease. The franchise tax was set at 10 per cent of net railway operating income allocated to New Jersey on a track mile basis with minimums of $4,000 and $100 for large and small systems. The franchise tax is for state use.

In 1955 railroad taxes were levied as follows: [39]

Property tax	$17,261,782
Franchise tax	1,164,247

The apportionment to state and local uses was as follows:

State use	$ 4,187,882
Local use	14,238,146

Perhaps the most striking effect of constitutional revision and subsequent legislation upon the railroad tax picture has been the shift of revenues from the state to the municipalities. In 1947 municipal revenues were $6,500,000, or 43.5 per cent of the total railroad tax. In 1955 the municipal share of $14,238,146 constituted 77 per cent of the total.

The burden of New Jersey's taxes upon its railroads has long been a troublesome question. At a public hearing before the Commission on State Tax Policy in December, 1949, the representative of the Associated

Commission on State Tax Policy, The Taxation of New Jersey Railroads (Trenton, 1948), p. 28.
* In 1948 the credit was 18 per cent; in 1949, 15 per cent; in 1950, 10 per cent; in 1951, 5 per cent. L., 1948, ch. 40, p. 114. By the 1948 act there are three classes of property: Class I, main stem; Class II, other real estate used for railroad purposes such as tracks, other than main stem, buildings, docks, etc.; Class III, tangible personal property.

Railroads of New Jersey demonstrated that the taxes per mile of track in this state were much in excess of those of other northeastern states.[40] However, track mileage is but one of many evidences of taxable capacity. The Federal Board of Investigation and Research, established pursuant to the Transportation Act of 1940, reported in 1944 that railroad taxes in New Jersey were the highest in the country based on three different factors. These factors were taxes per mile of road, taxes per mile of track, and taxes per dollar of reproduction cost less depreciation. But there was no evidence available on three other factors which the Federal board also considered important—taxes per car and locomotive mile, taxes per ton and passenger mile, and taxes per dollar of gross revenue. The board concluded:

It is not permissible, even on this showing, to say that New Jersey taxes its railroads more heavily than any other State, although it has acquired this reputation. It is quite possible that, mile for mile, the New Jersey railroads are worth more than the roads of any other state.[41]

OTHER TAXES

Inheritance and Estate Taxes

The inheritance tax on the estates of resident decedents applies to real and tangible personal property located in this state and to intangible personal property regardless of location. The tax on the estates of nonresident decedents applies to real property and tangible personal property located in New Jersey. First passed in 1892, the inheritance tax has been a fluctuating source of revenue, ranging over the past twenty years from a high of $21,500,000 in 1936 to $5,100,000 in 1940. The rate varies from 1 to 16 per cent depending upon the amount involved and the relationship of the beneficiary to the decedent.

An estate tax is levied also. The tax is the full amount of the difference between the credit allowed for Federal estate taxes and total state inheritance taxes. The yield of the tax is quite small. Of the $13,828,164 in death taxes received in 1955, the estate tax amounted to only $932,234.

Bank Stock Tax

Banks and trust companies, excluding savings banks, pay a tax of 0.75 per cent on the value of the shares of stock. The tax is paid to the county and is apportioned equally between the county and the municipality in which the bank is located. If there are branch banks, the municipality's share is apportioned on the basis of deposits in each branch to total deposits.

Alcoholic Beverage Tax

Alcoholic beverages have been taxed in New Jersey since 1933. At present, the tax is collected from manufacturers and distributors who sell or deliver beverages for consumption. The rate varies from three and one-third cents per gallon on beer to $1.50 per gallon on liquor.

Cigarette Tax

The cigarette tax, though relatively new in this state, is an important source of income. Established in 1948, the tax is levied at a rate of two and one-half cents per ten cigarettes and is collected through the sale of revenue stamps to distributors. License fees are collected annually from distributors, wholesalers, retailers, and for the use of vending machines.

An Unfair Cigarette Sales Act prohibits sales at less than cost. In addition, the act provides for a minimum sales price which guarantees the wholesaler a 4.25 per cent mark-up on delivered cigarettes and the retailer an 8 per cent mark-up on the "cost of doing business." [42] In form, the cigarette tax is a sales tax.*

Outdoor Advertising

Since 1930 license and permit fees have been collected from those engaged in outdoor advertising. A flat fee of $100 is paid for the license. In addition, a permit fee of from eighty cents to $25 is collected annually on each outdoor advertising structure depending upon the number of square feet in the billboard or other advertising space.

After administrative costs have been paid, the balance is distributed among the municipalities. Each municipality receives a sum based on the proportion of its permit fees to the total permit fees in the state.

Motor Fuels Tax and Motor Vehicle Licenses

Distributors of motor fuels pay a tax of four cents per gallon. Exemptions from payment of the tax are granted to persons using fuel in the operation of farm machinery, buses where the municipal street franchise tax has been paid, aircraft, stationary machinery, and motor boats used exclusively for commercial fishing.

Fees on motor vehicles constitute a major source of state revenue. The

---

* The retrogressive character of the cigarette tax was explained by Harry Kranz, Legislative Director of the New Jersey CIO, as follows: "It is, in effect, a discriminatory income tax on the low income groups. This may be illustrated simply. Neither a rich man nor a poor man can smoke much more than two packs of cigarettes daily. Assuming that both a $2,000 a year man and a $20,000 a year man each smokes two packs of cigarettes daily—and therefore each pays six cents a day or $21.60 a year in cigarette sales tax—the low income individual pays 1.08 per cent of his income for this one tax, while the upper-bracket individual pays only one-tenth of 1 per cent of his income in cigarette taxes." N.J. *Public Hearing Before Commission on State Tax Policy, December 14, 1949* (Trenton), pp. 63-64.

license fee on passenger cars is based on the manufacturer's shipping weight. Trucks pay a fee based on gross weight. Buses are taxed according to capacity. The director of motor vehicles acts as the license fee collection agency.

Bus Excise

Operators of intrastate buses are required to pay a monthly 5 per cent franchise tax on gross receipts. The ratio of the length of the route in each municipality to the operator's total route mileage serves as the basis for determining a municipality's share of the gross receipts tax.

Operators of interstate buses are required to pay a state excise tax of one-half cent per mile for the use of the highways. The operator is exempt from payment on mileage within municipalities where he has already paid the monthly franchise tax on gross receipts. This tax is also collected by the director of motor vehicles.

Unemployment Compensation Tax (Payroll)

The Unemployment Compensation Tax is not available for general purposes of government. Taxes collected are deposited in the United States Department of the Treasury for use in paying unemployment benefits. For an explanation of the unemployment compensation program see pages 313-16.

Pari-Mutuel Taxes

Holders of racing permits are required to pay commissions to the state on all pari-mutuel wagers; 7 per cent on all amounts under $40,000,000 and 8 per cent on amounts above $40,000,000. The state also collects the breakage, that is, the odd cents, and any sums held to cover uncashed tickets.

TAX ADMINISTRATION

The state administers nearly all nonproperty taxes whether for state or for local purposes. The municipalities have primary responsibility for the administration of the local property tax, except the tax on Class II railroad property, which is levied and collected by the state. In recent years the state has provided an increasing degree of supervision over the activities of local tax officials.

Property Tax Administration

Each municipality has a single assessor or a board of assessors. In 1952, the Commission on State Tax Policy obtained information concerning 532 taxing districts. There were single assessors in 363 districts and boards of assessors in 169 districts. The latter were appointed, except in

Elizabeth where there were thirteen elected assessors, one for each ward. Of the single assessors, 318 were elected and 45 appointed.[43] The assessor's principal function is the preparation of the assessment roll, that is, a listing and valuation of taxable property. The tax policy commission reported that in a large number of municipalities assessors were underpaid and that many of them lacked the elementary tools of good assessment practice such as a tax map or a card system. The commission recommended that an improved structure could be effected by establishing the county as the primary assessment district. This recommendation represented a considerable departure from traditional practice and probably will be slow of adoption.

At present there is a three-member board of taxation in each county, except in first class counties where the board consists of five members. The boards are appointed by the governor with Senate consent; compensation of board members is paid by the state. The functions of the county boards are to supervise the work of the municipal assessors, to equalize assessments among taxing districts, and to hear appeals by taxpayers or taxing districts. In its sixth report the tax policy commission declared that the county boards had failed to achieve tax equalization. The commission recommended that the boards be limited to the determination of appeals concerning valuations made by the proposed county assessors.

The administration of the property tax at the state level is divided between the Division of Taxation and the Division of Tax Appeals, both in the Department of the Treasury. In theory the Division of Taxation has had broad powers of supervision. In practice the statutory authority to supervise and to investigate meant nothing, since for approximately twenty years no funds were provided for a staff. However, in 1953 funds were appropriated, and a local property tax bureau was established. By means of a field staff, a monthly newsletter, and other measures, the bureau has endeavored to raise the level of assessment administration. The Division of Tax Appeals is a seven-member body appointed by the governor with Senate consent. No more than four members may belong to one political party. The division hears appeals from the county boards. It may also hear appeals from any ruling made by the director of the Division of Taxation.

The Administration of Taxes for State Purposes

The levy and collection of most nonproperty taxes is the responsibility of the Division of Taxation. In some instances, such as the franchise and gross receipts taxes on public utilities, the state levies and apportions the tax. Collection in these instances is the responsibility of the locality. Two major taxes are outside the jurisdiction of the division, the pari-mutuel tax, which is the function of the Racing Commission, and motor vehicle registration and license fees, which are administered by the Department of Law and Public Safety. Boxing and wrestling fees and taxes, a minor source of revenue, are administered by the secretary of state.

Tax Equity

In 1945 the State Commission on Taxation of Intangible Personal Property stated that "no industrial State has done so little in the past fifty years to bring its tax structure into line with its social, economic and political development as has New Jersey." [44] Although for years the cry of both political parties has been "no new taxes," a glance at the tax revenues shows not only that there have been new taxes but that old taxes have been substantially increased. For example, the rate on general property has gone from $4.62 in 1939 to $7.89 in 1956, an increase of 70 per cent.

Little attention has been given to the question of an equitable distribution of the tax burden. Since 1952 considerable strides forward have been taken in an effort to correct inequities in the assessment of the general property tax. But the modern concept of ability to pay is not reflected in New Jersey's revenue legislation. The observation of a tax commission in 1879 is equally true today: "Frequently the person who is most able to pay a tax is most able to escape it." [45]

NOTES

[1] *The Book of the States, 1956-57* (Chicago: The Council of State Governments, 1956), pp. 240-42.

[2] *Fifth Report of the Commission on State Tax Policy, Taxation and Public Policy in New Jersey* (Trenton, 1950), p. 27.

[3] U.S., The Commission on Intergovernmental Relations, *A Report to the President for Transmittal to the Congress* (Washington, 1955), pp. 300, 310.

[4] *Fifth Report . . . , op. cit.*, p. 49.

[5] *Sixth Report of the Commission on State Tax Policy, The General Property Tax in New Jersey; A Century of Inequities* (Trenton, 1953), pp. 28-29.

[6] *Fifth Report . . . , op. cit.*, p. 60.

[7] *Second Report of the Commission on State Tax Policy* (Trenton: 1947), p. 4.

[8] *Fifth Report . . . , op. cit.*, p. 64.

[9] *Ibid.*, p. 69.

[10] *Second Report . . . , op. cit.*, p. 48n.

[11] N.J. *Annual Report of the Division of Taxation, 1953* (Trenton, 1953), p. 16.

[12] N.J. *Report of the Commission on Taxation of Intangible Personal Property* (Trenton, 1945), p. 5.

[13] *Ibid.*, p. 15, and, for 1951 figures, N.J. *Fourteenth Annual Report of the Division of Local Government 1951* (Trenton), p. 147.

[14] *Report . . . Intangible Personal Property, op. cit.*, p. 18. For a summary of the defects, see p. 22.

[15] *Ibid.*, p. 46.

[16] *Ibid.*, p. 74.

[17] *Fifth Report . . . , op. cit.*, p. 72.

[18] U.S.C.A. 548. See also *Report . . . Intangible Personal Property, op. cit.*, p. 86.

[19] *First Report of the Commission on State Tax Policy* (Trenton, 1946), p. 29.

[20] L., 1946, ch. 174, p. 751.

[21] L., 1952, ch. 227.

[22] *Annual Report of the Division of Taxation, 1955* (Trenton, 1955), p. 33.

[23] John W. Cadman, Jr., *The Corporation in New Jersey, Business and Politics, 1791-1875* (Cambridge: Harvard University Press, 1949), p. 398.

[24] *Ibid.*, p. 401.

[25] N.J. *Senate Journal,* Appendix 1861, p. 576.

[26] L., 1873, ch. 450, p. 112.

[27] Harley L. Lutz, *The Taxation of Railroads in New Jersey* (Princeton: Princeton University Press, 1940), p. 5.

[28] *Ibid.*, p. 31. There was no change in the rates established by the 1873 law.

[29] L., 1897, ch. 69, p. 147.

[30] L., 1905, ch. 91, p. 189.

[31] L., 1906, ch. 82, p. 121. See also Lutz, *op. cit.,* pp. 32-42.

[32] L., 1921, ch. 138, p. 365.

[33] L., 1941, ch. 290, p. 768, and L., 1942, ch. 241, p. 651.

[34] See *Wilentz* v *Hendrickson* 133 N.J. Eq. 447 (1943), and 135 N.J. Eq. 244 (1944).

[35] For the total sums paid, see *Third Report of the Commission on State Tax Policy, The Taxation of New Jersey Railroads* (Trenton, 1948), p. 25.

[36] L., 1941, ch. 291, p. 776.

[37] *Third Report . . . , op. cit.,* p. 43.

[38] Art. VIII, par. 1.

[39] *Annual Report of the Division of Taxation, 1955, op. cit.,* p. 24.

[40] *Public Hearing before Commission on State Tax Policy, December 14, 1949* (Trenton, 1949), pp. 41-56.

[41] U.S. Transportation Investigation and Research Board, *Carrier Taxation,* 79th Cong., 1st sess., House Document No. 160, 1945, p. 164.

[42] L., 1952, ch. 247, p. 821.

[43] N.J. *Sixth Report . . . , op. cit.,* pp. 148-52.

[44] *Report . . . Intangible Personal Property, op. cit.,* p. xii.

[45] *Ibid.*, p. 8, quoting from N.J. *Report of the Special Tax Commission of the State of New Jersey,* Sen. Doc. 38 (Feb. 18, 1880), p. 14.

CHAPTER 11

Fiscal Administration

WITHIN THE last two decades the theory of a centralized fiscal administration has come to be generally accepted among the states. New Jersey is no exception. The organization for the control of state funds has been altered markedly since 1929 when the financial structure was described as "a most archaic and scrambled arrangement." [1]

The elements of executive fiscal control are now consolidated within the Department of the Treasury. The collection, custody, and disbursement of the tax dollar and other state revenues, the formulation and execution of the budget, the establishment of accounting procedures for all state agencies, controls over state purchase and property—all of these fall within the jurisdiction of one department.

THE DEPARTMENT OF THE TREASURY

The Reorganization Act of 1948 made the state treasurer the head of a large agency. Appointed by the governor, with the advice and consent of the Senate, the treasurer serves at the pleasure of the governor during his term of office and until a successor has been appointed and qualified.

Organization

The treasurer has general responsibility for the operations of the department. However, his authority is by no means complete. The law freezes the organization of the department by the provision that "the divisions, boards, commissions and offices, herein specifically provided shall be maintained." [2] The divisions established by law in 1948 were: Budget and Accounting, Purchase and Property, Local Government, Taxation, Tax Appeals, and the Division of the New Jersey Racing Commission. A Division of Investment was created in 1950, and a Division of Pensions in 1955. The treasurer is also the state director of the United New Jersey Railroad and Canal Company. The treasurer's appointive power is limited since, with one exception to be considered later, all division heads are appointed by the governor with Senate consent.

Revenue Management

General supervision over the collection of state revenues is centralized in the Department of the Treasury. However, the actual collection of funds is not centralized. About 70 per cent of revenues are collected by the Division of Taxation. The remainder is collected by other agencies outside the Department of the Treasury. Motor vehicle fees, for example, are collected by the director of motor vehicles. Boxing and wrestling taxes are collected by the secretary of state. Fees charged by the Department of Labor and Industry for boiler inspection are collected by that department. These funds must be deposited at once to the credit of the state. Only the treasurer may withdraw them. The customary procedure for departments collecting funds is to send the treasurer a monthly "transmittal of income" form together with an unsigned check drawn to the treasurer. He then signs the check thus transferring the funds from his "field account" to his "central working account." Departments are required to file monthly reports showing revenues collected together with amounts which are due.

The treasurer is the custodian of the public funds of the state. He receives, holds, and disburses state money. He is required to maintain accounts showing the revenues and expenditures and also the debts owed to or by the state. These accounts are subject to examination by a joint legislative committee shortly after the close of the fiscal year. A report of the finances of the state must be submitted to the legislature annually. Quarterly public records must be made available showing the balance of state funds on deposit in banks.[3] No money may be drawn from the treasury unless "it shall have been explicitly appropriated . . . to the purpose for which it was drawn." [4]

State Investments

Following severe criticism by a special committee investigating investment practices, the legislature, in 1950, established a Division of Investment within the Department of the Treasury. The boards and commissions in charge of retirement and other trust funds were brought into the new division.* A ten-member State Investment Council was created to

* The agencies concerned were: Board of Trustees of the State Employees' Retirement System; Prison Officers Pension Commission; Board of Trustees of the Teachers' Pension and Annuity Fund; Board of Trustees of the Police and Firemen's Retirement System of New Jersey; Board of Trustees of the State Disability Benefits Fund; and the Trustees for the Support of Public Schools. L., 1950, ch. 270, p. 917.

establish procedures governing the purchase and sale of securities. Five members of the council are selected annually by agencies constituting the division. The remaining five are selected by the governor for terms of five years.

The director of the division is appointed by the state treasurer for an indefinite term from lists submitted by the council. He may be removed by the state treasurer for cause and by the council upon the vote of seven members. The director is prohibited by law from engaging in any other occupation; he is required to devote his full time to the position.

Proposed purchases and sales of securities and other transactions involving the various funds must be submitted for approval to the state treasurer. Monthly reports of all investments bought, sold, or exchanged together with information about prices and dealers involved must be issued to the treasurer, the council, and the press.

BUDGET

The formulation and execution of the budget are the responsibility of the director of the Division of Budget and Accounting. By the Reorganization Act of 1948, the director was also named the state comptroller.

Development

Large strides in budget procedure have been made since the first budget measure was enacted in 1916. This early act was designed to provide executive leadership. But leadership was slow to develop, especially in the execution of the budget after the legislature had given its approval. This was due in part to the governor's weak constitutional position with respect to the independent department heads.

The state was subjected to severe criticism when the National Institute of Public Administration made an organizational survey in 1929.[5] The institute observed that the governor's message to the legislature covered only half of the expenditures. Continuing and indefinite appropriations and special funds, such as the separate highway fund, accounted for the remainder of state spending. The governor seemed to have little to do about the state's income. He was, the institute study noted, "largely detached from the state's financial management," once the legislature had acted.[6]

The institute recommended that one comprehensive budget be prepared including a budget document which contained the governor's discussion of major fiscal policies. Much more detailed estimates of the state's income and expenditures, backed by more complete information from the agencies concerning past and prospective workloads, were urged as matters of budget reform. The institute recommended fewer hearings by the agencies, a joint committee of the Assembly to consider both revenues and expenditures, and greater time for legislative consideration of budget bills to be presented to the legislature by the governor at the time of his budget message. Finally, the institute report recommended greatly increased attention to budget execution with quarterly allotments, control accounts, and more detailed financial reporting.[7] Over the next decade and a half, these recommendations were adopted by the state legislature.

Formulation

At present, all state agencies, through an official designated as the "request officer," are required to submit proposed budgets.* The agency must show its estimated revenues for the current year, and the actual amounts received during the past year. A breakdown must also be given of the purposes and amounts of the appropriations requested together with a statement of all amounts appropriated during the last fiscal year. This must include the annual appropriation or any allotments from the emergency fund. The unexpended balance must be indicated and all proposed encumbrances against this balance. Finally, the agency must estimate the amount of the proposed appropriation to be spent each quarter of the ensuing year.

After the agency budget requests have been received, a series of hearings are held. The law declares that these hearings "shall be open to the public." In practice, few people aside from the representatives of the interested agency attend.

The division director is required to submit his "findings, comments, and recommendations" to the governor prior to December 31, so that the governor may prepare the budget message and the necessary supporting documents for the consideration of the legislature. Ordinarily, the last weeks in December and the first days of January are a hectic period. Literally hundreds of final decisions must be made on the appropriations to be recommended. Each decision must take into account the over-all appropriation. This total amount is based on an estimate of many economic and political factors, including the sums spent in past years, revenue trends, the demands for increased state aid and state services, and the pressures for holding the tax line. When these decisions have been made, the budget message must be written and the budget document compiled and printed.

The budget document contains the state's complete financial program. The balances for the various funds are listed together with the anticipated revenues from all sources. The major portion of the budget document is concerned with the proposed appropriations. Departmental appropriations are broken down under five major objects of expenditure: salaries, materials and supplies, services other than personal, current repairs and

---

* The secretary of the Senate and the clerk of the Assembly serve as request officers for the legislature. The administrative director of the Supreme Court serves as request officer for the judiciary.

maintenance, and additions and improvements. For each item is listed the amount expended last year, the sums appropriated for the current year, the appropriation requests of the spending agencies, and the amounts recommended by the governor. Copies of the budget document are sent automatically to all members of the legislature, to each newspaper, and to public libraries.

Requests for supplemental appropriations follow about the same course as do requests for regular appropriations. In neither event is the governor permitted to recommend spending an amount in excess of the anticipated available funds.

Legislative Action

After the governor has presented the budget to the legislature in mid-January, one appropriations bill is prepared listing the proposed expenditures in about the same detail as appears in the budget document.* Hearings are held by a joint legislative committee, but only in connection with controversial budget items or upon the request of a dissatisfied department.

The director of the budget acts as technical adviser to the committee. At the same time he defends the governor's recommendations against legislative criticism. The deputy director of the budget serves as the secretary of the committee and assists in the preparation of the appropriations bill.

The legislature usually accepts, with minor revisions, the amounts proposed by the chief executive. Occasionally public pressure forces a change in this practice. In the fiscal year 1951, for example, the governor recommended a severe cut in the budgets of the state library and the state museum. The library request was reduced from $169,146 to $135,856. The museum request was reduced from $68,460 to zero. Public pressure upon the legislature caused these reductions to be eliminated, the library receiving $161,836 and the museum $65,120.

Execution †

After the passage of the annual appropriation act, an appropriation ledger sheet is set up for each account. Budget examiners then work out a fiscal expenditure program in conjunction with representatives of the spending agency. The appropriation for each account is alloted by quarters. An allotment sheet is credited with first quarter funds on July 1 and again on October 1, January 1, and April 1. The agency may make an amendment request if more funds are needed in a given quarter. If the

---

* The law requires the budget to be submitted on or before the third Tuesday in January, except in a year in which the governor is inaugurated when the final date is February 15.

† A dittoed memorandum prepared in 1951 by J. Lindsay DeValliere, then Director of the Division of Budgeting and Accounting, served as the basis for much of the material in this section.

request is approved, a subsequent quarterly allotment will be reduced or a transfer made from another account.

As a means of meeting emergencies, the director of the Division of Budget and Accounting is authorized to set aside a reserve out of each appropriation. No limitation is placed upon the amount which may be reserved. However, in actual practice this provision of the budget law has never been used. Nor has an even stronger provision which authorizes the governor to prohibit any expenditure. This drastic action was authorized in 1944 as a check against "extravagance, waste or mismanagement." [8]

As an additional control over expenditures, the director is given authority to pass upon requests for increased personnel. In order to exercise this control, a personnel sheet is set up for each employee. Agency requests for additional personnel must be approved both by the Department of Civil Service and by the budget office.

PROCUREMENT AND PROPERTY MANAGEMENT

Purchasing

The primary function of a central purchasing agency is to establish procedures designed to obtain high-quality merchandise at reasonable cost to the state. The Council of State Governments has pointed out that "The purchasing job properly done is not one of simply buying, but is a scientific search for maximum value through knowledge and analysis of the requirements of the using agencies and a thorough familiarity with materials and markets." [9]

Using agencies are required to submit schedules of the goods they wish to purchase. The director of the Division of Purchase and Property then establishes the conditions and specifications which must be met. Public bids are normally obtained and may not be waived without the written approval of the treasurer and written notice to the auditor. The lowest bidder meeting these specifications is ordinarily awarded the contract. The director has authority, however, to reject all bids and to award the contract anew "if deemed to the best interest of the State to do so." [10] As soon as the contract is awarded, an encumbrance request is sent to the Division of Budget and Accounting. The encumbrance indicates the appropriation or fund against which the contract is to be charged. Payment is made by warrant check signed by the director of the Division of Budget and Accounting and the state treasurer.

The head of the purchasing office is charged with the development of standard specifications for commodities and with testing goods purchased as to "service, quality, fitness and suitability." However, no testing laboratory is maintained.

All departments are required to do their buying through the purchasing officer. But provision is made also—by means of a direct purchase authorization—for agencies to purchase directly. This is especially necessary in the prisons and hospitals where perishable foods are purchased from day to day. The purchase division buys annually $8,000,000 to $10,000,000 worth of goods. The cost of operating the state's centralized purchasing office was estimated in 1950 to be 1.87 per cent of the goods purchased.[11]

Printing

Supervision and control of printing are the responsibility of the Division of Purchase and Property in the Department of the Treasury. The courts have recognized three types of printing: (a) general public printing which includes the General Assembly and Senate journals, and official reports and documents; (b) departmental printing which includes stationery and forms; and (c) the opinions of the courts. Preparation for printing of the journals and the laws is the responsibility of the secretary of state. The law requires that, with certain exceptions, state printing be done within New Jersey. The law also provides that no official report may be published until examined and edited by the state librarian and approved by the governor. This measure has not been enforced. Incidentally, another statute declares that any official who fails to submit his annual report to the governor as required by law before the thirtieth of November shall forfeit one half his salary from the due date until the report is presented.[12]

In practice the departments are given a considerable amount of freedom in connection with their printing needs. Often they have been hard-pressed for printing funds. As a consequence, agency personnel have been forced to reproduce annual reports and special studies in some form other than regular printing, such as mimeographing or lithoprinting.

Property Management

The maintenance and repair of state-owned buildings, other than those within the jurisdiction of the Department of Education and the Department of Institutions and Agencies, is the responsibility of the director of the Division of Purchase and Property. The purchase of all insurance necessary for the protection of state property, the rental of properties for the various departments, the assignment of office space, the disposition of personal property belonging to the state, and the use and disposition of property which has been seized or forfeited—all are functions of the division director.

ACCOUNTING, AUDITING, AND REPORTING

The accounting system "provides the documents needed to review, analyze, appraise, and criticize the fiscal affairs of the state and the wisdom with which they have been planned and conducted." [13]   This ideal has not always been fully realized in New Jersey.

Duplication of effort between the comptroller and the treasurer characterized the earlier system of accounting in the state.   It was not until 1944 that the functions of budgeting and accounting were brought together in one department.[14]

Present System

The director of the Division of Budget and Accounting is responsible for maintaining a uniform system of acounting in all state agencies.   He is responsible also for maintaining a centralized control of all accounts.   The law requires that a complete set of double entry accounts must be maintained on an accrual basis so as to reflect the financial condition of the state and of each accounting agency.*   Current practice is designed to establish effective pre-audit control.†   An allotment sheet is set up for each account.   Payrolls are charged automatically against the allotment sheet each pay day.   All other expenditures except minor travel expenses and items of petty cash, must be covered by previous commitments, either by purchasing agents' orders or by encumbrance requests.   When an encumbrance is placed against an account, the allotted funds can be spent for no other purpose.

Auditing

The Senate and General Assembly in joint session elect the state auditor for a five-year term.   His duty is to conduct a post-audit of all financial transactions and to make an independent verification of "all assets, liabilities, revenues and expenditures." [15]   County and municipal officials charged with the collection of funds for the state are also subject to examination.   The auditor is required to report both to the legislature and to

---

* The expression "double entry" means that an entry made on the debit side of one account is balanced by a similar entry on the credit side of one or more other accounts; "double entry is a method of analyzing the effect of transactions on fund assets, liabilities and equities, and of recording transactions so that each is self-balancing in its effect on the accounts. Through this system the records of all transactions are mathematically balanced or proved." Fladger F. Tannery, *State Accounting Procedures* (Chicago: Public Administrative Service, 1943), p. 10. By the term "accrual" is meant the recording of all commitments as encumbrances at the time the commitment is made. This is distinguished from what is sometimes called the cash basis system, which means simply the recording of funds actually received or disbursed. Potential revenues and commitments already made are not recorded. Cash basis in New Jersey municipal accounting, however, has a different meaning.

† Pre-auditing is concerned with the checking of documents by the executive department before any transaction is finally completed. It is to be distinguished from post-auditing, which is an independent review of the transaction by the auditor who is the representative of the legislature.

the governor. But if any malfeasance, misfeasance, or nonfeasance is disclosed, the auditor is required to report "forthwith" to the governor. However, the auditor's primary responsibility is to the legislature.

New Jersey follows the recommended practice with respect to the auditor's functions. He passes on the validity of financial conduct *after* the transactions are completed. He does not share in current financial management. The auditor is the one administrative officer who properly should be selected by the legislature. He is thus relieved of any obligation to the executive departments whose accounts he checks.

Audits are conducted by personnel on the staff of the state auditor. The policy of the office has been to audit the larger agencies and those taking in large amounts of money more often than the smaller units. For example, the motor vehicle and racing agencies have been audited annually, whereas a division handling few funds, such as the Division of Local Government, might not be audited more than twice in a decade.

A copy of each audit is sent to the governor, the department head concerned, the state library, the budget director, the Senate, and the Assembly. The audit includes recommendations regarding the fiscal practice of the department.

The need for increased cooperation among the state's fiscal agencies, including the auditor, was dramatically revealed in 1954. Former Governor Harold Hoffman died in June leaving a letter to his daughter in which he confessed to the embezzlement of $300,000 from the South Amboy Trust Company, a state-chartered bank. Hoffman was president of the bank and at the same time director of the Division of Employment Security in the Department of Labor and Industry. An investigation revealed that state disability benefit funds had been used to cover up the looting of the bank. The bank examiners had found no errors in the books of the bank, which indicated that state monies in the amount of $900,000 were on deposit. State records, however, showed that $1,200,000 had been deposited. Nor had the auditor or the state treasurer been aware of anything amiss in the employment security accounts. One consequence of the scandal was a series of changes in the procedures of three offices—the auditor, the treasurer, and the banking and insurance commissioner—in order to strengthen controls over state funds.

DEBT ADMINISTRATION

The Constitution of 1844 declared that the "credit of the State shall not be directly or indirectly loaned in any case," and established a debt limitation of $100,000.[16] Except for purposes of war, to repel invasion, or to suppress an insurrection, the legislature was prohibited from borrowing an amount greater than the constitutional limitation unless approved at a general election. The $100,000 limitation was roughly the equivalent of one year's annual appropriation in 1844. But it was only 0.05 per cent of a modern budget. At the Constitutional Convention of 1947 the dollar amount was eliminated in favor of a percentage figure. Now, the legislature may not borrow, without a public referendum, more than 1 per cent of the amount specified in the general appropriation law for that year. The new constitution retained the provision in the old which required that the measure placed before the people specify the means for paying the interest and discharging the principal of the loan. An additional clause in the 1947 document enables the legislature to borrow funds "to meet an emergency caused by disaster or act of God." [17]

Recent Constitutional Interpretations

The law establishing the New Jersey Turnpike Authority was quickly challenged on the ground that the provision for the issuance of bonds contravened the constitution. The supreme court declared that the Turnpike Authority Act did not create a debt of the state:

. . . the explicit and unambiguous language of the statute entirely negatives any possibility of the proposed bonds being in any manner debts or liabilities of the State . . . . [18]

The New Jersey Highway Authority Act also was attacked as violating the constitution. In this instance the people, by referendum, had approved a guarantee of the bonds of the authority. The act was challenged on the ground that the constitution prohibited a loan of the state's credit. The Superior Court observed that the constitutional prohibition was designed to prevent the loan of the state's credit for private ventures. It held that the highway authority was created for a "purely public as distinguished from a private purpose . . . ," and that it was not in violation of the constitution.[19] This view was upheld by the Supreme Court.[20]

In June, 1953, scarcely two weeks after the decision upholding the highway authority, the Supreme Court declared that legislation creating a state building authority was unconstitutional. The purpose of the building authority was to construct state office buildings, state police barracks, motor vehicle inspection stations, and other needed facilities which would be leased to the state. Annual rentals were to yield sufficient revenues to provide for the redemption of the bonds. The court held that had the state desired to construct these buildings directly, it would have been unable to do so without a public referendum in accordance with the debt limitation of the constitution. The court pointed out that the authority was "a contrivance to accomplish that which by the same means the State could not do directly." Further, the court observed:

The "rentals" constitute appropriations made by the State, not alone to provide operating expenses, but in *quantum* sufficient for the ultimate payment and retirement of the bonds. A true lease rental is compensation for the use of the property, not the consideration price for its purchase.[21]

Justice Jacobs in a strong dissenting opinion, in which he was joined by Justice Brennan, expressed his concern over "the adverse practical effects and the retrogressive implications of the action taken by the majority. . . ."

In authorizing and executing the actual leases in controversy before us the Legislative and Executive Branches have simply applied sound and economical current business practices without incurring any new state bonded indebtedness or imposing any new taxes, without endangering the State's credit, and without violating any restrictive constitutional policies expressed by the delegates [to the constitutional convention].[22]

Amount of State Debt

After an increase in the state's indebtedness has been approved by popular referendum, the "issuing officials"—the governor, state treasurer, and comptroller—carry out the provisions of the rather detailed law relating to bond issues. For example, the law concerning the construction of state teachers' college buildings provided that serial bonds be issued, the last installment to mature in fifteen years from the date of issuance. Provision was made in the law also for publication of the notice of sale, and the maximum interest rate. Within limitations established by law, the terms and conditions of the sale were to be prescribed by the issuing official.

At the close of the fiscal year 1955 the total long-term debt of the state amounted to $857,339,000. This sum was exceeded in but three states, New York, Pennsylvania, and California. On a per capita basis the New Jersey state debt of $161.67 ranked fifth among the states; Delaware had the highest per capita debt, $344.92, and South Dakota the smallest, $.29. Of New Jersey's total state debt, general obligations amounting to $117,976,000 and New Jersey Highway Authority bonds amounting to $285,000,000 were backed by the full faith and credit of the state. In

TABLE 12

LONG-TERM STATE DEBT, 1955

Function	Amount
Education: state institutions of higher education	$ 16,229,000
Highways	
State toll facilities	737,200,000
Other	38,170,000
Housing and community redevelopment	17,440,000
Miscellaneous (principally state institutional construction)	48,300,000
TOTAL	$857,339,000

Source: U.S. Department of Commerce, Bureau of the Census, *Compendium of State Government Finances in 1955* (Washington, 1955), p. 42.

addition there were $454,363,000 of nonguaranteed obligations representing sums used principally to finance the New Jersey Turnpike and its extensions. Table 12 indicates the long-term state debt by functions.

NOTES

[1] National Institute of Public Administration, *Report on a Survey of the Organization and Administration of the State Government of New Jersey* (Trenton: MacCrellish and Quigley, 1930), p. 39.

[2] L., 1948, ch. 92, p. 521.

[3] The state is not a preferred creditor. *Board of Chosen Freeholders of Middlesex Co.* v *State Bank at New Brunswick*, 30 N.J. Eq. 311 (1878).

[4] L., 1895, ch. 401, p. 788.

[5] National Institute of Public Administration, *op. cit.,* pp. 48-61.

[6] *Ibid.,* p. 49.

[7] *Ibid.,* p. 56.

[8] L., 1944, ch. 112, p. 287.

[9] *The Book of the States, 1950-51* (Chicago: The Council of State Governments, 1950), p. 179.

[10] L., 1948, ch. 92, p. 317.

[11] *The Book of the States, 1950-51,* p. 184.

[12] L., 1895, ch. 433, p. 826.

[13] Fladger F. Tannery, *State Accounting Procedures* (Chicago: Public Administration Service, 1943), p. 1.

[14] L., 1944, ch. 112, p. 287.

[15] L., 1948, ch. 29, p. 90.

[16] Art. IV, sec. VI, par. 3.

[17] Art. VIII, sec. II, par. 3.

[18] *New Jersey Turnpike Authority* v *Parsons*, 3 N.J. 235, 242 (1949).

[19] *Behnke* v *New Jersey Highway Authority*, 25 N.J. Super. 149, 166 (1953).

[20] *Behnke* v *New Jersey Highway Authority*, 13 N.J. 14 (1953).

[21] *McCutcheon* v *State Building Authority* 13 N.J. 46, 59, 60 (1953).

[22] *Ibid.,* p. 78.

CHAPTER 12

The Civil Service System

CIVIL SERVICE in New Jersey was first adopted in 1908. Legislation was enacted establishing a commission of four persons and providing for participation by any county or municipality which accepted the act by ordinance or referendum.[1] Essex County, Newark, Jersey City, and Bayonne were the first local governments to come under the new law.* The provisions of the law became fully effective in Essex County on June 28, 1908. Two days later an appeal was taken to the commission by one Ernest Joundt, an assistant engineer at the Essex County Hospital for the Insane. He alleged that he had been dismissed for no reason other than to make way for a brother of one of the county freeholders. Subsequently, the board admitted the correctness of the allegation and reinstated Joundt, thus ending the first serious controversy to come before the commission.[2]

In June, 1955, there were nearly 21,000 classified state employees and over 53,000 county and local employees under civil service. Although less than one fifth of the municipalities had come into the system at the end of the fiscal year 1955, the 104 which had done so represented over 70 per cent of the state's population.[3] Twenty counties had adopted civil service by 1956; only Somerset remained outside. The employees of five school districts are also under civil service.

* The constitutionality of the civil service law was upheld, but its adoption by ordinance of the municipal governing body was declared illegal in 1910. As a consequence, the law became inoperative in Essex County, and in Newark, Jersey City, Bayonne, New Brunswick, Rahway, and South Orange. The civil service law has since been adopted by referendum in all of the above except New Brunswick. *Booth v McGuinness*, 78 N.J.L. 346 (1910).

THE CIVIL SERVICE COMMISSION

The Civil Service Commission heads the Department of Civil Service. The commission consists of five persons appointed by the governor with the advice and consent of the Senate. All must be residents of New Jersey. The term of office of each member is five years and until a successor has been appointed and qualified. The commission is responsible for the adoption, after public hearing, of all rules and regulations affecting the civil service. It is charged also with the responsibility of conducting investigations concerning the observance of the regulations, with the adoption of classification and compensation plans, with the hearing and determination of appeals, and with establishing procedures for maintaining adequate employer-employee relationships in the state service.

The president of the commission is designated by the governor.* All executive powers of the commission are vested in the president who is charged with general supervision of the department. Actual operations of the department's staff are under the direction of the chief examiner and secretary who is appointed by the president with the approval of the governor.† A State Personnel Council, designed to establish standard personnel practices throughout the state service, was created by executive order in 1953. The council is composed of the personnel officers of all the principal departments, the president of the commission, and the budget director. In 1953, also, a five-member interdepartmental Advisory Council on In-Service Training was established to promote and coordinate the training of state employees.

RECRUITMENT, EXAMINATION AND APPOINTMENT

Recruitment

The commission's principal means of recruiting is the announcement bulletin. It provides a page of general information on such matters as applications, veterans' preference, examination centers, and employment lists. The bulletin contains a class specification for each position open to examination, including a "definition" of the work to be performed, and the educational and residence requirements. The statement also specifies the weight to be accorded the three examining factors: (1) education and experience, (2) the written test, and (3) the oral examination. The bulletin

---

* In the original law, the four-member commission selected one of its number to be president.

† The chief examiner and secretary holds office during the term of the president appointing him and until a successor has been appointed and qualified. He may be removed by the governor for cause. L., 1944, ch. 65, p. 125.

gives details on perhaps as many as 150 positions for which examinations are to be conducted. The following is illustrative:

Field Representative, Institutions and Agencies (Delinquency Prevention) (579)

Salary, 3840-4740 per annum

Open to male and female citizens, resident in the United States, with preference to eligibles, 12 months resident in New Jersey.

DEFINITION: Inspects the records kept by police departments, schools, courts and social agencies and interviews local officers to collect statistics as to the amount and kind of juvenile delinquency: gathers data as to the community conditions which result in juvenile delinquency and records opinions concerning potential methods of minimizing and alleviating unfavorable conditions; reports containing findings, conclusions and recommendations; attends public meetings; does related work as required.

REQUIREMENTS: 1. Formal education or other education or training showing attainment of the level represented by graduation from a college of recognized standing with specialization in sociology, social case work and/or medical social work.

2. One year of responsible experience in an accredited public or private agency doing work in the fields of child care, development, or general social case work.

Examination Weights: Education and Experience: 2; Written Test: 5: Oral Test: 3.⁴

The announcements of examinations are reprinted in the publications of the associations of civil service workers.

Rumors of positions to be filled spread quickly, particularly at the state capitol. During 1955, 1,837 tests were given for state, county, and municipal positions. The number of applicants was 45,328. The number who passed amounted to 14,373. However, in specialized fields the number of applicants is often quite small. Where the number of applicants is so small as to provide little or no competition, the applications may be processed on the basis of an evaluation of education and experience.

A criticism often leveled at state civil service systems, New Jersey included, is that positions are seldom established for the college graduate who has trained for government service. The recruitment process may encompass the beginning scientist, but there are few positions for the governmental "generalist." In 1956 New Jersey initiated a campaign to attract students graduating from college. The objective was to fill an increasingly large number of vacancies among several departments with individuals whose potential for growth was high. Consideration has been given also to an internship program, such as that of New York State. For some years New York has operated a program designed to feed into the state civil service a number of the country's most talented young people. A rigorous examination, unfettered by residence requirements, is used as the basis for the selection of prospective internes.

Examination

The rules of the commission prescribe three steps for entrance into the classified service: (1) the filing of a written application; (2) qualification, by the passage of required tests; and (3) certification.[5] Filing an application is a prerequisite to an entrance test. Examinations for state positions are limited to citizens of the United States who have been actual residents of the state for twelve months prior to the test.* The requirement of state residence may be waived if, because of technical qualifications, an adequate employment list cannot be obtained.

An applicant for admission to a test may be rejected providing he lacks the minimum qualifications for the position, is physically unfit, has falsified his application, makes excessive use of drugs, narcotics, or intoxicating beverages, or for other reasons.[6] An applicant must be notified in writing of the reason for his rejection. He may appeal the rejection by requesting the president of the commission to hear his case.

The commission has wide discretion in the giving of tests. The purpose of the tests is to "determine the relative fitness and ability of applicants actually to perform the duties of the class or position to which they seek appointment." † They may be oral, written, physical, or a demonstration of skill. They may be designed to measure abstract intelligence, mechanical aptitude, educational achievement, specialized knowledge, personal traits, and other qualifications. No questions may be asked nor may any recommendation be considered which involves an applicant's politics, religion, race, color, national origin, or ancestry. Three weeks' public notice must be given of all competitive tests. Following the examination, employment lists are prepared. Those who have obtained the minimum required average are listed, according to their average, in the following order: (1) disabled veterans and widows of disabled veterans, (2) veterans and wives or mothers of deceased veterans, (3) nonveterans.[7] Persons who fail an examination are given an opportunity to examine the test papers and to request a review of the test scores. The chief examiner and secretary may grant the review if, in his opinion, the request is justified. The order of names on an employment list may be changed only with the approval of the president.

The normal procedure for filling a vacancy is for the appointing authority to request the certification by the commission of the names of eligible

---

* Vacancies in domestic or laboring positions may be filled by qualified persons who have obtained their first citizenship papers in the event of a shortage of qualified citizens. N.J. *The Civil Service Law and Rules for the State of New Jersey* (Department of Civil Service, 1949), Rule 50.

† *Ibid.*, Rule 28. Personnel specialists emphasize a second objective of testing, to select persons capable of future growth. This objective is essential for the development of a career system. William E. Mosher, J. Donald Kingsley, O. Glenn Stahl, *Public Personnel Administration* (New York: Harper and Brothers, 1950), p. 97.

persons. These names may be on a re-employment list, an employment list resulting from an open competitive test, or an employment list resulting from a promotion test. For example, if the commission has only prospective new entrants to consider, the names of eligibles on the re-employment list are certified. If there is no re-employment list, the three persons highest on the employment list for the class of positions concerned are certified. The veteran whose name appears highest in the certification resulting from an open competitive test must be appointed, if interested. If the certification contains the names of nonveterans and the appointing authority exercises a choice and selects other than the highest in the certification, he must certify under oath that the appointment was not "by reason of race, color, political faith or creed."

Appointment

In order to give the agency making the appointment a feeling of participation in the selection process, probationary or working test periods of four months have been established. Reports must be filed with the commission at two- and three-month intervals. If the appointee is unsatisfactory, the agency's reason for dissatisfaction must be presented to the commission and an opportunity given for the probationer to defend himself. Local governments may terminate the service of an appointee at the end of a three-month probationary period.[8]

Temporary or provisional appointments may be made under certain conditions. The temporary appointment is, by civil service rule, to continue in force only until tests have been given, an employment list established, and the certification and appointment process completed. Temporary appointments in the state service are limited to four months and in the local government service to two months with the possibility of one extension for a similar period.[9] Emergency appointments may be made by the appointing authority for periods not exceeding ten days.[10]

CLASSIFICATION AND COMPENSATION

Classification

State employees and local employees in jurisdictions covered by civil service are divided into two broad categories—the classified service and the unclassified service. As of June 30, 1955, 7,030 of 81,818 employees were in the unclassified service. These included popularly elected officials, members of district boards of election, heads of municipal departments, municipal magistrates, and other positions in which the commission decided that it was not practicable to determine merit and fitness for appointment and promotion.

Employees in the classified service are assigned to the competitive division, the noncompetitive division, or the labor division. The first of these includes those positions in which the selection of eligibles is practicable on the basis of tests for merit and fitness. Subordinate positions involving housekeeping, custodial, and other duties or positions in which the conditions of employment make it difficult to obtain sufficient eligibles are placed in the noncompetitive division. Positions involving unskilled or semi-skilled labor are placed in the labor division.*

The purpose of classification is to focus attention upon the job to be done. Personnel specialists hold that if positions are organized into groups having similar duties and similar qualification requirements, it should be possible, theoretically, to devise an equitable compensation schedule. The rules of the commission reflect this theory by requiring the chief examiner and secretary to maintain up-to-date specifications for every class of positions. Specifications include:

(a) The title of the class;

(b) A statement of the duties performed and the responsibilities exercised in each class of positions;

(c) Examples of tasks performed by employees holding positions within the class;

(d) The minimum qualifications required of an incumbent for the satisfactory performance of such duties and tasks and the exercise of such responsibilities;

(e) As far as practicable the line of probable promotion; and

(f) The entrance rate, the maximum rate and the intermediate rates of the compensation schedule applying to the class.[11]

Civil service rules require the chief examiner and secretary to audit positions periodically. The president and the commission may change the allocation of a position to another class. However, the allocation may not be made until both the appointing authority and the person holding the position have been given an opportunity to be heard.[12] During the period July 1, 1954, to June 30, 1955, 482 positions in the state service were reclassified upward and 141 downward. Title changes were made in an additional 259 positions.[13]

When a county or municipality wishes to establish a new position, the appointing authority must present a statement of the duties and the proposed salary schedule to the chief examiner and secretary. The department then determines the title and the qualification requirements. A source of friction between the counties and the municipalities on the one hand, and the department on the other, has been the inability of the latter to maintain an up-to-date classification of positions in the local government service.

* The law originally provided for an exempt class. This class was eliminated from the state service in 1930 and from the local government services in 1948.

Compensation

The duties classification is a vital element in determining compensation levels. Rates of compensation are standardized for the various classes. The department has established forty-two salary ranges for the state service. The minimum in range one as of July 1, 1956, was $2,160. Five annual increments of $120 each were authorized, the maximum for the range being $2,760. The minimum in range forty-two was $13,200, the maximum $16,200. The annual increment for this range was $600. Employees are not entitled to the annual increment as a matter of right. Eligibility for the annual increment is determined or qualified on the basis of performance rating, provided the funds for the increases have been appropriated.

Counties and municipalities under civil service may establish salary schedules which are entirely independent of the state system. The department encourages local governing bodies to maintain an equitable schedule. Indeed, it may go so far as to investigate the rates of pay in a local jurisdiction. However, new schedules may not be established unless the local governing body adopts them. The department may require local authorities to provide uniform treatment with respect to entrance appointment rates, and minimum length of service before promotion.

CONDITIONS OF EMPLOYMENT

Hours of Work

State employees normally work a forty-hour week; office workers have a thirty-five-hour week. The determination of the work week is a matter of administrative regulation rather than of law. The commission's rule on the hours of work would seem to require a considerable amount of negotiation on the part of the president. The rule declares:

After consultation with appointing authorities the president, with the approval of the governor, shall formulate and administer, in conjunction with the budget officer, regulations for establishing and maintaining uniform and equitable hours of work required of all employees in the state classified service.[14]

The forty-hour week is a recent development. Formerly, many employees, particularly in some of the institutions, were required to work long hours. Although in some instances personnel shortages make a long work week inevitable for some staff members, they now receive overtime compensation.

Although the president of the commission may make recommendations to local governments concerning the hours of work, the actual determination is a local responsibility.

Leave System

State employees are granted vacations depending upon length of service. During the first year, the employee is entitled to one day per month. After twenty years of service, the vacation period is increased to sixteen days. With the president's approval, the leave of executive and administrative officers may be extended to one calendar month. Unused leave is cumulative through the next year only; that is, it must be taken in the next calendar year or lost. Sick leave with pay amounts to fifteen days per year and is cumulative. Disability leave with pay may be granted under certain conditions. Military leave for field training is in addition to the annual vacation period. Permanent employees are entitled to one year's leave of absence without pay. Leave regulations of the state service may also be applied to the local government services, providing the local authorities accept them.[15]

Transfers and Promotions

The commission has established detailed rules regarding the problem of transfers. The rules are restrictive in character and are designed to prevent abuses. For example, any transfer involving a change in compensation or a "substantial" change in duties requires the approval of the president of the commission. Transfers between departments may be made, providing there is no change in class or compensation, with the approval of the departments and the employee concerned. An interdepartmental transfer not exceeding six months may be made in order to permit an employee to obtain special training. The transfer of an employee from the noncompetitive or labor class to the classified service is prohibited.

A promotion involves a change to a higher class with a higher rate of compensation and an increase in the responsibility of the duties performed. The rules require that, as far as practicable, promotion tests be given and that an employment list be established. In 1955, 144 promotional tests were given at the state level involving 2,311 applicants. Of this number 1,167 passed.[16] A demotion, on the other hand, requires only a recommendation of the appointing authority and the approval of the president of the commission.

EMPLOYEE RELATIONS

Performance Ratings

A service rating plan is required to be kept current in the classified service of the state.[17] This requirement, one of the most difficult in personnel administration, was honored in the breach as much as in the observance until January, 1952, when a performance rating system was established,

The new plan is designed to answer the employee's questions concerning his performance, to bring out his strong and weak points, to reveal the need for training, and to provide a basis for counseling by the supervisor.

The employee is rated semiannually by his immediate supervisor. Seven performance factors are considered; quality of work, quantity of work, attitude toward work, personal relations, professional interest, supervisory effectiveness, and administrative effectiveness. No employee is rated on all seven. For example, clerical employees are rated on the first four factors while the last five factors are applied to administrative employees.

Five so-called "adjective levels" are used; unsatisfactory, fair, good, very good, and excellent. A numerical value of from 1 to 5 is given each level as follows:

4.67-5.00	Excellent
4.00-4.66	Very good
3.00-3.99	Good
2.00-2.99	Fair
0.00-1.99	Unsatisfactory

The employee's final numerical rating is the average of the several ratings he has received.[18]

Performance ratings may be appealed. The department head is required to send each employee a notification of his rating. If dissatisfied, the employee may request, in order, an interview with (1) his rating supervisor, (2) the section or division head, and (3) the department head or his representative. If the grievance remains unsettled, an appeal is made to a Performance Rating Appeals Committee composed of the chief examiner and secretary or his representative, a representative of the department head, and a representative selected by the employees of the division or department. The decision of the committee is final.

An employee may not receive a salary increment if his last two ratings average "unsatisfactory." This rating may also result in removal or demotion. In the event of a layoff within a department, the performance rating is used in conjunction with seniority credits as a basis for determining the employees to be released.[19] The adjective rating of 18,526 employees in 1955 is given in Table 13.

Suggestion Awards Program

A suggestion awards program was established in 1952 by executive order to recognize the accomplishments of individual employees. One year later legislation was enacted formalizing the program and creating within the Department of Civil Service a five-member New Jersey State Employees Awards Committee. No more than two members may represent the same department. Appointments are made by the governor for three-year terms upon nomination by the president of the Civil Service

TABLE 13

PERFORMANCE RATINGS

Adjective Rating	Number of Employees Rated	Per Cent	Change from Previous Rating
Unsatisfactory	54	.28	13
Fair	584	3.15	− 48
Good	6,194	33.44	166
Very good	8,587	46.36	−144
Excellent	3,107	16.77	151
TOTAL	18,526	100.00	

Source: N.J. *Forty-eighth Annual Report of the Civil Service Commission, 1954-1955,* p. 14.

Commission. The act declares that "awards programs may include any or all of the following: a suggestion awards program, awards for heroism, an efficiency and incentive award program, awards for professional accomplishment, and awards for service." [20] Cash, medals, certificates, insignia, or "other appropriate devices" may be awarded.

The central committee is responsible for the formulation and supervision of all programs. However, the law requires that three-member awards committees be appointed by the head of each of the principal departments. The judicial branch is included also; committee appointments are the responsibility of the chief justice. Permanent agencies of the legislative branch may appoint awards committees.

SEPARATION

Layoffs, Suspensions, and Removals

Lack of funds or a change in the volume or character of work performed may make necessary a reduction in the number of employees. The department affected is required first to lay off seasonal and temporary employees. If satisfactory service ratings exist, the least efficient permanent employees are the next to be laid off. In averaging the service rating to determine the order of layoff, the years of service are taken into account. Regardless of his service rating, a veteran is retained in preference to a nonveteran who has equal seniority. Seniority is the sole criterion in the absence of service ratings.

Permanent employees may be removed for any of a number of causes including inefficiency, insubordination, misconduct, intoxication, political activity during working hours, and others. The employee must be notified in writing of his dismissal and the reasons for his removal. He has thirty days in which to appeal to the commission for a public hearing at which he may be represented by counsel. The commission has wide discretion not only in investigating the case but in the conditions of its decision; that is, whether to approve the removal, to restore the employee to his position, or to fine, demote, suspend, or reprimand him. An employee may be suspended by the appointing authority as a disciplinary measure. When the suspension exceeds five days, the employee's right of appeal is the same as in the case of removal.[21]

Retirement

There is no direct relationship between civil service and retirement. The fact that a state or local government employee is under civil service does not automatically make him a member of the state retirement system. For example, county and municipal employees may be included in the retirement system only after a public referendum. Thus a county or municipality may choose to give its employees the benefits of the retirement system and at the same time remain outside the civil service. Conversely, a local government under state civil service need not become affiliated with the state retirement system.

The Public Employees' Retirement System is administered by a nine-member board of trustees within the Department of the Treasury.* The investment of pension fund monies is the responsibility of the director of the Division of Investments, whose operations are under the general supervision of the State Investment Council. However, the trustees of the retirement system may reject proposed investments. Records of the system are subject to examination by the Department of Banking and Insurance.[22]

The Public Employees' Retirement System was established in 1955 to replace the former State Employees' Retirement System. The new system is integrated with Federal Social Security. Regular contributions by the employer and the employee make up a fund which, with interest and with Social Security, will be sufficient to pay retirement benefits. The "retirement allowance" of the employee is made up of two elements: the "annuity" which is derived from contributions of the employee, and the "pension" resulting from the employer's contributions. Each employee has an individual account in the system.

New members are covered by a guaranteed benefit, upon retirement, of one-sixtieth of the average salary for the last five years of employment times the number of years of service. Retirement is optional at age sixty. The compulsory retirement age is seventy except in instances where the department head requests continuance. A member may, upon retirement, select one of several options. He may elect to receive the retirement allowance during his lifetime only or he may, by taking a reduced allowance, provide for his survivors.

* The governor appoints two members, three are elected by the state employee members, two by municipal employee members, and one by county employee members. The state treasurer is a member.

In the event a member is permanently disabled in line of duty, the annuity is based on accumulated deductions, but the pension is two thirds of his salary. However, for ordinary disability—that is, disability not in line of duty—a member must have had ten years continuous service before he is entitled to any retirement allowance. In such cases the retirement allowance is based upon the number of years of service.

Survivors' benefits vary according to whether the member's death was accidental and in line of duty or whether the death was from ordinary causes. If the former, the widow or children under eighteen receive the member's accumulated deductions and a pension of one-half final compensation. If the death were classified as ordinary, the beneficiary would receive the accumulated deductions, with interest, and a sum equal to one and one-half times the final compensation. For either accidental or ordinary death, the beneficiary would receive survivorship benefits payable under Social Security.

In addition to the Public Employees' Retirement System, there are three centrally administered retirement programs which include local employees: the Consolidated Police and Firemen's Pension Fund, the Police and Firemen's Retirement System, and the Teachers' Pension and Annuity Fund. In 1952, 211 local police and firemen's pension funds were brought into the new consolidated fund. All locally paid police and firemen are now under state-administered retirement systems. All teachers and full-time janitors are required to become members of the Teacher's Pension and Annuity Fund. The employer's share of the cost of the system is contributed by the state.

There are a number of contributory pension systems applicable to limited groups of public employees at both the state and local levels. Also, noncontributory pensions have been authorized in great abundance. These permit governing bodies to retire employees who meet specific requirements. Each law is written in general terms although but one person may qualify. For example, in 1941, a law authorized the freeholders of any third-class county having a population between 110,000 and 126,000 to pension the former secretary of the county board of taxation.[23] Although written to include all third-class counties within a given population range, this law in actual practice applied only to the secretary of the Morris County Board of Taxation. One over-all act integrated with Federal Social Security replaced over sixty of the noncontributory pensions early in 1956.

The noncontributory law, which until 1954 threatened to place a heavy financial burden upon the state, was the Veterans' Retirement Act. Any war veteran, after twenty years' service, at age sixty-two, or if disabled, was entitled to retire on a pension equal to one-half final salary. When originally enacted in 1906, the measure applied to Union veterans of the Civil War and required forty years of service.[24] In 1912 the length of service provision was cut in half.[25]   From time to time the act was amended to include veterans of other wars, until by the early 1950's it involved approximately 30,000 public employees.

The act setting up the Public Employees' Retirement System in 1955 put an end to the noncontributory feature.   Veterans must now contribute on the same basis as other employees.   However, after twenty years' service the veteran may retire at one-half his final salary upon reaching age sixty.

PROBLEMS OF CIVIL SERVICE

Over the years advocates of a system of civil service have had a hard struggle.   The fight for survival was particularly acute in the formative period of the commission.   Governors and legislators blew hot and cold. An investigation in 1916 revealed that the staff of the commission had been forced into quarters which "contained hardly sufficient cubic feet of air space to comply with the provisions of the tenement-house law. . . ." [26] The investigating group observed also that public confidence in civil service was endangered by one member of the commission who saw nothing inconsistent or harmful in his serving also as chairman of the Mercer County Democratic Committee.[27]

In recent years the position of the state employee has been greatly improved.   Increases in salary and adjustments in salary ranges have been designed to keep pace with the rising cost of living.   The forty-hour week with compensation for overtime has been made mandatory.   These are two of a number of changes which have been enacted into law.   They illustrate a degree of public acceptance of the civil service which is vastly different from that of a few decades ago.

But the experience at the state level has not carried over in the same degree to county and municipal governments.   In past years the commission has had a difficult time in keeping apace with its local responsibilities. Lack of sufficient personnel in the department to assist those municipalities and counties adopting civil service has had unfortunate results.   One consequence has been a tendency on the part of local officials to ignore civil service statutes and rules.[28]   This tendency, in turn, has acted to lower the morale of employees and to reduce public confidence in the merit system.

In September, 1953, new regulations were issued by the department concerning local payroll administration which should correct some abuses. Separate payrolls for permanent employees and temporary employees must now be submitted to the state for audit and approval.   The unit of the municipality or county in which the employee is working must be shown together with other specific data which will enable the department to check employment and disbursement records.

The Department of Civil Service is admittedly in a difficult position with respect to its supervision over local governments. Policing activities may be resented by local officials who set up the cry of home rule. On the other hand, when the people of a county or a municipality, by referendum, enter civil service, the state has an obligation to provide adequate supervision and assistance. Too often, this obligation has been met only in part.

Civil service was designed originally to eliminate the spoils system. Merit, rather than political affiliation, was the principal aim of reformers. This goal may have been achieved in large measure. However, other dangers threaten the public service. These dangers stem in part from the employees themselves. Forced, by neglect, to organize for their own protection, they have through their associations sometimes advocated measures which are opposed to the public interest. For example, employee organizations have insisted upon the promotion of the New Jersey employee to top administrative positions to the exclusion of the recruitment of persons from outside the state and have emphasized experience as the criterion for selection to the exclusion of educational and other qualifications. Overzealous action on the part of organizations of employees may reduce, rather than improve, the quality of civil service personnel and the prestige of public employment.

The organization of the commission itself has recently been the subject of criticism. A former president of the commission, Dr. William S. Carpenter, has observed that four of the five members are excluded by the terms of the law from any real participation in the direction of the system. As a consequence, their duties are limited chiefly to the holding of hearings:

Since the commissioners are confined to very meager duties, the result may be that they will become focal points in the political pressures which strive for irregular interference in the administration of the civil service system. Unless some way can be found for the commissioners to participate in the promotion of the merit system more significantly than at present, it will become increasingly difficult to justify the expenditure of public funds for their salaries.[29]

A considerably different evaluation was placed upon the work of the other commissioners by Dr. Lester H. Clee, the successor to Dr. Carpenter. After two and one-half years as president, Dr. Clee declared:

I have found the other four commissioners of real value and they are making a substantial contribution to civil service in our state. Their activities include holding of hearings, either individually, in pairs or by the entire commission; reading of voluminous transcripts of verbatim testimony; drafting of decisions and discussions thereon; individual handling of employee complaints, inquiries, etc., as well as attendance at bi-monthly commission meetings. Time and effort devoted by my fellow commissioners have been most helpful and I believe of inestimable value to the whole personnel program as now operating under civil service in our state.[30]

Many students of personnel administration favor placing complete responsibility for operating the agency in the hands of a single commissioner responsible to the chief executive. Under this plan the commission would not endeavor to operate as a policy-making body at all but would be limited to appeals and advisory functions.

In recent practice in New Jersey, leadership with reference to the development of new personnel policies stems from the head of the commission. The other commissioners serve only on a part-time basis. They cannot be expected to have a thorough acquaintance with day-to-day operations. So long as they are willing to accept this natural division of responsibility, the existing arrangement would seem to offer the advantages of a single head. At the same time, the commission as a whole is in a position to act as a buffer against political interference and to serve to advantage as a high level appeals agency.

NOTES

[1] L., 1908, ch. 156, p. 235. The commission was made a five-member body in 1917. L., 1917, ch. 105, p. 218.

[2] N.J. *First Annual Report of the Civil Service Commission* (Trenton: MacCrellish and Quigley, 1908), pp. 7-8.

[3] N.J. *Forty-eighth Annual Report of the Civil Service Commission, 1954-1955,* p. 21.

[4] N.J. *Announcement Bulletin No. 3,* (Trenton: Department of Civil Service, Nov. 4, 1953), pp. 4-5.

[5] N.J. *The Civil Service Law and Rules for the State of New Jersey* (Department of Civil Service, 1949), Rule 22.

[6] *Ibid.,* Rule 26.

[7] For the details of the listing of veterans, see *ibid.,* Rule 34.

[8] *Ibid.,* Rule 45.

[9] *Ibid.,* Rule 47.

[10] *Ibid.,* Rule 49.

[11] *Ibid.,* Rule 11.

[12] *Ibid.,* Rule 14.

[13] *Forty-eighth Annual Report . . . , op. cit.,* p. 10.

[14] *The Civil Service Law . . . , op. cit.,* Rule 54.

[15] *Ibid.,* Rule 55.

[16] *Forty-eighth Annual Report . . . , op. cit.,* p. 28.

[17] *The Civil Service Law . . . , op. cit.,* Rule 56.

[18] Department of Civil Service, *Performance Rating Manual* (Mimeographed, n.d.), p. 4.

[19] *Ibid.,* p. 8.

[20] L., 1953, ch. 125, p. 1321.

[21] *The Civil Service Law . . . , op. cit.,* Rules 57-59.

[22] For a summary to 1950 of the various laws relating to retirement, see Bureau of Government Research, Rutgers University, *Pension Legislation for Public Employees in New Jersey* (New Brunswick: Processed, 1950).

[23] L., 1941, ch. 369, p. 966. This act was repealed by L., 1955, ch. 263.

[24] L., 1906, ch. 252, p. 531.

[25] L., 1912, ch. 84, p. 115.

[26] *Report of the New Jersey State Civil Service Investigating Committee* (Trenton: MacCrellish and Quigley, 1917), p. 12.

27 *Ibid.,* p. 43.

28 N.J. *Forty-fourth Annual Report of the Civil Service Commission, 1950-51,* p. 3. For a recent careful description of state services to local governments see Ralph P. Shaw, Jr., "Personnel Services for Local Government: The New Jersey Program," *Public Personnel Review,* XVII (October, 1955), 222-26.

29 William Seal Carpenter, *The Unfinished Business of Civil Service Reform* (Princeton: Princeton University Press, 1952), p. 41.

30 Letter to the author dated August 19, 1953.

CHAPTER 13

The Courts

THE CONSTITUTIONAL CONVENTION of 1947 set the stage for a drastically modified court system. The extensive hearings by the committee on the judiciary and the final decision of the convention to make substantial changes in the court structure were the climax to a 100-year battle for reform. However, the words of the new constitution tell only part of the story. New legislation and especially the new administrative rules governing the courts have supplemented the constitutional changes. All of this has been done in order to improve "Jersey Justice." To obtain some appreciation of the present judicial system, it seems essential to review the development of the courts under the preceding constitutions.

THE COURTS UNDER THE CONSTITUTION OF 1776

The judiciary received scant attention in the Constitution of 1776. Freedom from Great Britain did not mean the abandonment of the British judicial heritage. On the contrary, the judicial system of the colony was retained virtually intact. Article I provided "that the government of this province shall be vested in a governor, legislative council, and general assembly." The courts were not mentioned. In later articles the governor was made chancellor, and ordinary or surrogate general. The first of these titles gave the governor judicial jurisdiction similar to that of the chancellor of England; the position of ordinary or surrogate general gave him jurisdiction in matters pertaining to wills and estates. The governor and the Council (Senate) were made the highest court of appeal and the court of pardons. Other provisions governed the terms of the various classes of judicial officers all of whom were elected by the council and assembly in joint session.

The selection of the judiciary by the legislature, especially county judges and justices of the peace, was constantly cited as an evil which should be eliminated. Justices of the peace were elected at times in large numbers in order to strengthen party control. Governor William Livingston in 1786 severely indicted the system:

I have seen justices of the peace who were a burlesque upon a magistracy, justices illiterate, justices partial, justices groggy, justices courting popularity to be chosen assemblymen, and justices encouraging litigiousness. But I have not seen any joint meeting sufficiently cautious against appointing such justices of the peace.[1]

Attacks were made with increasing frequency upon the Council's constitutional position as both a legislative and a judicial body. There was dissatisfaction also with the governor's dual status as chancellor and as chief executive. The separation of these functions in the Federal government served to stimulate demands for a similar separation at the state level. Finally, the fact that members of the Council, untrained in the law, sat as the court of last resort where they were in position to reverse the decisions of the Supreme Court seemed to observers a peculiar anomaly. This practice, it was argued, had the further disadvantage of eliminating all checks upon the passage of unconstitutional legislation. The members of the Council would not declare unconstitutional any act which, in their legislative capacity, they had already approved. As a consequence, when the opportunity for revision was presented in 1844, the question of judicial reform had a high priority on the agenda of the constitutional convention.

THE COURTS UNDER THE CONSTITUTION OF 1844

The Convention of 1844 made a number of changes designed to eliminate the criticisms enumerated above. The governor's heavy judicial duties were taken from him, and the new position of chancellor was established. However, appointments to the top offices of the judiciary were to be made by the governor.

Although the convention desired to eliminate the judicial function from the Legislative Council, the delegates were anxious to preserve the lay influence. They did not want the highest court composed solely of lawyers. The result was a greatly altered court of appeals. It was now to consist of the chancellor, the judges of the Supreme Court, and six persons to be "selected from the body of the people, for their integrity, their experience, and their plain, practical, sterling common sense." [2]

Judicial Structure

The changes made by the convention, although important, did not alter fundamentally the system of jurisprudence which had been brought from

England. After 1844 modifications were made from time to time by the legislature until by 1947 the number of courts completely confused the average citizen and questions of court jurisdiction baffled the most expert attorneys. Following is a brief summary of the court structure prior to the convention of 1947.

1. The Court of Errors and Appeals was the state's highest court. It was composed of the chancellor, the nine justices of the Supreme Court, and six so-called lay judges. The court had appellate jurisdiction only. The chancellor was not permitted to sit on appeals from the chancery court nor were justices of the Supreme Court permitted to sit on cases which they had previously decided individually, or as a panel.

2. The Court of Chancery technically consisted of one person, the chancellor. Ten vice-chancellors and fourteen advisory masters assisted him, the latter in recent years handling all matrimonial litigation. The jurisdiction of the court of chancery was concerned with "equity," a branch of jurisprudence designed to afford relief when none was available in the courts of law.

3. The Prerogative Court was headed by the chancellor, in this instance called the "ordinary." The vice-chancellors were vice-ordinaries. The court had jurisdiction over the probation of wills and matters pertaining to trusts and estates. Appeals from the orphans court were taken to the prerogative court although much of their jurisdiction was concurrent.

4. The Supreme Court was composed of the chief justice and eight associate justices. The duties of the justices were manifold. In addition to performing the original and appellate work of their own courts, the justices were members of the Court of Errors and Appeals. They were assigned also to counties as ex officio judges of the county courts. The charging of grand juries and, odd though it may seem, the appointment of park commissioners were additional functions of these justices.

5. A circuit court in each county had civil jurisdiction. It had neither criminal nor appellate jurisdiction. Otherwise, it could hear about the same types of cases as came before the Supreme Court or the county court of common pleas. Except for the judge, who was appointed by the governor and whose salary was paid by the state, the expense of the court was met largely from county funds.

6. The court of common pleas was a county court with original jurisdiction in civil cases. Some of the counties had more than one judge, all of whom were appointed by the governor. Appeals from workmen's compensation cases or from police and traffic courts could be taken to the court of common pleas. The same judge presided also over a number of other courts. First was the court of quarter sessions which had jurisdiction with a jury over indictable offenses of a criminal nature except murder and treason. The court of special sessions could hear similar cases

without a jury, provided the defendant waived his right. The court of oyer and terminer had jurisdiction over all criminal offenses. Cases relating to wills and estates were tried in the orphans court. Surrogates courts had a somewhat similar jurisdiction, although the surrogate was an elected official of the county.

7. There were a number of courts whose jurisdiction was limited both as to subject matter and to territory. These included civil district courts, criminal judicial district courts, county traffic courts, juvenile and domestic relations courts, and small cause courts. Municipalities were authorized by the legislature to establish justices of the peace courts, police courts, recorders courts, magistrates courts, and family courts.[3]

Defects

The complexities of the old system were brought out in the battle for revision during the 1940's. A slashing attack was made by the constitutional commission of 1941-42. It asserted that "New Jersey has the most complicated scheme of courts existing in any English-speaking state." [4] In the legislative hearings of 1942, and in the hearings of the committee on the judiciary in 1947, may be found page after page indicting the state for a system which had been simplified in England as long ago as 1873 and long since in nearly every state in America.

The major criticisms of the old New Jersey court system may be summarized as follows:

1. The Court of Errors and Appeals was unwieldy in size and unsatisfactory in composition. New Jersey had by far the largest top court. The sixteen judges were frequently referred to as a body "little larger than a jury, little less than a mob." [5]

2. The multiplicity of duties to be performed by members of the top court was unbusiness-like. For example, the chancellor was the Court of Chancery and ordinary or surrogate general. The Supreme Court justices could be only part time on the Court of Errors and Appeals since they had not only the work of the Supreme Court to do but also responsibility in the courts of the counties. The six "lay judges" in the top court were also members of the court of pardons. In addition, they were permitted to engage in private business.

3. Responsibility for properly administering the court system was lacking. Neither the chancellor nor the chief justice of the Supreme Court had adequate supervisory power. Work control records were nonexistent. As a consequence, the use of judicial manpower was uneven and wasteful.[6] The end result was delay in the disposition of cases and increased cost to the litigants. The point, often made, that justice delayed is justice denied had undeniable force when applied to the New Jersey courts before 1947.

4. The question which generated the greatest amount of discussion among the members of the legal profession was whether the New Jersey tradition of separate law and equity courts should be maintained or abandoned. The separate systems often made necessary resort to two trial courts in order to settle one controversy. Jurisdictional problems were frequently vexing. For example, suppose that a property owner brought suit in the Court of Chancery to halt trespassing on his property. The court would not have issued an injunction unless it was certain that title to the property was clear. If the title were not clear, the property owner would be forced to go to a court of law in order to establish his title. Then he would return to the Court of Chancery for the injunction. Or suppose that a suit were brought in the Court of Chancery to compel performance of a contract. Usually, if damages were involved, a separate suit had to be brought in a court of law. But not always. The question of which was the rule and which the exception proved embarrassing to the court and the legal profession.[7]

A study made of one volume of the *New Jersey Equity Reports* by a committee of the Essex County Bar Association demonstrated that "one out of every three of these reported cases illustrates the persistent, recurring and ineradicable conflict between the Court of Chancery and the various law courts." [8]   The merits of the parties to the suits were often a secondary issue. Those arguing for the abolition of the two separate systems held that the trial judge should be able to decide both equitable and legal issues. In 1908 Vice-Chancellor Eugene Stevenson, in commenting on the evils of the dual system, remarked:

After trying a nuisance case for three or four days and granting an injunction, it gives me no satisfaction, but, on the contrary, somewhat shocks my sense of justice to refuse to hear the complainant's appeal for his damages, and to require him to bring an action at law involving perhaps three or four days of trial in order that his damages may be assessed by a jury . . . .[9]

5. The procedure for appeals lacked uniformity and tended to delay a final decision. For example, a law case in the circuit court or the court of common pleas could be appealed twice, first to the Supreme Court and then to the Court of Errors and Appeals. A transfer inheritance tax case could be taken from the State Tax Commission to the Prerogative Court, then to the Supreme Court, and finally to the Court of Errors and Appeals. Tax assessment and workmen's compensation cases could be appealed three times. Conditions varied not only as to the number of appeals but also as to the basis for the appeal. In some cases an appeal could be made on the law only, in others on the facts only, in still others on both the law and the facts. "It is incredible, it is inexplicable, but it is true," was the cryptic summary of a prominent attorney before the legislative committee in 1942.[10]

A committee of the Essex County Bar Association concluded that

. . . in a substantial segment of New Jersey's judicial business, there is no assurance of adequate appellate review, and that, where review is available, the machinery therefor is characteristically inefficient, unwieldy, often needlessly duplicitous, inexcusably slow and costly to litigants, and in conflict with the public policy for expeditious final settlement of both public and private controversies.[11]

The Bar Association committee advocated the elimination of multiple appeals in favor of "one assured judicial review of all judicial actions and determinations, whether by courts or statutory tribunals." [12]

THE PRESENT JUDICIAL SYSTEM

The committee on the judiciary at the Constitutional Convention of 1947 agreed upon three basic principles as guides to a modern judicial system:

1. Unification of courts: The committee believed that only by a simplified and integrated court structure could jurisdictional controversies and delays be eliminated.

2. Flexibility of the court system: Flexibility would enable judicial business to be apportioned according to need thus utilizing judicial resources to the full.

3. Control over administration, practice, and procedure by rules of court: By this means business-like management together with simplified judicial procedures could be obtained.[13]

These objectives were achieved in large measure. "The judicial power," according to the new constitution, "shall be vested in a Supreme Court, a Superior Court, County Courts and inferior courts of limited jurisdiction." [14]

All members of the supreme, superior, and county courts are appointed by the governor with the advice and consent of the Senate. However, the governor is required to give seven days public notice before sending any nomination to the Senate. First appointments to the supreme and superior courts are for terms of seven years. After reappointment, the office is held during good behavior, with retirement at seventy years of age. County court judges hold office for a definite term of five years.* A distinctive feature of the old system, which has no constitutional status but

* In 1956 the chief justice received $25,000 annually. The associate justices received $24,000, and members of the Superior Court, $20,000. The judges of county courts received salaries ranging from $7,500 to $16,000 depending upon the population of the county or upon the number of judges. Where there is more than one judge the top salary is paid, but the position is considered a full-time one, and the practice of law is forbidden. Justices of the Supreme Court and judges of the Superior Court may be retired for disability on a pension of three fourths of their annual salary. The normal retirement of judicial officers is linked to a specified period of years of service. Normal retirement also carries a pension of three fourths of the annual salary.

which has been continued, is the practice of bipartisan appointments to courts having more than one judge. In 1948 appointments to county courts were required by law to be bipartisan where there are two or more judges.

Any member of the supreme, superior, or county courts is subject to impeachment. After impeachment, he may not continue to exercise his office until acquitted. A second means of removal applies only to the judges of the superior and county courts. The constitution provides that any member of the latter courts may be removed by the Supreme Court "for such causes and in such manner as shall be provided by law." [15] This clause has never been implemented by the legislature.

The Supreme Court

The Supreme Court of New Jersey, consisting of a chief justice and six associate justices, heads the state's judicial system. Five members constitute a quorum. The court has appellate jurisdiction in all causes provided for by the constitution and the laws. In general these include: causes involving an interpretation of the Constitution of the United States or the Constitution of New Jersey; causes marked by a dissent in the appellate division of the Superior Court; capital causes; causes certified to the Superior Court, the county courts, or other courts; and other causes provided by law. The court may exercise the original jurisdiction necessary to complete the determination of any case under review. In addition to its adjudicatory powers, the Supreme Court makes rules governing the administration of the courts and governing judicial practice and procedure. It also exercises jurisdiction over the admission to and discipline of the bar.

The Superior Court

Immediately below the Supreme Court is the Superior Court, which is divided into appellate, law, and chancery divisions. The appellate division sits in "parts" consisting of three judges each. The constitution provides for a minimum of twenty-four judges who are assigned by the chief justice of the Supreme Court to one of the three divisions. Since 1948 thirty-eight judges have been authorized by law.

With one stroke the delegates to the Constitutional Convention of 1947 settled the age-old controversy about the merger of the law and equity courts. According to the constitution, "the Superior Court shall have original general jurisdiction throughout the state in all causes." [16] This sentence spelled the end of the dual system. The constitution specifically authorized the law and chancery divisions, subject to the rules of the Supreme Court, to "exercise the powers and functions of the other division when the ends of justice so require, and legal and equitable relief shall be granted in any cause so that all matters in controversy between the parties may be completely determined." [17] The judiciary committee, in its report to the convention, emphasized that the constitutional provision for "divisions" and "parts" of the Superior Court was intended as a functional device designed to expedite the courts' business and not to effect a "permanent segregation of jurisdiction." [18] The committee was desirous of eliminating jurisdictional rivalries and therefore specifically avoided any constitutional apportionment of jurisdiction between the law and chancery divisions. It intended each division to have and exercise the powers of the court as a whole.

In practice, judges are regularly assigned to hear equity cases. For example, in the court year 1953-54 six judges of the Superior Court were regularly assigned to hear general equity matters and seven to hear matrimonial causes. Additional assistance was provided by the temporary assignment of judges from the appellate division and the law division.

The constitution authorized the appellate division to take appeals from the law and chancery divisions, from the county courts, and in other causes provided by law. The appellate division was also given the original jurisdiction necessary to complete a case.

The prerogative writs, *certiorari, mandamus,* and *quo warranto* were superseded by a hearing before the Superior Court. Under the old system it was necessary to get the permission of the court in advance before instituting proceedings for a prerogative writ. Now a decision of a lower court or of an administrative tribunal may be appealed "as of right" except in a criminal case where the Superior Court may exercise discretion.

County Courts

The inclusion of the county courts in the constitution destroyed the objective of a completely unified court system in which one court, the Superior Court, would exercise original jurisdiction in all important matters.

In the 1947 constitutional convention, representatives of the small counties wanted a county court with at least one judge whose primary business was to serve the interests of justice in that county. Otherwise, they argued, justice would be too remote.

As a consequence of the demand of the rural counties, the convention provided for county courts to exercise the jurisdiction formerly held by the court of common pleas, orphans court, court of oyer and terminer, court of quarter sessions, and court of special sessions.[19] The jurisdiction of the county courts may be altered by law. The chief justice of the Supreme Court is the administrative head with power to assign a county judge to sit temporarily in the Superior Court or in another county court.

Each county now has a county court. In some there is but one judge. Where there is more than one judge, appointments must be bipartisan in character, and the full time of each judge must be devoted to judicial duties.

The county courts are composed of two divisions, the probate division with jurisdiction over matters such as wills and estates, and the law division which exercises the remaining jurisdiction, both criminal and civil. The county surrogate serves as the clerk of the probate division and the county clerk serves as clerk of the law division.

District Courts

District courts were established by the legislature as early as 1873. At that time two special district courts were created for Newark. Later, county judicial districts were established by the legislature to exercise jurisdiction over counties or parts of counties. By an act passed in 1948 the district court system was reorganized and simplified. Counties with more than one district court were required to reorganize and establish one court with branches numbered according to the creation of the various districts. Designation of a presiding judge is made according to the rules of the Supreme Court.

The district court may hear actions of a civil nature where the matter in dispute does not exceed $1,000, in motor vehicle damage cases, $3,000. It may exercise criminal jurisdiction concurrently with the municipal courts. The county may establish a small claims division in the district court with jurisdiction in contractual disputes not exceeding $50. The district courts do a large volume of business. For example, in 1953-54 disposition was made of 134,103 cases and 50 per cent of all civil cases were determined in the district courts.[20]

Judges are appointed by the governor, with the consent of the Senate, for terms of five years. Judicial salaries, which are payable by the county, vary according to the classification of the county and the number of judges.

Juvenile and Domestic Relations Courts

A "court for the trial of juvenile offenders" was authorized by the legislature in 1903.[21] In 1912 the county juvenile courts were given jurisdiction over domestic disputes. Each county now has a juvenile and domestic relations court. Except where the appointment of a special judge is provided by law, the county judge presides.*

The jurisdiction of the court covers a wide range of offenses committed by persons under eighteen including felonies and misdemeanors, habitual vagrancy, incorrigibility, and immorality. Jurisdiction extends also to matters involving the abuse or neglect of children, their support and temporary custody, and the support of a wife and family.

Municipal Courts

The new constitution eliminated the constitutional status of the justice of the peace. This action paved the way for legislative abolition of the

* In 1952 Bergen, Essex, Hudson, Passaic, and Union counties had special judges. Other counties may provide by referendum for a special judge to preside over the court.

office.   Since January 1, 1949, New Jersey municipalities have had municipal courts instead of justices of the peace and small cause and other courts.   The municipal court is headed by a magistrate.   In mayor-council communities he is appointed by the mayor with the consent of the council. In other municipalities the magistrate is selected by the governing body. Whenever by agreement two or more municipalities agree to set up a municipal court, the magistrate is appointed by the governor.   Cities of over 200,000 population may have up to three additional magistrates.   In August, 1954, 482 municipal courts served 519 municipalities.

The new law setting up the municipal court will in time eliminate all former nonlawyer justices of the peace and police court judges.   However, at the time the law was passed, persons having actual experience as justices of the peace or police judges were made eligible to become magistrates. New appointees must be attorneys.

Magistrates receive a salary determined by ordinance.   They are prohibited from acting as defense counsel for an alleged criminal in any court of the state.

The jurisdiction of the court extends to minor civil actions and to violations of municipal ordinances, motor vehicle and traffic laws, fish and game laws, disorderly person offenses and other matters.   The court also has criminal jurisdiction over specified offenses where the person charged waives the right to indictment and trial by jury.   However, if the magistrate is not an attorney, he has no jurisdiction over an indictable offense.

Surrogate

Each county has an elected surrogate who presides over the surrogate court and who serves as clerk of the probate division of the county court. The Constitution of 1844 made the surrogate a constitutional officer. His constitutional status was retained in the convention of 1947.   The jurisdiction of the surrogate is concerned with wills and letters of administration and guardianship.   Orders or judgments made by the surrogate are subject to review in the county court.

JUDICIAL ADMINISTRATION

Vast administrative powers were placed in the hands of the Supreme Court and particularly in the hands of the chief justice.   The court was empowered to "make rules governing the administration of all courts in the state . . . ."   It was also given jurisdiction over admissions to the bar and the discipline of members of the legal profession.*

* Admission to the practice of law is supervised by a three-member Board of Bar Examiners appointed by the court.   According to Chief Justice Vanderbilt, New Jersey has "about 8,000 lawyers, an abnormally large number for our population. While New Jersey has 3.2 per cent of the population of the country, it has

The chief justice was made administrative head of all the courts with authority to appoint an administrative director to serve at his pleasure. He was also authorized to assign judges of the superior courts to the various divisions of the court and to make reassignments as needed.

Administrative Office of the Courts

The Administrative Office of the Courts was established in 1948.[22] The principal function of the office is to keep the members of the Supreme Court, particularly the chief justice, advised of the status of judicial business. Operational statistics are collected with a view to showing what the courts have done, what they are doing at the time of the report, and the work remaining to be done. Each judge is required to report weekly on such matters as the number of hours on the bench, the name and nature of each case heard, the result, and cases yet undecided.

Monthly reports are obtained from the clerks of the courts showing the number of cases on hand at the beginning of each month, the number of new cases, and the number settled or disposed of by trial. The reports are used in making assignments of judges to areas needing assistance and as a means of checking the handling of court calendars.

The chief justice has emphasized the gathering of statistics as perhaps the most fruitful activity of the administrative office.

I have been able to avail myself of these live records in performing the most difficult function confided to me as Chief Justice by the Constitution, the assigning of the trial judges "as need appears." Thus last month I was enabled to equalize the caseload throughout the State of the judges of the Law Division of the Superior Court, to rearrange the schedules of the Chancery Division and Matrimonial judges in the northern part of the State to meet two unusual situations, to reassign the division of the general equity work in the southern half of the State caused by an unanticipated illness, and to send aid to two county courts where the lists were especially congested.[23]

The administrative office acts as a clearing house in answering inquiries from officials, members of the bar, and the public concerning the operation of the courts.

In contrast with the five entirely separate court budgets under the old

---

4.7 per cent of the lawyers—or almost 50 per cent more than her share." Arthur T. Vanderbilt, "Our New Judicial Establishment: The Record of the First Year," *Rutgers Law Review* IV (January, 1950), 373.

As a consequence of the power given to the Supreme Court to regulate admission to the bar, examinations have been altered. Increased emphasis has been given to the development of tests of ability. The problems of legal draftsmanship and procedure also receive more attention. Examinations are now given three times a year, and the announcement of those who pass is made within three or four weeks, rather than five or six months as previously. In the first term of the new court disciplinary action, such as disbarment, suspension, or reprimand, was taken in twelve cases. David Stoffer, "Organization and Administration of the Courts," *Rutgers Law Review,* IV (September, 1949), 14.

system, the administrative office serves as the central budget agency of the courts. Other functions include (1) examining the administrative methods and systems of the judges, clerks, and stenographic reporters, (2) arranging accommodations for the courts, (3) purchasing supplies and equipment, (4) investigating complaints, and (5) public relations.[24]

Judicial Conference

As a means of improving the efficiency of the judicial machinery, the state now holds an annual judicial conference. The judges, top legislative officers, the attorney general, the county prosecutors, representatives of the law schools and bar associations, and ten laymen constitute the conference.[25] The administrative director is the secretary of the conference.

The Supreme Court has followed the practice of inviting suggestions for changes in the rules of the court. These are placed on the agenda for discussion at the conference. In 1952 sessions were also devoted to appellate procedures, the conduct of practicing attorneys, and standards of admission to the bar. Special committees reported on such subjects as improving the administration of criminal justice, sentencing and probation procedures, and the problem of processing habeas corpus applications. Subsequently, the Supreme Court issued new rules and amendments to the old rules.

Rules of practice and procedure provide the judicial machinery by which our substantial rights in life, liberty and property are protected and given effect. To keep pace with changing times such rules must be the subject at all times of continuing study and scrutiny by expert and trained minds under actual operating conditions, otherwise they will become obsolete and outmoded. The judicial conference is furnishing a most valuable service in its role as aid and advisor to the Supreme Court in this continuing task.[26]

There is also an annual conference of municipal magistrates and traffic court prosecutors. Through special committees the conference acts as an advisory body to the court. At the same time the conference performs a useful service in informing the magistrates of developments in current practice.

LEGAL PROCEDURE

Practice and procedure in all courts are now subject to the rules of the Supreme Court. Under the old constitution the rule-making power was divided; each court made rules of its own, and also the legislature enacted many rules although no effort was made to deal systematically with court procedures. As a consequence, "practice and procedure were needlessly complicated and rules on the same point were needlessly conflicting according to the court in which they arose." [27]

The Rule-making Power

The delegates to the Constitutional Convention of 1947 endeavored to eliminate the confusion concerning the rule-making power. The constitution now provides: "The Supreme Court shall make rules governing the administration of the courts in the state and, subject to law, the practice and procedure in all such courts." [28]

When the new Supreme Court was first organized, the decision was made to use the Federal Rules of Civil and Criminal Procedure as the basis for the new rules. Late in 1947 there began the collection of data from all over the country concerning the best judicial practice. Suggestions were invited from the members of the bench and bar, and a tentative draft was prepared for review and criticism.

Subsequently, on September 15, 1948, the new rules went into effect. Amendments were made from time to time, and in 1953 a general revision was accomplished. The rules are divided into eight parts:

I. Rules Relating to the Supreme Court and Rules of Administration;
II. Rules Governing Practice in the Appellate Division of the Superior Court;
III. Rules Governing Criminal Practice in the Superior Court and County Courts;
IV. Rules Governing Civil Practice in the Superior Court;
V. Rules Governing the County Courts and Surrogates;
VI. Rules Governing the Juvenile and Domestic Relations Court;
VII. Rules Governing Civil Practice in the County District Courts;
VIII. Rules Governing Practice in the Local Criminal Courts.[29]

The complete authority of the Supreme Court to make rules governing practice and procedure was not accomplished without a struggle. Differences of opinion developed over the constitutional phrase "subject to law." For example, could the court by rule set aside procedural legislation enacted prior to 1947? More particularly, could the court modify or overrule legislation of a procedural nature enacted after the adoption of the new constitution or enacted specifically to override a rule? In a case involving the allowance of counsel fees, the court held that its rules annulled preconstitution procedural legislation.[30]

Later, in connection with a suit involving the alleged libel of a deputy attorney general by a Middlesex County grand jury, the court held that its rule-making power was not subject to overriding legislation. The court declared that the phrase "subject to law" referred to substantive law. By this interpretation the limitation contained in the phrase "subject to law" means that the judicial rule of procedure may not alter the substantive law:

The phrase . . . thus serves as a continuous reminder that the rule making power as to practice and procedure must not invade the field of substantive law as such. While the courts necessarily make new substantive law through the decision of specific cases coming before them, they are not to make substantive law wholesale through the exercise of the rule making power.[31]

This opinion of the court has aroused a considerable amount of controversy.[32] The doctrine that a court rule cannot be overridden by the legislature may have large consequences in view of the narrow line that sometimes exists between what is substantive law and what is procedural law.[33]

Court Practice

The new rules have brought about many changes in court practice. They were designed to eliminate technicalities and to simplify judicial procedures.

The pretrial conference is one innovation which has been credited with improving the quality of the trial process and with speeding up considerably the output of the courts. The pretrial conference is prescribed for all contested issues except matrimonial cases. The purpose of the conference, which is held by the judge with the opposing attorneys in open court, is to prepare a chart or agenda of the forthcoming trial. In addition to saving time by agreeing on certain facts or the admission of certain documents, the conference gives the judge a view of the entire case before he begins to preside; "the perspective makes not only for better trials and surer justice, but also for fewer appeals." [34]

The new rules also radically altered the procedure for hearing appeals. Formerly there were three terms in the Court of Errors and Appeals. Oral arguments were presented continuously for about two weeks. This meant that from sixty to eighty cases were ready for consideration by the court after the term ended in addition to whatever backlog of cases the court had before the term opened. Now there is a single term with a few cases, perhaps a half dozen, argued orally each Monday. The result has been that "small, concentrated attacks on the ready calendar have replaced the diffuse methods of yesteryear which must have taxed even the trojans of the bench in trying to grasp, without prior examination of briefs or records, divers arguments day after day for successive weeks." [35]

In contrast to the practice of the appellate courts under the old constitution, where about half of all appeals were decided on the basis of briefs submitted by opposing attorneys, the new rules require oral arguments in every case. Each side has forty-five minutes. Prior to the oral argument, the judges study the briefs and at a Thursday conference of the court indicate to the presiding judge the points which need clarification. He, in turn, at the opening of the oral argument the following Monday, advises each side of the points with which the court is concerned. Once counsel has had an opportunity to state the issues, the court may ask questions. At a conference of the court the following Thursday, each judge discusses the case in turn and a tentative vote is taken. The presiding judge then assigns one member of the court to write a draft opinion. This is subjected to the criticism of the court before the opinion is put in final form and an official vote taken.[36]

The practice in this state of requiring all judges to read the record, hear oral argument and take part in court conferences prior to assignment of the case for writing of the decision, together with the elimination of any policy of rotation, represents the most thorough system of consideration in use in any appellate court.[37]

The courts have long since become big business. However, now they are able to cope with the volume of litigation which has been thrust upon them. A new structure, attention to the administrative side of judicial business, and simplified practice—these have resulted in a system of courts in New Jersey which serves as a guide to other states desiring to achieve judicial reform.[38]

NOTES

[1] N.J. *Proceedings of the New Jersey State Constitutional Convention of 1844, compiled and edited by the New Jersey Writers Project of the Works Projects Administration with an Introduction by John Bebout,* Sponsored by the New Jersey State House Commission, 1942, p. LI.

[2] *Proceedings . . . Convention of 1844, op. cit.,* p. 232.

[3] See Joseph Harrison, "New Jersey's New Court System," *Rutgers Law Review,* II (1948), 60-103. See also Edward B. McConnell, *A Brief History of the New Jersey Courts* (Trenton, 1954).

[4] N.J. *Report of the Commission on Revision of the New Jersey Constitution, May, 1942* (Trenton, 1942), p. 42.

[5] N.J. *Constitutional Convention of 1947,* IV, 6.

[6] For the administrative defects of the courts see the special study prepared by Ralph R. Temple, "Report on the Constitutional Courts of the State of New Jersey," in N.J. *Record of Proceedings before the Joint Committee of the New Jersey Legislature* (Trenton, 1942), pp. 1057-1121.

[7] Testimony of Russell Watson in *ibid.,* p. 284.

[8] *Report of Special Committee of Essex County Bar Association Concerning Constitutional Revision of Judicial Article* (Newark: Arthur W. Cross, Inc., Law Printers, 1947), p. 24.

[9] *L. Martin Co.* v *L. Martin and Wilkes Co.,* 75 N.J. Eq. 39, 56 (1908), quoted in testimony of Robert C. Hendrickson, N.J. *Constitutional Convention of 1947,* IV, 9.

[10] Testimony of Russell Watson, *op. cit.,* p. 283.

[11] *Report of Special Committee of Essex County Bar Association . . . , op. cit.,* p. 45.

[12] *Ibid.,* p. 50.

[13] *Convention of 1947, op. cit.,* II, 1180.

[14] Art. VI.

[15] Art. VI, sect. VI, par. 4.

[16] Art. VI, sec. III, par. 2.

[17] Art. VI, sec. III, par. 4.

[18] *Convention of 1947, op. cit.,* II, p. 1191.

[19] For the debate on this issue, see N.J. *Constitutional Convention of 1947,* I, 565-80.

20 N.J. *Annual Report of the Administrative Director of the Courts, 1953-1954* (Trenton: Administrative Office of the Courts, 1954), pp. 22-23.

21 L., 1903, ch. 219, p. 477.

22 L., 1948, ch. 354, p. 1419.

23 Arthur T. Vanderbilt, "Our New Judicial Establishment: The Record of the First Year," *Rutgers Law Review*, IV (January, 1950), 372.

24 Willard G. Woelper, "Administering the Courts in New Jersey," *Journal of the American Judicature Society*, XXXVI (1952), 70-74.

25 For the membership of the conference, see *Supreme Court Rules* 1:23-1.

26 Willard G. Woelper, "The Judicial Conference in Its Role in the Rule Making Process," *Rutgers Law Review*, V (1951), 357.

27 Roscoe Pound, "Procedure under Rules of Court in New Jersey," *Harvard Law Review*, LXVI (November, 1952), 30-31.

28 Art. VI, sec. II, par. 3.

29 N.J. *Rules Governing the Courts of the State of New Jersey* (Newark: Soney and Sage Co., 1953).

30 *John S. Westervelt's Sons* v *Regency Inc.*, 3 N.J. 472 (1950).

31 *Winberry* v *Salisbury*, 5 N.J. 240, 248 (1950).

32 See Benjamin Kaplan and Warren J. Greene, "The Legislature's Relation to Judicial Rule-making: An Appraisal of *Winberry* v *Salisbury*," *Harvard Law Review*, LXV (1951), 234-54. For a view upholding the court see Pound, *loc. cit.*, pp. 28-46.

33 For a recent attack on the court's rule-making power, see Governor Meyner's address before the Constitutional Convention Association as reported in the *Newark Sunday News*, January 22, 1956, pp. 1-2.

34 Henry E. Ackerson, Jr., "Pretrial Conferences and Calendar Control: The Keys to Effective Work in the Trial Courts," *Rutgers Law Review*, IV (January, 1950), 387.

35 David Stoffer, "Organization and Administration of the Courts," *Rutgers Law Review*, IV (September, 1949), 8.

36 Vanderbilt, *loc. cit.*, p. 359. "After considerable study of appellate methods elsewhere, I can truthfully say that I think there is no state in the Union in which each judge makes a greater contribution to every decision than in the appellate courts of New Jersey." *Ibid.*

37 George Warren, "New Jersey and National Judicial Standards—A Comparison," *Rutgers Law Review*, IV (June, 1950), 615.

38 For a review of the accomplishments of the new system and a bibliography of articles on the New Jersey courts see Arthur T. Vanderbilt, "The First Five Years of the New Jersey Courts under the Constitution of 1947," *Rutgers Law Review*, VIII (Spring 1954), 289-315.

CHAPTER 14

Law Enforcement

THE ORGANIZATIONAL structure of the state's law enforcement machinery has undergone widespread changes since 1948. Several independent agencies have been brought together under the supervision of the attorney general, a step which would not have been feasible prior to the adoption of the new constitution.

THE ATTORNEY GENERAL

The office of the attorney general was brought to the colonies from England. The Constitution of 1776 was silent concerning the powers of the office, but it did provide for a five-year term. This period of service, longer by two years than that of the governor, was retained in the Constitution of 1844. As a consequence, it would have been unwise politically for any governor to have asked for authority to bestow general administrative powers upon the attorney general. As it was, governors were frequently embarrassed by having on their hands holdovers appointed by previous chief executives. For example, Governor Driscoll, unable to persuade the incumbent attorney general to resign, shortly before his inauguration asked and obtained authority from the legislature to appoint a personal counsel.[1]

Powers and Duties

The enlargement of the attorney general's authority became politically feasible when his constitutional term of office was made concurrent with that of the governor. An increase in power, although a departure from tradition, involved nothing extraordinary since previous legislatures dating from 1812 had periodically altered the duties of the office.[2] As a part of the administrative reorganization in 1948, the attorney general was made responsible not only for the generally recognized functions of his office but also for the supervision of the previously independent departments of the state police, motor vehicles, alcoholic beverage control, and weights and measures. Each of these agencies was made a division within the Department of Law and Public Safety.

At the head of the department is the attorney general who is appointed by the governor, with the advice and consent of the Senate, to serve during the governor's term of office. The attorney general has "general responsibility" for the operations of the department. His authority includes the development of a program designed to promote efficient operations, the coordination of inspectional and law enforcement activities under the jurisdiction of the department, and the integration of departmental staff services. However, his control of the internal organization is limited in that the agencies receiving legislative recognition must be maintained. With certain exceptions, the attorney general may, providing he has the approval of the governor, exercise the power vested in the heads of the divisions of state police, alcoholic beverage control, weights and measures, and motor vehicles. To the extent that he exercises such power, the authority of the division head is superseded.[3]

Legal Functions

The state's legal services were consolidated in the office of the attorney general in 1944. Legislation was enacted after a special Commission on State Administrative Reorganization reported that a number of unsound practices had developed which were both costly and inefficient. These may be summarized as follows:

1. A number of agencies had their own legal departments. In 1942-43, $156,370 was appropriated for the salaries of the members of these departments while $80,728 was appropriated for the salaries of those in the attorney general's office. In addition, agencies often employed special counsel. Over a ten-year period this practice had cost an average of $100,000 annually. It was the opinion of the commission that all the legal business of the state should be conducted under the supervision of the attorney general.

2. Members of the attorney general's staff were being paid by county governments to prosecute criminal cases. The commission recommended that fees for professional services to other governmental units be paid into the state treasury.

3. The practice of departmental members in representing private clients before other state agencies was condemned.

4. The granting of tenure to part-time officials was declared to be a "travesty on the underlying principles of civil service." [4]

As a consequence of the commission's recommendations, and after considerable urging by Governor Edge, a Department of Law was established.

The powers of the department were declared to be those "now or hereafter conferred upon or required of the Attorney General." [5]   These include:

1. Providing legal advice to the governor, the legislature, and all other agencies of the state government.
2. Representing the state in all controversies in which its interests are involved.
3. Enforcing the provisions of the securities and civil rights laws.
4. Assisting the counties in the prosecution of criminal matters or, by request, assuming the functions of the county prosecutor.
5. Enforcing the constitution and the laws of the state.

The 1944 act followed closely the recommendations of the commission. All facilities for supplying legal services to the governor and to the various administrative agencies were consolidated.   Only those bodies charged with the hearing and determination of facts were authorized to employ full-time attorneys and in those cases the functions of the attorneys were limited.   The attorney general may assign one of his staff to work with an agency on a part-time or full-time basis, but the attorney general retains complete supervisory control.   The tenure question was solved by providing for deputy attorneys general and assistant deputy attorneys general. The former were to serve at the pleasure of the attorney general.   The latter were to obtain tenure after three years and were required to devote full time to their duties.

An interesting aspect of the 1944 act was the increase in the power of the governor over the prosecution of crime at the local level.   For years, the attorney general had had authority to serve in the capacity of prosecutor in a county having no prosecutor.*   He could intervene also at the request of the prosecutor, a judge of the Supreme Court, or the board of chosen freeholders.†   The 1944 act included the governor among those authorized to request action.

In 1954 there were thirty-six deputy attorneys general and two assistant

---

* This provision of the law was interpreted by the Supreme Court in 1947. The attorney general, in the absence of a Hudson County prosecutor, acted against members of the McFeely regime for failure to enforce the state gambling laws in the city of Hoboken.   The court held that "there is nothing inherently or constitutionally incompatible in the performance by the Attorney-General of the duties of a prosecutor of the pleas."   Further, said the court, "the legality of his acts while so serving may not be questioned in this proceeding upon the contention that the Governor violated the constitutional scheme in not earlier filling the vacancy in the prosecutor's office."   *State* v *McFeely,* 136 N.J.L. 102, 110 (1947).

† In 1947 an associate justice of the Court of Errors and Appeals called upon the attorney general for assistance in the prosecution of crime in Middlesex County. A bill for expenses submitted to the board of chosen freeholders by Deputy Attorney General John J. Winberry was disapproved on the ground that the county had made no appropriation to meet this expense. The Court of Errors and Appeals held that no discretion was vested in the county. On the contrary, the governing body had an absolute duty to pay. *Van Riper* v *Board of Chosen Freeholders,* 137 N.J.L. 715 (1948).

deputy attorneys general. Some were specialists in the legal problems of individual agencies; others prepared opinions on general problems coming before the attorney general. Formerly, most of the deputy attorneys general served on a part-time basis. In recent years greater emphasis has been placed upon full-time appointments.

STATE POLICE

The New Jersey Department of State Police was established in 1921 primarily to furnish protection to rural inhabitants.[6] Organized originally as an independent agency, the Department of State Police was transferred to the Department of Law and Public Safety in 1948 and renamed the Division of State Police.[7]

A superintendent of state police is the executive and administrative head of the division. He is appointed by the governor, with the advice and consent of the Senate, to serve during the term of the governor and until a successor to the superintendent has been appointed. The governor may remove him for cause.

The members of the state police are peace officers of the state and are subject to the governor's call. Their powers correspond to those of local police officers and include the prevention of crime, the pursuance and apprehension of offenders, the collection of evidence, and the execution of warrants. A limited number of troopers, not to exceed fifteen in any one county, may be used to enforce the election laws when a request is made by the county superintendent of elections. The state police are authorized by law also to act as motor vehicle inspectors and as wardens in protecting the forests and the fish and game of the state.[8]

The state police are organized on a semimilitary basis. The division consists of units concerned with operations, administration, and investigation. The field organization consists of four police commands.* The headquarters of Troop A, for example, is located at Hammonton. Troops A, B, and C have supervision of approximately one dozen substations each. Troop D consists of those assigned to patrol the New Jersey Turnpike and the Garden State Parkway. The authorized police strength of the division in 1956 was 866.

Personnel

Applicants for membership must be between twenty-two and thirty-five years of age, of good health and moral character, and preferably residents of the state. Competitive examinations consist of physical and mental

* A State Capitol police force was created in 1935. The force consists of those officers employed on the State Capitol grounds and adjoining parks. Duties of the force consist chiefly of the direction of traffic and parking around the Capitol and nearby state buildings. The force is supplemented and supervised by the state police. See L., 1935, ch. 271, p. 879.

tests, an oral interview, and a character investigation. A fifteen-week preservice course of training at the New Jersey Police Academy precedes a nine-month probationary appointment for the successful applicants. In 1953, of 1,528 men who applied for membership, 144 qualified by examination and 98 completed the preservice training program. After five years of service, members receive tenure. The State Police Retirement and Benevolent Fund, a separate contributory pension system, permits retirement at age fifty-five after twenty-five years of service. Salary ranges, formerly established by law, are now fixed by the Department of Civil Service.[9]

Operations

The investigation of crime in rural areas is considered the direct responsibility of the state police. In cities, the state troopers assist in investigations usually upon invitation of the local authorities. In special investigations, the state police cooperate with county prosecutors and with state and Federal agencies. The division headquarters, located at Wilburtha, near Trenton, maintains records of the results of each investigation. Division records also contain a classification of criminal arrests, stolen and recovered automobiles, traffic accident statistics, and motor vehicle arrests.[10]

Traffic control and traffic law enforcement are problems of increasing magnitude. The week-end traffic congestion on New Jersey's roads makes the policing function especially difficult. Troopers are assigned to those points where accident hazards are greatest. However, the large amount of traffic on existing road mileage produces a degree of congestion which no body of police could relieve effectively. Of 111,142 motor vehicle arrests made by the state police in the fiscal year 1955, 64,823 were the result of excessive speed.[11]

To facilitate police operations throughout the state, the division maintains the State Bureau of Identification. Local law enforcement agencies are required to send to the bureau fingerprints of all persons arrested for an indictable offense.[12] An attack upon this provision of the law as contravening the state constitution was denied by the Court of Errors and Appeals in 1946. The court held that the fingerprinting and photographing of an accused person prior to his trial and conviction did not deprive him of his constitutional rights.[13] A later chancery court ruling upheld the practice of distributing fingerprints before conviction to other states and to the Federal Bureau of Investigation:

. . . the statute in question is within the proper exercise of the police powers of the state for the purpose of facilitating crime detection and punishment in the interest of society generally and that one who has been indicted must submit to such slight invasion of his claimed right of privacy as may accompany the performance of the police duty required by the statute.[14]

An extensive communications system has been developed for the use not only of the state police but also for county and municipal police and for civilian defense purposes. A state-wide teletype system is made available, by law, to all enforcement agencies within the state.[15] Any government agency may connect, at its own expense with the basic system, which is, in turn, connected with twelve states and the District of Columbia. The state police radio network services about 180 mobile units of the division and forty cars operated by the Division of Motor Vehicles.

The Bureau of Identification acts as the connecting link between local agencies and the Federal Bureau of Investigation. A central file of missing and wanted persons in New Jersey is maintained, as well as files of sex offenders, registered and stolen firearms, laundry and drycleaning marks, and photographs of criminals. A crime detection laboratory is designed and equipped to do research and to make technical examinations of evidence.[16]

Training in law enforcement is assuming increasing importance. Legislation passed in 1948 required the superintendent of police to provide annually a training course for fish and game wardens.[17] Early in 1951 the division instituted a special six-week training course for municipal and county police officers. Designed for new appointees and young officers, it emphasized fundamental police practices and procedures.[18]

In addition to the investigation of crime and the control of traffic, the state police division engages in a variety of activities. One of the most important is the emergency service which the troopers endeavor to provide whenever life or property is endangered, or when accident or disaster strikes. The division is responsible also for the organization and supervision of about 450 school safety patrols. In 1953 these patrols furnished special highway crossing protection to approximately 140,000 children. The division cooperates with organizations desiring to give training in traffic safety, first aid, and lifesaving.

One of the more unusual activities of the Division of State Police is the maintenance of a registry of tattoo identifying marks for poultry. These are used just as branding marks are used on cattle—to prevent stealing. Approximately 1,000 tattoo marks have been registered.[19] The division also licenses private detectives, commissions railroad police, and enforces minimum fire safety standards in hotels.

As a part of the 1948 reorganization, the Board of Tenement House Supervision was transferred to the state police. The superintendent of state police was given the board's authority over the personnel of the agency. In 1953, however, the superintendent recommended that this function, together with such other special activities as hotel fire inspection, and the enforcement of regulations concerning liquefied petroleum gas, be removed from the jurisdiction of the state police as not being properly within their area of responsibility.

LAW ENFORCEMENT COUNCIL

In order to provide a continuing review of the effectiveness of the crimi-nal laws and the performance of the various enforcement agencies, a Law Enforcement Council was established in 1952.[20] The life of the council was originally limited to one year. However, a two-year extension was granted in 1953, and a one-year extension in 1955. Following a contro-versy with Governor Meyner over the right of the legislature to extend the terms of council members, the council, by concurrent resolution in 1956, was given the status of a legislative commission. The original act provided that the five members of the council be appointed by the gov-ernor with the advice and consent of the Senate. However, the 1956 resolution provides for the filling of vacancies by joint action of the presi-dent of the Senate and the speaker of the General Assembly. No more than three members may belong to the same political party. Government employees or officeholders are excluded from membership.

In 1953-54 the council conducted an investigation into the solicitation and collection of funds by organizations composed of law enforcement personnel. The results of the investigation, the council declared, "present a sordid picture . . . the effect of which is detrimental to proper law en-forcement, and, if allowed to continue unrestricted, will completely under-mine public confidence in law enforcement agencies." [21]

The council's report concerned the activities of eight associations. For example, in violation of the law, the Superior Police Officers Association of New Jersey had contracted with a professional solicitor to solicit ad-vertisements for the association's yearbook. By the terms of the contract the solicitor was to receive 70 per cent of all collections. Subsequently his share was reduced to 60 per cent. One of four assistants hired by the solicitor had a long criminal record, including convictions for robbery and for forgery. Posing as police officers, the solicitors telephoned prospects for advertisements and for contributions to be used for charitable purposes. Contributors received honorary memberships in the association. During the period 1949-1953 the solicitations amounted to approximately $164,-000. Over 60 per cent was retained by the professional solicitor. Only $1,353, or less than 1 per cent, was used for charitable purposes.[22]

Following the enforcement council's recommendations, legislation was enacted in 1954 designed to prevent the practices disclosed in the report.[23]

LEGALIZED GAMES OF CHANCE CONTROL COMMISSION

The first amendment to the Constitution of 1947 empowered the legis-lature to provide by law for the conduct of bingo and raffles in munici-palities which authorized games of chance by means of a public referendum. The constitutional amendment was adopted November 3, 1953. Enabling legislation was quickly approved. Early in 1954 three laws were enacted, the first authorizing raffles, the second authorizing bingo, and the third establishing a regulatory agency in the Department of State —the Legalized Games of Chance Control Commission.

Municipalities adopting the bingo and raffles laws by referendum may license the following:

bona fide organizations or associations of veterans of any war in which the United States has been engaged, churches or religious congregations and religious organizations, charitable, educational and fraternal organizations, civic and service clubs, officially recognized volunteer fire companies, and officially recognized first aid or rescue squads.[24]

The municipal governing body which issues a license has primary responsibility for supervising and controlling the games. They may suspend or, after hearing, revoke a license. The law provides that persons under eighteen may not participate. Restrictions on the amount of the prizes, the methods of advertising, and the kinds of reports are spelled out in the law.

In order to supervise the administration of the bingo and raffles licensing law, the legislature established the Legalized Games of Chance Control Commission. The commission consists of three members, no more than two of whom may belong to one political party. The term of office is five years. The members are entitled to receive expenses but they are required to serve without compensation.

The commission has extensive investigative and rule-making powers. It may suspend or revoke licenses, after hearing. It may hear appeals in instances where the governing body has refused to issue a license or has suspended or revoked a license. The commission is required to report annually to the governor, the president of the Senate, and the speaker of the General Assembly.

LOCAL LAW ENFORCEMENT

Law enforcement at the local level is the responsibility of a number of officials. The sheriff at the county level technically has broad powers of law enforcement. However, over the years he has had less and less to do with the apprehension of criminals. Local police officials are charged with the enforcement of the criminal laws. The courts have held that the mayor and other public officials have a "common responsibility." [25]

The County Prosecutor

Primary responsibility for the enforcement of the criminal laws rests with the county prosecutor. His principal function is "the detection, arrest, indictment and conviction of offenders." In discharging this function the prosecutor must use "all reasonable and lawful diligence." [26] Willful failure to discharge his duty makes him liable to indictment for official misconduct.

In past years local police officers had been inclined to cooperate with the county prosecutor as a matter of courtesy rather than as a matter of legal obligation. However, in 1953 the Supreme Court issued an opinion which placed great stress upon the dominant legal position of the prosecutor:

> The statutes reflect not a sporadic intent but a fixed legislative policy to cast on the county prosecutor responsiblility for the detection, apprehension, arrest and conviction of criminals in his county. Nor has the Legislature merely imposed duties of vast importance to the public on the county prosecutor. Not only has it seen to it that his office is staffed with assistant prosecutors, county detectives and county investigators. It has given him power not paralleled elsewhere in the county to incur expenses in the detection, arrest, indictment and conviction of offenders against the law . . . . Clearly the Legislature intended to give him dominant position and the primary responsibility for the enforcement of the criminal laws, not merely by conferring authority on him but by giving him the means of implementing such authority.[27]

The prosecutor is appointed by the governor with Senate consent for a term of five years.* He may be superseded by the attorney general who is authorized to exercise the powers of the prosecutor. At the request of the governor, the court, or the board of freeholders, the attorney general may designate one of his deputies to supersede the prosecutor in any county. On occasion the attorney general has superseded a prosecutor in connection with some phase of his activities, such as the investigation of gambling.

In order to enable the prosecutor's office to concentrate upon the more serious crimes, the legislature has classified a number of offenses as disorderly acts. A police officer may bring a disorderly person before a magistrate's court where the offender may be summarily sentenced. The maximum penalty is one year in jail and a fine of $1,000. Appeals from conviction may be taken to the county courts. However, for more serious offenses. the prosecutor must present the case before a grand jury.

The Grand Jury

The function of the grand jury is to hear the evidence of the prosecutor and to bring a formal accusation if, in its opinion, an accusation is merited.

---

* A prosecutor holds office until a successor has been appointed and qualified. L., 1948, ch. 54, p. 141. During the administration of Governor Driscoll prosecutors were often held over for months and in some cases years after their terms expired. The failure of party leaders within a county to agree upon an appointment was often cited as a cause for delay.

The grand jury may also issue a presentment, a statement of "derelictions in matters of public concern, particularly of officials, which may fall short of criminal offenses." [28]

Members of the grand jury are initially selected by two jury commissioners in each county. A "grand jury list" is prepared consisting of the name, occupation, and residence of from 125 to 300 persons as determined by the assignment judge of the Superior Court. In preparing the list, the jury commissioners are expected to exercise vigilance and impartiality. The community as a whole should be represented:

> This, of course, does not mean that each jury could or ought embody representatives of all groups. It does mean that each jury is to be selected without systematic or intentional exclusion of any qualified group . . . .[29]

A "grand jury panel" of thirty-five persons is drawn by lot in the presence of the assignment judge or a judge designated to meet with the jury commissioners. The panel is summoned for service by the sheriff, and the first twenty-three persons on the list, excluding those excused, constitute the grand jury.*

The grand jury has the status of an independent investigating body. Although it may look to the presiding judge and to the county prosecutor for guidance, investigations may be initiated by the grand jury under its own authority. But rarely is this done. Occasionally a grand jury is accused of being simply the puppet of the prosecutor. No objective study of the grand jury in New Jersey is available. However, it seems entirely probable that in most instances the responsible members of the community usually constituting the grand juries perform their duties in a thoroughly conscientious and satisfactory manner.

NOTES

[1] L., 1947, ch. 5, p. 19.

[2] For an account of the early changes in the authority of the attorney general, see *Public Utility Commissioners* v *Lehigh Valley Railroad Co.*, 106 N.J.L. 411 (1930).

[3] L., 1948, ch. 439, p. 1707.

[4] N.J. *Commission on State Administrative Reorganization*, Report Part 1, Submitted to Governor Walter E. Edge, February 1944, p. 2.

[5] L., 1944, ch. 20, p. 51.

[6] L., 1921, ch. 102, p. 167.

[7] L., 1948, ch. 439, p. 1707.

[8] L., 1940, ch. 198, p. 848.

[9] L., 1950, ch. 154, p. 336.

[10] N.J. *Annual Report, Fiscal Year 1952-53, Division of State Police, Department of Law and Public Safety*, pp. 26-35.

[11] *Ibid., 1955*, pp. 19, 22.

* A similar process is followed in the selection of the petit jury. The minimum number on the jury list is 250. A larger number may be determined by the assignment judge. Whether a jury is to be "struck"—that is, brought into being for the trial of a cause—is within the discretion of the Superior Court or a county court.

[12] L., 1930, ch. 65, p. 279.

[13] *McGovern* v *Van Riper*, 137 N.J. Eq., 548 (1946).

[14] *McGovern* v *Van Riper*, 140 N.J. Eq., 341, 347 (1947).

[15] L., 1930, ch. 64, p. 278.

[16] For a description of the laboratory, see New Jersey State Police, *Scientific Laboratory Services of the State Bureau of Identification*, 1946, pp. 5-21.

[17] L., 1948, ch. 439, p. 1707.

[18] Clinton A. Vance, "Municipal and County Police Complete First Basic Training Course," *New Jersey Municipalities*, XXVIII (April, 1951), 12-14.

[19] N.J. *Twenty-fifth Annual Report of the Department of State Police of New Jersey*, 1946, p. 18.

[20] L., 1952, ch. 253, p. 858.

[21] N.J. Second Report of the New Jersey Law Enforcement Council, *Law Enforcement and Solicitations* (Trenton, 1954), p. 1.

[22] *Ibid.*, pp. 12-18.

[23] L., 1954, ch. 181, p. 700.

[24] L., 1954, ch. 5, p. 17.

[25] *State* v *Weleck*, 10 N.J. 355, 368 (1952) quoted in *State* v *Winne*, 12 N.J. 152, 168 (1953).

[26] L., 1933, ch. 19, p. 35.

[27] *State* v *Winne, op. cit.*, p. 167.

[28] *In re Camden County Grand Jury*, 10 N.J. 23, 35 (1952).

[29] *State* v *Stewart*, 2 N.J. Super. 15, 26 (1949).

CHAPTER 15

Education

A CONSTITUTIONAL AMENDMENT guaranteeing a system of free public schools was adopted by the people of New Jersey in 1875.* The amendment stated that "the Legislature shall provide for the maintenance and support of a thorough and efficient system of free public schools for the instruction of all the children in the state between the ages of five and eighteen years." [1] This constitutional declaration of responsibility was made less than a decade after a comprehensive law was enacted establishing a state Board of Education. [2] The legislature has always had plenary powers in matters relating to education since the state constitution is silent concerning the organization of the school system.

THE STATE DEPARTMENT OF EDUCATION

Heading the organizational structure for public education in New Jersey is a Department of Education. The department consists of the State Board of Education and the commissioner of education in charge of administrative operations.

State Board of Education

The State Board of Education is a twelve-member body, three of whom must be women.† Members must have resided within the state for a

* A State School Fund was created by the legislature in 1817. This is reported to have been the first step in the development of a state educational system. See Carl Graydom Leech, *The Constitutional and Legal Basis of Education in New Jersey* (Lancaster, Pennsylvania: The Science Press Printing Co., 1932), p. 3.

† The law obviously was designed to afford women some representation. However, as it was written, men have no such guarantee. All the members could be women.

minimum of five years preceding their appointments. No more than one member may be appointed from any one county, a restriction which Governor Driscoll recommended be abolished in favor of selection from the state at large.[3] All are appointed by the governor, with the consent of the Senate, for six-year terms. The members receive expenses but no salary.

The board is charged with general supervision of public education as well as of the Department of Education. It is responsible also for making plans and recommendations concerning the development of public education including public higher education. The supervisory authority of the board has been spelled out by the legislature to cover such matters as making and enforcing administrative regulations, determining appeals from the commissioner's decisions, and prescribing a uniform bookkeeping system for school districts.[4] The courts have upheld the broad grant of powers to the state board and have approved such actions as setting aside the contract of a local board where lack of honesty was involved.[5] Although the state agency may withhold approval of secondary schools not meeting satisfactory standards, it may not usurp the general powers of a local board. For example, it may not make the first decision to close a school. This power is reserved by the local board.[6] Nor may it remove a school board member.[7]

New Jersey's State Board of Education, in common with the boards of thirty-three states, has general responsibility for various phases of educational policy, such as teacher education and certification. In twenty-five states the board determines the regulations governing the distribution of state school funds.[8] In New Jersey this power remains with the legislature.

Commissioner of Education

The administrative head of the Department of Education is the commissioner, appointed by the governor, with the consent of the senate, for a five-year term and until his successor is qualified. The commissioner is secretary and executive officer of the state board. His policy- and rule-making powers are subject to the approval of the board. Policy execution, however, is his function alone. His decisions concerning disputes arising under school law are binding unless an appeal is taken to the state board. However, action under the school law does not prevent an appeal to the courts once the remedies provided by the school law have been exhausted.[9]

In addition to enforcing the rules and regulations of the state board, the commissioner is charged with such duties as: supervising schools receiving state appropriations; serving as chairman of the board of examiners granting teaching certificates; reporting to the state board on the status of the public schools and all educational institutions receiving state support; prescribing minimum courses of study for elementary and high schools.[10]

The question of the appointment of the commissioner of education has proved to be a thorny issue in recent New Jersey politics.   The Department of Education was the last of the major agencies designated by law as a principal department after the adoption of the new constitution.[11] The law contained no statement about the method of selection of the commissioner.   Educational groups favored his appointment by the state board on the ground that this would insulate him from politics.   Governor Driscoll and citizen groups such as the League of Women Voters opposed this proposal, arguing that education was an integral function of government and should be made responsible to popular control.   As a consequence of this impasse, the legislature took no action. During the 1950 session the Governor declared in favor of appointment by the state board subject to his approval.[12]   However, the Senate refused to accept his recommendation.   To have done so would have resulted in their vacating control over an important position.   As a consequence, although the Department of Education was recognized as one of the principal departments, the existing provision for gubernatorial appointment of the commissioner continued in force.*

LEVELS OF EDUCATIONAL ORGANIZATION

Departmental Services

The services provided by the Department of Education may be classified as regulatory, leadership, and operational.[13]   For example, regulatory services relating to elementary instruction include accrediting public schools, approving schools for financial reimbursement, preparing and administering state examinations, and prescribing topics in the curriculum. Although the department has established courses of study, the local school districts are otherwise relatively free from state regulatory control at the elementary level.   However, a greater amount of control is exercised by the state over the secondary schools.

Leadership services include advising local officials in matters of organization, administration, and instruction; assisting the state teachers colleges in improving teacher education; and publishing resource materials for teachers and school administrators.   The department has operational control of the state teachers colleges and the New Jersey School for the Deaf.

---

* Originally, in 1866, the state board appointed the state superintendent.   L., 1866, ch. 222, p. 518.   The law was changed in 1889 giving the appointive power to the governor, with the advice and consent of the Senate.   L., 1889, ch. 5, p. 15.

In 1954 twenty-six states elected the chief state school officer; he was appointed by the state board in eighteen states, and by the governor in four.   The trend in the last decade has been toward appointment by the state board.   Whether the trend is good or bad is difficult to determine.   Students of public administration usually take the position that education is a part of government—just as health and welfare —and should be treated in the same manner as other functions.

County Superintendents of Schools

Paradoxical though it may appear, the county superintendent of schools is a state official; "he is the representative of the state, working in the county." [14] The appointment of the county superintendents of schools is the responsibility of the commissioner, with the advice and consent of the state board. To be eligible for the position, a candidate must hold an appropriate certificate. Three years' residence immediately preceding the appointment is also required. The term of office is three years. The salary of the county superintendent is paid by the state. However, his expenses, up to $900 annually, are the responsibility of the county.

The county is required to furnish office space for the superintendent, who is the custodian of all school records for the county. He is responsible for administering oaths to teachers and school officers; distributing state monies to the school districts; exercising general supervision of the schools of the county in accordance with policies of the state board; and counseling boards of education in such matters as courses, methods, discipline, management, and maintenance. He has no jurisdiction over city school districts, although his office acts as a service bureau on many matters affecting all teachers.

School Districts

A "school district" has been defined by the courts as a "generic term, conveniently used to designate the territory within which school lands and buildings are grouped." [15]   In general, each municipality is a separate school district. However, the school district is a corporate entity, distinct and apart from the municipal government. It is to be distinguished from one of the regular boards or departments. The courts have held that although board members in a city were appointed by the mayor, although the mayor and two councilmen sat as the board of estimate for raising money, and although school building bonds were city obligations, nevertheless, the board of education was a separate corporate entity.[16]

School districts operate under one of two series of laws. Each school system is popularly known either as a Chapter 6 or a Chapter 7 district, depending upon the laws under which it was organized. By referendum, a district operating under one chapter may change to the other.

The Chapter 6 district was intended for the city school system. The district board of education consists of five members unless, by referendum, in cities of at least 45,000, the board has been enlarged to nine. In first-class cities there are nine members. The members of the board are appointed by the mayor. Board appointees must be able to read and write, have no interest in any contract or claim, and have resided in the district for the preceding three years. The function of the board is to exercise "supervision, control and management" of the public schools and public

school property.[17]   By a majority vote of all the members, a superintendent
may be selected to supervise the schools.   A business manager may also
be appointed.

The control of the district board of education in financial matters is subject to the will of a board of estimate consisting of two members appointed
by the board of education, two members of the municipal governing body
appointed by that body, and the mayor.   The secretary of the board serves
also as the secretary of the board of estimate.   The board of school estimate must act upon the budget proposed by the board and determine the
amounts to be appropriated for school purposes.   As a practical matter,
in most districts, the governing body must also approve the school budget.
However, once the total amount is determined, the sum appropriated is at
the disposal of the school board.

The Chapter 7 district was intended for townships, towns, and boroughs.
The board of education consists of nine elected members unless at an
annual school meeting of the district the decision is made to reduce the
membership to seven, five, or three.   The qualifications of candidates are
the same as those of appointees in Chapter 6 districts.

The board may make rules for the management of the public schools
and public school property as long as those rules are not inconsistent with
the law and with the regulations of the state board.   The local board may
hire a superintendent of schools and teachers, select textbooks, prescribe
(with the county superintendent) the course of study, suspend or expel
pupils, and permit the school building to be used for other than school
purposes.   However, the school budget must be adopted by the voters.
If the proposed budget is rejected twice, the municipal governing body
must determine the amount necessary to operate the schools.   The state
commissioner fixes the appropriation in the event the governing body fails
to act.

A quarter of a century ago the district system was attacked by a study
commission authorized by the legislature.   The commission asserted that
"the two major problems are to control the creation of new school districts . . . and to stimulate the formation of larger units."   The commission continued:

> A study of conditions existing in rural schools leads inevitably to the con-
> clusion that a satisfactory schooling for the children of these schools cannot be
> provided under the present district system.   That a school district adequate for
> present day needs must be large enough to provide a standard 12 year course
> of study with a sufficiently differentiated curriculum to meet the major needs
> of the pupils is a principle that would be generally accepted as the ideal one
> in school organization.   Toward this end we should work.   If New Jersey can
> have a district system of this type under local control and with efficient super-
> vision and creative educational leadership, it will mark a new era in rural
> education for this State.[18]

At the time of this survey in 1928 there were 538 districts, twenty-three of which employed no teachers. In 1951-52 there were 555 districts, twenty-eight of which maintained no schools.[19]

In 1954-55 there were 540 "regular" school districts, 15 regional high school districts, and 7 county vocational schools.[20] The need for larger districts throughout the United States was recognized in 1948 by the National Commission on School District Reorganization, which recommended that a school administrative unit have "(a) At least 1200 pupils between the ages of 6 and 18; and (b) If possible as many as 10,000 pupils ages 6 to 18." [21] In New Jersey, as throughout the country, the movement for larger districts has made no conspicuous progress. However, consolidated districts and regional districts may be organized under present laws. Two or more Chapter 7 districts may, by referendum, form a consolidated district. The new board of education would consist of seven members elected for three-year terms. The membership of the board is apportioned by the county superintendent in accordance with the populations of the districts.[22] A regional district may be established by referendum to provide a special service, such as the establishment of a high school or a vocational school.[23] A separate nine-member board of education is required, apportioned by the county superintendent according to the populations of the constituent districts. However, each district must have one member.

New Jersey in 1951-52 had twenty one-teacher schools, which employed only 0.1 per cent of New Jersey's teachers, the smallest percentage of any state.[24] In 1947-48 New Jersey ranked first among all the states in percentage of high schools with more than 300 pupils. This number is considered the minimum in order to provide a comprehensive program without an undue financial burden. In New Jersey 90.5 per cent of all high schools enrolled more than 300 students. New Jersey was also first among the states in the percentage (1.1) of high schools with an enrollment of fewer than 100.[25]

The public schools of any school district are free to persons between the ages of five and twenty who are living in the district. The constitutional provision guaranteeing free public schools for children between five and eighteen having been interpreted as a minimum not a maximum, the legislature has extended the age limit to "under twenty" and has authorized local boards to provide free education to those over twenty as the board may determine. Children may not be excluded because of race, creed, color, national origin, or ancestry. Attendance in the public schools or in a day school giving equivalent instruction is compulsory for all children between the ages of seven and sixteen. Since 1903 school districts have been required to furnish textbooks and school supplies to all public school pupils free of charge.

SCHOOL FINANCE

Minimum Educational Program

Professional educators refer to the minimum educational program required by a state as the "foundation program." Most states provide funds to equalize the cost of the foundation program among the school districts. The program may be defined by law or by rules and regulations of the department of education. The definition of the program is usually in terms of educational opportunity or in terms of cost.[26] The statutory definition in New Jersey is related to costs, but the districts must comply with standards prescribed by the state Board of Education. The unit measure of educational need is the number of pupils in average daily enrollment. This figure is obtained by adding the number of days present to the number of days absent and dividing the total by the number of days the school was in session.

The foundation program is defined by law in New Jersey as one costing $200 per pupil in average daily enrollment. To assist the school districts in obtaining the amounts needed for the foundation program, the state provides equalization aid on the basis of a new formula adopted in 1954.[27] The formula, in brief, is:

State Aid = Foundation Program – Local Fair Share

In order to compute the amount of equalization aid, the "local fair share" must first be determined. Two calculations are necessary in order to arrive at the local fair share. First, a rate of fifty cents is applied to the equalized value of taxable property within the school district. Second, to this sum is added 25 per cent of the shared taxes payable to each municipality in the school district. The law declares that the shared taxes shall include the public utility franchise and gross receipts taxes, the financial business tax, the domestic life insurance and domestic casualty insurance tax, and the bank stock tax.

The provision in the law requiring the use of equalized value is designed to insure a uniform burden upon each district. Formerly, under the Pascoe Law, the large municipalities complained of discrimination. They contended that their properties were assessed at a higher ratio of true value than were rural properties. Now the director of the Division of Taxation of the Department of the Treasury is charged with certifying an equalized value for each district.

Once the local fair share has been computed, it is subtracted from the amount of the foundation program, that is, $200 times the average daily enrollment. The difference constitutes the equalization aid. No district may be paid less than $50 per pupil. However, a district which does not raise from local taxation an amount equal to its local fair share, and which does not spend $200 per pupil is not normally entitled to equalization aid.

The Commission on State Tax Policy estimated that the new formula will require school districts as a group to finance about 70 per cent of the foundation program. State equalization aid would amount to about 30 per cent, in contrast to 18.9 per cent in 1949-50. The commission estimated also that the tax resources used in determining the local fair share were no more than half of those actually in use under the old law. Thus districts would be free to use the remaining half for the enrichment of their educational program or for the payment of debt service requirements.[28]

In addition to equalization aid, the state pays 75 per cent of the cost of approved transportation. Special provision is made for atypical pupils, such as those who are mentally retarded or physically handicapped. County vocational schools are to receive $50 per pupil in state aid. The county is entitled to receive aid covering the salary and expenses of helping teachers, child study supervisors, and attendance officers. Emergency aid of $350,000 is to be appropriated annually to be distributed by the commissioner of education upon approval of the Board of Education.

Legislation providing for an annual building aid allowance was enacted in 1956. Once again a formula was used. The law requires that a capital foundation program be determined annually. To obtain this figure the average daily enrollment is multiplied by $30. From this sum is deducted the local fair share, five cents per $100 upon the "equalized full valuation of the taxing district." The remainder constitutes the building aid allowance which may be used for capital outlay, debt service, or as an addition to a capital reserve fund established by the state treasurer for each school district.[29]

Public School Revenues

In 1954-55 public elementary and secondary school revenues amounted to $461,948,420. This sum was obtained from a number of sources. The largest portion, $199,020,288, came from local taxing units. Over $93,-000,000 was obtained from bond issues. State aid paid directly to school districts accounted for about $37,000,000. Table 14 shows the per cent of revenue receipts by source for public elementary and secondary schools in New Jersey.

On a nation-wide basis, the average percentage state contribution for the support of the public elementary and secondary schools was 33.0 in 1943-44 and 41.4 in 1953-54. New Jersey's increase was more rapid than the national average, but the state's contribution was not yet half of the national average. New Jersey ranked forty-third in the proportion of state funds used for the support of the public schools. As a consequence of the School Aid Act of 1954 and the Building Aid Act of 1956, the state's position was scheduled for a marked change. State aid to be paid directly

TABLE 14

REVENUE RECEIPTS: PERCENTAGE DISTRIBUTION BY SOURCE

	Federal [a]	State	County	Local
1943-44	0.5	12.7	12.7	74.1
1953-54	1.0	16.6	0.8	81.6

Source: Clayton D. Hutchins and Albert R. Munse, *Public School Finance Programs of the United States* (Washington: U.S. Department of Health, Education and Welfare, Office of Education, Misc. No. 22, undated), p. 14.

[a] In 1952-53 direct Federal aid amounting to $1,097,986 was distributed by the state to local districts in connection with the operation of the National School Lunch program. The state's relationship to the program is primarily of a statistical and financial character. For example, a representative of the department audits accounts and assists in establishing bookkeeping systems. By June, 1953, sixty-seven districts were entitled to receive $837,047 in school construction aid as the result of the impact of Federal activities upon the school districts. N.J. Department of Education, *Annual Report 1953, Education Bulletin,* XXV (March, 1954), 110-11.

to school districts in the fiscal year 1957 is over $78,000,000, or double the amount paid three years previously.

The local property tax is the major source of revenue for the support of public education. In 1953-54, 81.6 per cent of local revenues for school purposes were derived from this source alone. The counties' financial participation in education extends only to appropriations by the board of freeholders for vocational schools operated by the county and to the office expenses of the county superintendents. As indicated previously, the salaries of the county superintendents are paid by state appropriation.

Public School Expenditures

The annual current expenditure per pupil in average daily attendance in New Jersey during 1954-55 was $328. A study by the United States Office of Education for 1951-52 indicated that New Jersey's $312.07 was the fourth highest in the country, exceeded only by New York, Delaware, and Oregon.[30] On an expenditure per capita of population basis, including capital outlay and interest costs, New Jersey's $48.46 ranked nineteenth among the forty-eight states.

PROBLEMS OF SCHOOL ADMINISTRATION

School Enrollment

In recent years public school enrollment has been increasing rapidly. In the five-year period 1948-1953 enrollment jumped from 615,000 to about 760,000, an increase of 23 per cent. One of the principal factors accounting for this change has been the increase in the number of births, from 55,059 in 1935 to 121,000 in 1955.

The rapid rise in enrollment which has occurred during the last few years will in all probability continue for at least a decade. The Department of Education has projected the enrollments to 1963, when 1,064,000 pupils are anticipated. The greatest numerical increases are expected in the lower grades. However, on a percentage basis senior high schools are expected to show a 67 per cent increase, grades 7-9 a 55 per cent increase and from kindergarten to sixth grade a 17 per cent increase.

The rapid growth of the public school enrollment has made necessary a number of administrative expedients. An estimated 64,000 pupils in 1953 were affected in some manner by such expedients as large classes, shortened school day, and classes in community buildings, school basements, or other locations not designed as classrooms. Another 70,000 pupils were taught by teachers with substandard certificates.

The need for increased facilities at once raises the question of the ability of the people of the state to support financially an enlarged school program. In 1947-48, the New Jersey population of school age was 16.8 per cent of the total population, the lowest among the states. Because of the low percentage, the income per school-age pupil was $8,776, which gave the state a ranking of seventh in the country as a whole.*

From the standpoint of the cost of education, in 1937-38, 3.6 per cent of the total income payments to individuals went for the support of the public school system at the state and local level. At that time New Jersey ranked eleventh among the states. In 1947-48 the percentage of income used for the public schools was 2.2, and New Jersey's rank was twenty-seventh. The drop from eleventh to twenty-seventh position does not necessarily mean that the people of New Jersey are spending a greatly reduced share of their income on education. The figures relate to public school education and do not take into account the growth of denominational and sectarian schools. In 1951-52 nonpublic schools in New Jersey provided for almost one quarter of the total number of elementary and secondary school students. However, it would appear that, expressed as a percentage of income, the total elementary and secondary school burden is relatively lighter than that of many states.

School Buildings

In 1953 New Jersey's public school pupils were housed in 1,855 buildings. Over one third of the buildings had been rehabilitated or newly con-

---

* *The Forty-eight State School Systems* (Chicago: The Council of State Governments, 1949), pp. 175-76. The Federal Office of Education, on the other hand, reports the average income per child from five to seventeen as $9,299. This amount gave New Jersey a ranking of fifth in the country. The report states that in 1937-38, 3.45 per cent of the total income payments to individuals were channeled into state and local revenues for public schools. In 1947-48 the percentage was 2.30. The study ranks New Jersey nineteenth in 1937-38 and thirty-fourth in 1947-48, with an estimated rank of thirty-one in 1949-50. Federal Security Agency, Office of Education, *Public School Finance Programs of the Forty-eight States*, Circular No. 274 (Washington, 1950), p. 87.

structed since 1945. In the period from January, 1945, to March, 1951, 1,076 new classrooms were constructed, and 2,005 more were added in the period from March, 1951, to September, 1953.

Notwithstanding an accelerating building program adequate facilities were lacking in many areas. A recent survey of public school facilities indicated that 125,000 pupils were in school plants rated unsatisfactory— that is, subject to one or more of the following deficiencies: "(1) structurally unsafe, (2) non-correctible fire hazard, (3) very poorly located with respect to school population and school organization, (4) completely inadequate site which cannot be enlarged, (5) unsatisfactory and hazardous environment, and (6) completely obsolete as to educational adequacy." [31]

Of 19,792 classrooms in February, 1953, 36.6 per cent had more than 30 pupils per classroom. There were 1,004 classrooms not in use, mostly in urban areas which had undergone shifts in population resulting in lower school enrollment. Another 1,098 classrooms were so crowded that the available space was less than 20 square feet per pupil.[32]

In order to relieve overcrowding, to house enrollment increases, and to replace obsolete buildings, the school facilities survey mentioned above declared that about $178,000,000 of new classroom construction was currently needed. This figure did not take into account projected enrollment increases. In May, 1954, the Department of Education estimated that new school construction would cost at least $50,000,000 annually for the next five years.[33] Plans and specifications for all new public school buildings and for modifications of existing structures must be approved by the department.

Transportation

Public school pupils are transported at public expense providing they live a certain distance from school; two or more miles for elementary school students and two and one-half miles for secondary school pupils. Transportation costs are subsidized by the state to the amount of 75 per cent. Transportation may also be provided on established public school bus routes for pupils attending other than a public school, if that school is not operated for profit.[34]

In 1953-54 approximately 143,000 pupils, or 19.6 per cent, were transported to school. The greater proportion of those transported, 74.3 per cent, rode in privately owned buses. School-owned buses accounted for 17.4 per cent, while the remaining 8.3 per cent used common carrier vehicles.[35]

THE SCHOOL STAFF

Public school districts in September, 1953, employed 30,828 teachers—

about three fifths in the elementary grades, about one quarter in the junior high schools, and the remainder in the senior high schools. The total public school enrollment was 759,131. There were also—as of 1951-52— 5,452 teachers and 191,569 elementary and secondary school pupils in nonpublic schools. Catholic schools alone accounted for 4,692 teachers and 179,016 pupils.[36]

Teacher Preparation

In 1947-48, 10,217, or 38.7 per cent, of New Jersey's public schoo! teachers had less than four years of college preparation. This percentage compared with 40.6 for the continental United States. Master's degrees or higher were held by 19.2 per cent, a figure exceeded in only seven states.[37]

Prospective teachers must be certified by the State Department of Education. Certificates are of four types. The limited certificate applies to those who have met the requirements of the state board for a given type of service, for example, the field of general instruction or that of administration and supervision. A permanent certificate may be obtained by those who have met the board's requirements and who have served three years. Provisional certificates are issued to those having some but not all the requirements for the limited certificate. Emergency certificates may be obtained for a limited time and for limited kinds of service upon the request of a board of education. Of 31,551 persons in the public schools during 1950-51, 9.2 per cent had substandard certificates.[38] Teachers with proper certificates receive tenure after three consecutive calendar years or after three consecutive academic years and employment for a fourth year.

Supply of Teachers

Qualified teachers have been in short supply since the end of World War II. In 1953-54 over 2,800 classes with an estimated 70,000 pupils were taught by persons with substandard certificates.

Of 4,695 teachers who were new to their districts in 1953, 1,074 had transferred from other districts in the state, and 560 had come from school districts out of the state. New Jersey colleges supplied 1,252, and colleges outside the state supplied 766. Aside from the 754, or 16 per cent, who returned to teaching from home duties, fewer than 6 per cent were recruited from other occupations.[39] The number of new teachers employed does not represent a net gain in the total teacher staff. During this same period 3,221 teachers left positions.* Of the 1,148 who transferred to

* Studies made over a four-year period showed a yearly turnover ranging from approximately 3 per cent in Hudson and 7 per cent in Passaic counties to approximately 20 per cent in Hunterdon, Somerset, and Ocean counties. The low turnover may be attributed to high salaries and attractive working conditions. N.J. Department of Education, Division of Higher Education, *The Demand and Supply of Teachers, 1952-1953*, p. 11.

other teaching positions, about 70 per cent remained within the state. Among other reasons for leaving were: to marry, 157; to assume home duties, 534; to retire, 384; to enter business, 163.[40]

In order to provide for the increasing school enrollments a number of positive steps have been taken. For example, school superintendents and the faculties of the New Jersey state teachers colleges have cooperated in a teacher recruitment campaign. Also, the state teachers colleges have expanded their facilities to provide for larger enrollments, and, in 1954, were in the process of arranging special programs designed to train graduates of liberal arts colleges as teachers. Several of the liberal arts colleges have been authorized to confer the degree of Bachelor of Science in Elementary Education.

In presenting data on the numbers entering and leaving the profession, one should not lose sight of the high average experience of New Jersey's teachers. In 1954 the average experience in teaching was 17.1 years. The average number of years in the present district was 13.7.[41]

Salaries

The estimated average teacher's salary in 1956-57 was $4,880,[42] a considerable increase over the average of $3,922 in 1951-52 when New Jersey's average was exceeded in four states and the District of Columbia.[43] The salaries paid in a number of the larger municipalities cause the expression "average salary" to be misleading. For example, a study made in 1954 showed that the average salary in seventeen of the twenty-one counties was below the state average of $4,360. The median salary, which has been worked out for a number of counties, gives a more accurate picture. The median salary for 1954-55 in Essex County was $5,492. This was $2,000 higher than Hunterdon County's median of $3,471. The highest paid teacher in Hunterdon County received less salary than 72 per cent of the teachers in Essex County. Throughout the state an estimated 2,500 teachers received in excess of $6,000. At the other end of the scale about 1,000 received less than $3,000. Over three-fifths of the districts had established salary guides with regular increments from the minimum to the maximum.[44] Legislation enacted in 1954, effective July 1, 1955, provided for a minimum salary of $3,000 and yearly employment increments of $150. The minimum for a teacher holding a master's degree and having seventeen years experience was set at $5,400. "Adjustment increments" of $150 annually were provided in order gradually to bring those below the schedule up to their proper place on the schedule, according to their years of employment.

Oath Legislation

Since 1935 teachers in public schools and colleges have been required to take an oath of allegiance to the Constitution of the United States and

the Constitution of New Jersey.[45]   In 1949 the oath was expanded to include a statement disavowing belief in force or any unconstitutional means
to overthrow the governments of the United States or of New Jersey.   The
oath required also a disavowal of membership in any such organization.[46]
The courts have upheld the law as "an entirely reasonable accommodation
of the fundamental personal rights—and the common interest—in the
safety of Government and the integrity of its educational processes." [47]

Retirement

An actuarial retirement system was established in 1919.   Teachers then
in service were permitted to join the Teachers' Pension and Annuity Fund.
Those entering after September 1, 1919, were required to become members.   Individual accounts are maintained for each member.   Each teacher
contributes a percentage of his salary designed to provide an annuity.   The
teachers' retirement allowance consists of the annuity and a pension paid
from state contributions.   Teachers may choose Class A or Class B membership, the first providing a retirement allowance amounting to half the
final average salary after thirty-five years of service and the second the
same retirement allowance after thirty years of service.   Retirement is
optional at age sixty; it is compulsory before the seventy-first birthday.

The retirement system is administered by a six-member board of trustees
consisting of three teacher representatives, one appointee of the governor,
the state treasurer, and one elected by the other trustees.   The board is
under the supervision of the Department of the Treasury.   The Teachers'
Pension and Annuity Fund was integrated with Social Security in 1955.[48]

PROGRAM OF INSTRUCTION

There is no hard and fast line drawn between elementary and secondary
education.   In some communities schools are organized on an 8-4 plan,
that is, eight elementary grades and four high school grades.   Many districts are organized on a 6-3-3 plan, with a junior high school for grades
seven through nine.   Others operate under a 6-6 plan, with a six-year high
school for grades seven through twelve.   All of these are approved by the
state Board of Education.

State leadership in curriculum development has stressed not only the
acquisition of knowledge and skills but also education for good character
and citizenship.   The ultimate objective of a "good education" has been
declared to be "the development of persons of honor, integrity, vision, and
high purpose—in short, persons of character." [49]

Special Education

Handicapped Children.   In recent years an increasing amount of attention has been given to the need for special programs for physically and

mentally handicapped children. As the consequence of a state-wide survey, a registry of all handicapped children has been established. In 1952-53, 17,411 handicapped children, 2.4 per cent of the resident enrollment, required special schooling. Of this number, over half were receiving adequate instruction. However, 1,746 were neither attending school nor receiving any type of formal training.[50]

School for the Deaf. The New Jersey School for the Deaf, located at Trenton, is directly under the supervision of the commissioner of education. He is responsible for the appointment of the superintendent, teachers, and all other employees; the care and maintenance of buildings; and the supply of textbooks and apparatus. Regulations concerning admission and management are delegated by law to the commissioner. Tuition is free, but the cost of maintenance is placed upon the parent or guardian to the degree deemed "just and equitable." The enrollment in 1953-54 was 317.

Vocational Education

The controlling purpose of vocational education is defined by New Jersey law as "to fit for profitable employment." [51] Any school district may establish industrial, agricultural, or household arts schools providing the district has obtained the approval of the commissioner of education; the commissioner is also responsible for the supervision of the school. Vocational schools may be established in any county by action of the freeholders upon recommendation by the State Board of Education. In counties under 100,000, the people may, by referendum, provide for the establishment of a vocational school. Courses of study must be approved by the commissioner of education although immediate supervision of the school is the responsibility of the county board consisting of the county superintendent and four appointed members.* A board of school estimate, consisting of the director and two members of the board of chosen freeholders and two members of the county school board, determines the annual budget.†
Funds are appropriated in the same manner as for other county functions. However, in some instances the tuition rate is established by the board of freeholders and is chargeable to the board of education of the sending district. Each county vocational school receives state support amounting to $50 per pupil. About one third of the counties have separate vocational institutions.

The commissioner of education is responsible for general supervision of

* In first-class counties the county supervisor makes the appointments; in second-class counties, and in third- and fifth-class counties having a population in excess of 180,000, the director of the board of chosen freeholders selects the four appointive members. In other counties appointive members are selected by the county court. In second-, third-, and fifth-class counties no more than two appointive members may belong to the same political party. L., 1929, ch. 321, p. 737.

† In first-class counties the county supervisor, rather than the director, sits on the board of estimate.

the many programs falling under the category of vocational education. In recent years the Department of Education has been concerned with the operation of apprentice training programs for veterans, the supervision of private trade schools, and the promotion of vocational agricultural education, trade and industrial education, home economics education, and occupational guidance and distributive education, that is, training for sales and promotional positions. The vocational education programs are financed in part by the Federal government under the George-Barden and Smith-Hughes acts. Federal aid amounts to approximately $500,000 annually.

HIGHER EDUCATION

Throughout the United States in 1949-50 one student was enrolled in college for every sixty-one members of the population. The ratio in New Jersey was one to fifty-six. Of the 85,787 college students who were residents of the state, 55.8 per cent were enrolled in institutions in other states:

	Number	Per Cent
Home state	37,951	44.2
Other states	47,836	55.8

New Jersey had the highest percentage of student residents migrating to other states for their college education. Delaware was next with a percentage of 43.7. At the other extreme, only 7.2 per cent of California's students attended colleges elsewhere.

New Jersey probably will always have a much higher than average percentage of its college population attending institutions in other states. A considerable number of colleges and universities in New York and Pennsylvania are within easy commuting distance of the densely populated areas of New Jersey, In past years there has been a dearth of educational facilities in the centers of population. The establishment of the State University, with centers in New Brunswick, Newark, and Camden, has resulted in increased educational offerings in these areas. It is significant that in 1930-31 only 30.5 per cent of New Jersey's college students attended institutions within the state in contrast with 44.2 per cent in 1949-50.[52]

The idea of public higher education in New Jersey has developed slowly. In common with many of the eastern states, New Jersey did little to promote any systematic plans. In recent years, the increased emphasis upon the desirability of a college education has virtually forced some of the older states—New York, Connecticut, Massachusetts, and New Jersey—to alter their traditional policy of relying upon private institutions and upon the great public universities of the Midwest.

The State University

Rutgers, The State University, is the eighth oldest institution for higher education in the United States, having been founded as Queen's College in 1766 by members of the Dutch Reformed Church. It is the only colonial college to have become a state university. The church relationship, which for all official purposes had ceased to exist before 1900, was terminated in an amendment adopted by the trustees in 1920.

In 1864 Rutgers was designated by the legislature as the Land Grant College of New Jersey to carry out the purposes of the Morrill Act passed by Congress in 1862. In succeeding years numerous laws were passed concerning scholarships at the State Agricultural College, the appointment of a Board of Visitors, the establishment of a State Agricultural Experiment Station (1880), a Department of Ceramics (1902), short courses in agriculture (1905), and the equipping of various buildings (1910-11). In 1917 the legislature declared the Agricultural College to be the State University of New Jersey.[53] The several departments of Rutgers were designated collectively as the State University of New Jersey in 1945.[54] By subsequent acts the University of Newark and the College of South Jersey were incorporated into the State University.[55]

In the years following the 1945 act the charge was frequently made that Rutgers was not "truly" the State University since there were only fourteen public trustees out of a total membership of fifty-six.[56] In order to meet this criticism, a major reorganization was effected in 1956. A Board of Governors was made responsible by law for the conduct of the university. The board consists of thirteen members. Of this number two, the president of the university and the commissioner of education, are ex officio members and have no vote. Of the eleven voting members, six are appointed by the governor with the advice and consent of the Senate and five are appointed by the Board of Trustees from among their members. The term of office is six years. The Board of Trustees was retained in an advisory capacity, and its membership was reduced to thirty-five.[57] In 1955-56 the university had about 13,000 students enrolled for credit in fifteen separate colleges and schools.

State Teachers Colleges

There are six state teachers colleges, located at Glassboro, Jersey City, Montclair, Newark, Paterson, and Trenton. They are under the operating control of the commissioner of education subject to the approval of the Board of Education. The commissioner is responsible for the educational program of each college and for making appointments, prescribing courses, granting diplomas, and making rules for the management of the six institutions. The primary function of the teachers colleges is to maintain a flow of graduates interested in public school teaching. Yearly enrollments of about 4,000 will be increased to 5,500 when an expansion program is completed. The increase in facilities was financed by a bond issue of $15,000,000 approved by popular referendum in 1952.

In addition to the teachers colleges and the State University, New Jersey appropriates sums for the operation of the Newark College of Engineering and the Trenton Junior College.

The Closing Door to College

Notwithstanding recent forward steps, the youth of New Jersey are still far from achieving the opportunities in higher education open to the youth of numbers of other states. In 1955 New Jersey ranked forty-fifth in net expenditures per capita for higher education. The expenditure of $2.06 per capita on higher education was less than half that of the national average and less than one-fourth that of several western states—in spite of the state's high per capita income (fourth in the Union in 1954).[58]

The enormous gap between the facilities for higher education which now exist, or are planned, and those which will be required—unless thousands of New Jersey youth are to be denied an opportunity for higher education—was revealed in a recent survey by Dr. Marshall P. Smith of the Trenton State Teachers College. He declared that unless new facilities were provided, over 25,000 New Jersey students by 1963 and over 80,000 by 1973 would have no place to go. Table 15 shows the deficit in facilities.

TABLE 15

PROJECTED UNDERGRADUATE FACILITIES AND ENROLLMENTS

Year	Out-of-State	Private N. J.	Public N. J.	Total Facilities	Probable Full-Time Enrollment	Deficit
1958	27,000	15,000	17,000	59,000	61,000	2,000
1963	28,000	21,000	17,000	66,000	94,000	28,000
1968	29,000	23,000	17,000	69,000	136,000	67,000
1973	30,000	25,000	17,000	72,000	155,000	83,000

Source: Marshall P. Smith, *New Jersey's Undergraduates 1954-1973* (Trenton: N.J. State Department of Education, 1956), p. 47.

CIVIL RIGHTS

In New Jersey the administration of civil rights legislation is primarily the responsibility of the Department of Education. The Constitution of 1947 retained the bill of rights which had been incorporated in the document of 1844. However, substantial additions were made. The first requires that "no person shall be denied the enjoyment of any civil or military right, nor be discriminated against in the exercise of any civil or military right, nor be segregated in the militia or in the public schools, because of religious principles, race, color, ancestry or national origin." A second addition relates to the rights of labor: "persons in private employment shall have the right to organize and bargain collectively. Persons in public employment shall have the right to organize, present to and make known to the state, or any of its political subdivisions or agencies, their grievances and proposals through representatives of their own choosing." [59]

Legislation prohibiting discrimination because of race or color was first passed in 1884. The Civil Rights Law provided that all persons should be entitled to the privileges of inns, public conveyances, and places of amusement and that any person aggrieved could bring action in the courts.[60] Seldom was the statute invoked. Most of those discriminated against preferred to suffer rather than to sue. The expense of litigation was a deterrent factor as was the unfavorable publicity associated with legal action of this type.

In 1944 the attorney general was charged with the enforcement of civil rights laws. Of much greater significance than the earlier civil rights legislation was the law against discrimination, passed in 1945, which declared that the opportunity to obtain employment without discrimination was a civil right. The act created a Division Against Discrimination in the Department of Education. Persons who felt themselves aggrieved in obtaining employment because of their race, creed, color, national origin, or ancestry were enabled to file a complaint. If, after investigation, the commissioner of education found the complaint was justified, he was required to endeavor to eliminate the practice by means of "conference, conciliation, and persuasion." If these methods failed, the commissioner could, after notice and hearing, issue a cease and desist order, an action enforceable in the courts.[61]

In 1949, following the recommendations of the Governor's Committee on Civil Liberties, the jurisdiction of the division was enlarged to encompass the original civil rights law. Thus, all civil rights protections were placed within one agency. For example, persons aggrieved because of discrimination in restaurants or in amusement places—and, since 1954, in public housing—may now turn to an administrative agency for assistance. The procedure is the same as in employment discrimination cases. The 1949 act also authorized the appointment of municipal commissions on civil rights.[62]

The state has acted positively and with considerable effectiveness in reducing discrimination in a number of areas. For example, the constitutional prohibition against segregation in the public schools did not automatically end that practice. In 1947-48 a survey was launched of fifty-two communities in ten counties. The board members of thirty school systems went on record to effect the elimination of segregation during that academic year. Nine requested an additional year. In nine others the survey group found that geography rather than institutional segregation was responsible for separate schools for Negroes and whites. By the school year 1950-51, thirty-nine of forty-three districts had completely eliminated segregation. Four districts at first showed little willingness to cooperate, but they have since taken steps to end segregation.[63]

An extensive study was made also of eighty-five general hospitals to determine the degree of discrimination in admission and employment practices. Major emphasis was placed upon the status of Negroes. The survey indicated that eighty-four of eighty-five hospitals admitted Negroes as patients, although six provided separate wards and thirteen did not permit Negroes to occupy semiprivate rooms. Thirty-seven hospitals employed Negro graduate nurses, a striking advance since 1940 when the number was so small as to be "negligible." Sixteen of forty-five hospitals having nursing schools admitted Negroes for training. Negro doctors had courtesy privileges in forty-six hospitals and were members of the medical staff in nineteen. The survey report pointed out that a hospital with no Negro doctor was not necessarily following discriminatory practices. In some areas, as in Sussex and Warren counties, there were no Negro doctors.[64]

The new agency has operated in an emotion-charged area where precedents were lacking. As a consequence, it has moved cautiously—endeavoring by persuasion rather than through public hearings and litigation to arrange satisfactory settlements. The Governor's Committee on Civil Liberties concluded its report with the observation that "the basic solution of the problems involved lies in constant education of the public concerning their civil rights, and more particularly their obligation to grant and safeguard those rights for others." [65] This has been the state's policy.

LIBRARIES AND MUSEUMS

State Library

New Jersey's state librarian, a position established in 1822, originally was appointed by the legislature in joint meeting.[66] In 1878 a board of commissioners consisting of the governor and other top officials was made responsible for selecting the librarian and for establishing rules regulating the library's operations. At the same time, a joint committee of the legislature, appointed annually, was to "order necessary repairs" and to "recommend additions and improvements . . . by exchange, purchase or otherwise . . . . " [67]

In 1900 a seven-member Public Library Commission was established to assist free public libraries.[68] Its jurisdiction was later extended to include control of state aid to school district libraries and to the operation of state traveling libraries. The commissioner of education and the state librarian were ex officio members of the commission. A Public Records Office was established in 1920.[69]

With the reorganization of the Department of Education in 1945, all of these separate units were merged into the Division of the State Library, Archives and History. An advisory council of five members, appointed by the governor with the advice and consent of the Senate, assists the division director.

Law and general reference libraries are maintained primarily for the use of state agencies. Reference and research services for the legislature are provided through a legislative bureau, attached to the law library. Inter-library loan facilities and technical and advisory services are furnished to the 289 public libraries, to school libraries, and to libraries in state institutions. The division is responsible also for authorizing the destruction of county and municipal records and for the operation of a records management program at the state level.

In recent years state services have been greatly strengthened. Emphasis has been placed upon raising the standards of libraries throughout New Jersey in terms of professionally trained staffs and in providing improved public services through county or regional library arrangements. In 1955 there were 258 free public libraries consisting of three basic types; 152 municipal libraries, 92 "association" libraries (private corporations which received municipal assistance), and 12 county libraries.[70]

The State Museum

Early museums, it has been said facetiously, had three objectives: first, storage; second, exhibition; and third, education. A bulletin of the New Jersey State Museum states that the first objective was achieved in full from 1890 when the Museum of the Geological Survey was established until 1915 when an enlarged program was initiated. However, in 1922 the museum was forced to relinquish its exhibit space and until 1929, when quarters were obtained in the State House Annex, it was forced to operate as a mail order agency sending to borrowers films, pictures, and specimens.[71]

The museum was governed after 1895 by a five-member commission.[72] In 1915 it was given divisional status in the Department of Conservation and Development, and in 1945 was transferred to the Department of Education.[73] The director has the assistance of an advisory council appointed by the governor with the advice and consent of the Senate.

The museum now provides a variety of services. Permanent collections relate to plant and animal life in New Jersey, to the state's archeological background, and to its topography and geology. Special exhibitions are arranged concerning present-day developments in the state. Recent subjects for public programs and displays have included research at the State University, developments in electronic research, and the contemporary arts in New Jersey. An extension service provides films and exhibits for schools and community organizations.

A principal and long-standing handicap of the museum has been lack of space. A building is needed designed to provide exhibition facilities and workshops and storage areas. In recent years approximately 100,000 persons annually have attended the exhibits and special programs of the museum. Many additional thousands—the museum has estimated 3,500,000 —have benefited from the visual aids made available to schools and community groups.

NOTES

[1] Art. VIII, sec. IV, par. 1.

[2] L., 1867, ch. 179, p. 360.

[3] *Second Inaugural Address,* January 17, 1950.

[4] For a comparison of New Jersey's Board of Education with that of other states see Federal Security Agency, Office of Education, *State Boards of Education and Chief State School Officers: Their Status and Legal Power,* Bulletin No. 12 (Washington, 1950).

[5] *Rankin v Board of Education of Egg Harbor Township,* 134 N.J.L. 342 (1946).

[6] *Boult v Board of Education of Passaic,* 136 N.J.L. 521 (1947).

[7] *Koven v Stanley,* 84 N.J.L. 446 (1913).

[8] *The Forty-eight State School Systems* (Chicago: The Council of State Governments, 1949), p. 184.

[9] See *Stockton v Board of Education,* 72 N.J.L. 80 (1905).

[10] For a list of the duties of the commissioner see N.J. *Manual of Organization and Administration of the Department of Education* (Trenton: Department of Education, 1950), pp. 4-6.

[11] L., 1950, ch. 254, p. 872.

[12] *Second Inaugural Address,* January 17, 1950.

[13] Federal Security Agency, Office of Education, *The Functions of State Departments of Education,* Misc., No. 12 (Washington, 1950), pp. 1-16.

[14] Quoted from Commissioner Kendall's State School Report of 1912 in Carl Graydom Leech, *The Constitutional and Legal Basis of Education in New Jersey* (Lancaster, Pennsylvania: The Science Press Printing Company, 1932), p. 20.

[15] *Falcone v Board of Education, Newark,* 17 N.J. Misc. 75, 78 (1939).

[16] *Merrey v Board of Education, City of Paterson,* 100 N.J.L. 273 (1924).

[17] L., 1903, ch. 1, p. 21 (2nd special sess.).

[18] N.J. *Report of the Commission to Survey Public Education* (1928), pp. 138-39.

[19] Department of Health, Education, and Welfare, Office of Education, *Biennial Survey of Education in the United States, 1950-52* (Washington, 1955), Ch. 2, "Statistics of State School Systems," p. 32.

[20] N.J. Department of Education, Division of Business, *Fourth Annual Report of the Commissioner of Education, Comparative Financial Statistics of School Districts, School Year 1954-55,* p. v.

[21] Quoted in *The Forty-eight State School Systems, op. cit.,* p. 52.

[22] L., 1947, ch. 86, p. 469.

[23] L., 1938, ch. 156, p. 315.

[24] *Biennial Survey . . . , op. cit.,* ch. 1, p. 54.

[25] *The Forty-eight State School Systems, op. cit.,* p. 195.

[26] "Statutory Bases of State Foundation Programs for Schools," *National Education Association Research* Bulletin, XXVI (1948), 49-51.

[27] L., 1954, ch. 85, p. 526.

[28] N.J. *Seventh Report of the Commission on State Tax Policy, Public School Financing in New Jersey* (Trenton, 1954), pp. 41, 99.

[29] L., 1956, ch. 8.

[30] *Biennial Survey . . . , op. cit.,* pp. 80-81.

[31] N.J. Department of Education, *Public School Facilities Survey* (1954), p. 10.

[32] *Ibid.,* p. 50.

33 N.J. Department of Education, *Education Bulletin,* XXV (May, 1954), 164.

34 *Everson* v *Board of Education,* 330 U.S. 1 (1946).

35 *Public School Facilities Survey, op. cit.,* p. 28.

36 *Biennial Survey . . . , op. cit.,* ch. 2 pp. 100-3.

37 California was far ahead of other states with 52 per cent. "Teachers in the Public Schools," *National Education Association Research Bulletin,* XXVII (December, 1949), 133.

38 N.J. Department of Education, *Annual Report of the State Board of Education and the Commissioner of Education to the Legislature of the State of New Jersey, 1952* (Trenton, 1953), p. 155.

39 N.J. Department of Education, Division of Higher Education, *The Demand and Supply of Teachers, 1953-1954,* Research Report Number 141 (March, 1954), p. 10.

40 *Ibid.,* p. 7.

41 S. Herbert Starkey, Jr., "Teacher Salaries in New Jersey, 1954-55," *New Jersey Education Association Review,* XXVIII (October, 1954), 64.

42 *NJEA Review,* XXX (October, 1956), 63.

43 *Biennial Survey . . . , op. cit.,* ch. 2, p. 70.

44 Elizabeth Ann Wright, "Teacher Salary Guides in New Jersey—1954-55," *NJEA Review,* XXVIII (September, 1954), 19.

45 L., 1935, ch. 155, p. 381.

46 L., 1949, ch. 22, p. 68.

47 *Thorp* v *Board of Trustees of Schools for Indus. Ed.,* 6 N.J. 498, 512 (1951).

48 L., 1955, ch. 37, p. 921.

49 Statement of Commissioner Frederick M. Raubinger in N.J. Department of Education, *Their Future Is in Our Hands; Education for Character and Citizenship* (1953), p. 5.

50 Charles M. Jochem, "State Survey on the Education of Handicapped Children," *Education Bulletin,* XXV (May, 1954), 151-52.

51 L., 1913, ch. 294, p. 596.

52 Federal Security Agency, Office of Education, *Residence and Migration of College Students, 1949-50,* prepared by Robert C. Story (Washington, 1951), p. 5.

53 L., 1917, ch. 32, p. 65.

54 L., 1945, ch. 49, p. 115.

55 L., 1946, ch. 217, p. 818; L., 1950, ch. 116, p. 216.

56 For the composition of the board under the 1945 act, see Albert E. Meder, Jr., "The Trustees," *Alumnae Bulletin, New Jersey College for Women,* XXVII (1951), 2-3.

57 L., 1956, ch. 61.

58 Marshall P. Smith, *New Jersey's Undergraduates 1954-1973* (Trenton: N.J. State Department of Education, 1956), p. 75.

59 Art. I, pars. 5, 19.

60 L., 1884, ch. 219, p. 339.

61 L., 1945, ch. 169, p. 589. The scope of the act was enlarged in 1951 to prohibit discrimination in employment to persons liable for military service. L., 1951, ch. 64, p. 418.

62 L., 1949, ch. 11, p. 37; L., 1954, ch. 198. See N.J. Committee on Civil Liberties, *Civil Liberties in New Jersey, a Report Submitted to the Honorable Alfred E. Driscoll, Governor of New Jersey* (1948).

63 N.J. Department of Education, Division against Discrimination, *Biennial Report 1949-1951* (Newark, 1951), p. 13.

64 N.J. Department of Education, Division against Discrimination, *Report on a Survey of Eighty-five General Hospitals in New Jersey* (Newark, 1949).

65 Committee on Civil Liberties, *op. cit.,* p. 21.

66 L., 1822, p. 26.

67 L., 1878, ch. 153, p. 228.

68 L., 1900, ch. 62, p. 95.

[69] L., 1920, ch. 46, p. 93.

[70] N.J. Commission to Study Library Services in New Jersey, *Better Libraries for New Jersey* (Trenton, 1956), p. 9.   See also N.J. *The Professional Education and Training of Library Personnel in New Jersey, a Report to the Commissioner of Education* (1951).

[71] *New Jersey State Museum, Portraying New Jersey's Story* (Trenton: Department of Education, 1946), Bulletin I.

[72] L., 1895, ch. 183, p. 349.

[73] L., 1915, ch. 241, p. 426; L., 1945, ch. 50, p. 132.

CHAPTER 16

Public Health

"THE WELFARE of the state is involved in the physical welfare of the citizen to a degree that should arrest the attention of every legislator," declared a special commission in 1874. The commission recommended the creation of a state board of health in order to provide a greater degree of protection to New Jersey citizens. Its functions were to be confined to compiling vital statistics and to "spreading information among the people." The legislature was asked to establish a board of health "because exemption from unnecessary exposure to disease is among the dearest rights of the citizen, and one of the noblest objects to which the attention of his representatives can be turned." [1]

THE STATE DEPARTMENT OF HEALTH

As an outgrowth of the commission's recommendations, legislation creating a State Board of Health was enacted in 1877. [2] A Bureau of Vital Statistics was established a decade later and the records of births, marriages, and deaths which had been collected on a state-wide basis by the secretary of state since 1848 were transferred to the new agency. In 1915 provision was made for an executive officer to be selected by the State Board of Health and to be called the director of health. The establishment of a state Sanitary Code was also authorized.

In recent years public health administration at the state level has undergone far-reaching changes both in organization and in program. In 1947, legislation was enacted eliminating the old twelve-member state board.*

---

* Previously the State Board of Health was the governing head of the department. The board was criticized as being unwieldy and as having a tendency to assume administrative duties. Members assigned to various bureaus were looked

A commissioner of health was designated as the chief administrative officer of the department.[3] Appointed by the governor, with the advice and consent of the Senate, the commissioner was required to be a licensed physician with five years' administrative experience in a public health agency. In 1948, the department was classified as one of the principal departments and the commissioner's term of office was made dependent upon the pleasure of the governor.[4]

A Public Health Council was created to replace the state board. This new seven-member body—enlarged in 1954 to eight members—was given authority to amend the Sanitary Code, to license health officers and inspectors, to advise the commissioner on public health problems, to make recommendations concerning the administration of the health department, and to study and investigate any public health activity of the state. The council has power also to modify or annul local regulations which have an effect extending beyond the boundary of the local jurisdiction. Appointments to the council are made by the governor, with the advice and consent of the Senate for terms of seven years. Two members must be licensed physicians and one a licensed dentist. The council receives expenses but no compensation. At least one meeting must be held each month.

As a result of the reorganization act of 1947, the authority and responsibility for administering the functions of the health department were placed squarely upon the commissioner. Although the council is required to approve the organization prescribed by the commissioner, it has no veto on his appointment of division heads; neither does the governor nor the Senate.

As administrative head of the department, the commissioner's responsibilities cover a broad field. These include internal management of the department, enforcement of the sanitary code and state health laws, maintaining liaison with other governmental agencies in matters of public health, and reporting public health conditions to the governor, the legislature, and the Public Health Council. He is required also to determine and to enforce minimum standards of performance for the public health activities of local health departments.

The commissioner has wide powers of inspection over any property, public or private, where he suspects a violation of the health laws or the Sanitary Code. In the event a local board fails to comply with state health laws or with the regulations of the Sanitary Code, the commissioner, after notice and hearing, is required to issue an order directing compliance. In the case of non-compliance with the order, he may institute legal proceedings or he may carry out the order himself. Whatever contracts he may

---

upon as unofficial heads of those bureaus. There was little coordination among the separate units. *The New Jersey State Department of Health, An Administrative Study of the Department by the United States Public Health Service, with supplementary recommendations by the State Board of Health* (1943), pp. 14-15.

THE STATE DEPARTMENT OF HEALTH

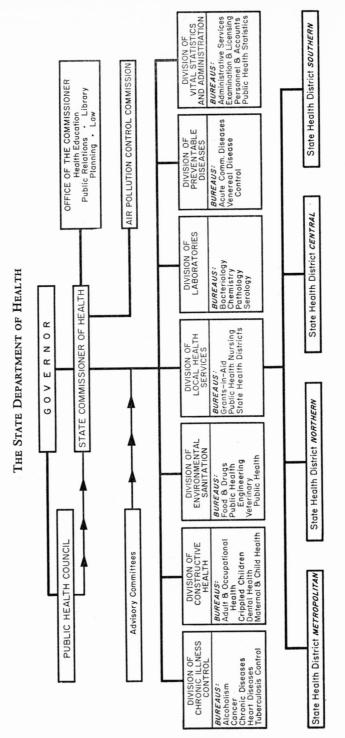

make in enforcing the order are binding upon the municipality. The commissioner may institute injunction proceedings to obtain the abatement of a nuisance. The courts are required to give emergency cases priority over pending litigation.

Departmental Reorganization

In the past, as new functions had been added to the department, little attempt had been made at integration. In 1947, eight bureaus, seven divisions, and two miscellaneous units reported to the director of health. During the period 1948-1950, the department was thoroughly reorganized. The commissioner was given a free hand by the legislature to provide the kind of organizational structure he thought best. The only exceptions were the Section of Examination, Licensing, and Registration, and the Crippled Children's Commission, both of which received statutory status.* Six major divisions were established.† As far as possible, related functions were placed under the same head. Personnel and housing changes were made with a view to bringing the units of a division together.

A major feature of the reorganization was the decision gradually to alter the character of the central office from one providing a variety of direct services to one providing consultative, advisory, educational, and promotional services. As a means of stimulating increased attention to public health problems at the local level, four state health district offices were established.‡ The major function of the district officer is to secure compliance with the Sanitary Code and the public health laws.

Sanitary Code

Regulations supplementing the health laws are contained in the state's Sanitary Code. The Public Health Council is authorized to establish, amend, or repeal regulations. Final adoption of a provision must be preceded by notice, publication of a summary of the text, and a public hearing. The regulations may concern any matter affecting public health such as water supply pollution, nuisance hazards to health, the control of communicable disease, standards of cleanliness for public eating establishments, and many others.

The provisions of the code have the force and effect of law. A local board may adopt additional health regulations for a particular community,

---

* Included in the new section were the state board of barber examiners, the department of beauty culture control, and the board of beauty culture control.

† Constructive Health, Environmental Sanitation, Laboratories, Local Health Services, Preventable Diseases, and Vital Statistics and Administration. In 1952, a division of chronic illness control was established by law. L., 1952, ch. 102, p. 438.

‡ District health offices had been maintained for a number of years in the rural areas of the state. In types of personnel and in work programs there was great variation. N.J. *Seventy-second Annual Report of the Department of Health, 1949* (Trenton, 1950), p. 15.

but these must be of a supplementary character. They may be more restrictive than the code, but they must not conflict with it. Enforcement of the sanitary code is the responsibility of the state commissioner of health, local boards of health, local police authorities, and other enforcement agencies. The department and the local boards are required to bring court action against violators. The penalty for each violation ranges from $25 to $100.

Health officers, and all inspectors—sanitary, food and drug, milk, meat, and plumbing—and public health laboratory technicians are licensed, after examination, by the health department. The public health council prescribes the qualifications. Licenses may be suspended or revoked by the council after notice and hearing.

LOCAL HEALTH ADMINISTRATION

The greatest single administrative problem has been that of obtaining adequate local health services throughout the state. Legislation passed in 1887 provided that each municipality, no matter what its size, should have a board of health.[5] At present, each board has a considerable amount of authority; it may hire personnel, enforce the state's Sanitary Code, and enact local health ordinances supplementing the state laws and the provisions of the code. The activities of the local boards are financed from municipal funds.

In 1954, there were 570 local boards of health providing health services varying greatly in scope. In addition, special health services were being provided by some counties, most school districts, and certain private voluntary agencies. The state also supplied several kinds of local health services directly. Local boards of health employed fifty-seven full-time licensed health officers serving ninety-three municipalities. Part-time licensed health officers served eighty-five municipalities. However, in 68.9 per cent of the municipalities there was no qualified, licensed health official. These municipalities accounted for about 28 per cent of the state's population. In 1949, average per capita amounts spent by local health boards ranged from $.18 in one county to $1.82 in another. The state-wide average in 1952 was $1.26.[6]

Over the past quarter of a century, a number of attempts have been made to obtain improved local health services. The proposals to improve local services have been based on the need for enlarging the jurisdictional units. Specialists in the field estimate that a population unit ranging from 35,000 to 50,000 is necessary in order to provide economical administration of a full-time staff. The recognized minimum staff includes a full-time health officer, a public health or sanitary engineer, sanitarians, public health nurses, laboratory technicians, and clerks.

A forward step was taken in 1951 with the passage of the Local Health

District Act, a permissive measure designed to encourage the formation of consolidated local health districts or county local health districts.[7] However, as of 1956 no county or group of municipalities had adopted the provisions of the act.

COMMUNICABLE DISEASE CONTROL

In New Jersey, a communicable disease is one so declared by law or by the state Department of Health.[8] The department may require a local board of health to take measures to prevent the spread of a communicable disease. Action may be brought in the courts in the event the local board fails to comply.

The elimination of tuberculosis, one of the most troublesome communicable diseases, has long been a major objective of the health department. Throughout the nation, the incidence of tuberculosis has shown a phenomenal decline, falling from 194.4 per 100,000 population in 1900 to 26.3 in 1949.[9] In New Jersey, the rate fell from 27.1 in 1949 to 16.8 in 1952.[10] The estimated national rate dropped to 16.1 in the same year. The white rate in New Jersey was 13.5, the nonwhite rate was 62.3.[11] The general decline in the rate of tuberculosis is considered to be the result of many factors including improved economic conditions and greatly increased general knowledge of the symptoms, sources of infection, and methods of control. Nevertheless, in spite of a tremendous decline, tuberculosis ranks as a leading cause of death in the state. In New Jersey, during 1953, there were 693 deaths. There were 6.0 reported tuberculosis cases per death.

The tuberculosis control program includes the provision of state-owned photofluorographic apparatus in clinics, mass X-rays in areas having a high incidence of tuberculosis, and the promotion as a standard procedure of the X-raying of all hospital admissions. The health department favors an intensification of its prevention program. To do so would result, it believes, in substantially lower expenditures for institutional care of tuberculosis patients.

The Department of Health also operates a venereal disease control program. Penicillin and other antibiotics and drugs are made available without charge to hospitals and private physicians for the treatment of syphilis. In recent years several special venereal disease clinics have been operated for migrant agricultural workers and migratory employees in the oyster industry.

ENVIRONMENTAL SANITATION

The oldest and most widely accepted phase of public health is that related to environmental sanitation. The early statutes were concerned with the power of the state and local boards of health in the elimination of nuisances and foul odors. In current usage, the term "sanitation" embraces all matters concerned with the hygiene of the environment. Today, the promotion of sanitation constitutes one of the basic functions of the New Jersey Department of Health.

Food and Drug Regulation

Food and drug laws have two basic purposes: to protect the public from adulterated or misbranded products, and to protect the individual conducting a legitimate business from the competition of those dealing in fraudulent merchandise. About 60 per cent of the foods, drugs, and cosmetics consumed by the public fall under the jurisdiction of the Federal government since they are moving in interstate commerce. However, it is estimated that 40 per cent are of an intrastate nature.[12] For example, if not shipped outside New Jersey, the products of a slaughterhouse in New Brunswick would not be inspected by the Bureau of Animal Industry of the United States Department of Agriculture. Nor would a beverage, manufactured and consumed locally, fall under the regulations of the Federal Food, Drug, and Cosmetic Act of 1938. Regulation of the 40 per cent moving in intrastate commerce depends upon the enforcement of state laws and regulations, principally the function of the Department of Health. Federal standards concerning the "identity, purity, quality, or strength" of foods and drugs may be adopted by the department.[13]

The New Jersey law prohibits the adulteration and misbranding of foods, drugs, and cosmetics. It provides for the licensing of a number of industries such as milk, ice cream, animal slaughtering, and narcotics. Under this legislation, state sanitary inspections are made of establishments which produce, prepare, pack, or store foods and drugs. State or local agents may inspect any food, drug, or cosmetic, obtain samples, and with the aid of the courts confiscate products intended for sale in violation of the law. Perishable foods may be summarily destroyed. Violators may be prosecuted in the courts for the collection of a penalty.

Responsibility for enforcement of the drug laws is placed not only upon the Department of Health but upon all peace officers within the state and all county prosecutors. In addition, the Board of Pharmacy is charged with enforcing the laws concerned with the handling of drugs by pharmacy establishments. Violation of the narcotics laws constitutes a high misdemeanor punishable by fine and imprisonment.

In his annual report for 1953, the United States Commissioner of Narcotics observed:

New Jersey has a model narcotic-control system, including adequate legislation, efficient personnel, and vigorous enforcement . . . . All States would do well to copy the narcotic enforcement machinery now functioning in New Jersey.[14]

Inspection Services

The Department of Health conducts thousands of sanitary inspections each year as part of its food and drug control program. The larger food processing establishments are checked for compliance with state sanitary regulations. In recent years, increased emphasis has been placed upon the inspection of out-of-state suppliers. Visitations of in-state dairies vary, those plants complying with regulations having fewer inspections than those with less satisfactory records. The inspection of ice-cream factories has become an accepted practice. Quality control of dairy products is measured by bacterial count. An unsatisfactory count, that is a sample containing more than the maximum permissible number of bacteria per cubic centimeter, invites an inspection of the premises by a representative of the department.[15]

There were 141 licensed slaughterhouses in New Jersey in 1953. These were inspected by the department for sanitation of buildings and facilities as were meat processing establishments and licensed cold storage warehouses. A sanitary shellfish control program was also operated. The program includes sampling of the growing waters and inspection of the handling practices of shellfish shipping and shucking establishments.

Public Health Engineering

The control of industrial wastes and the prevention of stream pollution constitute one of the state's greatest problems. Representatives of the department specializing in public health engineering inspect treatment plants for sewage and industrial wastes, conduct stream surveys, inspect bathing waters, and consult with municipalities and industries concerning the development of additional water supplies and increased facilities for the disposal of wastes.

The construction of sewerage facilities by a municipality may be hampered by the fact that the municipality has already borrowed to capacity. The department may issue "orders of necessity" so that the municipality may exceed its debt limitation and proceed with construction designed to eliminate a public health menace. Plans for the construction of water purification plants, whether by public or private agencies, must be approved by the health department which is also charged with responsibility for supervision and inspection of the plants. Sewerage construction plans must also be submitted to the department. The creation of special sewerage districts by two or more municipalities cannot proceed except upon favorable departmental action. Operators of public water treatment plants, public sewerage treatment plants, and public water supply systems are examined and licensed by the health department.

CONSTRUCTIVE HEALTH PROGRAMS

New Jersey has concerned itself increasingly with the concept of positive or constructive health. The objective is healthful living. The effectiveness of the program has an impact upon other activities such as the program for the prevention of chronic illness.

Maternal and Child Health

Public health programs usually give particular attention to the problems of expectant mothers and infants. This increased attention is one of a number of factors responsible for the remarkable decrease in maternal and infant mortality during the last two decades. The maternal death rate in New Jersey per 1,000 live births decreased from 5.3 in 1929 to 0.6 in 1952. This statistical difference meant that had the 1929 rate prevailed, 618 mothers would have died during child birth instead of 70.

Infant mortality also dropped amazingly during the period 1929 to 1952. In New Jersey, the rate fell from 60 to 24. Had the 1929 rate prevailed, 6,540 infants would have died instead of 2,633.

Maternal and child health activities of the department are for the most part designed to aid local communities. The state assists also in the development of educational programs for the field nurses and in the distribution of educational materials to expectant mothers. The health department also supplies a maternal and infant advisory service to hospitals, licenses and inspects maternity homes, and licenses midwives. The overall program of the department has been handicapped by the lack of adequate health departments in many communities of the state.

Nutrition

In the past, the promotion of sound nutrition has played a very small role in public health programs. Recently, the nutritionist has been recognized more widely for his part in helping to eliminate nutritional deficiencies. Through educational and training programs and pilot studies, the department has endeavored to emphasize the importance of proper nutrition in building up resistance to disease.

Dental Health

A state supervised dental health program has placed emphasis upon the prevention of tooth decay, "the most common of all our afflictions." [16] In the fiscal year 1953 demonstration dental treatment programs were provided in eighteen counties, and 98 dentists in mobile units, clinics, and private offices treated 6,874 children who were financially unable to obtain private care.[17] The state also assisted communities in planning for water fluoridation.

Adult and Industrial Health

In recent years the services of the health department designed to improve the health of the industrial worker have undergone a considerable change in emphasis. Fewer direct plant visitations are being made. Formerly—and there are still a considerable number—plant visitations were made for the purpose of determining potential health hazards and appraising the medical-nursing care provided.* More recently, emphasis has been placed upon the investigation and control of atmospheric pollution and the protection of the worker's health as a phase of civil defense. The health department provides consultative, educational, and training services in the field of radiological health. This program includes the detection, use and disposition of radiological materials.

Public Health Nursing

In recent years the character of public health nursing services provided by the state has changed markedly. Formerly, a small departmental staff of nurses provided specialized services. At present state efforts are being directed toward providing leadership, educational, and consultative services of a generalized nature to the approximately 1,500 full-time public health nurses employed by various agencies and governments in New Jersey. A grant-in-aid program has been developed to encourage municipalities, which formerly relied on state-paid personnel, to employ public health nurses directly.

Mental Health

For a number of years New Jersey has operated mental hygiene clinics designed for the early detection of mental disorders. These diagnostic services have been made available by the state's mental hospitals. However, the facilities provided were inadequate. In a supplement to his budget message for the fiscal year 1956, Governor Meyner called for the expansion and strengthening of these clinics in order to "nip mental illness in the bud whenever it is possible to do so." [18] He asked for increased funds for research together with monies for additional doctors, nurses, attendants, and psychiatric technicians in the state's hospitals and specialized institutions. Because of its institutional aspects, the prevention and treatment of mental illness has been the concern principally of the Department of Institutions and Agencies.†

* The law requires the department to "encourage the establishment of medical, dental, environmental engineering and nursing services in all industrial plants in the State . . . ." L., 1947, ch. 177, p. 807.

† See Chapter 18, page 245.

CARE OF THE ILL AND THE DISABLED

Chronic Illness

In 1951 a committee investigating the problems of the chronically ill reported that 856,510 individuals in New Jersey were wholly or partially incapacitated. Half of this number were under forty-five years of age and 17 per cent were under twenty-five.[19] The committee declared that in order to prevent, detect, and control chronic sickness and to rehabilitate the victims of chronic disease, the state was obliged to assume an increased degree of responsibility.

By focusing attention on the economic loss to society resulting from the large number of chronically ill, the committee was successful in obtaining the passage of legislation embodying some of its recommendations. Two of these enactments were of immediate concern to the Department of Health. One established a Division of Chronic Illness Control within the department and the second created an Advisory Council on the Chronic Sick.

Crippled Children

In the administrative reorganization following the adoption of the new constitution in 1947, the Crippled Children's Commission was transferred to the Department of Health.* The commission consists of ten members— the commissioner of health or some member of the department designated by him, one representative each from the Elks, Rotarians, Shrine, Kiwanis, Lions, and the Medical Society of New Jersey, one member from each house of the legislature, and one citizen appointed by the governor. Any member may be removed by the governor for cause.

The act effecting the transfer constitutes the commission as an agency within the Department of Health. However, the number of persons to be assigned to operate the agency and the duties they are to perform fall within the jurisdiction of the commissioner. He is required only to consult with the Crippled Children's Commission.[20]

The mandate of the commission is broad—to provide for the care, treatment, maintenance, education, and general welfare of the crippled children throughout the state. In carrying out this mandate, the commission has developed a program which endeavors to provide specialized medical, surgical, sociological, and psychological services. On January 1, 1953, 16,812 children were on the state register. Of this number 1,215 received clinic, hospital, and appliance services.[21]

Nursing services for crippled children are arranged by contract with

* The commission was set up on a temporary basis in 1926. Its permanent status stems from legislation passed in 1931. L., 1931, ch. 70, p. 126.

approved public health nursing agencies. The contract agencies and other non-official cooperating groups are supervised by state and regional public health nurses. During the fiscal year 1950, contracts with thirty agencies covered children in 318 municipalities. For example, contracts were made with the New Brunswick Visiting Nurse Association, the Bloomfield Red Cross Nursing Service, and the Hunterdon County Public Health Association.[22]

The Crippled Children's Commission, in cooperation with St. Michael's Hospital in Newark, operates a rheumatic fever demonstration unit and clinic. Several physical therapy treatment centers are maintained throughout the state and a number of clinics held each year for children afflicted with cerebral palsy.

Cancer and Heart Disease

Cancer control measures of the state include the distribution of literature on cancer, the payment of fees of dentists for courses in the detection and treatment of oral cancer, and research into the relationship between occupation and cancer of selected body sites such as the respiratory system. The research is supported by funds from the United States Public Health Service.

The heart disease control program is designed to assist physicians in earlier cardiac diagnosis. Training courses are provided from state funds. Cardiac demonstration centers are in operation at Newark, Trenton, Flemington, and Camden.

OTHER PROGRAMS

Vital Statistics

The Department of Health is charged by law with the responsibility not only of collecting facts regarding births, marriages, and deaths, but of obtaining information which may be of assistance in the solution of health problems and in the prevention of disease. The collection of vital statistics, the "bookkeeping of public health," has been accepted as a state responsibility since 1848.

Statistical data are centralized in one unit of the health department. All certificates of vital events have, since January 1, 1949, been coded and punched for mechanical tabulation. For example, if desired, a tabulation of deaths, by cause and by municipality, may quickly be made. More than 12,000,000 records on births, deaths, and marriages dating from 1848 are in the custody of the Registrar of Vital Statistics.[23] How accurate many of the older records are, especially of deaths, is a matter of conjecture. In order to minimize potential social stigma, the cause of death may not have been reported correctly. Inadequate reporting and faulty diagnosis also may have impaired the value of the official statistics. In order to reduce error, the health department now uses a widely accepted form, the International Classification of Diseases, Injuries and Causes of Death. The completeness of morbidity reporting depends also upon the adequacy of local health departments and the thoroughness of physicians.[24]

Laboratory Services

The health department's laboratory services are an important feature of the public health program. In the diagnosis of communicable diseases, and in determining their prevalence and the effectiveness of control measures, the laboratory performs an indispensable service. In the enforcement of the public health laws, samples of food, drugs, water, and sewage and trade wastes are subjected to chemical, bacteriological, and other examinations. Samples of dust are analyzed in connection with studies of health hazards in industrial plants. Control serums are prepared and distributed for use in various serological testing laboratories throughout the state.

Miscellaneous Activities

The interests of the Department of Health cover a wide range. Biological supplies including gamma globulin, and various vaccines are regularly made available to physicians and local health departments through approximately sixty distributing stations. A veterinary public health program has been initiated to supplement the work of the Department of Agriculture in controlling diseases transmissible to man. Pilot studies have been conducted in the technique of multi-phase screening; a battery of tests, for tuberculosis, anemia, diabetes, syphilis, and others were given each individual participating in the study, the objective being to develop a plan for early detection of disease. In cooperation with Alcoholics Anonymous, a limited program has been instituted in the field of alcoholism.* Pilot clinics have been established at Camden, Trenton, and Newark in an experiment to assist alcoholics through the out-patient service of a general hospital. In addition, packets of educational materials on the problem of alcoholism were distributed to public and school libraries.

In each program, much attention has been given to public health education. By means of training courses, publications, and conferences, and with the help of large numbers of citizen advisory committees and civic groups, the health department has endeavored to acquaint the people of New Jersey with the importance of an adequate public health program.

* The legislature granted broad statutory authorization for the rehabilitation of alcoholics in 1948. L., 1948, ch. 453, p. 1853.

NOTES

[1] *Report of the Health Commission of the State of New Jersey* for the Year 1874 (New Jersey Legislative Documents, 1875), p. 62.

[2] L., 1877, ch. 140, p. 220.

[3] L., 1947, ch. 177, p. 792.

[4] L., 1948, ch. 444, p. 1748.

[5] L., 1887, ch. 67, p. 80.

[6] N.J. *Seventy-sixth Annual Report of the Department of Health, 1953* (Trenton, 1954), p. 141.

[7] L., 1951, ch. 69, p. 431.

[8] L., 1895, ch. 260, p. 493.

[9] Department of Commerce, Bureau of the Census, *Statistical Abstract of the United States, 1952* (73rd ed., Washington, 1952), p. 73.

[10] *Seventy-sixth Annual Report . . . , op. cit.,* p. 166.

[11] *Ibid.,* p. 202.

[12] T. E. Sullivan, "Problems Encountered in Enforcing State Food, Drug, and Cosmetic Laws," *Food, Drug, Cosmetic Law Journal,* VI (November, 1951), 817-23.

[13] L., 1939, ch. 320, p. 786.

[14] Treasury Department, Bureau of Narcotics, *Traffic in Opium and Other Dangerous Drugs for the Year Ended December 31, 1953* (Washington, 1954), pp. 10-11.

[15] N.J. *Seventy-third Annual Report of the Department of Health, 1951* (Trenton, 1952), p. 66.

[16] *Ibid.,* p. 9.

[17] *Seventy-sixth Annual Report . . . , op. cit.,* p. 73.

[18] N.J. Second Supplementary Budget Message of Robert B. Meyner, Governor of New Jersey (Trenton, 1955), p. 9.

[19] N.J. *Report of the Temporary Committee on the Chronic Sick* (1951), p. 5.

[20] L., 1948, ch. 444, p. 1748.

[21] *Seventy-sixth Annual Report . . . , op. cit.,* pp. 57-69. See also *Children and Youth in New Jersey,* Report of the Governor's Committee on Youth (Trenton, 1949), p. 64.

[22] *Seventy-third Annual Report . . . , op. cit.,* p. 153.

[23] From 1848 to 1887 records were collected by the secretary of state. See also Walter R. Scott, "One Hundred Years of Vital Statistics in New Jersey and Their Value to Health Departments," *Public Health News,* XXIX (June, 1948), 167-70.

[24] For a general discussion of the pitfalls in the recording of vital statistics, see John J. Hanlon, *Principles of Public Health Administration* (St. Louis: C. V. Mosby Co., 1950), pp. 300-7.

CHAPTER 17

Public Welfare

WELFARE LEGISLATION in the colonial period made little differentiation between crime and poverty; "the popular notion that able-bodied pauperism was attributable solely to individual indolence gave rise at the very start to an intermingling of penology and poor relief." [1]

In 1798 the New Jersey legislature authorized the counties to construct almshouses for the poor and in 1799 provided for county workhouses to incarcerate offenders against the law. These measures laid the foundation for the separate development at the local level of the penal and poor laws. But at the state level, as various institutions were established to care for particular groups, there developed the theory that penal and charitable activities should be managed by a single agency. This theory has continued to the present day. As a consequence, one agency—the Department of Institutions and Agencies—not only is responsible for administering the usual welfare services, such as old age assistance and aid to dependent children but also operates the state's penal and correctional institutions and its mental hospitals.

DEPARTMENT OF INSTITUTIONS AND AGENCIES

A Council of Charities and Corrections was established in 1883 to collect statistics and to inspect institutions.[2] In 1905, the office of commissioner of charities and correction was established, with inspectional powers only.[3] A Dependency and Crime Commission was set up in 1908 to study the "causes of dependency and criminality." [4] Two separate investigating bodies were appointed in 1917, a Prison Inquiry Commission and a Commission to Investigate Conditions of the State Charitable Institutions.[5] Both commissions held that in order to promote, coordinate, and properly manage the state's welfare activities, one over-all administrative agency should be established. As a consequence, the legislature created the Department of Charities and Corrections in 1918; a year later the name was changed to the Department of Institutions and Agencies.[6] The 1948 reorganization made no fundamental change in the department's activities.

Organization

Heading the Department of Institutions and Agencies is a State Board of Control. An indication of the legislative intent to centralize all welfare activities under one jurisdiction may be obtained from the language of the 1948 statute setting up the department as one of the fourteen principal executive agencies:

Within the limitations imposed by general legislation applicable to all agencies of the State, the State Board is hereby granted complete and exclusive jurisdiction, supreme and final authority, and the requisite power to accomplish its aims and purposes in and upon the institutions, boards, commissions and other agencies, hereinafter in this section named, and designated as charitable, hospital, relief, training institutions and correctional institutions of this State, to the end that they shall be humanely, scientifically, efficiently and economically operated.[7]

The State Board of Control consists of nine members appointed by the governor, subject to Senate confirmation. The governor is an ex officio member. The law requires appointments to be made without reference to political belief. The term is eight years, but members may be removed by the governor for cause. No salary is paid in connection with the positions, although reimbursement is made for actual expenses. The board elects one of its members annually as president. There must be at least six regular meetings each year. Four members constitute a quorum.

The board has the right of visitation and inspection over all institutions, public and private, which receive state money. This includes the power to inspect county and city jails and hospitals and private institutions or agencies designed for physical and mental defectives, and dependent or convalescent children. In the event the laws governing the treatment of inmates are being violated, the state board may apply for a court order to remedy the improper conditions. Failure to comply constitutes contempt of court. Institutions conducted by church and fraternal societies for their own members are exempt.

A commissioner of institutions and agencies serves as the executive officer of the Board of Control and the administrative head of the department. The commissioner, who need not be a resident of the state, is appointed by the board subject to the governor's approval. He may be removed by the board, or by the governor, upon notice and opportunity to be heard. In addition to his responsibility for the supervision of all phases of the department's work, he is the budget officer, the fiscal officer, and the appointing authority under the civil service laws.

Institutional Management

Each state institution is required to operate within the general policy framework established by the State Board of Control. Notwithstanding the existence of a citizen body responsible for over-all policy determination, there is also a citizen board of managers for each institution. These boards, consisting of from five to seven members each, are appointed by the state board with the governor's approval for terms of three years. They are responsible for the "management, direction and control" of the various institutions. Members of these boards receive expenses but no compensation. They may be removed by the state board for cause.

The executive officer of an institution is selected by the board of managers of that institution with the approval of the state board. In practice this means that the standards established by the department for the selection of top personnel are accorded great weight. The executive officer of the institution is responsible for the appointment, with the approval of the managing board, of all officers and employees. His discretion is limited by the recruitment regulations and practices of the Department of Civil Service. Employees who are not within the civil service may be dismissed either by the board of managers, with the approval of the state board, or by action of the state board alone.*

Actual day-to-day management of an institution rests upon the executive officer. He is responsible to the board of managers for proper maintenance of the plant and equipment, for the conduct of institutional employees, and for the care and treatment of all inmates.†

---

* For the case of a prison employee whose dismissal was upheld by the Civil Service Commission and then by the courts, see *Ristow* v *Civil Service Commission of New Jersey*, 6 N.J. Misc., 444 (1928). In a more recent case the commission upheld the superintendent of the State Village for Epileptics at Skillman who dismissed an attendant for sleeping on duty. The commission declared: "the lives of patients were at stake. The penalty of dismissal for gross neglect of duty under such circumstances can hardly be deemed too severe." *The Welfare Reporter*, V (August, 1950), 18.

† A 1945 court case illustrates the trying problems coming before the executive officer of an institution. A child was born to an unmarried woman after her commitment to the Clinton Reformatory in 1938. The executive officer filed a petition in the Bergen County Juvenile and Domestic Relations Court asking that the infant be placed under the care of the State Board of Children's Guardians. Notice of a hearing on the petition was served on the executive officer but not on the mother. After the hearing the court awarded custody of the child to the board. Six years later the mother brought suit to vacate the order. The Court of Errors and Appeals ruled that although by law the executive officer had custody of every person admitted to the institution, in this instance the infant had not been admitted or committed to the institution. As a consequence, service of notice upon the executive

New Jersey has direct operating control over approximately two dozen institutions. About twenty fall into two easily defined categories, penal or correctional and mental. These will be described briefly later. In addition there are two specialized institutions, two homes for veterans, and one home for firemen.

Originally established as the State Village for Epileptics, the New Jersey Neuropsychiatric Institute, located at Skillman, cares for a number of special groups such as epileptics, alcoholics, child psychotics, and cerebral palsy cases. In recent years facilities at the institute have been expanded considerably.

The State Sanatorium at Glen Gardner is the only state institution operated for victims of tuberculosis. Most facilities for the treatment of tuberculosis are operated by county governments. A study published by the Department of Institutions and Agencies in 1955 (Research Bulletin No. 122) indicated that of 2,489 persons in public sanatoriums, 2,265 were in county and city hospitals and 224 in Glen Gardner. Charitable and proprietary hospitals accounted for an additional 10 per cent. In addition a number of tuberculosis victims who suffered also from mental illness were patients in the state's mental hospitals.

The Home for Disabled Soldiers at Menlo Park cares for a limited number of honorably discharged needy veterans. At Vineland, the New Jersey Memorial Home provides facilities for over 100 veterans and their wives and widows of veterans. The New Jersey Home for Firemen at Boonton is supervised by the Department of Institutions and Agencies although the home is financed from nonbudgeted funds.

The control of the state over its own institutions is complete. In addition to the twenty-odd state institutions, there are approximately 700 county, municipal, and private institutions which fall under the visitation and inspection powers of the state board. These include county jails, municipal lock-ups, hospitals, nursing homes, children's institutions, and homes for the aged. The counties alone operate seventy institutions with a daily population of about 14,000. All of these are subject to inspection by the Department of Institutions and Agencies. Private hospitals and nursing homes are subject to licensing by the Hospital Licensing Board.* The licensing procedure serves to buttress the work of the inspectional staff. Otherwise, in order to insure compliance, a court order must be obtained, violation of which constitutes contempt.

---

officer rather than the mother was improper and the Juvenile and Domestic Relations Court had no power to place the child under the State Board of Children's Guardians. *Gregg* v *Juvenile and Domestic Relations Court*, 133 N.J.L. 89 (1945).

* So are county and municipal institutions applying for Federal funds. The Hospital Licensing Board was created in 1947; licenses have been required since 1927.

PENAL AND CORRECTIONAL INSTITUTIONS

New Jersey's penal and correctional institutions are operated with a view to providing the degree of custody necessary for each individual committed to the institution by the criminal courts. The purpose in providing varying degrees of custody is twofold, as an aid in the study and treatment of offenders and as a means of reducing prison construction and operating costs. Three categories of custody for inmates have been established:

1. A close custody inmate is one who might be expected to plot escape and to carry out escape plans at considerable risk to his own safety and that of others.
2. A medium security inmate is one who might seize an opportunity to run away if he found himself unobserved but who would not plot or run the risk to get away.
3. A minimum custody inmate is one who might be expected to observe the limits of confinement without supervision or physical barriers to escape.[8]

Minimum and medium security units are believed to afford a better atmosphere for prisoner rehabilitation than do the maximum security units which are reserved for recidivists (repeaters) and offenders difficult to control.

Prisoners are committed to the penal and correctional institutions only after conviction by a criminal court. Sentences are usually for minimum and maximum terms. A sentence to a reformatory may be for an indefinite term. The maximum indeterminate sentence is five years. After commitment, new prisoners are sent to the quarantine wing of the state prison at Trenton where they are classified.

The classification system, sometimes referred to as "man-analysis," was established following the report of a prison inquiry commission in 1917. Classification involves a thorough study of each individual. In developing the prisoner's case history, he is interviewed by staff specialists including the physician, the psychiatrist, the psychologist, the chaplain, the director of education, the industrial supervisor, and others.[9] A complete study is made of each individual's personal, social, educational, and occupational life. The classification committee then decides upon the treatment and training to be accorded each person. Periodic reclassification is designed to provide an opportunity for adjustment in the assigned program. An indication of the importance of correct classification and treatment may be obtained from the fact that 97 per cent of all prisoners are ultimately released to the community.

One of the principal administrative problems is the organization and supervision of productive employment in the penal and correctional institutions. The kinds of work to be performed and the standards of work such as hours, compensation, and selling prices are within the jurisdiction of the State Board of Control. However, the State House Commission must approve new industries or the enlargement of existing plants. The state board may act as an independent contractor in the use of prison labor for public works.

The products of prison labor are used by state and local governmental agencies. The State Use Industries provide training opportunities of considerable value. In addition to assisting inmates in the development of valuable skills, the goods manufactured enable the state to recoup some of the costs incident to the confinement of prisoners. Manufactured articles include license plates, highway signs, shoes, clothing, furniture, washing compounds, and insecticides. Prison personnel participate also in baking, canning, and farm production. By setting up a number of small industries, vocational training opportunities are increased.

The State Prison

In New Jersey the "State Prison" is a collective term which includes all institutions, "farms, camps, quarries or grounds," designated by the State Board of Control "where convicts sentenced to the State Prison may from time to time be kept, housed or employed." [10] The institutional executive officer is called the "principal keeper." * Women may not be confined in the state prison, nor males under sixteen except for conviction of murder. The prison consists of the institution at Trenton and the Rahway and Leesburg Prison Farms.

The State Prison at Trenton provides maximum security detention. Older and more serious male offenders are housed here with the emphasis being placed on confinement and work rather than on rehabilitation. However, the shops—shoe manufacturing, binding, woodworking—although permitting close custody, also provide some vocational training.

The Prison Farm at Rahway is a medium security institution. In addition to a substantial agricultural program, industrial training is given in foundry work, shoe and textile manufacturing, and certain phases of printing.†

The 1,000-acre Prison Farm at Leesburg provides minimum security. It has no walls, cells, or even a fence. The more trustworthy prisoners and those soon to be released are transferred to Leesburg for farming and canning operations.

* For many years, the office of principal keeper was a thorn in the side of the department. Control of the prison was difficult so long as the "keeper," a constitutional officer, was a patronage appointment. Since 1951 the Board of Managers has had the appointive authority, subject to approval by the State Board of Control.

† On June 1, 1948, what formerly were the State Reformatory at Rahway and the State Prison Farm at Bordentown exchanged functions.

Reformatories

The New Jersey Reformatory is also a collective term which includes any institution, designated by the State Board of Control, to keep persons sentenced to the reformatory. Males between sixteen and thirty who have been convicted of crimes punishable in prison but who have never previously been sentenced to prison may be committed to a reformatory.

The Bordentown Reformatory provides medium and minimum security for the more unstable younger prisoners. Emphasis in recent years has been placed upon rehabilitation with broadened programs in psychiatric treatment, clinical psychology, and education. Considerable national prominence has been given a program called "guided group interaction," a means of reshaping the attitudes of offenders through group therapy.* Work activities are principally of an agricultural nature with some industrial and vocational training.

At Annandale Farms the inmates live in separate cottages. The institution was developed for first offenders. In the absence of a penal atmosphere, emphasis may be placed on individual training. A farm, dairy, piggery, and cannery combine training and productive work.

The New Jersey Reformatory for Women includes any institution so designated. The only women's reformatory is that at Clinton Farms. Most offenders live in cottage-type barracks without locks, fences, or other escape barriers. However, a new building has recently been constructed to house security risks. The institution has attained national recognition for its "honor system," a successful plan for handling inmates.

The State Home for Boys at Jamesburg and the State Home for Girls at Trenton provide care and training for delinquents between eight and sixteen years of age. An accredited school is in operation at each institution. In addition, vocational training is offered in a number of fields. These schools have been described as "resident schools specializing in handling young delinquents and behavior problems." [11]

An entirely new type of institution was opened in 1949 at Menlo Park. The State Diagnostic Center provides special facilities and staff for the study of various classes of offenders. For example, persons convicted of sex offenses are sent to the Diagnostic Center prior to sentence by the court. The center has a staff of specialists in psychiatry, psychology, and social work.

* The plan has been described as "an effort to capture the intellectual interest of the participant and to examine individual and group attitudes and their reciprocal reaction. As applied to the offender, it is an attempt to reeducate him, to help him discover for himself that conformity to social rules is more satisfying than the delinquent behavior which led to his incarceration. This is accomplished by creating an atmosphere of free discussion under a skilled leader who encourages discussion without trying to secure acceptance of his own views." F. Lovell Bixby, "Guided Group Interaction," *The Welfare Reporter*, V (August, 1950), 15.

In 1950 a new institution was established on an experimental basis. Highfields, the former Lindbergh estate, now provides specialized short-term treatment, chiefly group psychotherapy, for a small number of youthful offenders who are recommended for care by the State Diagnostic Center.[12]

Prison Reform

In 1952 a series of riots and disturbances at both the Trenton Prison and the Rahway Prison Farm resulted in the appointment by Governor Driscoll of a special committee to investigate the administration of the prison system and the operation of the parole board.

The committee reported that the institutional plants were inadequate, the Trenton Prison being "the most archaic in the United States." [13] Many prisoners were confined behind solid doors in overcrowded and poorly ventilated cells; prison yards were too small, the shops were fire hazards, and the construction of the wings prevented proper segregation.

Large numbers of men were found to be idle, a factor destructive of prisoner morale. The committee absolved the Department of Institutions and Agencies of blame for this condition. Instead the responsibility was placed upon those labor and industrial groups who have opposed the production of prison goods. For example, the Union Printers League of New Jersey opposed the repair or replacement of printing equipment damaged in the riots, in spite of the fact that only 15.5 per cent of the state government's printing was done in the prison shop. Enforced idleness was declared to be a serious problem also at Rahway and at Bordentown.

A substantial contributory factor to the disturbances, the committee found, was the problem of obtaining and keeping stable custodial personnel. In 1951 there was a turnover of 64 per cent among the custodial force. Over half of the correction officers were temporary appointees who had not passed any civil service examination. Inadequate salaries were declared to be the principal reason for the department's inability to recruit and retain qualified personnel.

The committee condemned the "unevenness of discipline," the lack of careful work assignment, and the absence of educational and vocational training programs. They emphasized the necessity for a forward-looking fiscal policy which would permit the employment of competent professional and technical personnel.

The procedures of the Parole Board and the actual workings of the parole law were the subject of bitter complaint by the prisoners. The committee found that there were serious inequities in the law itself. For example, fourth offenders were given less consideration for parole than a person sentenced for life on a first degree murder charge. Incorrect administrative interpretations of the parole law also worked injustices. Judges often violated the principle of the indeterminate sentence by making minimum and maximum sentences of equal length. The Parole Board's practice of giving only brief interviews to prisoners did not accord with the committee's idea of a proper hearing. However, the function of parole supervision gave parolee's "in ample measure the guidance, direction, and enlightened assistance requisite for the critical transition to a useful and self-sustaining place in community life.[14]

The state hastened to correct the deficiencies brought out in the investigating committee's report. Salaries of correction officers were increased and additions were made to the staff. An effort was made to reduce idleness and increased funds were made available for recreation and clothing. Finally, changes in legislation and in policy were effected with reference to the administration of paroles.

PROBLEMS IN CRIME CONTROL

Probation

Not every person who has been convicted of an offense is placed in a correctional institution. The courts of the state may suspend imposition of a sentence and place the offender on probation:

Probation is the status of a person convicted of a crime or adjudged guilty of delinquency during a period of suspension of sentence or corrective treatment in which he is given liberty conditioned on his good behavior and in which the state through its agents by personal supervision attempts to assist him during good behavior.[15]

If the conditions of the probation are violated, the offender may be arrested and sentenced to jail.

Probation is primarily a county function. The county court is empowered to appoint a chief probation officer in accordance with regulations of the Civil Service Commision. The salaries of the probation officer and his staff are paid from the county treasury.

The ultimate goal of probation is the rehabilitation of offenders. The inherent difficulty of achieving this goal was stated by the authors of a recent study of 1,000 persons who had been released on probation in Essex County in 1937:

What must be resolved is the paradoxical situation of having the probationer at liberty in a delinquent environment and at the same time expect him to forego his delinquency and undergo profound changes of character.[16]

The authors of the study declared that the success of probation as a device for rehabilitating offenders depended upon meeting five needs:

1. Better selection of cases for probation treatment
2. Better qualified and more expert personnel

3. Improved casework techniques and skills, including the reduction of case loads

4. More effective community agencies and resources for the care and guidance of people in trouble

5. Wider public understanding of probation procedure as well as of the causes and motivations of deviant behavior.[17]

Parole

The conditional release of prisoners is accomplished by means of a parole system. A parole bears no relationship to a pardon, nor should it be interpreted as leniency or as a means of escaping the punishment of the court. Former Commissioner of Institutions and Agencies Sanford Bates has said that men are not granted paroles; they are subjected to parole after finishing the institutional portion of a sentence. Both the prisoner and the public benefit from the supervision and guidance surrounding the individual released on parole. It serves as a bridge to assist him over the period of adjustment from institutional life to an independent existence.*

The system for paroles is administered by a State Parole Board consisting of a full-time chairman and two associate members appointed by the governor with the consent of the Senate. Established by law in 1948, the board is attached administratively to the Department of Institutions and Agencies. The board has jurisdiction over the release on parole of all persons in correctional institutions who have been sentenced to fixed minimum and maximum terms or to life imprisonment. Prisoners in reformatories may be released on parole by the board of managers of the correctional institution. The State Parole Board is responsible for determining the conditions of parole, that is, whether the parolee may leave the state, whether he shall contribute to the support of dependents, and whether he

* Bates lists the advantages of a parole system over the definite sentence plan as follows:

"1. The date of release can be adjusted, timed to a day when the prisoner has best prepared himself for release.

"2. The date of release may also be adjusted to a suitable environmental situation in the outer community.

"3. The amount of time served may be made commensurate with the prisoner's success in readjusting himself.

"4. The parole system makes possible the preparation of a program of employment and home surroundings most advantageous to continued rehabilitation.

"5. The release is always a conditional one and may be summarily terminated and the prisoner promptly returned without the delay of apprehension and trial.

"6. Mistakes made by the trial court or the prosecution may be properly rectified without recourse to the unusual method of pardon or other clemency.

"7. The limited control of the state over the prisoner may be continued at very much less expense and the difficult transition from institution life to free life undertaken with less risks to the public."

"How Should the Conditional Release of Prisoners be Regulated?" *The Welfare Reporter*, V (September, 1950), 4. For a recent study, see N.J. *Fourth Report of the New Jersey Law Enforcement Council, Strengthening Parole Services* (1956).

evidences the good conduct necessary to remain at liberty. No inmate may be considered for parole until he has served one third of the maximum sentence or the minimum sentence less commutation time for good conduct and time credits for work. The board is required to maintain a record of each prisoner's eligibility for parole and to review each case after public notice. The review must include an evaluation by the Department of Institutions and Agencies together with a report from the institution where the prisoner was confined. Finally, the review must include a general interview with the prisoner himself. A unanimous vote of the board is required.

The State Parole Board is the advisor of the governor with respect to applications for commutation of sentence, pardons, restoration of citizenship, and reprieves; and the governor may ask the board for help in any matter of executive clemency. Actual supervision of parolees is the function of the Department of Institutions and Agencies, operating through district parole supervisors in nine geographic areas.

Juvenile Delinquency

State action in the field of delinquency prevention takes the form of providing advice, information, and stimulation to local community efforts. Staff members recognize "no one universal sovereign panacea," which will eliminate juvenile delinquency.[18] Instead their operations are designed to assist other state and local agencies, and community groups who are concerned with youth welfare and the improvement of community life.

Through the cooperation of an advisory group called the Governor's Committee on Youth, the Division of Community Services for Delinquency Prevention periodically conducts a state-wide Governor's Conference on Youth. Other services include supplying technical assistance to local youth welfare groups and to municipal youth guidance councils, the preparation and distribution of printed materials such as *Delinquency Can Be Prevented,* and the compilation of statistics concerning children brought before the courts.

MENTAL HEALTH

Decade after decade, the rate of hospitalization for the mentally ill has continued to increase. The New Jersey rate in 1890 was 187 per 100,000 population. In 1950 the number had increased to 394.8 per 100,000.[19] Several factors account for this increase: (1) the public has become more aware of mental illness, and cases are more quickly recognized; (2) proper classification of cases has resulted in commitment to a mental hospital rather than to a jail or an almshouse; (3) the higher proportion of aged persons in the population has resulted in a greater number of senile admissions; (4) small homes and modern apartments prevent families from caring for mentally ill relatives; and (5) modern hospital care and treatment are recognized as more productive of beneficial results.

The increased recognition of the problems of the mentally ill has been accompanied by a demand for state acceptance of the institutional responsibility. For example, of 7,025 admissions in 1954, 5,166 or over 70 per cent were to the state hospitals. The remainder were admitted to county mental hospitals.[20] The average census in the state hospitals in 1954 was over 14,000.

State Mental Institutions

The State Hospital at Trenton, founded in 1846 as the State Insane Asylum, receives patients from Warren, Hunterdon, Somerset, and Mercer counties and from eastern Essex County. In addition it provides for all of the state's criminally insane. The State Hospital at Greystone Park, established as an insane asylum in 1876, receives patients from Sussex, Passaic, Morris, and Bergen counties and from western Essex. The State Hospital at Marlboro, founded in 1931, receives patients from Union, Middlesex, and Monmouth counties. To the extent existing facilities permit, patients are housed in small cottage groups. A fourth institution, the newly constructed State Hospital at Ancora, serves the southern counties. The children's unit of the hospital at Marlboro was transferred in 1946 and a year later was recognized by the legislature as a separate institution. Designated the Arthur Brisbane Child Treatment Center at Allaire, located near Farmingdale, it is used for the examination and treatment of emotionally disturbed children.

One of the most distressing problems at the state hospitals has been the shortage of nurses, technicians, and attendants. Turnover of service personnel has for some years been a serious problem. For example, in 1955, at Greystone Park there were 1,613 persons full-time and 23 part-time taking care of 6,583 patients. During the year 1,095 employees had been hired and 1,006 had left service. At the same time there were about 250 vacancies in the position of institutional attendant. Increases in salaries and the initiation of the forty-hour week have failed to reduce materially the personnel shortages.

A contributing factor to the personnel shortages has been the lack of proper physical facilities. The state hospitals have become increasingly overcrowded. Practically all available space has been used for beds, including day rooms, dining room areas, and in some instances parts of corridors. An excerpt from an annual report of the medical director at Marlboro indicates some of the operational problems:

Despite our earnest and unremitting efforts, the resident population of this hospital has continued to grow by accretion so that it is now at an all time peak. Senile admissions continue to rise while senile deaths have been markedly decreased through the use of penicillin, sulfonamides, et cetera. Thus we have a constantly growing senile population, requiring a great deal of nursing care, many of them constantly bed-ridden, and most in no way able to contribute any useful activity to the institution. Also, by reason of the over-crowding, they are more and more exposed to the hazards of being housed with young, physically strong psychotics, which inevitably results in injuries to them at the latter's hands. Personnel necessary for the specific treatment of these younger psychotics with hopeful prognosis has to be diverted to such senile care. Without such treatment, the recovery rate of the younger psychotics is reduced; this further increases overcrowding, and so the vicious circle grows.[21]

The construction of the new state hospital at Ancora should relieve, at least temporarily, the severe overcrowding of patients. Whether this de-velopment will solve the problems of personnel shortages, or tend to ac-centuate them by adding a fourth institution to be staffed, remains to be seen.

In 1949 New Jersey ranked eighth among the states in expenditures per resident patient. The states having the highest and lowest expenditures and certain neighboring states are listed below.[22]

State	Expenditures per Patient	Rank
New Jersey	$ 779.23	8
Wisconsin	1089.01	1
Tennessee	323.65	48
New York	960.84	2
Pennsylvania	643.51	22
Connecticut	901.04	4

Maintenance paid by patients amounted to 7.2 per cent of the mainte-nance expenditures compared with a national average of 8.9 per cent.[23]

Since 1921 the state hospitals have provided mental hygiene clinical services to communities. Teams consisting of a psychiatrist, a psycholo-gist, social workers, and clerical assistants treat maladjusted persons re-ferred by physicians, teachers, welfare agencies, and others. The passage of the National Mental Health Act in 1946 made available Federal funds for the expansion of community mental health programs. The ratio is one dollar of state money for two of Federal funds. Because of its pre-vious community activity in the mental hygiene field, the Department of Institutions and Agencies was designated as the state agency to administer the program. The operation of effective community psychiatric clinics has been called "the core of a state's mental health program" which would produce dividends in improved health, reduced commitments to institu-tions, and a consequent savings in costs.

Mental Deficiency

Mental deficiency is a continuing affliction affecting approximately 1 per cent of the population. For New Jersey this means in the neighborhood of 45,000-50,000 persons. Many of these are cared for by their families either at home or in special schools. The deficiency of some is relatively slight, and they are able to make adjustments within the community. However, in 1950, 4,600 were in state institutions.

New Jersey operates five institutions, each specializing in the training of particular types of deficient children. An order of commitment by the courts is necessary before the department will admit a child or an adult to any one of the schools. Parents able to pay maintenance charges are required to do so.

The North Jersey Training School at Totowa receives less highly retarded girls from six through twenty years of age who are believed capable of benefiting from special instruction. An individual program is developed for each of approximately 600 girls housed in cottages. Training is both academic and vocational and includes food preparation, domestic work, operating power sewers and looms, and dairy operation. In 1948 a nursery unit was opened for boys and girls under five years of age.

The Vineland State School has approximately 1,800 girls who are more seriously deficient mentally. As in Totowa, the cottage plan of housing is used, which facilitates classification by age, personality, and mental development. Elementary subjects and crafts, such as textile weaving, are taught; also domestic and garden activities. The state also subsidizes the training of 350 boys and girls at the Vineland Training School, a private institution specializing in research and training for the mentally deficient.

The New Lisbon State Colony cares for approximately 950 boys. Academic and vocational training is provided for those able to benefit. The vocational training includes work in woodworking, baking, canning, shoe and automobile repair, and farming. A considerable number are released under supervision for work in the community.

Seriously handicapped males are housed and trained at the Woodbine State Colony. Of about 950 in the institution, the average mental age is about two and one-third years although the average chronological age is eighteen years. The emphasis in training is upon assisting each patient to develop himself to the maximum of his ability. In the more serious cases this may mean nothing more than the ability to eat or to dress without assistance.

A fifth institution, the Edward R. Johnstone Research and Training Center was opened in 1956. Formerly the Bordentown Manual Training School, the facilities were converted for the care of the mentally retarded.

In 1954 a special commission established four years earlier by the governor and the legislature submitted an extensive report on the problems of mental deficiency in New Jersey. The committee declared that the state institutions for the mentally deficient were "bulging far beyond their physical capacities." The lack of adequate supervisory and training personnel was condemned as "false economy":

. . . a cottage at New Lisbon, with 50 rambunctious teenagers with the minds of six year olds is supervised by a single attendant. This kind of scene may be duplicated in all of the institutions. There are just not enough employees to do the kind of day-to-day work with the mentally deficient that will achieve the greatest benefit for the individual and the institution . . . .

If New Jersey is to operate "training" schools and not "custodial" institutions, it is absolutely necessary that many more attendants be hired who can work directly with the population.[24]

Low salary scales, inadequate housing, the lack of promotional opportunities, and the remoteness of the institutions from potential labor markets were listed by the committee as factors contributing to the difficulty of obtaining qualified employees. Job dissatisfaction was heightened also by the excessive number of patients. Overcrowding made difficult the operation of a positive rehabilitation program. This, in turn, prevented employees from obtaining a sense of accomplishment, and accentuated the problem of employee turnover.

Increased salaries and improved conditions for the staff were recommended together with additional facilities and an expanded program for the mentally deficient. The committee's recommendations pertained also to (1) establishing more flexible admission policies in order that parents need not be forced to obtain a formal court order, (2) providing the public with more information about institutional operations, (3) forming a separate commission to study the weaknesses in the existing system of assessing maintenance charges, and (4) providing budget allocations for institutions housing the mentally deficient comparable to those for the state's institutional population as a whole.

PUBLIC WELFARE SERVICES

Public welfare services of a wide variety are available to the people of New Jersey. The administration of these services follows no single pattern. For example, the Old Age and Survivors Insurance system is exclusively a Federal program. Established by the Federal Social Security Act of 1936, the Old Age and Survivors Insurance system now provides almost all employed persons with basic protection against loss of income in old age together with survivorship benefits in the event of a worker's death.

Another program arising out of the Social Security Act—Unemployment Compensation—is described in Chapter 21. The program is administered by the state under standards established by the Federal government.

Old age assistance, aid to the blind, aid to dependent children, and aid for the permanently disabled are administered by the state and county governments in accordance with Federal standards. The state alone operates certain child welfare services, although the counties share the cost. General assistance is fundamentally the responsibility of the municipalities, although the state supplies grants-in-aid.

Old Age Assistance

A formal program of state participation in old age assistance was begun in 1932, four years before the passage of the Federal Social Security Act.* Payments were based on a ratio of 75 per cent by the state and 25 per cent by the county. The age and residence requirements at that time substantially limited the eligible group. In 1936 eligibility requirements were liberalized in order to permit the state to qualify for Federal aid. However, the ratio of state-local participation was retained.

The Department of Institutions and Agencies is responsible for supervising all aspects of the program, which is administered at the local level by the county welfare boards. The functions of the department include (1) prescribing uniform standards, records, and accounts; (2) preparing regulations with reference to all operating problems such as processing applications, affording fair hearings, regulating disbursements, and making reimbursements; and (3) establishing, in cooperation with the Department of Civil Service, personnel standards in accordance with Federal requirements.

There are no regional offices. The department works directly with the county welfare boards. State field representatives supervise the activities of the county agencies in order to promote uniform practices. Case workers, who are county employees selected on a merit basis, constitute the link between the director of the county board and the recipient of old age assistance.

To be eligible for old age assistance, a prospective recipient must meet both Federal and state requirements. For example, in order to receive Federal aid, a state may not impose an age requirement of more than 65 years. The Federal law also requires that the recipient be a "needy" person. The standard of determination of a needy person is left up to the states. As a consequence, in December, 1954, recipient rates varied widely from 46 per 1,000 persons aged 65 or over in New Jersey, to 579 in Louisiana. New Jersey had the lowest recipient rate among the forty-

---

* Prior to that time relief for the aged was simply a part of general relief which was controlled by the individual municipalities. A special commission appointed in 1930 declared that the system was inadequate and recommended recognition of the principle of state aid for aged persons similar to the long established principle of state aid for dependent children. "Report of the Pension Survey Commission," N.J. *Minutes of the Assembly, 1931,* pp. 145-58.

eight states.*   The actual number of recipients in July, 1956, was 19,639.

Citizenship and residence requirements for old age assistance, the principal state additions to Federal rules of eligibility, vary considerably throughout the United States.   New Jersey, in common with her neighboring states of New York and Pennsylvania, has no citizenship requirement.   On the other hand, Connecticut and Massachusetts disqualify all noncitizens.   New Jersey's requirement of one-year residence is considerably more strict than that of New York where the applicant may simply indicate his intention to remain in the state.   Reciprocal agreements with other states make possible the elimination of the residence requirement.

New Jersey follows a strict policy with reference to reimbursement.   The recipient must agree to repay the sums received.   This agreement is, in effect, a lien upon the recipient's estate.   Although this practice is common among the states, few enforce the reimbursement provision with the vigor of New Jersey.   For example, in 1948 New Jersey recovered $700,998.17 or an average of $30.10 for each enrolled recipient.   In contrast, the average recovery in Massachusetts was sixty-nine cents, and that state made no attempt to recover from estates under $3,000.   In the fiscal year 1954 New Jersey recovered $958,131.

The aged in New Jersey must be reduced to circumstances where they are devoid of cash resources sufficient for their immediate requirements before they may receive assistance.   Thus, an applicant who has $200 on hand is not immediately eligible for old age assistance; on the other hand, an applicant who owns a home worth substantially more but who is lacking immediate cash resources will be granted assistance.

New Jersey follows a strict policy also with respect to the responsibility of relatives.   An aged person's parents, his spouse, and his children are legally responsible for his support.   All income of the relations, above an amount determined by the state to be required for their own cost of living at a reasonable standard, must be made available for the aged person's budgeted needs.   This cost of living standard is modified in relation to extraordinary medical or education expenses and other special obligations which the relative can demonstrate.   Court action to compel support may be brought by the county director of welfare.

Each applicant for old age assistance is investigated by the county welfare office.   Both needs and resources are studied.   A budget prepared by the state is used as a basis for the evaluation of the individual's food, clothing, shelter, medical, and other needs.   Grants are based upon the

---

* Several factors account for this low rate: (1) New Jersey is a high-income state.   (2) Because of its heavy industrialization, the state has a large number of recipients of Old Age and Survivors Insurance.   Further, there are more private pension plans.   (3) " Need " must be established to the satisfaction of an investigative and administrative staff accustomed to full enforcement of strict regulations, as, for example, the regulation pertaining to the responsibility of relatives.

difference between the applicant's needs and his resources. There is no maximum grant. In September, 1954, the average monthly grant amounted to approximately $67; grants ranged from $1.00 to $594 per month.

The cost of old age assistance is shared by the Federal, state, and county governments in the ratio of approximately 50, 34, and 16 per cent. In addition, one half of administrative costs are paid by the Federal government. Federal grants are made directly to the state and are based on a formula of "four-fifths of the first $25 of the average payment per recipient and one-half the balance." [25] However, the maximum Federal payment is $55 per month. Amounts above the maximum are paid from state and local funds.

Aid to the Blind

In 1909 a Commission for the Amelioration of the Condition of the Blind was created.[26] The commission was directed to prepare a register of the blind, and physicians were required to report cases of defective vision which might lead to blindness. Later, the commission was authorized to make loans of "such sums as shall be appropriated" for the assistance of the blind in establishing businesses. In 1921 eligibility standards were established. Needy blind persons over twenty-one years of age who could meet residence requirements and who had no responsible relatives were entitled to apply for aid. Actual assistance funds were made available by the county upon the recommendation of, and for the use of, the commission. First established as an independent agency, the commission was placed under the general supervision of the Department of Institutions and Agencies in 1922.

After Federal funds became available, through the Social Security Act, the age limit was lowered to eighteen and the residence qualification reduced to one year. The pattern of expenditure was retained. The county welfare board was required to operate under regulations of the commission, which kept a tight hold on the monies made available by the counties. However, the commission was required to return to the counties any Federal funds received. Emergency assistance could be supplied by the county director of welfare, subject to the approval of the commission.

Of $653,083 spent in the fiscal year ending June 30, 1954, the Federal portion amounted approximately to 50 per cent, the state to 2 per cent, and the county to 48. In none of the forty-five states participating in the Federal program was the percentage of state expenditure so low or the local share so high. In July, 1956, there were 912 recipients of Federal aid. The average monthly payment amounted to about $70.[27] The basis of Federal aid is the same as that for old age assistance.

Services provided under the program for the approximately 4,500 persons registered with the commission include educational and vocational training, employment surveys and placement assistance, financial aid, home industry development, and a variety of special activities designed to promote the well being of blind children.

Child Welfare

The State Board of Child Welfare is responsible for providing assistance to needy children. The board was created in 1899 as the New Jersey State Board of Children's Guardians. At that time two commissions of inquiry had revealed the inadequate care received by children who had become public charges and who had been placed in county or city almshouses. As a result, the board was given supervision over "all indigent, helpless, dependent, abandoned, friendless and poor children." [28] At first the work of the board was almost exclusively with children whose parents were dead or institutionalized or where the courts had separated a child from his parents because of neglect, abuse, or desertion. In recent years the scope of the state's work has been greatly enlarged, particularly since 1951 when a comprehensive law was enacted.[29]

At present the title "State Board of Child Welfare" refers to the unit in the Department of Institutions and Agencies which administers the care and custody, guardianship, home life assistance, and other state programs. A seven-member nonsalaried Board of Managers appointed by the State Board of Control with the approval of the governor serves as a policy-making and advisory body.

The care and custody program is designed to provide counseling, supervisory, and financial services. Upon application, the state determines by investigation whether (1) the welfare of the child is endangered, (2) any other welfare or child-caring agency will provide the services required, (3) financial assistance is available under any other law, (4) any legally responsible person is willing and able to provide for the child. If the answer to the first question is in the affirmative and the answer to the others is in the negative, and providing also that institutional care is unnecessary, the state may provide such care and custody as may be required. "Care" may involve services to the family including expenditures for the child's maintenance, or it may also involve placement outside the home. "Custody" involves supervisory services also. However, it is of a more formal nature, requiring a signed document from the parent or person exercising control over the child authorizing the state to assume control. In February, 1955, there were 1,288 children under state supervision.

Under the guardianship program, the State Board of Child Welfare may assume control of a child upon the basis of a court order. If the parents have been convicted of an offense against their children such as abuse, abandonment, or neglect, or if the child has been convicted of delinquency, or the best interests of a child under the care and custody program require state guardianship, then a petition may be made to the juvenile and domestic relations court of the county concerned. After notice and hearing to the appropriate parties, the court may commit the child to the guardianship of the state. Children are placed with foster parents who receive funds from the state for maintenance, including food, clothing, and medical, dental, and hospital care. If necessary, the child may be placed in an institution. Of 5,035 children under the guardianship program in February, 1955, maintenance costs were paid for 3,410. The others were old enough to maintain themselves or were being assisted by the foster families without charge to the state. The average monthly payment per boarding child was $47.75. Both the care and custody and the guardianship programs are financed by the state and the counties, each unit paying half the cost.

The state also operates a program referred to as the home life assistance program, known on a national basis as "aid to dependent children." This phase of child welfare was established in 1913 when the board was authorized to provide financial assistance to needy widows who otherwise would have been compelled to place their children under institutional care. On the theory that the greatest benefit to their children would be gained through the maintenance of family life, the attorney general earlier had ruled that money paid as board to a mother for her own children was a legal expenditure under the original act. The "Law to Promote Home Life for Dependent Children," passed in 1913, was liberalized from time to time both as to qualifications for assistance and in respect to means of finance.[30] Originally, administrative costs were paid by the state, and the entire assistance cost was placed on the counties. When the program was brought under the Social Security Act, all three levels of government shared the financial burden. In December, 1954, New Jersey had nine recipients in the aid to dependent children programs per 1,000 population under eighteen years of age. This ratio was lowest among the forty-seven states receiving Federal funds. In July, 1956, 6,458 families involving 16,075 children received assistance amounting to an average monthly payment of $121.09 per family.

No longer is it necessary for a person seeking aid to qualify under one of the specific programs. Any person may now obtain counseling and other services from any of the district offices of the State Board of Child Welfare. Of perhaps greatest significance is the fact that the state may now take measures to help children without the necessity of first seeking court intervention.

The state endeavors also to provide special protection for children in connection with placement for adoption. Persons or associations engaged in the placement of children for adoption must have the approval of the Department of Institutions and Agencies. Legislation enacted in 1953 required the department to establish standards concerning the professional training, experience, and practices of placement agencies.[31]

Permanent Disability

In 1950 Federal grants to the states became available for certain disabled persons. An individual between eighteen and sixty-five who is permanently and totally disabled for any reason other than blindness is entitled to aid from his county welfare board. Federal funds are made available on the same basis as the programs for old age assistance and aid to the blind. The state's share is one half of any sum spent by the county in excess of the Federal participation. In July, 1956, 4,046 persons received an average of $86.53 monthly.

General Assistance

Needy persons not covered under any state law may apply to the municipalities for assistance. Aid given by the municipalities is called public assistance or, more commonly, general assistance.

Grants-in-aid are supplied by the state; no Federal funds are involved. The amount of the grants for each municipality is determined on a sliding scale. The "preceding year's public assistance millage" is first obtained. This millage multiplied by net valuations taxable would equal the amount spent on public assistance the preceding year. The state share ranges from 40 per cent, where the preceding year's millage did not exceed 1.6, to 60 per cent in municipalities where the millage was in excess of 4.0.

Municipalities desiring to obtain state aid are required to operate under rules prescribed by the state. The program at the local level is administered by a local assistance board of from three to five persons. A director of welfare, selected by the local board, serves as the executive officer.

In recent years much consideration has been given to proposals to consolidate general assistance functions in the county which has operating jurisdiction over the categorical programs. However, legislation to effect this change has failed repeatedly.

NOTES

[1] Paul T. Stafford, *Government and the Needy, A Study of Public Assistance in New Jersey* (Princeton: Princeton University Press, 1941) p. 24.
[2] L., 1883, ch. 205, p. 249.
[3] L., 1905, ch. 57, p. 92.
[4] L., 1908, ch. 140, p. 209.
[5] L., 1917, pp. 989, 992.
[6] L., 1918, ch. 147, p. 343; L., 1919, ch. 97, p. 222.
[7] L., 1948, ch. 60, p. 147.
[8] F. Lovell Bixby, "New Jersey's Penal and Correctional Institutions," *The Welfare Reporter,* V (October, 1950), 11.
[9] Emil Frankel, "Crime Treatment in New Jersey, 1668-1934," *Journal of Criminal Law and Criminology,* XXVIII (1937), 103.
[10] L., 1948, ch. 60, p. 149.
[11] Bixby, *loc. cit.,* p. 13.

[12] F. Lovell Bixby, "Highfields," *The Welfare Reporter*, V (June, 1950), 3.

[13] N.J. *Report of the Committee to Examine and Investigate the Prison and Parole Systems of New Jersey to His Excellency Alfred E. Driscoll, Governor of the State of New Jersey* (1952), p. 13.

[14] *Ibid.*, pp. 93-94.

[15] Jay Rumney and Joseph P. Murphy, *Probation and Social Adjustment* (New Brunswick: Rutgers University Press, 1952), p. 6.

[16] *Ibid.*, p. 249.

[17] *Ibid.*, p. 266.   See also N.J. *Third Report of the New Jersey Law Enforcement Council, Strengthening Probation Services* (1956).

[18] Douglas H. MacNeil, "State Government and Prevention of Delinquency," *State Government*, XXII (May, 1949), 142.

[19] For the trend from 1930 to 1946 see N.J. Department of Institutions and Agencies, *Hospital and Public Health Resources in New Jersey* (Trenton, 1947), p. 45.   The earlier figure is given in N.J. Department of Institutions and Agencies, *A Report, 1934-43 and Handbook* (Trenton ?, 1943?), p. 47.   The rate in 1950 is found in N.J. Department of Institutions and Agencies, *The Trend in Mental Hospital Patients in New Jersey, 1930-1950, A Statistical Analysis*, Research Bulletin No. 102 (Trenton, 1951), p. 1.

[20] *Hospital and Public Health Resources in New Jersey, op. cit.*, p. 41.

[21] N.J. *The Eighteenth Annual Report of the New Jersey State Hospital at Marlboro for the year ended June 30, 1948* (mimeographed), p. 19.

[22] *The Mental Health Programs of the Forty-eight States* (Chicago: The Council of State Governments, 1950), p. 262.

[23] *Ibid.*, p. 263.

[24] N.J. *Mental Deficiency in New Jersey, A Report to Governor Robert B. Meyner and the Members of the Senate and General Assembly by the Commission to Study the Problems and Needs of Mentally Deficient Persons* (Trenton, 1954), p. 108.

[25] U.S. Department of Health, Education, and Welfare, Social Security Administration, *Social Security, A Brief Exploration of the Social Security Act* (Washington, 1953), p. 24.

[26] L., 1909, ch. 136, p. 208.

[27] *Social Security Bulletin*, XIX (October, 1956), 34.

[28] L., 1899, ch. 165, p. 362.

[29] L., 1951, ch. 138, p. 574.

[30] L., 1913, ch. 281, p. 578.

[31] L., 1953, ch. 264, p. 1769.

CHAPTER 18

Agriculture

AGRICULTURE is an important industry, notwithstanding New Jersey's position as the most highly urbanized state in the Union. In 1954 the state ranked fifth in the value of its commercial vegetables and fourth in the value of eggs produced. Milk production per cow was second only to California.[1] The state's most important commodity in 1953 was eggs, with a farm value of over $132,454,000. The total value of all agricultural products was $404,187,000.[2]

In 1950 there were 24,838 farms consisting of 35.8 per cent of New Jersey's total land area of 4,814,080 acres. Table 16 indicates the acreage of farms in various categories.

STATE BOARD OF AGRICULTURE

The early promotion of agriculture was carried on by local or county agricultural societies. They sponsored fairs, special exhibits, and lectures to disseminate agricultural information and spread new ideas. The New Jersey State Agricultural Society, founded in 1781, came to be widely recognized after 1855 as the representative of all the local groups. At the request of the state society, the legislature on several occasions appropriated funds to aid the farmers in controlling animal and plant diseases.

In 1872, the New Jersey State Board of Agriculture was established. It was authorized to investigate any subject "relating to the improvement of lands and agriculture . . . ." [3] The law was vague concerning the composition of the board and there was much uncertainty concerning the societies which could participate in its deliberations. In an effort to achieve a stable and representative membership, amending legislation was passed on several occasions during the period 1882-1887.[4] The board was instru-

TABLE 16

ACREAGE OF NEW JERSEY FARMS, 1951

All Land in Farms, By Size of Farm	Acres
Under ten acres	28,309
10 to 49 acres	196,953
50 to 99 acres	288,322
100 to 179 acres	509,410
180 to 259 acres	268,442
260 to 499 acres	230,050
Over 500 acres	203,955
TOTAL LAND IN FARMS	1,725,441

Source: U.S. Bureau of the Census, *U.S. Census of Agriculture: 1950*, Vol. I, Counties and State Economic Areas, Part 2 (Washington, 1952), pp. 273, 310.

mental in obtaining legislative authorization for a State Agricultural Experiment Station and in establishing county boards of agriculture. It was active, also, in seeking good roads, lower freight rates, and rural free delivery.

The board promoted farmers' institutes, sponsored the establishment of a commission to fight tuberculosis in animals, and obtained legislation, such as the nursery inspection law, designed to protect agricultural interests.

A major reorganization of the board occurred in 1916, when a Department of Agriculture was established. The department consisted of a board, a secretary and an assistant secretary, and three bureaus: animal industry, plant industry, and markets. The board consisted of eight persons chosen by delegates to the annual convention of the various agricultural associations. Two members of the board were elected each year. The governor was required by law to issue commissions to the persons elected at the convention. The secretary of agriculture was then appointed by the board.[5]

The reorganization act of 1948 constituted the Department of Agriculture as one of the fourteen principal departments.[6] The eight-member board was continued. However, by virtue of a change in 1944, there must be at all times one member representing each of the four leading agricultural commodities. Membership on the board is restricted to those actually engaged in "the production of farm crops or livestock products . . . ."[7] The two members elected each year by the convention are now recommended to the governor for appointment, with the advice and consent of the Senate. In accordance with the new constitution, members of the board may be removed by the governor for cause, upon notice and opportunity to be heard. Only notice and hearing are required to remove the secretary.

The assignment of functions to the operating units of the department is the responsibility of the board. Supervision and control may be exercised directly or through the secretary. The board is also responsible for the appointment, with the governor's approval, of the secretary, and together with the secretary, for the appointment of division heads and other employees of the department.[8]

ANIMAL INDUSTRY

State legislation designed to prevent the spread of contagious diseases in animals was first introduced in 1880.[9] Owners suspecting the presence of an infectious disease were required to notify the Board of Health. Provision was made for indemnifying the owner if the diseased animal was killed.

Animal Disease Control

The most important program, dating from 1894, has been that of tuberculosis elimination. For many years official efforts were confined largely to testing cattle shipped into the state. In 1917-18 cooperative arrangements were made with the Bureau of Animal Industry, United States Department of Agriculture, to establish accredited herds free from tuberculosis. Public demand for milk from accredited herds caused farmers to realize the economic advantages in eliminating bovine tuberculosis. In 1918-19, state and Federal veterinarians tested 2,920 cattle. Of this number, 9.5 per cent reacted. In the fiscal year 1954, 238,747 animals were tested. The reaction percentage was 0.10.[10] The state department may quarantine all cattle within a county or municipality if the reaction exceeds 0.5 per cent.[11] The average state indemnity paid in the fiscal year 1954 to farmers with diseased cattle was $82.10. An average Federal indemnity of $27.72 plus an average salvage value of $108.89 enabled owners to recoup a total of $218.70 per head on condemned animals.[12]

In cooperation with the Federal Bureau of Animal Industry, an extensive testing program is carried on, designed to eliminate brucellosis. This disease, common to cattle and swine, is transmissible to man. The relationship between diseased cattle and undulant fever was officially recognized in 1931 when the state board required special tests of dairy animals shipped into the state. Indemnities were established by the Federal government in 1934 and by the state on a limited basis in 1940.[13] In 1954, the salvage value and the Federal and state indemnities amounted to a total of $205.00, or approximately 65 per cent of the appraised value of each condemned animal.[14]

Bovine tuberculosis and brucellosis are but two of a host of animal diseases. The state endeavors to assist farmers in the prevention, diagnosis, and cure of any disease which may prove harmful to the animal industry. For example, a suspicion of the disease of anthrax in a cow would probably result in a laboratory examination by the state. The Lederle Laboratories in New York State and the United States Pathological

Laboratories in Washington are frequently asked for a confirming diagnosis. If tests confirm the presence of anthrax, the farm is quarantined; infected pastures are burned; barns, yards, and utensils are cleaned and disinfected; and other animals are immunized.

An outbreak of vesicular exanthema in hogs, caused by the feeding of raw garbage, was the source of much concern in 1952. Whatever the disease, in order to protect the public and the industry, the state endeavors to work closely with representatives of the Federal Bureau of Animal Industry. Federal personnel together with representatives of the Bureau of Swine Disease Control—established in 1953—conducted an extensive inspection program. By the end of the fiscal year 1954 the incidence of the disease had been reduced, although all or parts of eighteen counties were under Federal quarantine. As a consequence of the quarantine, restrictions are placed upon the movement of swine.[15]

Not all of the agricultural department's activities are of a purely preventive nature. Legislation was enacted in 1953 requiring the department to "encourage and promote education and interest in the production of pure bred livestock." [16]

Poultry

The state may establish regulations restricting the importation of poultry as a means of preventing the spread of infectious diseases. For example, at the Newark poultry terminal a state inspector checks truck lots. He is authorized to order the destruction of all fowl unfit for human consumption. During the period 1953-54, 5,886,000 birds were inspected at poultry terminals and over 39,000 were condemned.[17] Departmental representatives also inspect poultry markets and individual flocks throughout the state. Tests are made to discover the presence of Newcastle, Pullorum, and other diseases.

A fresh egg in New Jersey is required by law to be something more than an egg of recent origin.* In 1934 the State Poultry Association was instrumental in obtaining the passage of a law defining a fresh egg, New Jersey fancy grade, as one with an air cell one-eighth inch or less in depth, the yolk visible, the white firm and clear, and the germ showing no visible development.[18] The enforcement of the fresh egg law was made the responsibility of the secretary of agriculture, who was authorized to examine the eggs offered for sale in any store or market. A person violating the law was made subject to a penalty of up to $25 for the first offense and up to $50 for each subsequent offense, the penalty to be obtained through action in a court of law. State inspectors and state-licensed inspectors assist in the enforcement of the fresh egg law. During 1953-54, out of 9,469 stores inspected, there were 1,458 violations. There were no prose-

* New Jersey State Certified Fresh Eggs are specially packaged, high-quality eggs which are candled under state supervision.

cutions although warnings were issued by the department in 441 instances. Thirteen violations resulted in hearings.[19]

LICENSING OF DEALERS

Persons engaging in the business of buying or selling cattle, poultry, milk, and perishable agricultural commodities are required to be licensed by the secretary of agriculture. For example, the secretary may investigate the record of an applicant who wishes to deal in cattle. If he finds that the individual has violated the laws or regulations governing the movement of cattle, the application may be denied. The secretary may also revoke a license. However, a hearing must be granted the holder of the license, and he must be given a copy of the complaint at least ten days prior to the hearing. The secretary's action in refusing to grant a license or in revoking a license is subject to review by the Superior Court.

PLANT INDUSTRY

Legislation to prevent the introduction and spread of insects injurious to plants was first passed in 1898 when the office of state entomologist was created.[20] In 1911 the office of state plant pathologist was established to control dangerous plant diseases.[21] When the Department of Agriculture was set up in 1916, insect and plant inspectional activities were combined.

Nursery Inspection

The department now inspects annually all nurseries within the state. If the nursery is found to be free of injurious insects and plant diseases, a certificate of inspection is issued. Nurserymen and dealers are required to attach a copy of the certificate to parcels of stock which are being sold. During 1953-54, 602 nurseries were inspected.[22] Where diseases dangerous to plants are found, the department may require remedial action, it may embargo the shipment of the plants, or it may order the plants destroyed.

Nursery stock shipped in from other states is frequently checked notwithstanding the presence of a certificate of inspection. Although imported plants may be inspected, the department relies upon the work of Federal inspectors at ports of entry. Persons who bring plants into the state are required to notify the department within twenty-four hours.

Insect Pest Control

Perhaps the largest single effort in protecting the state's plant life was the successful battle waged against the gypsy moth during the twelve year period 1920-1932. In cooperation with the United States Department of Agriculture, the department organized a special crew to cover an infested area of over 400 square miles centering around Somerville. In 1923, 423 men were employed on this one project. The state and Federal governments each spent over $1,000,000 in eliminating, at least temporarily, gypsy moth infestations. The Japanese beetle has proved to be a more formidable foe. A somewhat similar cooperative project has retarded, but not eliminated, this enemy of plant life.[23] Annual surveys are conducted to determine the action to be taken against the European corn borer and the golden nematode of potatoes.

Seed Certification

Certification programs have been developed in order to make possible the use of high-quality seed. Departmental inspectors examine and certify seed tomatoes, potatoes, corn, rye, oats, and other grains. Certified seed has been declared to be "the foundation of good agriculture."

MARKETING

The Department of Agriculture conducts a broad program of marketing services, both promotional and regulatory. Farmer groups are well organized. The poultry association, the potato association, the horticultural society, the grange, the farm bureau, and the farmers' union—these illustrate the horizontal and vertical methods of organization through which farmers make their wants known both as a collective group and as specialized producers. The department works closely with these organizations in an effort to assist the individual farmer and to promote the demand for New Jersey's agricultural products.

Crop Reporting Services

Information on market conditions and prices is disseminated by telephone, radio, and departmental publications. By means of the *Weekly Market Review, Auction News, Truck Crop News,* and *Market Conditions,* agricultural information of both a general and specialized nature is sent to farmers on a seasonal and year round basis.

Farmers have several means of selling their products. The state assists in the organization of "farmers markets" in the metropolitan areas and in some of the larger cities. Produce is made available both to the wholesale and retail trade. At special "shipping point markets" farmers may bring products for purchase by wholesalers. Most fruits and vegetables are sold through these farmer-owned cooperative associations, although a number of specialty products such as apples, white potatoes, and sweet potatoes are sold through private dealers. State services include the developing of new marketing programs, advising on improved selling practices such as the choice of package and the method of packing, and promoting discussion meetings of marketing groups.

The state has long preached to farmers the dollars and cents value of standardized grading and packing. Legislation in 1921 authorized the department to establish grades and to collect inspection service fees from groups which adopted the grading system.[24] State and Federal grades are identical except where special categories seem desirable for New Jersey producers.

Cooperatives

For many years the state has taken an active part in the promotion and operation of farmers' cooperative associations. In addition to assisting in the organization and incorporation of these cooperatives, state representatives have helped in the establishment of accounting procedures and in standardizing the grades of fruits and vegetables. Nine fruit and vegetable auction markets owned and controlled by farmers in 1954 sold 3,917,621 packages valued at $8,012,772. Livestock auction markets are both cooperative and private in character while poultry and egg auction markets are exclusively cooperative. Marketing, selling, and service agricultural cooperatives totalled 114 in 1955.*

Each cooperative is required to file copies of the certificate of incorporation with the secretary of state and the secretary of agriculture. Copies of financial statements must be submitted annually. In order to obtain compliance with this law, the legislature in 1951 provided for the dissolution by proclamation of any cooperative which failed to submit a report three years in succession.[25]

Milk Control

State controls were first imposed upon the dairy industry in 1933. New Jersey producers shared in the general chaos which resulted from the falling off of consumer purchasing during the depression. The legislature declared that unjust, destructive, and demoralizing practices in the production and distribution of milk constituted a danger to the public peace and safety. In an effort to stabilize the industry, a Milk Control Board was created with authority to license dealers and fix prices. The board operated as an independent agency until 1949, when it was transferred to the Department of Agriculture and renamed the Office of Milk Industry.†

* Most cooperatives are organized under the Agricultural Cooperative Association Act. Others are incorporated under the Associations not for Pecuniary Profits Act or the General Corporation Law. *Thirty-fourth Annual Report,* p. 87.

† The number of members on the board has fluctuated. Originally there were three, the secretary of the Board of Agriculture, a member of the State Board of Health, and one person appointed by the governor. L., 1933, ch. 169, p. 353. The number was increased to five in 1935, all appointed by the governor to serve at his pleasure. L., 1935, ch. 175, p. 412. In 1941, the board was reduced to three members named in the act. Their successors were to be appointed by the legislature in joint session. A director of milk control, appointed by the board, was authorized to issue and enforce orders, rules and regulations. L., 1941, ch. 274, p. 713. Under the reorganization of 1948, the board was abolished, and an Office of

The problem of establishing effective controls has proved to be extremely vexing. The state must endeavor to protect three groups, producers, processors and distributors, and consumers. Each group is interested primarily in its own welfare, and a regulation designed to assist one group may work severe hardship upon one or both of the others.

Controls to assist the producer involve obtaining a price for his milk which provides a fair return, enforcing payment for milk purchased, establishing quality standards, and regulating the quantity of milk produced. Controls to help the processors and distributors must take into account the interests of (1) the processor who is responsible for pasteurizing, refrigerating, bottling and transporting the milk; (2) the dealer, who may also be a processor, and who sells to subdealers, stores, and perhaps directly to the consumer; (3) the subdealer; and (4) the store. These groups are interested in controls which allow a sufficient spread between the amount paid to the producer and the amount charged the consumer so that the processing and distribution function may be carried on at a profit. The consumer's main interest is in obtaining a plentiful supply of wholesome milk at a reasonable price.

Prices may be fixed by regulation of the Office of Milk Industry. A change in price may not be made without notice of the proposed change and public hearings. For some years price controls applied to dealer relationships and to consumers as well as to the producer. Mounting costs of production and surpluses in the supply have complicated the problems of control.

Persons directly affected by an order of the Office of Milk Industry are entitled to judicial review. The appellate division of the Superior Court is authorized to affirm, suspend, reverse, vacate, or modify the order if the "substantial rights of the appellant have been prejudiced . . . . " [26]

OTHER ACTIVITIES

Agricultural Education and Research

Agricultural education and research in New Jersey was formally begun in 1864 when the Scientific School operated by Rutgers College was designated to receive the interest from the funds made possible by the land grant college [Morrill] act of 1862.[27] Federal grants of land were made to those states agreeing to establish and support schools for the promotion of agriculture, and the mechanic arts.[28] An Agricultural Experiment Station was established by the state in 1880 with headquarters on the Rutgers campus.[29]

Milk Industry was created in the Department of Agriculture. The director of the office is appointed by the governor with the advice and consent of the Senate. L., 1948, ch. 447, p. 1777.

Eight years later a second experiment station was also located on the Rutgers campus. This resulted from the decision of Congress to promote research at each of the state agricultural colleges. New Jersey accepted the provisions of the Hatch Act, and the Agricultural College Experiment Station was established.[30] The two stations were immediately placed under one director. At present, the two are operated as a single unit under the title New Jersey Agricultural Experiment Station.

The College of Agriculture and the Experiment Station operate an educational program of wide scope. The college offers undergraduates the choice of five programs in agriculture, and one each in agricultural engineering, pre-forestry, and wildlife conservation. In addition, it offers short courses carrying no college credit, and programs of graduate study leading to advanced degrees. The Extension Service acts as a "field teaching arm" making available to the people of the state, both rural and urban, a variety of educational services. The Extension Service programs may be classified in three broad categories: (1) work with adults in all phases of agriculture, (2) work with adults in the field of home economics, and (3) youth programs in agriculture and home economics.[31]

The research program of the college and the Experiment Station has been of a twofold character. An effort has been made to balance experimentation designed to solve immediate agricultural problems with research of a more fundamental nature.

The Experiment Station serves as a regulatory and control agency in connection with the inspection, analysis and sale, of seeds, fertilizers, and insecticides. Distributors of so called "economic poisons," that is, insecticides, fungicides, rodenticides, and herbicides, are required to register their products with the state chemist at the Agricultural Experiment Station. He is empowered, after notice and hearing, to issue rules and regulations concerning their sale and distribution.[32]

Soil Conservation

The value and use of land depends upon a number of factors. For agricultural purposes, the type and quality of soil, the slope of the land, and the degree of erosion are important. Improper land use has resulted in water and wind erosion which in turn have reduced productivity by as much as twenty to fifty per cent.

In order to combat improper land use, soil conservation districts have been established in a number of areas. The governing body of the district is a committee of three supervisors appointed by a State Soil Conservation Committee.[33] Technicians of the Federal Soil Conservation Service are assigned to the districts. For example, the Freehold Soil Conservation District includes Monmouth, Middlesex, and Mercer counties.[34] In 1947 there were six districts covering eighteen counties. Each district is a governmental subdivision of the state empowered to adopt and enforce land use regulations. The supervisors are authorized to present a bill of complaint to the court against landowners who refuse to observe the regulations. Contour farming, the provision of windbreaks, crop rotation, and forest planting are among the conservation practices designed to increase the productivity of the land.

NOTES

[1] U.S. Department of Agriculture, *Agricultural Statistics, 1955* (Washington, 1956), pp. 203, 373, 421.

[2] N.J. Department of Agriculture, *Thirty-ninth Annual Report of the New Jersey State Department of Agriculture, July 1, 1953, to June 30, 1954* (Trenton, 1954), p. 7. For a recent account of farming in New Jersey, see John T. Cunningham, *Garden State* (New Brunswick: Rutgers University Press, 1955).

[3] L., 1872, ch. 546, p. 97.

[4] Harry B. Weiss, *History of the New Jersey State Board of Agriculture, 1872-1916* (Trenton: New Jersey Agricultural Society, 1949), pp. 31-36.

[5] L., 1916, ch. 268, p. 561.

[6] L., 1948, ch. 447, p. 1777.

[7] L., 1944, ch. 202, p. 722.

[8] L., 1950, ch. 293, p. 990.

[9] L., 1880, ch. 220, p. 322.

[10] *Thirty-ninth Annual Report . . . , op. cit.,* p. 48.

[11] L., 1945, ch. 204, p. 701.

[12] *Thirty-seventh Annual Report of the New Jersey State Department of Agriculture, July 1, 1951 to June 30, 1952* (Trenton, 1952), p. 46.

[13] L., 1940, ch. 231, p. 903. The state will not indemnify an owner for more than 8 per cent of the herd in any one year.

[14] *Thirty-ninth Annual Report . . . , op. cit.,* pp. 80-81.

[15] *Ibid.,* pp. 61-66.

[16] L., 1953, ch. 302, p. 1843.

[17] *Thirty-ninth Annual Report . . . , op. cit.,* p. 31.

[18] L., 1934, ch. 146, p. 383.

[19] *Thirty-ninth Annual Report . . . , op. cit.,* p. 140.

[20] L., 1898, ch. 104, p. 166.

[21] L., 1911, ch. 54, p. 80.

[22] *Thirty-ninth Annual Report . . . , op. cit.,* p. 147.

[23] Harry B. Weiss, *The New Jersey Department of Agriculture, 1916-1949* (Trenton: New Jersey Agricultural Society, 1950), pp. 167-89, 224-28.

[24] L., 1921, ch. 83, p. 134.

[25] L., 1951, ch. 303, p. 1085.

[26] L., 1948, ch. 447, p. 1782.

[27] L., 1864, ch. 369, p. 650.

[28] U.S. Statutes-at-Large, 1862, ch. 130, p. 503.

[29] L., 1880, ch. 106, p. 137.

[30] L., 1888, ch. 97, p. 129.

[31] *Science and the Land, the 71st Annual Report of the New Jersey Agricultural Experiment Station, 1949-50* (New Brunswick: Rutgers University, n.d.), p. 134.

[32] L., 1951, ch. 316, p. 1123.

[33] L., 1937, ch. 139, p. 319.

[34] *Monmouth County Soils, Their Nature, Conservation, and Use,* College of Agriculture and Experiment Station, Rutgers University, New Brunswick, New Jersey, in cooperation with The Soil Conservation Service, U.S. Department of Agriculture, Bulletin 738, 1948, p. 16.

CHAPTER 19

Conservation and Economic Development

THE PROTECTION and development of the state's natural and economic resources include a host of separate programs. Prior to 1944 each program was operated independently. At that time seven agencies * were brought together in the Department of Economic Development.[1] The following year eleven agencies † were merged into the Department of Conservation.[2] In 1948 these departments and the Department of Aviation were merged to form the Department of Conservation and Economic Development.[3]

The department is headed by a commissioner who is charged with organizing and administering its work. He is appointed by the governor, with the advice and consent of the Senate, to serve at the pleasure of the governor during his term of office and until a successor has been appointed and qualified. The 1948 reorganization law established five operating divisions.‡ Four of five division heads are appointed by the governor with the advice and consent of the Senate. The fifth is appointed by an advisory

---

* State Planning Board, State Housing Authority, New Jersey Council, South Jersey Transit Commission, Port Raritan District Commission, State Service Officer, Municipal Aid Administration.

† Board of Fish and Game Commissioners, Board of Shell Fisheries, Department of Conservation and Development, Commission on Historic Sites, Commissioners of High Point Park, Grover Cleveland Birth-Place Association, New Jersey Veterans of All Wars Memorial Association, Commissioners of Edison Park, State Water Policy Commission, Passaic Valley Flood Control Commission, Department of Commerce and Navigation.

‡ Planning and Development, Veterans Services, Fish and Game, Shell Fisheries, Water Policy and Supply. The law authorized the establishment of an Administrative Division at the discretion of the commissioner.

council with the approval of the governor. The director of any division may be removed by the governor for cause, after notice and opportunity to be heard.

FOREST MANAGEMENT

Approximately 3,200 square miles or over 40 per cent of the state's land area consists of forests and scrub growth. The forests of North Jersey are principally mixed hardwoods with oak predominating; the pine region of South Jersey is practically a wilderness area. In many parts of the state the wooded areas are in poor condition as a result of improper cutting and forest fires.

The problem of protecting the forestland was recognized as early as 1885. The legislature authorized a special survey in 1894 and eleven years later made provision for a Forest Park Reservation Commission to obtain lands for state forests and to combat the forest fire menace.[4] The functions of the commission were transferred to the Department of Conservation and Development in 1915.[5] At present, state functions pertaining to forest management cover a wide range of activities.

Protection Against Fires

Efforts to improve forest land are useless unless fires can be prevented or controlled. Fire ruins the timber, injures the soil, destroys the wildlife, and affects the water supply. The control of forest fires has been called the "basic problem of conservation in New Jersey." [6] The number of fires and the acreage burned are shown in Table 17.

TABLE 17

FOREST FIRES, 1914-1950

Period	Average Annual No. of Fires	Average Annual Acreage Burned
1914-1923	836	86,000
1924-1933	1,210	70,000
1934-1943	1,636	36,000
1944-1950	1,216	20,057

Source: William J. Seidel, "New Jersey Defense and Forest Fires," *New Jersey Municipalities,* XXVIII (November, 1951), 14.

The state operates a Forest Fire Service headed by a state firewarden. Section firewardens are responsible for sections of approximately 100,000 acres each. These, in turn, are subdivided into districts. Section and district firewardens are responsible for the supervision of the crews of radio-equipped motorized units and portable pumping units. Alarms are transmitted to the wardens chiefly through watchers in over twenty strategically located lookout towers. The fire service makes use of powered pumping equipment, tractors, plows, a two-way radio communication system covering about ninety stations, and other modern fire-fighting devices.[7]

During a dry season, the governor may, by proclamation, close the forests to the public. He may also suspend or curtail the open seasons for fish and game. The proclamation becomes effective upon twenty-four hours notice.[8]

Reforestation

Almost one quarter of the land area of New Jersey is unproductive. Much of the unproductive area is privately owned and consists of abandoned farms in North Jersey and cut over or burned areas in South Jersey. Most of the abandoned farm land is of a marginal character for agricultural purposes.

The state enedavors to promote the rehabilitation of those areas which have potential value for forestry, recreation, and wildlife. For example, owners of forest properties have been encouraged to establish "tree farms."

State Forest Nursery. Seedlings for reforestation may be obtained from a state nursery at Washington Crossing in Mercer County. The seedlings are used in state forests, parks, and on the grounds of state institutions, and are sold to private landowners. Since 1926, when the state nursery was established, over 40,000,000 seedlings have been distributed for reforestation.

Private Forest Management. Timber cutting on private lands is not subject to public regulation. However, the state offers technical guidance to private owners concerning problems such as the best species of tree for the location; planting and cutting practices; rates of growth and yield; and marketing methods. The state also operates sample plots where studies are conducted on various phases of forest management such as thinning and improvement cutting, and the effects of cutting on wildlife.

STATE LANDS AND PARKS

The state has broad powers to acquire lands for forest park reserves and reservations. It may purchase, lease, sell, or exchange lands or it may exercise the power of eminent domain. However, New Jersey has been slow to obtain and develop public recreational facilities. In 1950 the state owned 129,907 acres of forests, parks, and fish and game preserves. This total amounted to 26 acres per one thousand people. By contrast, Pennsylvania owned 289 acres and New York 208 acres per thousand population.[9]

In order to obtain a greater degree of utilization of public lands, a Land Use Committee was established in 1954. The committee consists of staff members from units of the Department of Conservation and Economic Development. Previously, land purchased for public shooting and fishing grounds was usually limited to that one purpose alone. Summer recreational use was not considered. The function of the Land Use Committee is to develop a program by means of which the state's forests, parks, historic sites, hunting and fishing grounds, and other lands may serve a wider public use.[10]

State Forests

In 1955 New Jersey had eleven state forests totalling approximately 150,000 acres. The management of the forests has been designed to accomplish four objectives: (1) to provide public recreation facilities, (2) to produce timber, (3) to protect the water supply and control erosion, and (4) to support wildlife. The forests serve also as laboratory and demonstration areas for management studies. The location, date of acquisition, and acreage of the state forests are listed in Table 18.

TABLE 18

STATE FORESTS

State Forest	Acquired	County	Acreage
Bass River	1905	Burlington and Ocean	9,270
Belleplain	1928	Cape May and Cumberland	6,492
Green Bank	1930	Burlington and Atlantic	1,833
Jackson	1915	Ocean	43
Jenny Jump	1931	Warren	967
Lebanon	1908	Burlington and Ocean	22,185
Norvin Green	1947	Passaic	2,260
Penn	1910	Burlington	2,958
Stokes	1907	Sussex	12,429
Abraham S. Hewitt	1951	Passaic	1,890
Wharton Estate	1954	Atlantic, Burlington and Camden	90,000
TOTAL			150,327

State Parks

The state maintained twenty-three parks in 1955. Several had been developed primarily for recreational purposes. Others had some historic significance. Not all areas designated as parks had been developed for public use. Table 19 lists the state parks by date of acquisition, by county, and by acreage.

Historic Sites

The state also owns and maintains a number of historic sites. In 1954 there were seventeen homes, monuments, or other places of historic interest under the administration of the Department of Conservation and Economic Development.

TABLE 19

STATE PARKS

State Park	Acquired	County	Acreage
Allaire	1940	Monmouth	1,170
Barnegat Lighthouse	1951	Ocean	32
Cheesequake	1938	Middlesex	962
Cranberry Lake	1925	Sussex	109
Edison	1947	Middlesex	30
Farny	1944	Morris	803
Fort Mott	1947	Salem	104
Hacklebarney	1924	Morris	193
High Point	1923	Sussex	10,935
Hopatcong	1925	Sussex-Morris	107
Island Beach	1953	Ocean	2,200
Mt. Laurel	1908	Burlington	20
Musconetcong	1925	Sussex-Morris	343
Parvin	1931	Salem	967
Princeton Battlefield	1946	Mercer	39
Ringwood Manor	1936	Passaic	545
Saxton Falls	1925	Morris-Warren	9
Stephens	1937	Morris-Warren	237
Swartswood	1914	Sussex	704
Voorhees	1929	Hunterdon	428
Washington Crossing	1912	Mercer	373
Washington Rock	1947	Somerset	27
Worthington	1954	Warren	6,200
TOTAL			26,337

Riparian Lands

Land under the tidal waters within the state belongs to the state. The owner of the bank or ripa has no legal claim to lands between the high and low water mark. However, the legislature has given the riparian owner a "preemptive right." That is, he may obtain a grant or lease from the state. If he takes no action, the state may make the grant to another person or to a corporation. However, the grant is not effective until six months after the riparian proprietor has been notified. He receives compensation for his interest in an amount set by the state.[11] The State permits utility companies to lay underwater cables, water mains and pipe lines for oil and gas. These permits are called "easements." Title to the state's land is not conveyed as in the case of a grant. Instead the corporation has a permanent crossing right.

Cases of illegal occupancy of the state's riparian lands, called purprestures, are frequently discovered. Often owners of residential properties, unfamiliar with the necessity for obtaining riparian rights, build piers on the state's property. Cases are referred to the attorney general when the owner ignores the state's notice of his illegal occupancy.

By means of price maps and field investigations, the state establishes riparian values.*   The sale and lease of riparian lands, together with the income from invested funds, has resulted in an average annual state income of $500,000 over the last twenty years.[12]

Coast Protection

The ocean front resort industry is the primary source of income to the people of the counties bordering on the Atlantic Ocean.   One of the great threats to the welfare of that industry is beach erosion, a fearsome term to the owners of coastal recreational properties.   Disappearing beaches and unstable dwellings and boardwalks threaten doom to the recreation industry.   A beach eroded is a beach abandoned.

Although the state entered the coast protection field in the early 1920's, it has been only since 1944 that any substantial financial aid has been available to the municipalities.[13]   Projects receiving state approval are eligible for state aid covering one-half of the cost of construction.   However, because of limited state funds no comprehensive plan has been undertaken.   Instead, the policy has been to approve municipal projects on the basis of the urgency of the problem and in the light of available state and municipal funds.   A comprehensive program to solve the erosion problem, it has been estimated, would cost an average of one million dollars per mile of beach.†

A permanent State Beach Erosion Commission was established in 1949. The commission was authorized to provide "ways and means" of preserving the state's 185.9 miles of beachfront.   There are twelve members on the commission, four senators appointed by the president of the Senate, four assemblymen appointed by the speaker of the House, and four public members appointed by the governor.

WATER POLICY

The state's most vital natural resource is water.   Severe droughts in 1944 and again in 1949 focused public attention upon the need for a greatly increased water supply.   The problem was not a new one.   Governor Stokes in 1907 declared that "our potable water supply presents the most important problem before the people of the state . . . .   The use of

---

* The fee charged by the state for a riparian grant is based upon front footage. The location, the stream, the possibilities for development—all are factors in the determination of the rate.   See Frank D. Holmes, "Functions of Division of Navigation Affect Most Counties," *New Jersey Counties,* V (May, 1946), 7.

† At present the accepted practice is to construct all-stone jetties.   Timber and sheet metal have largely been abandoned as a result of the damage caused by sand abrasion, heavy waves, and normal deterioration.   Instead, a center mount of small stone is now enveloped by large stones of from two to seven and in some instances twelve tons each.

this water is so necessary to life that a direct and active control over the diversion thereof for domestic and municipal purposes should be exercised by the state." [14]

Development of State Policy

The legislature authorized the creation of a Water-Supply Commission in 1907 consisting of five persons appointed by the governor.[15] One of the principal functions of the commission was the determination of the watersheds and water sources which municipalities and corporations should be permitted to acquire and develop.

Prior to the passage of the act, private water companies had laid claim to vast watershed areas. The status of their claims was thrown into doubt by an opinion of the court that "in our potable waters we have a vast natural asset belonging to the people, the conservation and purity of which is indispensable to their health and well being." [16] Governor Stokes gave his assurance that legitimate claims would be protected in the pending legislation:

New Jersey deals out equity. She does not confiscate property on technical grounds. Her justice is founded upon right and not upon might. The corporations will receive fair treatment, but they, too, must be fair, and they must not attempt, while their rights are protected, to claim a jurisdiction which would interfere with this necessary public work on the part of the State in the interests of its people.[17]

The new laws fulfilled the governor's promise by providing that municipalities or corporations acquiring lands or water or constructing new works, such as reservoirs, in good faith should be permitted to continue without interference. Future developments were to be approved by the commission. Annual payments to the state were to be made for all diversions of water from streams, lakes, or other sources in excess of the amount being diverted at the time of the passage of the act. No payment was required for a per capita diversion of less than one-hundred gallons daily.*

The principle of state control over the development and diversion of the water supply was extended in 1929 to include "surface, subsurface and percolating waters." A Water Policy Commission inherited the functions of the Water-Supply Commission. This body was charged with "general supervision over all sources of potable and public water supplies." [18] Specific control over large users of wells and artesian water supplies was granted to the Department of Conservation and Economic Development in 1947.[19] As a consequence of the reorganizations of 1945 and 1948, the powers of the water commission are now exercised by the conservation

---

* The city of Trenton challenged the constitutionality of the 1907 statute on the ground that the statute violated the contract clause of the Constitution of the United States. The Supreme Court of the United States upheld a judgment for $14,310 against the city. *City of Trenton* v *New Jersey* 262 U.S. 182 (1922).

department. A Water Policy and Supply Council of nine members performs important operating functions such as determining, after public hearing, the merits of applications for new or additional water supplies by municipalities, private water companies, or industries. The members of the council are appointed by the governor with the advice and consent of the Senate for terms of four years.[20]

State Supervision

State supervision of water resources includes a number of functions designed to conserve and develop those resources. In addition to control over diversion, the state encourages and may require the inter-connection of public water supply systems whether owned by a governmental unit or a private corporation. Automatic recording gauges are maintained at seventy-six stream-gauging stations. Ground water investigations are conducted to obtain data on such problems as the intrusion of salt water into wells, the use of ground water for irrigation, and the possibility of storing excess surface water underground.* State permits are required for the construction of dams and stream encroachments. Dams are inspected periodically in the interest of safety and for flood control. Recently, the state has rehabilitated the Delaware and Raritan Canal and has converted it into a source of industrial water supply.

Water is in short supply in three areas: the northern and southern metropolitan districts and the seashore resort district. The daily volume consumed in 1954 totaled more than 588,000,000 gallons; the breakdown by regions was:[21]

Area	Daily Consumption (millions of gallons)
Northeastern region	435
Southwestern region	84
Coastal region	59
Northwestern region	10
TOTAL	588

The amount of water consumed has increased much more rapidly than the safe yield. For example, in North Jersey the demand and safe yield in millions of gallons daily were as follows:

	Demand	Safe Yield
1940	271	355
1948	390	374
1954	418	420

* Stream gauging and ground water investigations are conducted in cooperation with the United States Geological Survey. The cost is shared equally between the state and Federal Governments.

Throughout the state surface supply sources are used to meet 70 per cent of the demand while underground supplies meet 30 per cent of the need.[22]   The Water Policy Commission has declared that surface water has the advantages of dependability and economy over sub-surface sources. Artesian wells have been resorted to in certain areas because of the lack of storage capacity and the pollution of surface waters.

The supply of water has not kept pace with the increased demands. Industry, particularly, needs large quantities.   For example, an estimated 50 gallons of water are required in processing a case of canned peas; 70,000 gallons are needed to produce one ton of paper.   The lack of adequate supplies acts as a deterrent to industrial development, and is a continuing threat to the health and welfare of the people.   A principal problem is one of obtaining greater storage facilities.[23]   Proposals to establish the Round Valley Reservoir Project in Hunterdon County and the Wharton Water Supply System in South Jersey would, if carried to completion, provide the necessary storage.   However, disagreements over the types of state controls and the possible effects upon the supply of water in the lake regions have prevented legislative approval of any comprehensive project. Legislative authorization in 1956 to purchase the Round Valley site was coupled with a restriction that only Delaware River water could be channeled into the reservoir.

FISH AND GAME

Roughly one person in eighteen in New Jersey has a hunting or fishing license.   The issuance of a quarter million licenses to sportsmen is one means of state control of the supply of fish and game.   A second means is through the establishment and operation of public hunting and shooting grounds.   Over 100,000 acres are available for this purpose.   A third measure of control is by means of fish and game management practices.

Management

The enforcement of the laws is the responsibility of fish and game wardens.   In 1955 a protector, two district protectors, and four assistant district protectors supervised over thirty regular fish and game wardens.   The wardens have the power of summary arrest.   The State Police are also authorized to enforce the fish and game laws.   A small Coastal Patrol Service operates two forty-foot seagoing cruisers and other patrol boats. The coastal patrol is concerned principally with those who violate the commercial fishing laws.

Fish and game are distributed by the state to hunting areas.   For this purpose, pheasants and quail are raised on state-owned farms.   Fish are propagated and distributed from state-owned hatcheries.   Rabbits are purchased in the west.   In the fiscal year 1952, the market value of fish and game liberated was $751,869.[24]   Receipts from hunter's and angler's licenses amounted to $889,065.

Wildlife management activities include the improvement and maintenance of an adequate food supply, the distribution of shrubs to provide cover, the installation of walls and dikes for ponds, and the control of predatory animals such as foxes, hawks, and weasels.   For example, in 1953 a staff of six "predator controlmen" was assigned to protect the state's game and wildlife, and the farmers poultry and livestock, from predators. Incidentally, the great horned owl was listed as the most destructive of all animals and birds of prey.[25]

The sportsmen of the state are well organized and constitute a potent force in the determination of policy and in the administration of the fish and game laws.   An eleven-member Fish and Game Council is charged by law with the formulation of "comprehensive policies" for the protection and propagation of fish and game.   Its actions are subject to the approval of the commissioner of conservation and economic development.   However, the council is not directly responsible to the commissioner.   The governor appoints the Fish and Game Council, with the advice and consent of the Senate, from recommendations submitted by agricultural and sportsmen's groups.*   It is charged with advising the commissioner and the director of the Division of Fish and Game.   Hearings may be held with respect to the activities of the division.   The council is required to report annually to the governor and to the legislature.   The New Jersey Fish and Game Code consists of regulations adopted by the council after public hearings.

The council is responsible for the appointment, subject to the governor's approval, of the director of fish and game.   The director serves at the pleasure of the council.   However, his work is subject to the supervision of the commissioner of conservation and economic development.

Shell Fisheries

Oyster and clam beds lying under the tidal waters are owned by the state.   Any citizen who obtains a license may harvest from the approximately 50,000 acres of shellfish-producing bottom.†   The importance of the shellfish industry may be gauged from the fact that in 1947 it was the principal business in sixty-three of the municipalities of South Jersey.[26]   At one time New Jersey ranked first among the states producing oysters and clams.   At present it ranks fifth.

---

* Three members must be farmers recommended by the agricultural convention, six must be sportsmen recommended by the New Jersey State Federation of Sportsmen's Clubs, and two are required to be commercial fishermen.   Farmer and sportsmen representatives are chosen on a geographical basis. L., 1948, ch. 448, p. 1783.

† Nonresident licenses are issued during the period June-September.   However, the nonresident may not sell oysters and clams. L., 1950, ch. 217, p. 543.

State control of the shellfish industry includes the leasing and protection of lands for the planting and cultivation of oysters and clams and the licensing and regulation of persons taking shellfish from the natural beds. Control is exercised through a Division of Shell Fisheries and a Shell Fisheries Council of nine members.[27] The director of the division is appointed by the governor, with the advice and consent of the Senate, to serve during the governor's term of office and until a successor has been appointed and qualified. The members of the council are appointed by the governor, with the advice and consent of the Senate, for terms of four years. The chairman of the council is designated by the governor. The council sits in two sections, the Maurice River Cove Section and the Atlantic Coast Section.

GEOLOGICAL SURVEY

The need for a geological survey was first recognized by the legislature in 1854. The governor was directed to employ "some competent person or persons" to make the survey and to

. . . describe in sections of one township each, accompanied by proper maps, diagrams, profiles and references, with a full, scientific and practical description of the rocks, minerals, ores, sands, clays, marls, peat, fossils, soils and other substances . . . which may be valuable to the people in the several townships of this state.[28]

The venture proved a too ambitious one and was suspended. A decade later the position of state geologist was created together with an eleven-member Board of Managers of the Geological Survey.[29] Through subsequent legislative changes the board was abolished and the functions of the geological survey absorbed in the Department of Conservation and Economic Development.

The state geologist analyzes rocks and minerals with a view to determining their properties and their uses. Geologic studies and maps are made of areas in which there is particular interest. In recent years ground-water problems have been a source of hundreds of requests for information. The state maintains a list of bench marks showing the height above sea level of many hundreds of places.[30] The exact positions, both horizontally and vertically, of approximately 6,000 points have been determined and made available for public use. These positions or monuments are of particular value to engineers. Detailed topographic maps are published showing data such as the location of the monuments, political boundaries, and land and water areas.

PLANNING AND ZONING

State Planning

Planning was given recognition as a separate function of the state in 1934 when the legislature created an independent State Planning Board.[31] The board consisted of nine members appointed by the governor with the advice and consent of the Senate. Four of the nine were required to be appointed from among the heads of chief executive offices of state agencies. Governor Moore's appointments failed to be confirmed in the Senate, and it was not until March, 1935, that the board began to function. In the meantime, unofficial studies were carried forward by a staff supplied through the Federal Emergency Relief Administration, a practice which continued for several years.

The board was abolished in 1944 when planning functions and personnel were transferred to the Department of Economic Development.[32] In the 1948 reorganization, planning was included in the functions of the Department of Conservation and Economic Development.

The original act charged the board with coordinating physical development plans of state and local authorities particularly with relation to plans for highways, airports, forests and parks, water supply, flood control, recreation, and land use. A master plan was to be prepared for the over-all development of the state. This plan was published in 1950.[33] It was intended as a long range policy guide in such matters as the acquisition of public lands, highway and institutional construction, and the conservation and development of natural resources.

In 1954 greatly increased emphasis was placed upon the planning function. Consultants were retained to assist an expanded staff in developing over-all state programs in conservation, recreation, and other fields. The planning office was used also as an instrument of the governor in stimulating other state agencies to consider their program needs on a long range basis.

County and Municipal Planning and Zoning

The state has endeavored to stimulate planning in counties and municipalities. It furnishes advisory assistance by means of informative literature, special studies, and an annual survey of the status of planning and zoning. Municipal planning boards were first authorized in 1930.[34] Permissive legislation was passed in 1935 authorizing the establishment of county and regional planning boards.[35] In 1955 there were 343 municipal planning boards and 12 county planning boards.

Zoning, a phase of planning, was authorized by constitutional amendment in 1927. By 1955, 386 municipalities had enacted zoning ordinances. These were designed to promote the orderly use of properties and to protect communities from harmful development.[36]

A major revision of the planning laws was enacted in 1953. The legislature permits municipalities to have as much or as little planning as they may wish. The governing body of a municipality may, by ordinance, create a planning board to consist of from five to nine members. The mayor is required to be a member, together with one of the governing body selected by it. The other planning board members are appointed by the mayor from citizens of the municipality. The chairman of the board is selected by the members from among the appointed citizens. No member may act on any matter in which he has any personal or financial interest. The planning board is also the zoning commission.

Under the new law the governing body is the final planning authority. Subdivision regulations in effect at the time of the passage of the act were required to be adopted by ordinance of the governing body by July 1, 1954. If not adopted, they were of no effect. If, under the new law, the governing body authorizes the planning board to regulate subdivisions, the governing body is required, by ordinance, to establish standards for the board's guidance. Any person aggrieved by the action of the board may appeal to the governing body and to the courts.[37]

Housing and Slum Clearance

Public housing as a function of the state stems from the creation of the New Jersey State Housing Authority in 1933.[38] The powers and duties of the authority were vested in a five-member governing body whose primary function was to provide housing for families of low income. Slum clearance projects were approved by the authority for Atlantic City and Camden. Construction costs were financed primarily by Federal funds. In 1938, the legislature authorized the creation of local housing authorities. The state agency then limited itself to cooperating with the United States Housing Authority and to advising and assisting local authorities.[39] In 1944 the New Jersey Housing Authority was abolished and its functions transferred to the Department of Economic Development.

The state adopted a more vigorous policy following World War II. A public emergency was declared to exist with reference to housing for veterans. Individual municipalities were required to assume responsibility for determining the need, the type of structure, and the site. State financial grants were made available exclusively for construction. Other costs, such as land acquisition and the installation of streets and utilities, were to be paid by the municipality. A total of 41 million dollars of state money was made available for construction. The legislature appropriated 6 million dollars in 1946 out of a post-war reserve account. In the same year, public approval was given for a $35,000,000 bond issue.

Management of the completed projects was made the responsibility of the municipality. State laws required that veterans be given first preference; otherwise the selection of tenants was handled by the local community. The amount of rent to be charged was fixed by agreement between the municipality and the state. Rent proceeds, after the deduction of maintenance costs and in lieu tax payments, were to be divided between the state and the municipality according to the amount each had invested.

All told, 7,733 units were constructed in approximately 125 municipalities and in four state educational institutions—Rutgers University and the state teachers colleges at Glassboro, Montclair, and Trenton. Construction was of several types, from converted barracks to permanent apartment buildings. Over 4,000 of the units were classified as temporary. The state investment amounted approximately to $38,000,000 while the municipalities expended over $14,000,000.[40]

A more ambitious state housing project was proposed by the legislature in 1949.[41] Funds were to be allocated by a public housing and development authority for several types of housing. The funds were to be obtained from the sale of $100,000,000 in state bonds. The project collapsed when the public referendum to increase the state debt failed of approval.

The state has enacted legislation which authorizes municipalities to proceed with the rehabilitation of blighted areas. The Urban Redevelopment Law of 1946 provided that municipalities could acquire lands on which were located "substandard, unsafe, unsanitary, dilapidated or obsolescent" dwellings.[42] These lands could then be leased to insurance companies and banking institutions under a contract providing for the rehabilitation of the blighted area. A municipality, by ordinance, may also create a redevelopment agency. Regional development agencies may be established by two or more municipalities.[43] After a determination by the municipal governing body that a blighted area exists, the agency may proceed with the rehabilitation of the area. Plans of the agency must be approved by the municipality. Financial assistance may be obtained from the Federal government upon the presentation of a satisfactory program of urban renewal.[44]

ECONOMIC PROMOTIONAL ACTIVITIES

State action to attract commerce and industry has changed markedly over the years. The present-day approach is a far cry from the nineteenth century practice of providing special charters. The generous terms of these charters were in themselves an enticement to locate or at least to incorporate in New Jersey. After 1875, liberal general incorporation laws were enacted. Thereafter, an application to the secretary of state accompanied by a relatively inconsequential fee and the payment of a small franchise tax provided the applicant with a corporate charter. By the early twentieth century the state had become notorious for its easy policies toward the chartering of business corporations. In more recent years New Jersey has given way to other states.[45]

Efforts to "sell" New Jersey are now of a much different type. Illustrated brochures are distributed and newspaper and radio advertising is used to depict New Jersey's advantages, such as its proximity to mass markets and its skilled manpower. The emphasis is upon attracting industry and upon bringing out-of-state capital into New Jersey. However, other facets of the economy are not neglected. For example, industries and farm associations cooperate with the state in the promotion of farm produce; and New Jersey's advantages as a recreation and resort area have been widely heralded. An effort is made also to promote local pride in New Jersey through a variety of intrastate educational activities.

NOTES

[1] L., 1944, ch. 85, p. 168.

[2] L., 1945, ch. 22, p. 62.

[3] L., 1948, ch. 448, p. 1783.

[4] E. B. Moore, *Forest Management in New Jersey* (Trenton: N.J. Department of Conservation and Development, 1939), p. 13.

[5] L., 1915, ch. 241, p. 426.

[6] Moore, *op. cit.*, p. 10.

[7] William J. Seidel, "Forest Fires in New Jersey," *New Jersey Municipalities,* XXVII (March, 1950), 10-12.

[8] L., 1948, ch. 11, p. 59.

[9] *Development Plan for New Jersey, A Report upon Planning Surveys, Planning Studies, and a Comprehensive Plan for the State of New Jersey* (Trenton: Planning Section, Bureau of Planning and Development, Department of Conservation and Economic Development, 1950), p. 24.

[10] For a summary of the condition of the state's forests, parks, and other lands in 1954, see "Address of Commissioner Joseph E. McLean," *New Jersey Recreation Development,* V (January, 1955), 1-5.

[11] L., 1869, ch. 383, p. 1017. See *Landis v Sea Isle City,* 129 N.J. Eq. 217 (1941). For a statement of the state ownership of lands under water, see *Stevens v Paterson and Newark Railroad Co.,* 34 N.J.L. 532 (1870).

[12] N.J. *Second Annual Report of the Commissioner of Conservation for the Period July 1, 1946, to June 30, 1947* (1948), p. 62.

[13] L., 1944, ch. 93, p. 242.

[14] N.J. *Report of the State Water-Supply Commission to the Legislature of New Jersey, 1908* (Trenton: The John L. Murphy Publishing Co., Printers, 1908), p. 6.

[15] L., 1907, ch. 252, p. 633. Prior to this act the state geologist had been charged with a "general oversight" of the streams and lakes to insure their use for the benefit of all the people. L., 1905, ch. 238, p. 461.

[16] Quoted in *Report of State Water-Supply Commission . . . , op. cit.,* p. 6.

[17] Quoted in *ibid.,* p. 8-9.

[18] L., 1929, ch. 267, p. 635.

[19] L., 1947, ch. 375, p. 1192.

[20] L., 1948, ch. 448, p. 1783.

[21] Tippetts, Abbett, McCarthy, and Stratton, *Survey of New Jersey Water Resources Development,* Legislative Commission on Water Supply, State of New Jersey (New York, 1955), IV-13.

[22] *Development Plan for New Jersey . . . , op. cit.,* p. 18.

[23] Statement of Dr. Thurlow C. Nelson, Chairman, Water Policy and Supply Council, in *Public Hearing* on Assembly Bill 246 (Trenton, May 17, 1954, mimeographed), p. 4. For an annotated bibliography on the subject of water supply, see New Jersey Taxpayers Association, *Water Supply Studies in New Jersey* (Trenton, 1954).

[24] *Annual Report New Jersey Department of Conservation and Economic Development Division of Fish and Game, 1952* (Trenton), p. 9.

[25] *New Jersey Outdoors,* III (March, 1953), 5.

[26] N.J. *Second Annual Report* . . . , *op. cit.,* p. 77.

[27] L., 1948, ch. 448, p. 783.

[28] L., 1854, ch. 74, p. 176.

[29] L., 1864, ch. 337, p. 591.

[30] N.J. Report of the Department of Conservation and Development, Bulletin 21 (Geologic Series), *A List of Bench Marks in New Jersey* (Trenton, 1921).

[31] L., 1934, ch. 178, p. 429.

[32] L., 1944, ch. 85, p. 168.

[33] *Development Plan for New Jersey* . . . , *op. cit.*

[34] L., 1930, ch. 235, p. 1039.

[35] L., 1935, ch. 251, p. 767.

[36] N.J. Department of Conservation and Economic Development, *Annual Report, 1954-55* (Trenton), p. 10.

[37] L., 1953, ch. 433, p. 2168.

[38] L., 1933, ch. 444, p. 175.

[39] Dorothy Schaffter, *State Housing Agencies* (New York: Columbia University Press), pp. 405-50.

[40] N.J. Department of Conservation and Economic Development, *Annual Report, 1954-55* (Trenton), p. 75.

[41] L., 1949, ch. 303, p. 929.

[42] L., 1946, ch. 52, p. 109.

[43] L., 1949, ch. 306, p. 976.

[44] Randy Haskell Hamilton, "The New Look in Slum Clearance and Urban Development," *New Jersey Municipalities,* XXXI (October, 1954), 15-19.

[45] John W. Cadman, Jr., *The Corporation in New Jersey* (Cambridge: Harvard University Press, 1949), pp. 419-41.

CHAPTER 20

Transportation

THE HIGHWAYS of New Jersey are among the most heavily traveled in the world. Three factors are responsible. As one of the most densely populated and industrialized areas in the nation, there is within the state a natural movement of people and commerce which in itself is the source of a great volume of passenger car, bus, and truck traffic. Although one of the smallest states in area, New Jersey in 1954 had a total of 1,928,077 automobiles, buses, and trucks, and ranked eighth in total motor vehicle registration.[1] A considerable part of the state's traffic arises from the normal commuting of many hundreds of thousands of New Jersey residents who work in New York and Philadelphia. A second factor is that New Jersey acts as a corridor for the Atlantic seaboard, carrying a large part of the commerce flowing to and from the south and west. Finally, New Jersey's seashore resorts attract not only vacationers from many parts of the country but serve as a magnet for weekly excursions of literally millions in the metropolitan areas of New York and Philadelphia.

DEPARTMENT OF HIGHWAYS

Organization

New Jersey was the first state in the union officially to recognize the highway problem as one which was, in part, the responsibility of the state itself. Legislation passed in 1891 provided state aid for roads improved under the auspices of the boards of chosen freeholders.[2] In 1894 the office of state commissioner of public roads was created, a position paying five dollars a day and expenses when the incumbent was actually working.[3]

A highway department was established in 1917. At that time, a commission of eight members, plus the governor in an ex officio capacity, was charged with administering the department.[4]   The commission was authorized to delegate the hiring of employees to a state highway engineer or his assistant, both of whom were appointed by the commission. It was charged also with laying out a highway system for the state, the general pattern of which was already established by the legislature's action in designating fifteen routes.[5]   In 1923, shortly after Governor George S. Silzer took office, the membership of the commission was reduced to four.[6]   Following a series of administrative studies, in each of which the highway department came in for a considerable amount of criticism, commission control was abolished.   In 1935, after Governor Harold Hoffman, in his inaugural address, had called for an end to the practice of mixing "politics, cement, and tar in our highway construction and maintenance," [7] a law was passed establishing a single commissioner as head of the department.*

State Highway Commissioner

The state highway commissioner is nominated and appointed by the governor with Senate consent to serve at the governor's pleasure and until a successor has been appointed and qualified.[8]   As the administrative and executive head of the department, he is required by law to devote full time to his office.

The highway commissioner has full authority to organize the department as he may desire.   The only legislative commands with reference to the departmental organization are that the commissioner shall appoint a state highway engineer and an assistant state highway engineer.   These officials may be removed by the commissioner for cause.

The broad powers of the commissioner over the internal organization and operations of the department extend also to the substantive field of highway construction and maintenance.   He may acquire lands by gift, purchase, or condemnation according to law.   He has authority to determine rules and specifications and to make contracts "covering all matters and things incident to the acquisition, improvement, betterment, construction, reconstruction, maintenance, and repair of state highways." [9]

HIGHWAY SYSTEM

There are approximately 28,000 miles of roads and streets under the jurisdiction of the various governmental units of the state. A classification by type of unit is shown below.

Type of Unit	Mileage
State	1,740
County	6,266

---

* L., 1935, ch. 178, p. 440. The first appointee to the new office was the Governor's secretary, who happened also to be the Republican state chairman.

Township	12,368
Borough	3,568
City	3,154
Town	828
Village	117
TOTAL	28,041 *

The selection of a road as a state highway is accomplished by law or by action of the commissioner. The route number may or may not be specified in the act which spells out the beginning point of the route, the towns through which it passes, and the terminal point. Before the commissioner may take over a road as a part of the state highway, he must give notice to the appropriate governing body and conduct a hearing. However, nearly all of the state system has been determined by action of the legislature. In past years legislated highways were designated often without reference to the highway department's recommendations. Need was sometimes secondary to sectional political considerations.

Of the state-administered roads and streets in 1952, the type of surface was classified as indicated in Table 20. Although the state highway sys-

TABLE 20

STATE-ADMINISTERED HIGHWAYS CLASSIFIED BY TYPE OF SURFACE

Type of Surface	Mileage
Non-surfaced mileage	122
Soil-surfaced	15
Slag, gravel, or stone	212
Bituminous surface treated	55
Mixed bituminous	4
Bituminous penetration	76
Bituminous concrete and sheet asphalt	521
Portland cement concrete	1315
Brick	2
Block	9
TOTAL	2331

Source: U.S. Department of Commerce, Bureau of Public Roads, *Highway Statistics 1952*, p. 117.

tem comprises less than 10 per cent of the total mileage of roads and streets, it carries a large share of the total traffic. The volume of traffic is said to be seven times the national average, over twice that of New York,

* The state mileage in the table is taken from U.S. Department of Commerce, Bureau of Public Roads, *Highway Statistics 1950*, p. 115. The mileage for the other governmental units is taken from N.J. *Road Mileage Survey, as of July 1, 1943* (Trenton: New Jersey State Highway Department, 1943), p. 3. The total mileage, therefore, is an approximation.

and five times that of Pennsylvania.[10]   For example, in 1954 the average daily volume of traffic on Route 1 near Newark was over 68,000 cars.[11] Estimates by the highway department of increased auto registration and travel indicate a need for a two billion dollar highway construction and modernization program over a ten-year period.

Highway Design and Construction

Extensive planning is essential in determining the constituent elements of a comprehensive State highway system and in determining the priority to be given each element.   Several types of traffic data are needed.   These include: traffic counts, surveys of types of traffic, origin and destination surveys, and measures of the weight and wheel loads of trucks.   This information is considered by the highway department in relation to present and prospective land use, development trends, geographical distribution, and other factors.[12]

Research and testing operations are also important not only for determining the quality of materials used in construction, but for assessing the value of newer techniques and interpreting the results of the use of different materials and methods.   Thousands of tests are run each year by the highway department on cement, reinforcing steel, pipe, asphalts and other materials used in construction.   Cores are cut from pavements to determine whether construction specifications are being met.   Field inspectors check a number of items such as sand, stone, and bituminous materials at the point of production.   Basic highway research is carried on by the highway department and by contract with the state university and other institutions with research facilities.

Not the least of the technical problems surrounding the design and construction of a highway system is that of land acquisition.   Lands which cannot be obtained by gift or purchase must be condemned.   For either purchase or condemnation, an analysis of the value of the properties concerned must be made.   The analysis must include such matters as the use of the property, the changes that will result following the enlargement or creation of a highway, the right of ingress and egress, and other factors making up the question of total property damage.   Problems of appraisal, of negotiation with the owner, of obtaining clear title, of litigating contested cases—all must be solved not only to the satisfaction of the highway department but also to the satisfaction of the community in which the right of way is sought.[13]   Condemnation proceedings are resorted to only in a relatively small portion of total land acquisitions, probably not exceeding 20 per cent.   A condemnation proceeding does not necessarily indicate the refusal of an owner to sell his property.   Inability to locate an owner or an involved title may result in a condemnation.

Road design increases in complexity as the volume and speed of traffic increase. A well constructed two or three lane highway may become obsolete quickly in a rapidly expanding community. In addition, an obsolete highway may constitute a serious hazard to safety. Highway design includes a host of individual considerations each of which must be fitted into a general pattern suited for the volume and type of traffic in a given area. Adequate width, well-maintained shoulders, the absence of roadside obstacles, proper grades and curves, a minimum of intersections and access and egress points, a smooth, nonskid surface—all are elements in increasing highway capacity, that is, in increasing the ability of a highway to accommodate traffic.

An illustration of the changes in design brought about by the growth in traffic volume may be seen in the highway department's virtual abandonment of the rotary intersection.* Designed to expedite the flow of traffic, it may actually slow traffic flow where the volume is exceptionally heavy. The rotary intersection requires a large area for development, yet it cannot handle the volume of a more simply designed intersection.[14]

Another illustration of the changes in design brought about by heavy traffic volume is the increased median strip in the newer divided highways. In 1954 New Jersey had 427 miles of divided highways under state control, a figure exceeded only by California, Texas, and Ohio.[15] This is remarkable in view of the fact that in terms of the mileage of roads and streets under state control, New Jersey ranked forty-fifth among the states.[16] However, on some of the divided highways the median strip is so narrow that vehicles have no protective area for making left turns at intersecting roads. The design of the newer divided highways makes provision for a larger median strip and protected area, thus speeding up traffic and at the same time decreasing the accident hazard.

A major problem of highway design has been that of providing uninterrupted travel in areas where the density of traffic is heavy. One solution has been the Turnpike Authority, described later. A second solution, made possible by legislation passed in 1945, is the construction of limited access freeways and parkways.[17] The freeway is designed for both passenger and truck traffic; the parkway is confined chiefly to passenger cars.

Great difficulty has been encountered in protecting existing highways from spoilage by undesirable advertising and roadside developments. Efforts of garden clubs and other citizens groups to beautify the state's major highways have had some success. The highway department has been handicapped in working with these groups by the lack of adequate roadside zoning controls. A study made in 1947 of a fifty-mile portion of the Blue Star Memorial Highway between Phillipsburg and Newark indicated that municipal zoning regulations covered less than half the mileage.

* A rotary intersection is one in which traffic merges into and flows out of a central island.

Had the 132 gasoline stations and garages in this stretch of highway been evenly spaced, the motorist could have purchased gasoline every four-tenths of a mile.[18]

The destruction of the scenic possibilities of a highway is but one result of inadequate controls. Also, the many exits and entrances to the highway occasioned by the various roadside establishments greatly reduce the efficiency of the highway. As a result, traffic capacity is lessened and the hazards of driving increased. A third factor, to be balanced against an increase in commercial enterprise, is the blight upon large areas for purposes of residential development. Uncontrolled roadside development discourages desirable residential building.

Maintenance

The highway commissioner is charged with maintaining the highway system of the state "in good order." [19] Keeping existing roads in proper condition requires continuous action. Hazards arise daily in a variety of ways, but especially through gradual deterioration and disintegration. It has been said that "the most permanent thing about a highway is the cost of keeping it up." [20]

The term "maintenance" embraces the work performed to keep a highway in good condition after it has been constructed. This includes snow removal and ice control. Actual construction, according to New Jersey law, must be done by private contract or by institutional labor.[21] Maintenance work may be done either by the state or by private firms on a contract basis.

The state is divided into districts, each in charge of a supervisor of highway maintenance. In addition there are a bridge maintenance organization and a landscape organization. A mere listing of some of the apparatus used is sufficient to indicate the high degree of mechanization in road maintenance. Compressors, graders, spreaders, rollers, bituminous kettles and finishers, tractors, mixers, snow plows, traffic line markers, and a variety of specially equipped automobiles and trucks are used to keep the highways in condition.

Each type of construction presents special maintenance problems. For example, in a concrete highway cracks and joints must be sealed, and proper drainage assured. If excessive moisture collects under the pavement, heavy traffic will cause cracking and ultimate disintegration. Minor breaks or scaling may be repaired by the application of bituminous materials. There is "cold mix patching" and "hot mix patching." With larger breaks, the proper solution may be to cut out and replace the concrete. Where the slabs of concrete have settled, due to water in the sub-grade, mudjacking may be used to return the slab to its original position. The department has carried on extensive operations in this technique which consists of pumping a "slurry" of cement, water and soil through holes drilled in the pavement.*

A major problem for the highway department in recent years has been manpower. Compensation for highway work has lagged behind wages paid in industry. As a consequence, the department has experienced difficulty in recruiting personnel.

HIGHWAY FINANCES

Fiscal Administration

The budget of the highway department is now an integral part of the entire state budget. However, for over two decades, from 1923 until 1945, the highway budget was on a calendar year basis, entirely separate from the state's July 1–June 30 fiscal year. Furthermore, the department operated under a separate budget. As a consequence, it acquired a remarkable degree of independence. But in 1945 the separate budget was abolished.[22] The highway fund, as an entity apart from the general fund, ceased to exist.

The proposed budget of the department is now considered by the state fiscal officers in the same light as the requests of all other state agencies. The needs of the highway department are measured as one element of all the needs of all departments. Total needs are then considered in the light of total revenues. In former years the department had revenue sources which in theory were reserved exclusively for highway use. Monies were received from the sale of bonds, the gasoline tax, registration fees, Federal aid, and other sources. These were deposited in the highway fund which rivaled the general state fund in size. The principle of dedicated funds was severely condemned in a Princeton Survey report:

* From nation-wide data the Federal Public Roads Administration has summarized maintenance operations and the distribution of maintenance expenditures as follows:

	Percentage
"A. Traveled way-surface	48
B. Shoulders	10
C. Drainage—ditches, culverts	10
D. Roadside—mowing, erosion control, vegetation, footpaths, recreation areas	8
E. Traffic service—guardrail, signs, signals	5
F. Snow and ice control	10
G. Bridges—superstructure, substructure, stream bed, signs	7
H. Special service—permits, load limitations, detours, public relations	2"

Highway Practice in the United States of America (Washington: Public Roads Administration, Federal Works Agency, 1949), p. 207.

It is not proper that any unit of government should live to itself alone. Each one is a part of a vast machine operating for the benefit of the people as a whole. It is unthinkable that any agency should be allowed to spend all it can collect, while another agency, relying upon specific appropriations, starves its essential services . . . . The single factor in determining what a department is to be allowed to spend should be the public value of its services.[23]

As a matter of fact, the state has seldom practiced the principle that all revenues from highway users were to be expended solely for highway purposes. For example, during the period 1931-1940, highway funds were used to service bond issues concerned with state institutions, education, and relief. During this same period, over $36,000,000 of highway funds were appropriated for emergency relief.[24]

Since 1945, New Jersey has operated under the principle of a single state fund, into which all revenues are paid and from which all monies are appropriated. Nevertheless, the theory that highway revenues should be used for highway purposes is still the subject of considerable debate. Proponents of the dedicated fund principle point to the fact that the constitutions of many states prevent the diversion of highway monies. The argument of those opposed to anti-diversion centers chiefly about the need for a greatly enlarged state highway program. A second factor in the argument is the discriminatory feature of taxes extracted from motorists and used for general state operations. However, these arguments are not, in fact, arguments to support the principle of a dedicated fund. Rather, they are evidences of a need for overhauling the entire revenue structure in order that the state may have sufficient funds, obtained equitably, to perform the increased services demanded by changed conditions.[25]

State Aid to Local Governments

As indicated previously, New Jersey was the first state to assist local governments in the building of roads. From a $20,000 appropriation in 1891, state aid for county and municipal highways had risen to over $17,000,000 annually by the fiscal year 1957.

State monies are granted both to counties and municipalities. Counties receive funds based on a legislative formula. The simplest phase of the formula is a straight legislative apportionment to each county of $55,000— a total of $1,155,000—for the construction, maintenance, and repair of county roads and bridges.[26] A second apportionment is on the basis of area, population, and county road mileage. In 1956 the sum apportioned on this basis was $6,000,000. Another sum of $2,000,000 was apportioned on the basis of population and road mileage only. The apportionment of the total State aid to Atlantic County, chosen here for purposes of illustration, is shown in Table 21.

In addition to the sums granted to counties by the State, two appropriations are made also for municipal roads. The first appropriation is dis-

TABLE 21

APPORTIONMENT OF STATE AID TO ATLANTIC COUNTY, 1956

County Road Mileage	361,680
% of Total County Mileage	5.448
Population 1950	132,399
% of Total Population	2.738
Area in square miles	610,310
% of Total Area	7.421
Average % of county road mileage area and population	5.202
Apportionment of $6,000,000	$312,120
Average % of county road mileage and population	4.093
Apportionment of $2,000,000	$81,860
Apportionment of $1,155,000	$55,000
TOTAL	$448,980

Source: N.J. State Highway Department, *Apportionment of Motor Vehicle Aid Fund to Counties* (Mimeographed, 1956).

tributed on the basis of the average of two percentages: (1) municipal population to State population, and (2) municipal road mileage to total municipal road mileage in the State.[27]   In 1956 this amounted to $4,470,000. The second appropriation is a flat legislative apportionment of $100,000 for each county.   The municipalities must share 10 per cent of the cost of all work performed.

Federal Aid

State and local governments in New Jersey receive federal funds for four classes of highways—primary, secondary, urban, and the interstate system. The oldest class, called the Federal aid primary system, was established following the Federal Highway Act of 1921.   In June, 1953, 1,696 miles of New Jersey's highways, including 1,155 miles in rural areas and 541 miles in urban areas, were declared eligible for Federal aid in the primary highway system.[28]   Most of the state routes are included in the primary system.

The Federal-Aid Highway Act of 1944 established a secondary system of roads eligible for Federal funds.   Each county was allocated a certain mileage by the Federal Public Roads Administration, and specific routes were selected by county, state, and Federal highway officials.   Their selections were based on a number of factors including the rural population of each county, the vehicle-mileage, the number of farms, and the number of mail routes, bus routes, and recreational establishments.[29]   In 1953 there were 1,921 miles in the secondary system of New Jersey.

In recent years, Federal highway aid funds have been made available for the improvement of highway facilities in cities with a population over

5,000. Primary system funds are also available for the urban mileage in the primary system.

Federal funds are distributed for the various systems on a percentage basis. The primary system receives 45 per cent of aid funds, the secondary system 30 per cent, and the urban system 25 per cent. However, this percentage distribution need not be applied in a given state. Almost 50 per cent of New Jersey's total apportionment of Federal highway monies in the fiscal year ending June 30, 1953, was for urban roads. The Federal Highway Act of 1954 authorized substantially larger sums beginning in 1956 for the primary, secondary, and urban roads. The states are required to match these grants on a 50-50 basis. In addition, funds for the interstate system—first established in 1952 and applying to important routes connecting metropolitan areas—were increased for the country as a whole from $25,000,000 in 1952 to $175,000,000 in the 1954 act, and to $2,500,000,000 in the 1956 act. Ninety per cent of the cost of the interstate system will be borne by the Federal government.

The grants to New Jersey under the Federal-Aid Highway Act of 1956 are shown in Table 22.

TABLE 22

FEDERAL AID FOR HIGHWAYS APPORTIONED TO NEW JERSEY

Type of Aid	Amount, 1957	Amount, 1958
Primary	$ 6,879,051	$ 5,076,800
Secondary	1,622,120	1,719,295
Urban	7,910,850	9,356,635
Interstate	28,675,021	37,235,749
TOTAL	$45,087,042	$53,388,479

Source: N.J. State Highway Department, *Federal Apportionments to the State of New Jersey and State Matching Funds Required* (Trenton, August 20, 1956, mimeographed).

HIGHWAY AUTHORITIES

New Jersey Turnpike Authority

Traditional state practices of highway construction and finance were discarded in 1950 when the New Jersey Turnpike Authority was established. The objective of the authority was described in the enabling act as follows:

to facilitate vehicular traffic and remove the present handicaps and hazards on the congested highways in the state, and to provide for the construction of modern express highways embodying every known safety device including center divisions, ample shoulder widths, longsight distances, multiple lanes in each direction and grade separations at all intersections with other highways and railroads . . . .[30]

The authority was established as "a body corporate and politic" in the Highway Department. Therefore, on an organization chart the authority would be classified within one of the fourteen major departments. However, in practice, the highway commissioner has no jurisdiction whatsoever over the authority. The supreme court has held that the authority is "in but not of the State Highway Department and that fact does not make it any the less an independent entity . . . ." [31]

The authority consists of three members, each of whom is required to be a resident of the state and a qualified elector of at least one year's standing. The members are appointed by the governor with the advice and consent of the Senate for terms of five years. Members may be removed by the governor for cause, following a public hearing. The governor is responsible also for designating one member as chairman and one as vice-chairman. The members receive expenses but no compensation.

The authority is empowered "to construct, maintain, repair and operate turnpike projects at such locations as shall be established by law," to sue and be sued, to issue revenue bonds, to charge transit tolls, and to exercise the power of eminent domain.[32] The enabling act stated that the bonds of the authority were in no sense a liability of the state nor a pledge of the state's credit. The act provided that each bond was to contain a similar statement. Counsel for the highway commissioner, in a friendly suit, argued that these statements meant little; the state had created the authority and was responsible for its debts. However, the supreme court upheld the act asserting that, in the eyes of the law, the authority was an independent public corporation.

A bond purchase agreement was arranged whereby subscribing investors, such as insurance companies, state fund agencies, and others, made commitment to purchase $220,000,000 of thirty-five year turnpike revenue bonds bearing interest of three and one-quarter per cent. As a means of saving an estimated twelve million dollars in interest, the authority borrowed the money only as needed paying one half of one per cent annually on the unissued portion of the total loan.[33] Opponents of the authority were quick to point out that had the state itself borrowed the money and constructed the turnpike, the difference in interest rates would have permitted a saving of several million dollars, since the state is able to borrow money at a lower rate of interest.

As a means of speeding the design and construction of the 118-mile express thoroughfare, the turnpike was divided into seven sections. For example, grading and drainage work was divided so that contractors could bid on twenty-mile sections or on half of a twenty-mile section. The division of work among a number of engineering firms and contracting firms made possible simultaneous construction operations.

The turnpike, depending upon the traffic density of a given area, has from two to four twelve-foot lanes in each direction. Motorists may enter or leave the turnpike at eighteen traffic interchange points. Tolls are based on an average of one and one-half cents per mile for passenger cars, with trucks and buses paying about four cents per mile. The pavement is of asphaltic concrete.

The administration building, located at the New Brunswick interchange, is the nerve center for all turnpike operations. For maintenance purposes, the turnpike is divided into twelve sections centered about six divisional headquarters. Policing is a function of the State Police with the turnpike authority compensating the state for actual costs.

Traffic volume at the end of 1955 averaged over 70,000 vehicles daily. Tolls amounted to over $21,000,000. The fatality rate was 2.47 per 100,000,000 vehicle miles in 1954, a figure which is considerably lower than the state average of 5.3. About 90 per cent of the traffic consists of passenger cars, a large part of which are from out of state.[34]

Additional projects of the authority include a spur to connect with the Pennsylvania Turnpike, an extension from the Newark Airport interchange to the Holland Tunnel (both completed in 1956), a spur to the New York State Thruway, and an east-west road between the Hudson and Delaware rivers crossing the state from Hudson County through Warren County.

New Jersey Highway Authority

The success of the New Jersey Turnpike led to the establishment of a second three-member agency in 1952, the New Jersey Highway Authority.[35] The qualifications for membership and the provision for appointment and removal are identical with those of the turnpike authority, except that membership in the new agency is for nine years. This time the authority was integrated more closely with the highway department.

Although the authority was authorized to issue its own bonds, criticism of the high interest rates in connection with the turnpike's operations led to the adoption of a new procedure. By public referendum, in November, 1952, the credit of the state was pledged for the guarantee of bonds up to $285,000,000 in connection with the authority's first project, the Garden State Parkway, running from Bergen and Passaic counties to Cape May. The constitutionality of this procedure was upheld by the Supreme Court.[36] The parkway began full-scale operations in 1955.

MOTOR VEHICLE CONTROL

State regulation of motor vehicles began in 1906. The term "motor vehicle" was determined by law to include "all vehicles propelled otherwise than by muscular power, excepting such vehicles as run only upon rails or tracks." [37] The assistant secretary of state was made ex officio commissioner of motor vehicles in charge of a Department of Motor Vehicle Registration and Regulation. In 1926 the agency was given independent status as a

Department of Motor Vehicles.[38] By the reorganization act of 1948 the department was transferred to the newly created Department of Law and Public Safety and reconstituted as one of six divisions under a director of motor vehicles.[39] The director is appointed by the governor, with Senate advice and consent, to serve during the governor's term and until a successor has been appointed and qualified. The director may be removed by the governor for cause.

Registration

State authority in the field of motor vehicle control begins with the licensing of car dealers and the registration and licensing of vehicles. Instead of the state performing the operations incident to registering vehicles and issuing licenses, agents were appointed in various communities to act for the director of motor vehicles. These private individuals were paid on a fee basis depending upon their volume of business. The agents rented quarters, hired personnel, and issued license plates, registration certificates, and drivers licenses. Despite numerous attacks upon the system as uneconomical, and as promoting abuses, fundamental changes were not acceptable to the legislature until 1955 when a centralized mail order system operated by the State was authorized.[40] The agency system was not eliminated completely. The law requires one agent in each county for every 300,000 inhabitants or any fraction of that number.

Motor vehicle fees constitute one of the largest sources of State revenues. For the registration year ending March 31, 1955, gross revenues totaled $56,721,192. Some of the larger elements making up this sum are shown in Table 23.

TABLE 23

REVENUES FROM MOTOR VEHICLE LICENSES AND REGISTRATIONS, 1954

Passenger vehicles	$22,691,062
Commercial vehicles	10,980,110
Auto drivers licenses	6,841,437
Trailer Registrations	2,818,555
Unsatisfied Claim and Judgment Fund Fees	2,745,415
Vehicle inspections	1,687,286

Source: N.J. Department of Law and Public Safety, *Forty-Ninth Annual Report of the Director of Motor Vehicles of the State of New Jersey for the year 1954*, pp. 9-10.

Highway Safety

The state promotes a broad program of safety education. By means of publications, motion pictures, and the various media of public information, an effort is made to develop proper driving attitudes. These programs are coordinated by a Bureau of Traffic Safety established by executive order in 1951. Another factor designed to contribute to safe driving is the practice of license revocation. This may be accomplished through hearings by state officials or by municipal magistrates. In 1954, the state held 1,940 hearings. Municipal magistrates and divisional hearing officers together accounted for 16,879 license revocations. In 1952 the point system was introduced to provide increased control over motorists who repeatedly violate the traffic laws. A schedule of points was established by administrative regulation covering each type of violation. A motorist who accumulates twelve points during a three year period may, following a hearing, have his license revoked.

One source of complaint of law enforcement officials has been the statute concerning fatal traffic accidents. The law reads as follows: "Any person who shall cause the death of another by driving any vehicle carelessly or heedlessly in wilful or wanton disregard of the rights of safety of others shall be guilty of a misdemeanor." [41] During the four year period 1947-50, only 204 indictments were returned out of a total of 1,825 cases presented for grand jury investigation. The low ratio of about one indictment per eleven deaths was attributed to the interpretation placed upon the words "wilful or wanton." Half of those indicted were convicted.[42]

Detailed statistics are maintained on traffic accidents. For example, the mileage-death rate has been maintained since 1928. This rate is determined on the basis of the number of deaths per hundred million miles of vehicle travel. The mileage is obtained by multiplying the average miles per gallon of gasoline, a figure computed on a national basis by the Bureau of Public Roads, times the annual gasoline consumption in New Jersey. In spite of a threefold increase in gasoline consumption during the period 1928 through 1951, traffic fatalities were reduced markedly, as may be demonstrated from divisional reports summarized in Table 24.

TABLE 24

RATE OF TRAFFIC FATALITIES

Year	Traffic Fatalities	Gasoline Consumption	Deaths per 100,000,000 Vehicle Miles
1928	1075	422,346,478	19.58
1938	865	810,952,855	8.21
1951	763	1,329,566,990	4.41

Source: N.J. *Forty-Sixth Annual Report of the Director of Motor Vehicles*, 1951, p. 39.

In 1952, the national traffic death rate was 7.3. New Jersey, with 4.4, had the sixth lowest rate in the United States.[43]

The state is responsible by law for the control and operation of traffic signals and signs. In this connection the Bureau of Traffic Safety supplies traffic engineering services particularly to county and municipal governments. Requests by local governments for traffic control signals and ordinances for no passing zones, or other desired local regulations to govern public highways, must be approved by the bureau.

Enforcement and Inspection

In New Jersey, the enforcement of highway regulations is the function of two agencies. In addition to the state police, a separate inspector force under the director of motor vehicles also performs road patrol activities such as issuing summonses to violators, making investigations, and recovering stolen cars. A major activity of the inspector force, which in 1954 had an authorized complement of 145, is the examination of applicants for drivers' licenses. A minor activity is the enforcement of the law requiring the licensing and supervision of junk yards adjacent to state highways.

Motor vehicles registered in New Jersey are required to be inspected annually. When the owner is unable to present his car for inspection, his registration certificate and license plates must be surrendered. The same procedure is followed for owners of cars which on reexamination do not pass inspection. In 1956, the state operated approximately thirty inspection stations and employed over 500 examiners.

Accident Compensation

A series of financial responsibility laws was passed in 1952 designed to assure compensation to the victims of motor vehicle accidents. Under earlier legislation adopted in 1929, a person who failed to satisfy a court judgment had his license revoked.[44] The license was restored after the judgment had been satisfied and proof of financial responsibility had been supplied in the event of future accidents. In 1949, there were 8,324 license revocations for failure to comply with the laws relating to financial responsibility and 5,032 restorations. During that same year sixty per cent of the reported vehicles involved in accidents were insured. This figure compared favorably with only 27 per cent in 1938. But it was far below the figure in states with more stringent legislation.

The new Security Responsibility Law requires an owner or operator of a motor vehicle involved in an accident to furnish proof of his ability to meet a claim for damages up to $10,000 for injuries or death to more than one person and up to $1,000 for damage to property. Failure to do so results in a suspension of his motoring privilege.[45] The motorist is not compelled to purchase insurance. But persons who suffer loss at the hands of an uninsured motorist who is unable to pay may be compensated up to $11,000 from a fund administered by the Unsatisfied Claim and Judgment Fund Board.[46] The board consists of the Director of the Division of Motor Vehicles, the Commissioner of Banking and Insurance, and four representatives of insurers. The fund is obtained by a levy of three dollars upon uninsured motor vehicle owners, one dollar upon insured motorists, and not more than one-half of one per cent upon the premiums on automobile liability insurance written in New Jersey. Uninsured motorists are not eligible for benefits. The cost of administering the Security Responsibility Law is met by the insurance companies.[47] The insurance companies must also establish a fund under the control of the commissioner of banking and insurance to provide protection against the insolvency of any company.[48]

OTHER FORMS OF TRANSPORTATION

Aviation

New Jersey had five military and eighty-five commercial airports in 1950. In addition there were ten seaplane bases and thirty-three private landing strips. Eleven of the commercial fields were owned by public agencies. Relatively few of the airports provided scheduled passenger or freight service. Most were concerned with air schools, charter flying or industrial aircraft operations. In 1950 there were 4.9 aircraft owners per 10,000 population.[49]

In the interest of public safety and to promote "aeronautical progress" a Department of Aviation was established in 1931.[50] An aviation commission and the office of director of aviation were also created. All were absorbed by the Department of Conservation and Economic Development as a consequence of the reorganization of 1948.

The state's regulation of aviation is geared in as closely as possible with Federal standards and rules. For example, an aircraft or a pilot licensed by the United States is automatically deemed to be licensed by the state. A state license must be obtained for air races or air meets, and for the establishment of airports, landing strips, air schools, and other facilities. The licensing of an airport requires a public hearing, and the proceedings must meet the requirements of due process of law.[51]

The rapid urbanization of New Jersey has increased the potential expansion of commercial and private aviation. At the same time, the opportunities for suitable airport locations have diminished. The state Development Plan has recommended the acquisition of new sites to meet future requirements together with continued regulation of the "location, size, use and management" in the interest of traffic safety both for those on the ground and those in the air.

Navigation

The state has a variety of problems arising out of its title to and its interests in tidal and navigable waters. For a long period the accepted method of meeting each problem was to create a new and independent agency. Thus there were the Board of Riparian Commissioners, the Department of Inland Waterways, the inspectors of power vessels, and the New Jersey Harbor Commission. In 1915 these agencies were consolidated in a Department of Commerce and Navigation governed by a Board of Commerce and Navigation.[52] The functions of the department and board were vested in the Department of Conservation in 1945. In the reorganization of 1948 the navigation functions were included in the work of the Department of Conservation and Economic Development.

New Jersey has an inland waterway system extending 123 miles from Manasquan Inlet, in Monmouth County to Cold Spring in Cape May County. In addition to the main stem channel there are 178 miles of branch channels. The waterway system is used for recreational purposes by many thousands of small boat owners. For some years, state boats patrolled the waterway, maintaining lights, removing channel debris, and assisting the boating public. Small state dredging crews endeavored to keep the channels open. Major dredging operations were done by contract. In 1950, the state agreed to turn over to the Federal Government the responsibility for maintaining and developing the intracoastal waterway.[53]

The state operates public yacht basins at Forked River in Ocean County, at Leonardo in Monmouth County, and at Atlantic City. Additional docking facilities, called marinas, according to the state Development Plan, could be made self-sustaining through service charges and would assist in the promotion of recreational businesses.

NOTES

[1] U.S. Department of Commerce, Bureau of Public Roads, *Highway Statistics 1954* (Washington, 1955), p. 14.

[2] L., 1891, ch. 201, p. 378. Under this act the state was to pay one third of the cost provided the total sum spent by the state for all construction in any one year did not exceed $20,000. For an exceptionally thorough treatment of the state's highway administration, see Sidney Goldmann and Thomas J. Graves, *The Organization and Administration of the New Jersey State Highway Department*. Prepared for Roger Hinds, Governor's Examiner of the New Jersey State Highway Department (Trenton, 1942).

[3] L., 1894, ch. 276, p. 409.

[4] L., 1917, ch. 15, p. 35. A commission of four members including the state commissioner of public roads was established in 1909 to lay out an ocean boulevard. The authority of this commission was gradually expanded. See Goldmann and Graves, *op. cit.*, pp. 4-6.

[5] L., 1917, ch. 14, p. 25.

[6] L., 1923, ch. 6, p. 19.

[7] N.J. *Senate Journal*, 1935, p. 93.

[8] L., 1948, ch. 91, p. 508.

[9] L., 1929, ch. 221, p. 413.

[10] W. Carman Davis, "New Jersey's Highway Problems," *New Jersey Municipalities*, XXXIII (May, 1956), 13.

[11] N.J. Department of Law and Public Safety, Bureau of Traffic Safety, *Highway Accident Factors, 1954*, p. 3.

[12] Sigvald Johannesson, "Highway Planning," *New Jersey Counties*, November 1947, pp. 7-8, 11. See also *Highway Practice in the United States of America* (Washington: Public Roads Administration, Federal Works Agency, 1949), pp. 49-59.

[13] For an account of departmental appraisal practices in the 1930's see Goldmann and Graves, *op. cit.*, pp. 310-23.

[14] *Highway Practice . . . , op. cit.,* pp. 102-3.   Also see Goldmann and Graves, *op. cit.,* pp. 393-95.

[15] *Highway Statistics, 1954, op. cit.,* p. 108.

[16] *Ibid.,* p. 102.

[17] L., 1945, ch. 83, p. 419.

[18] Institute of Local and State Government, "A Report on Roadside Protection on New Jersey State Highway Routes 28-29 (U.S. 22), The Blue Star Drive and the Proposed Blue Star Memorial Highway," reported in Highway Research Board Bulletin No. 18, *Land Acquisition and Control of Highway Access and Adjacent Areas* (Washington, 1949), p. 11.

[19] L., 1927, ch. 319, p. 722.

[20] *Highway Practice . . . , op. cit.,* p. 204.

[21] L., 1931, ch. 225, p. 564.

[22] L., 1945, ch. 33, p. 90.

[23] Quoted in Goldmann and Graves, *op. cit.,* p. 184.

[24] *Ibid.,* p. 186.

[25] Stanley W. Ackley, "Highway Finance Problems in New Jersey," *Review of New Jersey Business,* V (July, 1949), 6-7, 12.

[26] L., 1946, ch. 207, p. 804.

[27] L., 1947, ch. 62, p. 202.

[28] U.S. Department of Commerce, *Annual Report, Bureau of Public Roads, Fiscal Year 1953* (Washington), p. 70.

[29] N.J. *Highway Department, 1947-48.*

[30] L., 1948, ch. 454, p. 1857.

[31] *N.J. Turnpike Authority* v *Parsons,* 3 N.J. 237, 244 (1949).

[32] L., 1948, ch. 454, p. 1861.

[33] New Jersey Turnpike Authority, *Annual Report 1950* (Trenton, 1951), pp. 17-20.

[34] New Jersey Turnpike Authority, *Annual Report 1955* (New Brunswick, 1956), p. 8.   For the state fatality rate see *Highway Accident Factors, 1954, op. cit.,* p. 2.

[35] L., 1952, ch. 16, p. 65.

[36] *Behnke* v *N.J. Highway Authority* 11 N.J. 579 (1953).

[37] L., 1906, ch. 113, p. 177.

[38] L., 1926, ch. 147, p. 228.

[39] L., 1948, ch. 439, p. 1707.

[40] L., 1955, ch. 8, p. 33.

[41] L., 1935, ch. 282, p. 913.

[42] N.J. Department of Law and Public Safety, *Forty-Sixth Annual Report of the Director of Motor Vehicles of the State of New Jersey for the Year 1951,* p. 26.

[43] N.J. Department of Law and Public Safety, *First Annual Report of the Bureau of Traffic Safety and the State Coordinating Council on Traffic and Safety of the State of New Jersey* (Trenton, 1953), p. 10.

[44] L., 1929, ch. 116, p. 195.

[45] L., 1952, ch. 173, p. 548.

[46] L., 1952, ch. 174, p. 570.

[47] L., 1952, ch. 176, p. 598.

[48] L., 1952, ch. 175, p. 591.

[49] *Development Plan for New Jersey, A Report upon Planning Surveys, Planning Studies, and a Comprehensive Plan for the State of New Jersey* (Trenton: Planning Section, Bureau of Planning and Development, Department of Conservation and Economic Development, 1950), p. 23.

[50] L., 1931, ch. 190, p. 475.

[51] *Penna. R.R. Co.* v *N.J. State Aviation Com.* 2 N.J. 64 (1949).

[52] L., 1915, ch. 242, p. 432.

[53] L., 1950, ch. 333, p. 1109.

CHAPTER 21

Labor

THE PRESENT Department of Labor and Industry had its genesis in a Bureau of Statistics established in 1878. The bureau was required to report to the legislature on the "commercial, industrial, social, educational, and sanitary conditions of the laboring classes," and to "foster and enlarge our manufacturing and every other class of productive industry." [1]   In 1904 a Department of Labor, under a commissioner, was organized. At the time it had no relationship to the Bureau of Statistics but was designed to enforce state regulations concerning hours and conditions of work.[2] From time to time additional functions were added. In 1916, the Bureau of Statistics was made one of the constituent units of the enlarged labor department.[3]   It was not until the reorganization of 1948 that the existing title, Department of Labor and Industry, came into use.[4]

The labor department is headed by a commissioner who is appointed by the governor, with the advice and consent of the Senate, to serve at the governor's pleasure and until a successor has been appointed and qualified. The commissioner is charged with responsibility for administration, including the issuance of rules and regulations authorized by law for the operation of the various programs of the department. The commissioner is required to initiate enforcement proceedings and to make an annual report to the governor and to the legislature.

Operating programs are organized in three divisions: labor, workman's compensation, and employment security. The director of each division is appointed by the governor, with Senate consent, to serve during his term of office. Each director is subject to the governor's removal, for cause, upon notice and opportunity to be heard.

PROTECTION OF EMPLOYEES

Inspection Services

New Jersey has a host of laws and a number of industrial codes having the force of law designed to protect the health and safety of its 1,850,000 industrial workers (for the occupational groups, see the chart on page opposite). Factories and workshops in "productive industry" are required to register with the commissioner of labor and industry.[5] He must approve industrial building plans in such matters as the installation of stairways, elevator shafts, fire alarm systems, lighting, sanitation, and ventilation. Machinery must be safeguarded. Steam boilers must be inspected either by a representative of the department or by an insurance company inspector licensed by the department. Industrial accidents and occupational diseases must be reported by the employer.

During the fiscal year 1955 labor department personnel conducted approximately 36,000 factory inspections. Over 8,000 orders were issued designed to require compliance with state statutes or regulations. These orders concerned such matters as guards for machines, electrical wiring, fire protection, and sanitation.[6]

Legislation enacted in 1954 provides for state regulation and inspection of mines and quarries. The law requires an inspection of underground mines every three months. There are four iron mines and one zinc mine in New Jersey. Other mines, including quarries, and sand, gravel, clay, and shale pits, must be inspected twice each year. In the interest of safety, the commisioner of labor and industry may order all work stopped.[7]

Protection of Women and Children

The law regulates also the hours of work of children and of female employees.[8] The statutes relating to women afford a limited protection only. Women may not be employed in a manufacturing establishment, bakery, or laundry before 7:00 A.M. or after 12:00 P.M. This limitation may be suspended by the governor in time of national emergency. The maximum work day is ten hours and the maximum work-week is six days or fifty-four hours. However, this provision of the law does not apply to hotels or businesses of a continuous nature where a single day's work does not exceed eight hours. Nor do the restrictions of the law apply to canneries packing perishable fruits and vegetables.

New Jersey's first law applying specifically to child labor was passed in 1851, following Governor George F. Fort's plea that "infant laborers in factories . . . be protected from such excessive exactions as are calculated to destroy their physical and mental capacity for health and usefulness." [9] The first child labor law prohibited work for minors under ten with a maxi-

OCCUPATIONAL GROUPS: PERCENTAGE OF EMPLOYED PERSONS IN
UNITED STATES AND NEW JERSEY, 1950

OCCUPATIONAL GROUP	PER CENT OF EMPLOYED PERSONS
	5 10 15 20
OPERATIVES AND KINDRED WORKERS	19.8 / 24.1
CRAFTSMEN, FOREMEN, AND KINDRED WORKERS	13.8 / 15.8
CLERICAL AND KINDRED WORKERS	12.0 / 14.9
MANAGERS, OFFICIALS, AND PROPRIETORS, EXCEPT FARM	8.6 / 10.2
PROFESSIONAL, TECHNICAL, AND KINDRED WORKERS	8.5 / 10.1
SERVICE WORKERS, EXCEPT PRIVATE HOUSEHOLD	7.6 / 7.1
SALES WORKERS	6.9 / 6.7
LABORERS, EXCEPT FARM AND MINE	6.4 / 5.5
PRIVATE HOUSEHOLD WORKERS	2.5 / 2.1
FARMERS AND FARM MANAGERS	7.3 / 1.1
FARM LABORERS AND FOREMEN, INCLUDING UNPAID FAMILY WORKERS	4.3 / 1.1
NOT REPORTED	2.3 / 1.0

UNITED STATES

NEW JERSEY

Reproduced with permission from John E. Brush, *The Population of New Jersey* (New Brunswick: Rutgers University Press, 1956), p. 53.

mum for minors above that age of ten hours per day and sixty hours per week.[10]   Although the minimum age was increased in 1883, it was not until 1904 that a comprehensive child labor law was enacted. This legislation resulted from the revelations, made by reform groups, of children working under extraordinarily bad conditions.[11]   Agricultural work by minors was not regulated until 1940, the last major revision of the state's child labor laws.*

At present the minimum age at which a minor may legally take a job varies from twelve to eighteen depending upon the nature of the work involved. In general, the minimum age is sixteen. This limit applies to work in a factory at any time or in any gainful occupation during school hours. Outside school hours and during vacation periods the minimum age is fourteen for work not prohibited by law or regulation. The minimum age in agricultural work is twelve with a maximum of ten hours per day. Newsboys also have a twelve year minimum.

The eighteen year minimum applies to work in connection with power driven machinery, certain occupations specified by law, and other occupations and places of employment deemed by the commissioner, after public hearing, to be hazardous or injurious to "the life, safety, or welfare" of minors.[12]   Employers of minors under nineteen are required to maintain records covering each minor's hours, wages, and other working conditions. This law does not apply to agricultural labor and to domestic service in private homes.

Minors under sixteen engaged in "street trade" activities such as selling newspapers, or engaged in farm work must have special permits obtained from a school district "issuing officer." The permit must be requested by a parent or guardian and the conditions of work must be indicated.

Minors under eighteen, unless in agriculture, must obtain from the issuing officer an employment certificate in order to work in any authorized gainful occupation. Before the employment certificate is issued, the minor is required to submit proof of his age and the prospective employer must submit a promise of employment indicating the nature of the work, the hours, and the wages. A physician's certificate is required together with the minor's school record. Upon the basis of these four documents, the issuing officer may approve the minor's application for a certificate.†

Any violation of the child labor laws is a criminal offense. Each day

* The Federal government also has controls relating to child labor. The Fair Labor Standards Act, for example, prohibits the employment of "oppressive child labor in commerce or in the production of goods for commerce." *Federal Code Annotated* 29:212(c).

† In 1942 a State Commission on Student Service was created. The law creating the commission was to expire upon the conclusion of treaties of peace. The commissioner's function was to survey labor requirements and to make a determination of the need for student labor in agriculture. L., 1942, ch. 23, p. 52. Minors over 16 were authorized to work longer hours by an act passed in 1943 to be effective during the war emergency. L., 1943, ch. 146, p. 396.

in which a violation occurs constitutes a separate offense as does each minor employed in violation of the law.[13]   An injured minor who is illegally employed may collect double the compensation to which he ordinarily is entitled.[14]

Regulation of Wages and Hours

Employers are required by law to pay their employees in cash every two weeks.[15]   Permission to pay by check may be granted by the commissioner of labor and industry.   In certain instances the department may require the employer to post bond.   Employees failing to receive wages may file a claim with the department for the enforcement of the wage laws.

Minimum wage legislation enacted in 1933 requires the commissioner, upon the petition of fifty or more residents, to investigate the wages being paid women and minors in any occupation.[16]   If he finds, upon information in his possession and with or without the investigation, that wages are "oppressive and unreasonable," he is required to appoint a wage board. The board, consisting of representatives of the employer, the employees, and the public, has the obligation of recommending a minimum fair wage. After hearing, the commissioner may issue a wage order.   The order specifies the basic minimum wage, and usually also overtime provisions and the rate for learners.   Minimum fair wage mandatory orders now cover the following occupations: light manufacturing, wearing apparel and allied occupations; beauty culture, restaurants, laundry and cleaning and dyeing, and retail trade.

Migrant Labor

Throughout the United States, the migrant labor problem is almost exclusively a farm problem.[17]   New Jersey is no exception.   Migrant workers maintain no stable home.   Indeed, by law, any person who maintains an "all-year-round dwelling place in this state for one year or longer" is not a migrant worker even though his labor is temporary and seasonal.[18]   Negroes and Puerto Ricans constitute the major portion of New Jersey's migrant labor force.

Following a typical migrant labor pattern, crews migrate north from Florida, harvesting potatoes in North Carolina and Virginia before the New Jersey crop is ready in July.   After about twenty days in this state, they move to New York.   Their harvesting season ends with the picking of the Maine potato crop in October.

In recent years considerable numbers of Puerto Ricans have been brought directly to this state on contract.   In 1946 the Gloucester County Board of Agriculture and several farm employer associations joined with the board to form the Garden State Service Cooperative Association. New York and Michigan groups joined the association in 1950 when the Gloucester County Board's project, now the Glassboro Service Associa-

tion, became simply a constituent member. The Garden State Association in 1950 employed 4,600 Puerto Ricans. Of this number 2,319 were
recruited in Puerto Rico. The remainder were classed as "walk ins." [19]
The manager of the Glassboro Association told the President's Commission on Migratory Labor that employment contracts are made lasting several months to cover the harvesting of a number of crops such as aspar-
agus, tomatoes, and potatoes.[20]

The regulation of migrant labor received state-wide recognition in 1945
with the passage of the Migrant Labor Act.[21] A migrant labor board was
established consisting of twelve persons, seven of whom were department
heads ex-officio, or their deputies. Of the remaining five, to be appointed
by the governor with the advice and consent of the Senate, two were required to be representatives of farmers and one of organized labor. In
addition, a separate division was created, now the Bureau of Migrant
Labor. It was charged with enforcing the labor laws with respect to migrant labor camps and with providing inspectional services designed to
encourage improved housing and sanitation. Other functions included
making cooperative arrangements with executive agencies concerning problems such as the protection, health and welfare of migrant workers and the
education of their children. Existing law does little to regulate individual
labor contractors, a source of exploitation of the migratory worker in many
states.[22]

In the fiscal year 1955 there were approximately 22,000 migrant workers in the state, most of whom lived in the 2,736 registered migrant camps.
The camps range in size from cabins housing one or two workers to large
barracks structures housing four or five hundred. The legal capacity of all
camps in 1955 totaled 32,615.[23] Regular and seasonal inspectors of the
department check the camps for compliance with state laws and regulations.

SETTLEMENT OF LABOR DISPUTES

State machinery to arbitrate disputes between management and labor
was first established in 1892. Provision was made for local arbitration
boards approved by the county courts and representing management, labor,
and the public. A state board, appointed by the governor, was empowered
to decide appeals from the local boards or to hear cases in the first instance if the parties to the disputes so desired.[24] The work of the incumbent board became a political issue, and in 1895 it was replaced by persons of the legislature's choosing.[25] Shortly after 1900 the board ceased to
function.

Mediation

New machinery at the state level was not created until 1941 when the
New Jersey State Board of Mediation was established. As now con-

stituted, the board consists of seven persons appointed by the governor
with the advice and consent of the Senate, two representing employers,
two representing employees, and three representing the public. The chairman of the board, a public representative, is designated by the governor.

The board may, on its own initiative or at the request of either party to
a dispute, take steps to "effect a voluntary, amicable and expeditious adjustment and settlement of the differences and issues between employer
and employees. . . ." [27] The board may arrange conferences, discuss
grievances, and, through negotiation, endeavor to obtain a settlement of
the dispute. The board has no authority of compulsion. By agreement
of the disputants, a case may be submitted to arbitration, a device which
over the years has gradually increased in popularity. The board maintains
a panel of arbitrators.

Of 541 cases classified as closed during the fiscal year 1955, 79.3 per
cent were referred to the mediation board by labor unions. The sources
of cases accepted by the board are shown below.[26]

SOURCES OF CASES HANDLED BY BOARD OF MEDIATION

Referred by	Number of Cases	Per Cent
Management	40	7.4
Labor	429	79.3
Management and labor	57	10.5
Public agencies	1	0.2
Board intervention	14	2.6

The issues involved varied, the most numerous being wages, group insurance and hospitalization, vacations and holidays with pay, discharges,
union recognition, and shop relationships. The manner in which disputes
were settled in 1955 is shown below.

METHOD OF SETTLEMENT OF LABOR DISPUTES

	Number of Cases	Per Cent
Adjusted by conciliation	135	25.0
Adjusted by mediation of board alone	180	33.2
Adjusted by arbitration	139	25.7
Cases closed by board (election com-pleted, case dropped by company or union, and others.)	87	16.1

Compulsory Arbitration

Labor disputes in public utilities are regulated by separate legislation.
In 1946 "heat, light, power, sanitation, transportation, communication,
and water" were declared to be "life essentials of the people," and subject,
therefore, to regulation in the public interest.[28] As originally enacted the
statute provided for collective bargaining, the certification of bargaining

representatives by the Board of Mediation, the setting up of an advisory board of arbitration, and finally, seizure of a plant or facility by the governor upon his finding that "the public interest, health and welfare are jeopardized, and that the exercise of such authority is necessary to insure the operation of such public utility. . . ." [29]

In 1947, just as 12,000 telephone workers throughout the state were going on strike, the act was amended prohibiting strikes after seizure and making compulsory the decision of the board of arbitration. Heavy penalties were provided for violations.[30] The supreme court of the state subsequently declared the act unconstitutional on the ground that the legislature had delegated its powers to the boards of arbitration without providing adequate standards to guide the agency.[31] In 1949 the legislature established standards for the operations of the boards, and the act was again placed in full effect. However, the validity of the act has since been questioned by virtue of the decision of the United States Supreme Court outlawing a somewhat similar Wisconsin statute on the ground that the state act infringed upon the Federal Labor Management Relations Act of 1947.[32]

The arbitration boards established following state seizure consist of five members. Each party to the dispute appoints one. The two partisan members then select three others. Failure to reach an agreement results in appointments by the governor. In practice, the governor's appointments have been made from lists prepared by the board of mediation which were then submitted to the disputing parties for rating. The three persons nearest to being acceptable to both parties were then selected.

The approach of these boards has been one of mediation as distinguished from adjudication. The power of decision has resided in the public members. Their practice of caucusing by themselves was condemned by the court.[33] A study made in 1951 concluded that compulsory arbitration "has apparently functioned successfully. . . ." The report declared that the administration of the act had been conducted with skill and impartiality.[34]

Since 1951 the act has been little used. In 1954 the Governor's Committee on Legislation Relating to Public Utility Labor Disputes recommended the repeal of the statute. The committee declared that the act had not been applied consistently, and that it had "definitely contributed toward the inability or unwillingness of the parties to settle their differences directly and expeditiously." [35]

WORKMEN'S COMPENSATION

Workmen's compensation legislation in New Jersey dates from 1911 when the state passed an employers' liability act, one of the first of its kind in the country.[36] The act greatly improved an injured workman's chances of obtaining compensation through legal action since it removed the employer's long standing common law defenses of (1) negligence on the part of the employee, (2) negligence of a fellow servant, and (3) the employee's assumption of risk. However, awards still depended upon court action after the passage of the new act.

In his 1911 gubernatorial inaugural address, Woodrow Wilson called for legislation which would free the workman from the necessity of resorting to the courts:

We must have a workingman's compensation act which will not put upon him the burden of fighting powerful composite employers to obtain his rights, but which will give him his rights without suit, directly, and without contest, by automatic operation of law, as if of a law of insurance.[37]

Not until 1918 was Wilson's challenge heeded. In that year, a Workmen's Compensation Bureau was established. A commissioner of labor, deputy commissioners of compensation, and referees were granted "exclusive original jurisdiction" of claims for compensation.[38]

New Jersey is classified as one of the twenty-six states having an "elective" as distinguished from a compulsory compensation law. By this is meant that the employer—and the employee—may choose to reject Article 2 of the act, entitled elective compensation, as distinguished from Article 1, labelled actions at law. This must be done by affirmative action. An employer making this choice loses the defenses previously mentioned—contributory negligence, negligence of fellow servant, and assumption of risk.

Closely related to the question of compensating the injured employee, is that of the source of the funds from which he is paid. In 1917 New Jersey passed an employers' liability insurance law compelling every employer, except a governmental agency, to make provision for the payment of obligations to injured workers. The employer was given the choice of obtaining liability insurance or of carrying his own risk.[39] The latter alternative was made contingent upon proof of financial ability.*

The employers of two large categories of workers, farm laborers and domestic help, are not required to obtain coverage. They may elect to obtain insurance covering their employees if they so wish. All other regular employees are covered. Workers in casual employment and newspaper vendors are excluded. Although the law is elective as far as private employment is concerned, public employees other than those holding elective office are covered on a compulsory basis.

Willful negligence acts as a bar to the receipt of compensation. This is defined by law as "(1) deliberate act or deliberate failure to act, or (2) such conduct as evidences reckless indifference to safety, or (3) intoxication, operating as the proximate cause of injury." [40]

---

* State insurance systems exist in eighteen states. In New York and Pennsylvania, for example, an employer may choose to insure in either the state system or with a private company. In some states the employer is required to insure in the state fund. State Workmen's Compensation Laws as of September, 1950, Bulletin 125 (U.S. Department of Labor, Bureau of Labor Standards, 1950), p. 4.

An injury may result in one of three forms of disability: temporary, permanent total, or permanent partial. The amount of compensation paid an injured worker for a disability arising out of and in the course of employment depends on three factors: the worker's weekly wage, the period of time over which payment is made, and the minimum or maximum payment per week. For example, compensation on a temporary disability is based upon a statutory wage and compensation schedule for a period not to exceed 300 weeks. However, the maximum payment is forty dollars per week. For an injury "total in character and permanent in quality" the rates noted above are continued during a period of 450 weeks. Periodic extensions may be obtained which in effect make the grant indefinite.

Permanent partial disability carries a compensation schedule for a stated period. For example, an individual losing a thumb is compensated for seventy-five weeks. The maximum is thirty-five dollars per week. Death payment benefits are compensated on a graduated scale according to the number of dependents. The weekly maximum is forty dollars to be paid over a period of 350 weeks. Additional compensation is paid if at the end of 350 weeks there are children under eighteen. All occupational diseases are compensable.

The law requires a waiting period of seven days before compensation is due. If the disability does not extend beyond the waiting period, the injured employee is not entitled to other than medical aid.* If this disability extends beyond four weeks, the employee may collect for the waiting period also.

Notice to the employer is a condition which precedes the enforcement of any claim for compensation. Unless given within fourteen days, compensation is not due until the employer is notified. An injury is not compensable unless the employer knows of the incident within ninety days.† The courts have held that the purpose of the notice is to enable the employer to make a "timely investigation" of the accident.[41]

In the event of a dispute between an employer and an employee arising out of a claim for compensation, either party may submit the case to the Department of Labor and Industry. Questions of fact, the kind of injury and its effect, and the amount of compensation—all may be brought up for adjudication.

In a majority of instances, compensation cases are settled by agreement between the injured employee and his employer. The agreement must be filed with the department and is not binding until approved. If no volun-

---

* Medical, surgical, and hospitalization costs are chargeable to the employer and are not a part of the compensation award. *Aiello* v *Borough of Verona* 18 N.J. Misc. 176 (1940).

† The fact that a fellow worker or a shop steward knows of an injury does not constitute notice. *Magnuson* v *George Peterson Inc.* 132 N.J.L. 243 (1944). However, a foreman or plant physician's knowledge is also the employer's knowledge. *Kardos* v *American Smelting and Refining Co.* 132 N.J.L. 577 (1944).

tary agreement is reached within a period of twenty-one days, the department may institute an inquiry and file a petition for compensation. This petition is then reviewed in the same manner as a petition from the employee.

Claimants must file petitions within two years of the date the injury occurred. There are special provisions concerning occupational diseases. The employer is served a copy by the Department of Labor and Industry, together with a notice directing him to file an answer admitting or denying the substance of the petition. From four to six weeks after the filing of the petition, a hearing must be held. Ten days notice of the hearing must be given each party. Although not bound by the technical rules of evidence, the department is required to determine "the substantial rights of the parties from competent evidence." [42] For example, the court has held that the failure of a worker to prove the exact time of an accident was not a bar to compensation, providing he could establish the time with reasonable certainty.[43]

The findings and determinations made by the Division of Workmen's Compensation have the same standing as a judgment of the county court when filed in the county clerk's office. Representatives of the division hearing the case have power equal to that of the courts also in compelling the attendance of witnesses and the production of necessary records. All hearings are required to be open to the public.

The decision in a particular case may be appealed to the county court. The party making the appeal must send to the court a transcript of the record and testimony in the case certified by the division. After a hearing on the appeal during which each side has an opportunity to present arguments based exclusively on the transcript, a judgment is given which is "conclusive and binding," except as a higher court may call up a case for review. The hearing held by the court "is a trial de novo upon the record as presented and is for the purpose of providing a new mind for the consideration of the testimony adduced." [44]

During the fiscal year 1955 there were 56,245 compensation cases. Of this number 37,658 were settled by agreement; the remainder, after hearings. Total benefits, exclusive of medical expenses, amounted to $32,172,496.[45]

REHABILITATION OF THE HANDICAPPED

Since 1919 the state has conducted a program for the rehabilitation of the physically handicapped.[46] The Rehabilitation Commission consists of the commissioners of education, labor, and institutions and agencies together with eight persons appointed by the governor. Of the eight, one is to represent the employers of labor, one to represent organized labor, and two—one a woman—are to be selected because of their interest in the treatment and education of crippled children. In 1948, the commission was transferred to the Department of Labor and Industry.[47]

To be eligible for assistance, a handicapped person must be a resident of the state with some chance of successful rehabilitation. The commission is prohibited by law from assisting the aged or helpless who require permanent custodial care, the blind and deaf who are being assisted by other state agencies, and "persons who in the judgment of the commission are not susceptible of rehabilitation." [48]

Physical handicaps may arise from (1) disease, such as poliomyelitis or arrested tuberculosis, (2) congenital deformity, (3) accident or other causes. In its efforts to rehabilitate the handicapped, the commission is authorized by law to provide medical and social service care, furnish artificial limbs and other appliances, and establish special training schools. The ultimate objective of the rehabilitation process is to develop or restore the handicapped individual's work capacity and to place him in satisfactory employment so that he may be self-sustaining.

One indication of the success of the program may be obtained from the records of those rehabilitated. For example, in 1952, 977 citizens who had been returned to remunerative employment the preceding year paid $227,853.60 in payroll tax deductions. Of this number 802 earned an average of over $30 per week. Thus physically handicapped, non-productive citizens became productive members of society.[49]

Federal grants-in-aid cover administrative and counseling and placement costs plus half the cost of the various services provided for the individual.

EMPLOYMENT SECURITY

Through its employment service, the Department of Labor and Industry maintains a state-wide registration of unemployed workers. The major function of the service is to help the unemployed find jobs.

A state public employment service was first established in 1915 when a bureau of employment was authorized to bring together employers seeking labor and workers seeking employment.[50] After World War I, the bureau was given the task of assisting veterans in obtaining employment. When the federal unemployment compensation program was initiated, the employment service acted as the field organization for processing claims. During World War II, the entire organization was transferred to the United States Employment Service. By presidential directive in September, 1942, the War Manpower Commission assumed jurisdiction. When Federal controls ended in 1946, state operations were resumed. Since January 1, 1949, the Department of Labor and Industry has had responsibility for the employment security program.

The state's employment service is tied in closely with the Bureau of

Employment Security in the United States Department of Labor. New Jersey is now a part of Region II of thirteen Federal defense regions. Since September, 1950, all costs of administering the employment service and its thirty-six local public employment offices have been paid from Federal grants.*

The basic objective of the employment service is "the placement of qualified unemployed men and women, particularly veterans, in suitable employment." [51]

UNEMPLOYMENT COMPENSATION

In 1936 the legislature issued a declaration of public policy to the effect that "involuntary unemployment" was the "greatest hazard of our economic life." [52] Modeled to conform with the provisions of the Federal Social Security Act, the state established machinery for the payment of benefits to the unemployed.

Prior to the adoption of the Social Security Act, Wisconsin was the only state having any form of unemployment insurance. Although the Federal law was passed in 1935, the states were slow to enact enabling legislation. However, within six weeks after the reelection of President Roosevelt in 1936, a large number of states passed unemployment compensation laws and by mid-1937, all had enacted enabling legislation. The major reasons for this sudden change was the provision of the Social Security Act imposing an annual excise tax of three per cent on payrolls, and an annual offset on funds paid to a state for the operation of a system of unemployment compensation. The first application of the tax was to the 1936 payrolls of employers of eight or more. Ninety per cent of the first year's tax could be offset by payments to a state unemployment compensation fund prior to January 1, 1937. Federal funds were authorized for aid to the states in the administration of their laws. The pattern thus established quickly brought the states into line.[53]

The Social Security Act placed the responsibility for administration of unemployment compensation upon the states. New Jersey collects the funds, determines the eligible claimants, and disburses payments. The states were required to establish merit systems for those employees concerned with administering the unemployment compensation laws. They were also required to deposit unemployment compensation funds in the Federal Treasury and to invest those funds in Federal securities.† Bene-

* Under the original Wagner-Peyser Act of 1933 the states were required to match Federal appropriations.

† The amount of funds for administrative purposes has been a constant source of friction between the Federal and state authorities. A tax of three tenths of one per cent on wages is paid to the Federal government by New Jersey employers of eight or more. The state contends that this sum should be used to administer the

fits are paid on the basis of requisitions against the account of New Jersey in the unemployment trust fund.

Prior to the reorganization of 1948, jurisdiction of the laws relating to unemployment compensation was vested in an Unemployment Compensation Commission of seven members. As a consequence of the reorganization act, the powers and duties of the commission were assigned to the Division of Employment Security in the Department of Labor and Industry. The commission was abolished and the membership reconstituted as the Employment Security Council to act in an advisory capacity concerning the operation of the unemployment compensation laws.[54]

Eligibility and Benefits

To be eligible for benefits an individual must be registered with an employment office, he must have filed a claim, and he must be able, available, and actively seeking work. Further, he must have earned at least $15 per week during seventeen weeks of his base year, a period defined as the first fifty-two of the fifty-three calendar weeks preceding the week in which the claim was filed. The weekly benefit rate is two-thirds of his average weekly wage. Benefits in 1955 ranged from a weekly $10 minimum to a $35 maximum over a period of from 13 to 26 weeks in any benefit year.* A one-week waiting period before benefits are payable is paid retroactively after four weeks of unemployment.[55]

An individual may disqualify himself for benefits by (1) quitting his job, (2) being discharged for improper conduct, and (3) not applying for work when directed or for refusing to accept suitable work when offered. Participation in a labor dispute is also a disqualifying factor for the duration of the dispute.

Claims for benefits must be filed in accordance with regulations of the Division of Employment Security. An initial determination is made by a representative of the division who then requests the most recent employer or employers to supply information necessary to determine the claimants eligibility and benefit rights. If the employer fails to reply within seven days, the divisional representative is required to make an initial determination based upon information available, including the claimant's affidavit. An appeal may be taken by any one of the interested parties within seven days. A disputed claim is heard before an appeal tribunal consisting either of a salaried examiner of the division or of a three-member panel made up of the examiner and one representative each from industry and labor. Above the appeal tribunal sits a Board of Review which may on its own

---

employment security programs. From 1938 to 1950 the tax on New Jersey employers amounted to $91,380,000. The total amount returned to the state, however, was less than half that sum, $41,674,281.

* A benefit year is defined as the 364 calendar days following the filing of a claim for benefits.

action affirm, deny, or modify the former's decision. It may ask also for additional evidence. The board is required to accept an appeal if the decision of the lower tribunal was not unanimous or if the initial determination was overruled or modified. Decisions of the board are subject to judicial review.*

Approximately 1,450,000 workers are covered under the New Jersey law. Agricultural laborers, domestic servants, and governmental employees are among the categories of workers not covered. New Jersey is one of two states requiring contributions by the employee. Originally the rate was one per cent of wages. At present, the rate is one fourth of 1 per cent of the first $3000. Worker contributions in 1954 amounted approximately to $10,150,000. In 1954, 294,288 claimants received one or more payments totalling $117,662,644.[56]

Experience Rating

A separate account is maintained for each employer. The employer must pay a tax of 2.7 per cent on all wages for a period of three years. After the initial period he is assigned a rate depending upon his employment experience. If he has a reserve balance—that is, if his contributions exceed the benefits paid—his tax is reduced. The reserve ratio is computed as follows:

$$\frac{\text{Contributions paid} - \text{Benefits charged}}{\text{Average annual payroll}} = \text{Reserve ratio}$$

The higher the reserve ratio, the lower the tax. Illustrations of the tax rates are shown below.

Ratio	Tax Rate (per cent of payroll)
6% but less than 7%	1.8
9% but less than 10%	.9
11% or above	.3

These rates may be reduced still further providing the balance in the Unemployment Trust Fund exceeds 10 per cent of total taxable wages. The experience rating distribution assigned for the 44,864 employer accounts during the fiscal period July, 1952–June, 1953 is shown in Table 25.

Experience rating is based upon two theories, first that employers may be encouraged to stabilize their operations thus reducing unemployment and second that the employer responsible for unemployment should pay a

* In 1952, 21,609 New Jersey cases and 892 cases for other states were taken to the appeal tribunals. About 60 per cent were filed by employees and 40 per cent by employers. The Board of Review received 4,060 appeals. Of this number, 55 were taken to the superior court, 25 by employees and 30 by employers. N.J. *Sixteenth Annual Employment Security Report, 1952* (Department of Labor and Industry, Division of Employment Security, 1952), p. 15.

TABLE 25

EXPERIENCE RATING IN NEW JERSEY, 1952-53

Employer Accounts	Rating		Per Cent of All Accounts
6,304	.3		14.05
2,295	.6		5.12
2,900	.9		6.46
3,018	1.2		6.73
2,819	1.5		6.28
2,308	1.8		5.14
1,678	2.1		3.74
3,796	2.4		8.46
6,446	2.7	(overdrawn [a])	14.37
13,300	2.7	(not rated)	29.65

Source: N.J. *Sixteenth Annual Employment Security Report*, 1952, Table 22.
[a] Where the benefits charged exceed the contributions credited, penalty rates may be assigned.

proportionate share of the costs. How effectively the theories have operated is a subject of much debate.[57] A practical result has been to lower substantially the unemployment compensation tax paid by industry. The effective rate in New Jersey during 1954 was 1.53 per cent of payrolls. Total employer contributions amounted to $61,916,156.[58]

TEMPORARY DISABILITY BENEFITS

Although New Jersey has an unemployment compensation law designed to provide payments during periods of involuntary unemployment, the law has no application for individuals thrown out of work because of illness or accident unrelated to their employment. To be eligible for benefits under the unemployment compensation act, a worker must be "available" for employment. Nor do the payments under the workmen's compensation laws provide for wage loss in the event of non-occupational illness or accident. Voluntary cash sickness benefit plans fill this gap only partially. The legislature has declared that the voluntary benefit plans provided "uneven, unequal and sometimes uncertain protection . . . ."[59]

In 1948 a Temporary Disability Benefits Law was enacted, establishing a system for the payment of individuals disabled during unemployment or for accident or illness not compensable under workmen's compensation. The act is tied in with the unemployment compensation law. The worker is entitled to disability benefits during a period of unemployment, provided he has wage credits for previous covered employment. If employed, he is entitled to benefits for non-occupational illness or accident.

Temporary disability benefits may be paid through a state plan or through private plans. The state plan includes all covered workers who are not entitled to disability payments under a private plan. Weekly benefits are based upon the employee's wage credits and ranged in 1955 from ten to thirty-five dollars. Maximum total benefits may not exceed twenty-six times the weekly benefit. An individual is not eligible for benefits covering the first seven days of disability.

Benefits under the state plan are paid from the Disability Benefits Fund. The fund was established initially by the transfer of $50,000,000 from the Unemployment Trust Fund. Employer contributions are based on annual experience ratings. Employee contributions are one-half of 1 per cent. Separate accounts are maintained for those claiming disability benefits not compensable under workmen's compensation and for disabled unemployed claimants. Benefits paid in the fiscal year 1955, exclusive of private plans, were as follows: [60]

State plan	$8,064,126
Disabled unemployed	$1,166,965

A private plan may be established by any covered employer. At present, the employer may provide for the payment of benefits through one of three types of private plans. The first and most widely used is by means of a contract of insurance with an authorized agency. Self-insurance by the employer constitutes a second method. A third is by an agreement between the employer and a union. Benefit payments under the private plans must be at least equal to those under the state plan. If a part of the cost is to be met by the contributions of employees, a majority must agree to the plan.

An advisory council assists in administering the law. The council consists of four labor representatives and two representatives each for employers, the medical profession, and the insurance industry. These are appointed by the governor with the advice and consent of the Senate. In addition there are representatives of the Department of Labor and Industry and the Department of Banking and Insurance. Administration of the disability benefits law includes not only the operation of the state plan but general supervision and approval of the various private plans.

NOTES

[1] L., 1878, ch. 105, p. 169. The title used by the new agency was Bureau of Statistics of Labor and Industries. N.J. *Legislative Documents, 1879*, II, No. 55.
[2] L., 1904, ch. 64, p. 152.
[3] L., 1916, ch. 40, p. 67.
[4] L., 1948, ch. 446, p. 1762.
[5] L., 1925, ch. 117, p. 338.
[6] N.J. *Annual Report of the New Jersey Department of Labor and Industry, July 1, 1954-June 30, 1955*, p. 11.
[7] L., 1954, ch. 197, p. 730.
[8] L., 1912, ch. 216, p. 337.
[9] N.J. *Minutes of Assembly, 1851*, p. 129.
[10] L., 1851, p. 321.

[11] See articles by Hugh F. Fox in *The Annals*, "Child Labor in New Jersey," XX (1902), 191-99, and "The Operation of the New Child Labor Law in New Jersey," XXV (1905), 522-27. See Philip Charles Newman, *The Labor Legislation of New Jersey* (Washington: American Council on Public Affairs, 1943), ch. IX.

[12] L., 1940, ch. 153, pp. 344-45.

[13] *Ibid.*, p. 331.

[14] L., 1945, ch. 74, p. 378.

[15] L., 1932, ch. 249, p. 546.

[16] L., 1933, ch. 152, p. 304.

[17] For population characteristics, employment, and earnings see Louis J. Ducoff, "Migratory Farm Workers in 1949," *Agriculture Information Bulletin*, No. 25 (Bureau of Agricultural Economics, United States Department of Agriculture, 1950).

[18] L., 1945, ch. 71, p. 351.

[19] *Migratory Labor in American Agriculture* (Report of the President's Commission on Migratory Labor, 1951), p. 108.

[20] *Ibid.*, p. 111.

[21] Since 1918 the Bureau of Employment had been required to assist and counsel migrant laborers. L., 1918, ch. 235, p. 845.

[22] *Migratory Labor in American Agriculture, op. cit.*, pp. 92-93.

[23] *Annual Report . . . , op. cit.*, p. 118.

[24] L., 1892, ch. 137, p. 238. See Newman, *op. cit.*, pp. 50-54.

[25] L., 1895, ch. 341, p. 688.

[26] *Annual Report . . . , op. cit.*, pp. 131-34.

[27] *Ibid.*, p. 230.

[28] L., 1946, ch. 38, p. 87.

[29] *Ibid.*, p. 93.

[30] L., 1947, ch. 47, p. 160. Individual penalties providing fine and imprisonment were later removed. L., 1947, ch. 75, p. 443.

[31] *Van Riper* v *Traffic Tel. Workers' Fed. of N.J.* 2 N.J. 335 (1949).

[32] *Amalgamated Association, etc.* v *Wisconsin Emp. Rel. Bd.* 340 U.S. 383 (1951). For an analysis of the differences between the Wisconsin and New Jersey acts, see Jack Pincus and Eli J. Warach, "The New Jersey Public Utilities Labor Disputes Act: Some Considerations as to its Validity," *Rutgers Law Review*, V (Spring, 1951), 531-38.

[33] *N.J. Bell Tel. Co.* v *Communications Workers, etc.*, 5 N.J. 354, 380 (1950).

[34] Robert R. France and Richard A. Lester, *Compulsory Arbitration of Utility Disputes in New Jersey and Pennsylvania* (Princeton: Industrial Relations Section, Department of Economics and Social Institutions, Princeton University, 1951), p. 57.

[35] N.J. *Report to Governor Robert B. Meyner by the Governor's Committee on Legislation Relating to Public Utility Labor Disputes* (Trenton, 1954), p. 18.

[36] L., 1911, ch. 95, p. 134.

[37] N.J. *Senate Journal*, 1911, p. 61.

[38] L., 1918, ch. 149, p. 429.

[39] L., 1917, ch. 178, p. 522.

[40] L., 1945, ch. 74, pp. 391-92.

[41] *Brown* v *Brann and Stuart Co.* 20 N.J. Misc. 405 (1942).

[42] *Andricsak* v *National Fireproofing Corp.* 3 N.J. 471 (1950).

[43] *Schafer* v *Bernard* 18 N.J. Misc. 119 (1940).

[44] *Huber* v *New England Tree Expert Co.* 137 N.J.L. 549, 552 (1948).

[45] *Annual Report . . . , op. cit.*, pp. 157, 201.

[46] L., 1919, ch. 74, p. 138.

[47] L., 1948, ch. 446, p. 1762.

[48] L., 1946, ch. 263, p. 922.

[49] N.J. Department of Labor and Industry, *Rehabilitation Commission, Annual Report,* July 1, 1951—June 30, 1952, pp. 1, 21.

[50] L., 1915, ch. 47, p. 87.

51 *Synopsis of Plan of Operations and Employment Service Seven Point Program,*
Release of Bureau of Public Relations, Department of Labor and Industry
(mimeographed, undated), p. 1.

52 L., 1936, ch. 270, pp. 1045-46.

53 Edwin E. Witte, "Development of Unemployment Compensation," *The Yale
Law Journal,* LV (December, 1945), 21-52.

54 L., 1948, ch. 446, p. 1762.

55 L., 1952, ch. 187, p. 616.

56 *Annual Report . . . , op. cit.,* p. 226.

57 See, for example, Almon R. Arnold, "Experience Rating," *The Yale Law
Journal,* 55 (December, 1945), 218-41.

58 *Annual Report . . . , op. cit.,* p. 225.

59 L., 1948, ch. 110, p. 587.

60 *Annual Report . . . , op. cit.,* p. 215.

CHAPTER 22

The Regulation of Business and Industry

THE FUNCTIONS OF the New Jersey state government vary greatly in their scope and purpose. At one extreme, the state acts positively—to establish and operate the School for the Deaf or to assist farmers in the distribution of agricultural products. At the other extreme, the state acts negatively— to punish the individual who violates one of the criminal laws. But the state operates also in a middle ground—where standards and guide lines are necessary as a means of preventing the few from acting against the general public interest. State regulation of certain types of business and industry illustrates this middle area of governmental action.

FINANCIAL INSTITUTIONS

The state endeavors to prevent unsafe and unethical practices by banks, insurance companies, real estate agencies, and other organizations and individuals engaged in financial operations. Originally a function of the secretary of state, regulatory activities were placed in a Department of Banking and Insurance in 1891. The agency was designated a principal department in 1948.[1] The internal organization is specified by law.

At the head of the department is a commissioner of banking and insurance who is appointed by the governor, with Senate consent, to serve at the governor's pleasure or until a successor has been appointed and qualified. The commissioner may not be connected with the control of any of the corporations regulated by the department.

Banks

In 1955, 109 commercial banks, with assets totaling over $2,600,000,000, were operating under state authorization. In addition, there were twenty-three mutual savings banks with assets of over $1,000,000,000. Out-of-state banks authorized to do business in New Jersey totaled thirty-four. The number of national banks in New Jersey was 188, with assets of over $3,400,000,000.[2]

A minimum of seven persons, "of full age," may incorporate a bank.* They are required to execute a certificate of incorporation setting forth the ownership, the amount of capital stock, the initial surplus, and other information specified by law. When the certificate of incorporation, together with an affidavit by each incorporator, is submitted to the commissioner of banking and insurance, it constitutes an application for a bank charter. After a public hearing, the commissioner is required to approve or reject the application and to file with the department a statement of the reasons for his decision. Upon approval of the charter, the bank may proceed with its organization, but no business may be transacted until a certificate of authority has been issued by the commissioner. Failure to issue the certificate is subject to review in the Superior Court.[3] Branch banks and auxiliary offices may be established in the municipality or county of the parent organization. However, there are a number of legislative restrictions surrounding the setting up of branch banks.

In 1948 a comprehensive revision of the banking laws was enacted.[4] The powers of banks are prescribed by statute. The law prohibits banks from engaging in certain activities. For example, except under specified circumstances, a bank may not purchase its own capital stock. Violations of prohibited practices may be enjoined by the court upon suit of the commissioner.

Every bank is required to file at least two reports annually with the commissioner. He may examine a bank at any time and may, by subpoena, compel the appearance of persons and papers. If any person refuses to obey the subpoena, the commissioner may apply to the Superior Court for an order compelling compliance.

The commissioner may order a bank to cease unlawful or unsafe practices. Such an order is subject to review by the Superior Court. He may also take possession of any bank which in his opinion is in an unsound

---

* L., 1948, ch. 67, p. 181. Nine persons are required to incorporate a savings bank. In 1856 Charles Sanford and seven associates established the Cataract City Bank in Paterson, a commercial bank. Sanford owned 2,965 shares and each of his associates five shares. When the bank failed four years later, the argument was advanced that there had been no incorporation. The Supreme Court held to the contrary. At that time it was necessary only to file and record the certificate of incorporation with the secretary of state and the clerk of the county. *Rafferty, Receiver, etc.* v *Bank of Jersey City* 33 N.J.L. 368 (1869).

condition. The bank may apply to the court for an order directing the commissioner to show cause why the property should not be retained.

The commissioner has a Banking Advisory Board to assist him in determining policy. It consists of the commissioner, ex officio, and eight unsalaried members appointed by the governor with Senate consent for terms of four years. Within the framework of the commissioner's powers and subject to his approval, the board may, by a two-thirds vote, make, amend, or repeal regulations governing certain phases of the banking business.

Securities Regulation

The New Jersey securities law, or Blue Sky Law as it is commonly called, is designed to prevent fraud in the sale of securities:

The opportunity for fraud in the sale or exchange of securities is manifest, and bitter have been the experiences of many who have relied upon the representations of dishonest dealers, and even upon the representations of honest dealers, in the handling of dishonest securities.[5]

Fraud is defined by statute as misrepresentation, omissions in disclosing facts, promises which are beyond reasonable expectation, and attempting to gain profits "so large and exorbitant as to be unconscionable and unreasonable." [6] The use of fraud in connection with the sale of securities "within or from" New Jersey is prohibited.

Enforcement of the securities law is the responsibility of the attorney general. Whenever he considers that the public interest would be served by an investigation, he may require statements and reports under oath covering the business of the enterprise in question. He may, by subpoena, order the production of records or compel the attendance of witnesses. The attorney general may apply to the courts for assistance in the event of a failure to comply with his order. He may also apply to the courts for an injunction, or the appointment of a receiver, to restrain the continuance of illegal practices. The attorney general is authorized to recover for state use the costs of any proceeding.

Building and Loan and Savings and Loan Associations

In 1955 there were 448 active state-chartered building and loan and savings and loan associations in New Jersey. For over a century these associations have been given legislative recognition for their importance in encouraging thrift, frugality, and home ownership. Comprehensive legislation was first enacted in 1903 to correct a "public scandal" in the loose operation of building and loan associations.[7]

Any nine or more citizens of the state may apply for a certificate of incorporation. The application is subject to the approval of the commissioner of banking and insurance. After a public hearing, and perhaps an independent investigation, the commissioner approves or rejects the application. Such factors as the area to be served, the character of the incorporators, and whether the proposed association would be of service to the public are to be weighed in making the decision.

Associations are regulated by state law with respect to their powers, management, membership plans, and assessments. An annual financial statement must be filed with the commissioner who is required to examine each association at least once every two years. He has the power to subpoena books and records of the association, but if any person refuses to obey, an application must be made to the court for an order to compel production of the documents.

The state, through the commissioner of banking and insurance, has extensive powers of supervision. He may order an association to discontinue unsafe or illegal practices. Refusal to comply makes the association liable to a fine of $500, to be recovered, however, not by the commissioner directly but through the courts after prosecution by the attorney general. Foreign associations—that is, those not incorporated under New Jersey law—may have their authority to do business revoked. The commissioner may apply to the court for an injunction to prohibit further business transactions, or he may take immediate possession of an association pending its merger, reorganization, dissolution, or liquidation. The association, or any member, may appeal to the Superior Court for appropriate relief. The court has authority to determine both the law and the facts in the case and to issue any order it considers proper.

Small Loan Companies

The commissioner of banking and insurance supervises persons operating under the state's small loan law: "The object [of the law] was the eradication of the abuses and evil practices that had attended the conduct of this business, primarily the unconscionable and oppressive interest exactions." [8] The statute permits a maximum interest rate of 2.5 per cent per month on balances of $300 or less and 0.5 per cent per month on that portion of the balance exceeding $300 and not over $500.

Those engaged in the business of making loans of $500 or less must be licensed and bonded. The commissioner is required to investigate the applications and issue licenses. He may deny an application or, upon notice and hearing, revoke a license. He is authorized also to make rules and regulations governing the small loan business. In 1955 there were 235 licensed small loan offices.

Credit Unions and Other Agencies

Credit unions are also supervised by the commissioner of banking and insurance. Supervision includes approving the certificate of incorporation and the by-laws of the credit union; examining the organization at least once every two years; receiving a report annually; and, if necessary, taking possession of the property and business of the credit union. However, this drastic action may be taken only with the approval of the Superior Court.

First authorized in 1938, credit unions are cooperative associations formed for the promotion of thrift and to create a mutual fund from which loans are made to members. There were seventy-five state-chartered credit unions in 1955. In general, membership is limited to groups having a common employer, members of a church congregation, employees of a governmental unit, or residents of a rural area having a population of no more than 2,500.[9]

Investment companies and sales finance companies are subject to regulation by the commissioner, as are the provident loan associations which make loans secured by a pledge on personal property. The licensing and regulation of pawnbrokers, the inspection of special trust funds of cemetery associations, the licensing of persons making a business of cashing checks, and the authorization of persons to engage in the business of transmitting money overseas fall within the purview of the Department of Banking and Insurance.

INSURANCE

Early state interest in insurance was confined to granting special charters to companies insuring against fire and marine risks. In 1826 an act was passed regulating and taxing New Jersey agents of out-of-state companies. Legislation enacted in 1852 required life insurance companies to submit an annual report to the secretary of state. The law required also that this report be published daily for two weeks in a Trenton newspaper.[10] The supervisory relationship of the secretary of state was terminated in 1891 with the creation of the Department of Banking and Insurance.

State law regulates the formation of insurance companies and the kinds of insurance which may be sold. Persons wishing to incorporate are required to sign a certificate setting forth the name of the proposed company, the location of the principal office, the kinds of insurance to be sold, whether a stock or mutual company, the amount of capital stock, and other information. Both the attorney general and the commissioner of banking and insurance must give their approval before the new company may transact business. The function of the attorney general is to determine whether the certificate of incorporation is consistent with state law. The commissioner of banking and insurance must determine whether the company's proposed methods of operation constitute a hazard to its policy-holders or to the public. He is responsible also for the regulation of the insurance business.

Supervision of Companies

The commissioner may issue a cease and desist order against companies violating the insurance laws. Notice and hearing are required, after which a statement of specific violations must be served upon the company. Cease and desist orders may be reviewed by the courts.

Insurance agents, brokers, and solicitors are required to be licensed. The commissioner may revoke a license, after notice and hearing, providing he finds fraud or misrepresentation in obtaining the license. Illegal withholding of premiums or other violations of the insurance laws, as well as improper services to the public, are also causes for revocation.

Every insurance company licensed to do business in New Jersey is required to submit an annual statement to the commissioner showing the amount of business transacted and its financial condition including premiums written, losses paid, assets, liabilities, capital stock, surplus, and other matters prescribed by the commissioner. In 1952 statements were received from 446 fire and casualty companies, seventy-seven life insurance companies, eighty-two fraternal beneficiary associations, three mutual benefit associations, three hospital service corporations, and nineteen mutual benefit associations.

The state prescribes by law the kinds of investments insurance companies may make. Legal restrictions are placed upon loans, investments, and deposits. For example, no life insurance company may invest more than 2 per cent of its assets in any one corporation nor loan money upon its own stock.[11]

As a check in determining the value of securities held by the companies, the state works through the Committee on Valuation of Securities of the National Association of Insurance Commissioners.* The committee investigates, analyzes, and evaluates securities. The information obtained is made available to other states as an aid in supplying supervision over insurance companies. The costs of the evaluations are met through assessments on the companies.

Rating organizations—that is, those engaged in insurance rate-making—must also be licensed. They may not discriminate in the services provided to members and subscribers. The rates established by the rating organization must be reasonable and at the same time adequate for the "safety and soundness" of the company.[12] The rating systems used by an insurer are required to be filed with the commissioner, who may within ninety days disapprove them as being excessive, inadequate, or discriminatory. Rebates or other departures from the rating system are prohibited unless

---

* The National Association of Insurance Commissioners is a voluntary organization of the top state officials concerned with insurance supervision. For a brief description of its activities, see "State Regulation of Insurance," *The Book of the States, 1952-53* (Chicago: The Council of State Governments, 1952), pp. 444-46.

specifically approved by the commissioner. He is required to examine the methods of operation of each rating organization at least every five years. Insurance advisory organizations, which assist insurers and rating organizations by the collection of loss and expense information, are also subject to examination by the commissioner.

Special legislation was enacted in 1947 prohibiting unfair trade practices. False advertising and misrepresentation of policy contracts, disseminating false information, defamation, boycotts, coercion, intimidation, rebates, and unfair discrimination were forbidden. The commissioner was empowered, after notice and hearing, to issue a cease and desist order. By petition, a court review of the decision may be obtained. If the practice deemed unfair is not specifically mentioned in the act, the commissioner may petition, through the attorney general, for the assistance of the court. Under this circumstance, the court assumes jurisdiction of the case and, if it finds an unfair practice, issues the restraining order. This measure was adopted in order to supply an increased degree of state regulation.

Federal versus State Control

Insurance companies had been free of Federal intervention under the Sherman Antitrust Act by virtue of the decision of the United States Supreme Court that "issuing a policy of insurance is not a transaction of commerce." [13]   However, in 1944 the court reversed itself.[14]   Both the insurance companies and the states feared that the insurance rating organizations would fall within the Sherman Act's prohibition of price-fixing agreements.   Congress removed this fear to a considerable degree by the passage of the McCarran Act in 1945 which declared that the Sherman Act, the Clayton Act, the Federal Trade Commission Act, and the Robinson-Patman Anti-Discrimination Act were to apply to insurance only "to the extent that such business is not regulated by State law." [15]   New Jersey, in 1944, had enacted regulatory measures designed to insure reasonable, adequate, and non-discriminatory rates.[16]   This legislation was supplemented in 1947 by the statute concerning unfair trade practices.[17]   Taken together, these measures may sufficiently protect New Jersey insurance organizations from the operations of the antitrust laws.[18]

PUBLIC UTILITIES

At the urging of Governor Woodrow Wilson, New Jersey enacted comprehensive public utility legislation in 1911.[19]   Corporations supplying transportation, water, light, heat, and power, Wilson observed, "render a public and common service of which it is necessary that practically everybody should avail himself." [20]   Effective regulation of these businesses, he contended, was in the interest both of the public and of the corporations themselves.   Based upon a New York statute of 1906, the Public Utility

Law of 1911 established a three-member Board of Public Utility Commissioners with rate-making and other powers designed to assure adequate state supervision. With some modification, this system of control still prevails.

One of the reorganization acts of 1948 designated the Board of Public Utility Commissioners as a principal department. The board was declared to be the head of the department. Appointments to the board are made by the governor with the advice and consent of the Senate for terms of six years. No more than two of the three members may belong to the same political party.[21] One member is designated by the governor to serve at his pleasure as president. The president is the chief administrative officer of the department.

The jurisdiction of the department in 1953 extended in small or large degree to 828 public utilities. Of this number, 186 water utilities, ten electric, and one gas utility were municipally operated. Municipal utilities are under the department's jurisdiction in a casual way only, with reference to (1) the filing of annual reports and (2) rates for service beyond municipal boundaries.[22] There were 631 privately owned utilities under the jurisdiction of the board. This number included eight electric utilities, nine gas, nine telephone, 113 water, eight sewerage, and 492 local transportation companies. In general, the supervisory activities of the board are concerned with the problems of (1) rates, (2) quality of service, (3) adequacy of facilities, and (4) the issuance of securities.

Standards of Service

One of the major interests of the board concerns the adequacy, safety, and quality of service provided by the public utilities. The Board of Public Utility Commissioners is authorized to issue regulations establishing standards of service which the utility must follow. For example, companies are required to conduct periodic tests of their meters and to file summaries of the tests.* The public utility department has its own testing equipment calibrated regularly by the United States Bureau of Standards. These instruments are used to check the testing equipment of the utilities.

A utility may not abandon its operations without authorization. An application to do so must show that the public convenience and necessity are not affected adversely and that the particular service is no longer feasible. Railroads and buses, because of changing operating conditions, frequently request the discontinuance of service. After public hearing, the public utilities board approves or rejects the application for discontinuance. In 1950 there were twenty-two applications for change in the status of rail-

* In 1953 the number of meters was approximately as follows: 1,850,000 electric, 1,300,000 gas, and 350,000 water. *Forty-fourth Annual Report of the Board of Public Utility Commissioners to Hon. Robert B. Meyner, Governor, for the year 1953* (Trenton, 1954), pp. 26, 32, 37.

road stations—that is, to change the station from an agency to a non-agency status, to remove the station building, or to abandon the station completely. Seventeen applications were approved, one was denied, and four held open for further examination.

Decisions of the Board of Public Utility Commissioners may be appealed to the courts. One of the most interesting cases interpreting the board's right to permit the abandonment of railroad service concerned the twenty-mile branch line between Woodbury and Penns Grove. The board granted the request of the Pennsylvania-Reading Seashore Lines to discontinue passenger service. Parallel bus service was available, and revenues were not sufficient to cover operating costs. From January 1, 1938, to August 31, 1939, there were on the average only twelve passengers per train. The decision of the board was appealed. In 1942 the Supreme Court upheld the board. The Court of Errors and Appeals reversed the decision, holding that since the railroad's franchise authorized the carriage of both passengers and freight, the cessation of the carriage of passengers was a breach of contract which the board had no right to waive.[23] In 1949 the railroad again tried to abandon the passenger service. Evidence at the public hearing showed that the number of passengers averaged 6.2 on one train and 8.1 on another. The board found that:

Continued operation of non-essential service at a substantial continuing loss, particularly where as here another means of reasonably convenient public transportation is available, is, in our opinion, not justified as in the public interest.[24]

In spite of this finding, the board ordered the passenger service continued because of what appeared to be the binding decision of the court.

TABLE 26

TYPES OF COMPLAINTS

	No. of Complaints
Railroads	
Rates and fares	54
Station facilities and train service	97
Conditions at grade crossings	15
Street Transportation	191
Electric, Gas, Water, Telephone, and Sewer	
Service extensions	169
Rate schedules	119
Billing practices	165
Meter Tests	22
Quality of service	84
Miscellaneous	44

Source: N.J. *Forty-first Annual Report of the Board of Public Utility Commissioners to Hon. Alfred E. Driscoll, Governor, for the year 1950* (Trenton, 1951), pp. 38-40.

The order was affirmed by the appellate division of the Superior Court. The Supreme Court, however, took a different view. In holding that the top court's decision in 1942 was unsound, the chief justice observed that the principle of *stare decisis* was entitled to respect but was "not an idol to be worshipped . . . ." [25] The court held also that the board's order to continue the service constituted an arbitrary taking of property in violation of the due process clause of both the state and Federal constitutions. It declared also that by forcing the railroad to operate the branch line at a deficit, all the system's service was jeopardized thus imposing an undue burden on interstate commerce.

Complaints relating to service are referred to departmental inspectors who conduct an investigation. If the company is at fault, an effort is made through informal negotiations to effect an adjustment. Either the complainant or the company may apply for a formal hearing before the board. The types of complaints received by the board are illustrated in Table 26.

Safety

Departmental representatives inspect railroad tracks and structures annually to determine whether the facilities are proper and safe for the traffic they bear. The board may require the railroad companies to make repairs or improvements. This authority extends to ordering the installation of automatic electric crossing gates and to the elimination of grade crossings. Serious accidents must be reported. They are usually investigated by members of the staff.

Reports are required of bus operators who are involved in an accident. Representatives of the utilities board normally investigate fatal accidents or those involving an unusual incident. Departmental inspectors in 1954 made 10,573 inspections of buses to determine whether they were safe and were being properly maintained.[26] Periodic inspection is made of out-of-state buses which operate in New Jersey. Reciprocal agreements have been negotiated with New York and Pennsylvania under which a certificate of inspection of one of the states is accepted by the other two. Bus operators are required by law to carry insurance against liability for property damage and personal injury. Evidence of this insurance must be filed with the board.

Grade crossing accidents resulted in death to twenty-two persons and injury to eighty-seven during 1954.[27] Over a period of years the board has endeavored to eliminate the more hazardous crossings and where elimination was impractical, to promote the installation of protective devices.* Sepa-

* Signals and safety devices are under the jurisdiction of the Federal Interstate Commerce Commission. Track and structural changes are under the jurisdiction of the state public utility board. An application to the Interstate Commerce Commission for a signal change would be referred to the board for investigation. If the investigation showed that the proposed change would adversely affect the service, a hearing would be held and a determination made by the board prior to a decision by the Interstate Commerce Commission.

ration of railroads and highways furnishes the only positive protection. However, the high cost factor has made rapid progress difficult. The board's policy is to withhold approval of application for new grade crossings except at industrial sidings where normally the expense of a bridge would be prohibitive.

In 1938 there were about 3,740 public and private grade crossings. The kind of protection afforded at these crossings falls within the jurisdiction of the public utilities board. However, its authority to order the elimination of grade crossings is limited to other than state highways. These are under the jurisdiction of the State Highway Department.

Prior to 1930 the entire cost of grade separation was borne by the railroads. With the aid of the state and later of the Federal government, a considerable number of projects was completed during the 1930's. At present, the railroad company is required to pay only 15 per cent of the cost incident to the elimination of a grade crossing.[28]

Control of Security Issues

No utility may issue securities without the approval of the Board of Public Utility Commissioners. The Public Utility Law of 1911 required that an application be made to the board and that the application be approved prior to the issuance of any stocks or bonds. The purpose of this regulation was to lessen and, if possible, to eliminate the abuse of overcapitalization. Prior to 1911 overcapitalization was extensive. Particularly when utilities were consolidated, large quantities of new stock were issued which bore little relation to the value of the properties involved or to the earning power of the new companies.

Approval by the board furnishes no guarantee of the intrinsic value of the security. Board approval of new issues is designed to assure that there is a legitimate need for the money to be raised, that the corporation will obtain assets approximately equal to the value of the securities, and that the company probably will be able to meet the fiscal charges imposed by the security.[29] In 1954 the board received 85 applications requesting approval of the sale of property and of the issuance or transfer of stocks, bonds, and notes.

The board must also approve the sale of a utility. It endeavors to determine such matters as the reasonableness of the sales price, the question of continued safe and adequate service, and other aspects of the sale affecting the public interest.

Rate Regulation

The determination of rates for service constitutes the board's greatest problem. It is authorized by law to fix "just and reasonable" rates. In general, two steps must precede the determination of the actual charge for a given utility service. The first involves establishing a rate base, that is, the amount in dollars upon which the utility is entitled to earn a reasonable return; the second involves establishing a rate of return, that is, an annual percentage of the rate base. The rate base multiplied by the rate of return gives an amount which the board considers the utility is entitled to earn. Unfortunately, for all parties concerned—the utility, the public, and the board—the determination of the rate base of an electric power, telephone, or railroad company has for three quarters of a century proved to be a complex and baffling problem.

In arriving at the value of a utility's property, the board has followed the practice of considering the original cost adjusted to what the courts have referred to as prudent investment cost. Reproduction cost is also taken into account. Thus the termination of fair value involves a reasonable judgment of the property's value as distinguished from the result of any single or arbitrary formula.[30]

There are a number of formulae useful in the determination of fair value: depreciated original cost, depreciated prudent investment, reproduction cost of the property less depreciation, cost of reproducing the service as distinct from the property, and there are undoubtedly others. But the Board is not bound to and, indeed, should not use any single formula or combination of formulae in arriving at a proper rate base, for the determination of fair value is not controlled by arbitrary rules or formulae, but should reflect the reasonable judgment of the board based upon all the relevant facts.[31]

Determination of the rate of return is also a somewhat complicated problem. Utilities require large amounts of investment money. The return must be sufficient to induce investors to risk their funds.[32] In recent years rising costs have resulted in large numbers of requests for increases in the rate or fare charged. The board's practice in each instance involving rates or fares is to hold a public hearing. In order to speed up the hearing process, the board may designate certain members of its staff as hearing examiners.

Procedures

In any proceeding requiring a formal order or a certificate, an investigation is made, a staff report is prepared, public hearings are held, and, finally, the utility board makes a decision. Technical rules of evidence are not required. In 1954, 575 decisions, orders, and certificates were issued.[33] In some of these, one day's work by a staff member was sufficient for the board to make a determination. In others, the investigative work and the public hearings extended over a period of months. This lengthy study was necessary in order to meet the requirement of the courts that there be sufficient evidence to support the board's determination.

For over a decade the annual reports of the board have pointed up the necessity of a qualified staff sufficiently large to perform properly the work of the agency. In 1940 the total personnel was eighty-six; in 1956 ninety-one positions were authorized. This increase would seem to bear little relationship to the vastly increased regulatory burden resulting from New Jersey's industrial development.

ALCOHOLIC BEVERAGE CONTROL

New Jersey is known as an "open licensing" state; that is, it has no operating responsibilities, aside from the controls related to licensing, in connection with the manufacture, sale, and distribution of alcoholic beverages. However, licenses and permits are required for every commercial activity.[34] The system in New Jersey is in contrast to that in seventeen "monopoly" states, such as Pennsylvania, where the retail sale of packaged liquor is in the hands of state-owned "package stores." [35]

A few weeks prior to the enactment of the Twenty-first Amendment in December, 1933, a New Jersey state commission recommended a plan for "rigid control over what should hereafter be a legitimate and not an outcast industry . . . ." [36] At the suggestion of the commission, a Department of Alcoholic Beverage Control was established by law. The purposes in providing control were defined by the first commissioner of the new department as follows:

to regulate manufacture, sale and distribution, to police an industry, to chart the business through defined tax channels, to remedy abuses inherent in liquor traffic, to promote decency, sobriety and order, and the power to compel obedience to orders. It means not only that licensees shall obey, but that everybody else must respect the law . . . . The major problem of control is to stop everybody else from doing the same thing that only legitimate licensees may do.[37]

Administration

The department continued as an independent agency until the reorganization in 1948.[38] At that time it was constituted a division of the Department of Law and Public Safety.* The organizational structure of the department was retained except that the old divisions were by law reconstituted as bureaus in the new division.

The director is charged with the appointment of inspectors, investigators, and executive assistants. These officials are not under civil service although they obtain tenure after a three-year probationary period.[39] The alcoholic beverage laws permit the director, his deputies, and the inspectors and investigators to make arrests without warrant for violations committed in

* The director of the division is appointed by the governor, subject to Senate confirmation, to serve during the governor's term of office and until a successor has qualified. The director may be removed by the governor for cause. Three deputy directors are appointed by the division head.

their presence. In the enforcement of these laws, they have the authority of peace officers.

Any municipality of over 15,000 population may establish a board of alcoholic beverage control. In municipalities having a population of 100,000 or more and having also a board of finance, there may be established a municipal excise commission.[40]

The director may make rules and regulations designed to control the alcoholic beverage industry. These rules cover licensing, appeals, disciplinary proceedings, labeling, fair trade contracts, and a host of other subjects.[41] However, in promulgating and interpreting these rules the courts have held that the "administrative authority is not vested with unlimited discretion; it is restrained by the principle of the statute and by the means and methods provided for its execution." [42]

Licensing

The following five classes of licenses are established by law:

Class A — manufacturer's license
Class B — wholesaler's license
Class C — retailer's license
Class D — transportation license
Class E — public warehouse license

Classes A, B, and C have several subdivisions. "State licenses" are issued by the division for classes A, B, D, and E and for the plenary retail transit license, a subdivision of class C; most other class C licenses are issued by the municipal governing bodies or by municipal boards of alcoholic beverage control in accordance with the regulations of the division. Fees range from $5,000 for the Class A plenary distilling license authorizing the manufacture, sale, and distribution of any distilled alcoholic beverage to $10 for a Class C plenary retail transit license covering boats under five tons.

In 1947 the legislature placed a limitation upon the issuance of new retail licenses in a community. No new plenary retail consumption license or seasonal retail consumption license may be issued in any municipality until the total of these licenses is fewer than one for each 1,000 population.[43] This does not mean that there are now no more retail liquor establishments than one per 1,000 population. On the contrary, there are municipalities with as many as one per 74 persons.* The act does nothing to prevent renewals or transferals with the result that in many areas a

* In 1947 the Borough of Highlands had 28 licensed establishments and a population of 2,076 by the 1940 census. In a case before the Supreme Court the point was made that the summer population increased to 15,000. The court held that "the facts as revealed by the record here show a total lack of any public need or necessity for the issuance of additional licenses." *Brush* v *Hock* 137 N.J.L. 257, 259 (1948).

transfer brings a high price. A municipality may, on its own initiative, limit the number of retail licenses. It may also, by referendum, limit the hours of sale or even prohibit the retail sale of all kinds of alcoholic beverages.

The director of the division or the issuing authority may revoke or suspend any license in the event the holder of the license has violated state laws, local ordinances, or the rules and regulations of the division. The licensee must be given a five-day notice of the charges against him and a "reasonable opportunity" to be heard. He must be notified in writing of the suspension or revocation. An appeal may be taken to the director from decisions of a municipal body. The courts have long held that a liquor license is no contract. Rather, it is a privilege which the state, under its police power, may terminate.[44] Persons engaged in illegal alcoholic beverage activity may be subjected to arrest and criminal prosecution. Illicit stills and other unlawful property may be seized and, after hearing, be forfeited to the state.

WEIGHTS AND MEASURES

The Biblical injunction "let me be weighed in an even balance, that God may know mine integrity" is of more than casual interest to New Jersey's weights and measures enforcement officers. To them, merchants engaging in short weight and short measurement deserve the appellation "thief" just as surely as does the second story artist or the pickpocket.[45]

In 1911 the state created a Department of Weights and Measures and made the standards of weights and measures those recognized or supplied by the United States.[46] The statute was unusual in that county and municipal superintendents of weights and measures, although selected by their respective governing bodies, were included in the department. The jurisdiction of the county superintendent normally extended only to municipalities having no local superintendent.

As a result of the reorganization of 1948, the department was constituted a division of the Department of Law and Public Safety.[47] The division is headed by a superintendent who has general supervision over the administration of all weights and measures laws.* His powers extend also to the work of the county and municipal superintendents.† He is custodian of all standards. He is required to compare county and municipal stand-

---

* The superintendent is appointed by the governor, with the advice and consent of the Senate, to serve during the governor's term of office and until a successor has been appointed and qualified. The superintendent may be removed by the governor for cause.

† Municipalities of over 60,000 population are required to have a superintendent of weights and measures. Other municipalities may by ordinance provide for the office. In 1951 there were eighteen municipal superintendents. N.J. *Fortieth Annual Report of the Division of Weights and Measures, Department of Law and Public Safety*, 1951, p. 8.

ards with those of the state at least once in every five years and to check state standards with those of the National Bureau of Standards once in every ten years. He is authorized to establish rules and regulations governing the sale of commodities.

The major responsibility of the division is the elimination of faulty or fraudulent weighing and measuring equipment. For example, scales through constant service may wear out. Or, through premeditation, they may be adjusted to give short weight. Packages may be short weight due to carelessness or to intent to defraud. Failure to check milk cartons may mean that every package filled by machine is short weight.* Any person who "sells or exposes for sale less than the quantity he represents" violates the law.[48]

The law requires also that the net weight of any article of food sold in package form must be clearly indicated on the outside of the package. Violations of these statutes are frequent, due perhaps as much to indifference on the part of the producer as to deliberately fraudulent action. Potato growers who weigh, bag, and ship new potatoes without proper allowance for shrinkage are the source of many complaints. The sale of prepackaged meats lends itself to careless and dishonest practices. The division holds merchants responsible for the true weight marked on the package. Shrinkage losses may not legally be passed on to the consumer in the form of a short weight package.

Penalties are provided for violation of the various laws relating to weights and measures. For example, the punishment for failing to mark the net quantity on a food package is a fine of from $25 to $50 for the first offense, $50 to $100 for the second offense, and $100 to $200 thereafter. Efforts of the division to increase the penalties have met with failure in the legislature. Packaged goods other than food are not covered by existing law. A proposed net weight container law has also been sidetracked. Indeed, a considerable number of the weights and measures statutes are in need of revision if the consumer is to receive adequate protection.[49]

Except for personnel to man four newly established truck weighing stations, the operating staff at the state level has not been increased in any substantial degree since organized weights and measures work began in

* In 1948 the division received complaints that one of the large oil companies was distributing canned lubricating oil in short weight. Representatives of the division called the company's attention to the complaint. In the next two weeks 39,000 cases of motor oil were checked (twenty-four cans per case). Short measure beyond permissible tolerance was found in over 300 cases, the errors ranging from one ounce to over six ounces. Two sealed cans were found in which there was no oil at all. Subsequent investigation revealed that trapped air in the lines of the oil filling machine had caused the short measure condition. Laxity in inspection methods resulted in a large loss to the company not only in the cost of making restitution for the faulty cans but in the prestige value of the company name. N.J. *Thirty-seventh Annual Report of the Department of Weights and Measures,* 1948, pp. 27-28.

1912. As a consequence, supervisory and inspectional duties are of necessity spread too thin adequately to protect consumer welfare.[50]

RACING

The racing of horses has become one of the leading businesses in New Jersey. In 1954, the pari-mutuel track wagers of 2,822,606 patrons amounted to $260,786,625.

The courts have declared that "the business of horse racing and pari-mutuel wagering is so definitely affected with a quasi-public interest that legislative supervision, control and regulation is without question required." [51]

The government of the state regulates the business through the New Jersey Racing Commission, a bipartisan agency attached for administrative purposes to the Department of the Treasury. The four members of the commission are appointed by the governor, with the advice and consent of the Senate, for six-year terms. They serve without compensation. The members of the commission elect a chairman annually.

The commission is required to approve applications for racing sites and to approve the officials supervising the races. It also licenses owners, trainers, jockeys, agents, and others concerned with the operation of the tracks. The commission has full authority to prescribe the rules and conditions governing racing. Running races are required by law to conform to the rules of the Jockey Club, steeplechase races to the rules of the National Steeplechase and Hunt Association, and harness races to the rules of the United States Trotting Association. These rules may be modified by the commission, but only after the associations have been given an opportunity to be heard.

An application for a racing site may be approved provisionally by the commission following a public hearing. However, final approval rests in the hands of the public. The question of permitting racing in a particular municipality and county must be voted upon in a general election. A majority of the voters both of the municipality and of the county concerned must approve the proposal.

The dates for horse race meets are subject to the commission's approval. The number of days of racing at each track has been increased substantially in recent years as shown below:

	1947	1950	1955
Atlantic City	42	45	50
Monmouth Park	36	47	50
Garden State	42	50	50
Freehold (harness racing)	24	24	50

In thirteen years of pari-mutuel operations, through 1953, state racing revenues amounted to $111,000,000.[52]

In order to protect the racing public, the commission retains private groups to conduct laboratory tests of the saliva and urine of horses. Evidence of the use of drugs may result in suspension of the owner. Employees of the racing association and of concessionaires are fingerprinted in order to exclude those with criminal records.

The supervision of racing involves other state agencies. Many stable employees are migrant laborers. The living quarters of these employees fall under the inspection authority of the Department of Labor, as does also investigation of the employment of minors. The Department of Health is interested in the problem of venereal disease control. The State Police assist in controlling traffic and work with private agencies in policing the tracks. In order to reduce the problem of illegal betting away from the tracks, the attorney general has endeavored to prevent the wagering of lay-off money—that is, bets made to protect bookmakers—at the mutuel windows. The protection of the public by the various state and local enforcement agencies requires a considerably greater effort than might be suspected from the New Jersey Racing Commission's reports indicating an actual out-of-pocket supervisory cost of less than one per cent of the revenues received.

NOTES

[1] L., 1891, ch. 6, p. 17, and L., 1948, ch. 88, p. 499.

[2] *Annual Report, Bureau of Banking,* 1955, pp. v-xv.

[3] For a sharp criticism of the method of granting bank charters in the 1920's, see *Report of Joint Legislative Commission to Investigate Department of Banking and Insurance,* 1929.

[4] L., 1948, ch. 67, p. 178.

[5] *Wilentz* v *Edwards* 134 N.J.Eq. 522, 528 (1943).

[6] L., 1930, ch. 52, p. 251.

[7] L., 1903, ch. 218, p. 457. See *Bucsi* v *Longworth Building and Loan Ass'n* 119 N.J.L. 120, 124 (1937).

[8] *Maellaro* v *Madison Finance Co. of Jersey City* 142 N.J.L. 140, 143 (1943).

[9] L., 1938, ch. 293, p. 632.

[10] L., 1852, ch. 69, p. 174. A general law for the incorporation of insurance companies was enacted the same year. L., 1852, ch. 64, p. 159. See John W. Cadman, Jr., *The Corporation in New Jersey, Business and Politics 1791-1875* (Cambridge: Harvard University Press, 1949), pp. 70-72, 217-18. See also John S. Thompson, "The Business of Insurance in New Jersey," in William Starr Myers (ed.), *The Story of New Jersey* (New York: Lewis Historical Publishing Company, Inc., 1945), pp. 493-546.

[11] L., 1937, ch. 164, p. 396.

[12] L., 1944, ch. 27, p. 72.

[13] *Paul* v *Virginia,* 8 Wall. 168, 183 (1868). The prohibitions in the Sherman Act were supplemented by those in the Federal Trade Commission Act, and the Robinson-Patman Act.

[14] *U.S.* v *Underwriters Association,* 322 U.S. 533 (1944).

[15] 59 U.S. Statutes-at-Large 33, 34.

[16] L., 1944, ch. 27, p. 69.

[17] L., 1947, ch. 379, p. 1200.

[18] "Is New Jersey's Insurance Legislation Sufficient to Comply with the Requirements of the McCarran Act?" *Rutgers Law Review,* III (February, 1949), 95-109.

[19] L., 1911, ch. 195, p. 374. Occasional laws regulating some phase of the business of a specific utility had been passed from time to time. Standards relating to the quality of gas, for example, were established in 1876. L., 1876, ch. 192, p. 309. A Public Utilities Commission was established in 1910, but it had only moderate regulatory powers. L., 1910, ch. 41, p. 56.

[20] N.J. *Senate Journal,* 1911, p. 63.

[21] L., 1948, ch. 90, p. 506. Members must be citizens of the state and not under age 30.

[22] N.J. *Forty-fourth Annual Report of the Board of Public Utility Commissioners to Hon. Robert B. Meyner, Governor, for the year 1953* (Trenton, 1954), p. 1.

[23] *O'Connor* v *Board of Public Utility Commissioners* 128 N.J.L. 35 (1942); Reversed, 129 N.J.L. 263 (1942).

[24] Quoted in *Penna.-Reading S.S. Lines* v *Board of Public Utility Commissioners* 6 N.J. 114, 117-18 (1950).

[25] *Ibid.,* p. 123.

[26] N.J. *Forty-fifth Annual Report of the Board of Public Utility Commissioners to Hon. Robert B. Meyner, Governor, for the year 1954* (Trenton, 1955), p. 62.

[27] *Ibid.,* p. 47.

[28] L., 1947, ch. 178, p. 817.

[29] M. C. Waltersdorf, *Regulation of Public Utilities in New Jersey* (Waverly Press, Inc., 1936), pp. 105-9.

[30] N.J. *Twenty-ninth Annual Report of the Board of Public Utility Commissioners to Hon. A. Harry Moore, Governor, for the year 1938* (Trenton, 1938), p. 12.

[31] *Public Service Coordinated Transport* v *State* 5 N.J. 196, 217 (1950).

[32] *Ibid.* "The public is not to be laden with unreasonable or extortionate rates in order that dividends may be provided for the utility's stockholders."

[33] *Forty-fifth Annual Report . . . , op. cit.,* p. 13.

[34] L., 1933, ch. 436, p. 1180.

[35] For the statutory provisions of other states, see *The Book of the States, 1952-53* (Chicago: The Council of State Governments, 1952), p. 447.

[36] N.J. *Report on Alcoholic Beverage Control and Taxation prepared and submitted by the Alcoholic Beverage Commission to the One Hundred and Fifty-seventh Legislature of the State of New Jersey,* 1933, p. 12.

[37] *Report to the Governor and Legislature of the State of New Jersey* by D. Frederick Burnett, Commissioner, Department of Alcoholic Beverage Control, 1935, p. 3.

[38] L., 1948, ch. 439, p. 1707.

[39] L., 1945, ch. 229, p. 743.

[40] L., 1940, ch. 63, p. 175.

[41] N.J. Department of Alcoholic Beverage Control, *Rules and Regulations,* 1945.

[42] *Duff* v *Trenton Beverage Co.* 4 N.J. 595, 608 (1950).

[43] L., 1947, ch. 94, p. 501. An exception was made for new hotels.

[44] *Meehan* v *Board of Excise Commissioners of Jersey City* 73 N.J.L. 382 (1906). But the legislative provision for notice and an opportunity to be heard must be observed. *Drozdowski* v *Sayreville* 133 N.J.L. 536 (1946).

[45] N.J. *Thirty-eighth Annual Report of the Division of Weights and Measures, Department of Law and Public Safety,* 1949, p. 5.

[46] L., 1911, ch. 201, p. 414.

[47] L., 1948, ch. 439, p. 1707.

[48] L., 1911, ch. 201, p. 414.

[49] For the legislative recommendations of the division, see N.J. *Forty-third Annual Report of the Division of Weights and Measures, Department of Law and Public Safety,* 1954, pp. 32-34.

[50] *Ibid.,* p. 11.

[51] *State* v *Garden State Racing Association* 136 N.J.L. 173, 175 (1947).

[52] N.J. *Fourteenth Annual Report of the New Jersey Racing Commission to the Governor of New Jersey* (Trenton: Department of Treasury, Division of New Jersey Racing Commission, 1953), p. 4.

CHAPTER 23

State Occupational Licensing

FEW PEOPLE realize the extent to which state law governs admission to the practice of particular trades and professions. A directory compiled by the New Jersey State Employment Service in 1947 listed 214 occupations which required a state license prior to employment.[1] In some instances the requirements for a license are inconsequential. In others, years of formal training and experience are necessary before an individual is permitted to practice on his own.

The state government has a dual role in licensing occupations. It is obligated on the one hand to protect the public from those who profess to practice certain trades or professions, and who in fact are lacking in integrity or in competence. At the same time the government is obligated to prevent the licensing function from being abused. The law or regulations governing admission to practice may be so restrictive as to give those already in the occupation a monopoly position.

The determination of the trades or professions which properly should be licensed is not an easy one. All states license some occupational groups such as accountants, attorneys, dentists, pharmacists, and physicians.[2] In these fields there has been general public acceptance of the necessity for state action. But some occupations are licensed, not so much because of special problems which justify licensing legislation as because of the demands of the occupational group. In each occupational area controlled by a licensing system, governmental vigilance is necessary to protect the public generally, and to safeguard the interests of those seeking admission.

ORGANIZATION FOR LICENSING

Occupational licenses are issued by a number of state agencies. Prior to 1948, responsibility was vested chiefly in independent boards, each representing a particular occupation. When the Department of Law and Public Safety was created, the following eleven boards were placed in a Division of Professional Boards responsible to the attorney general:

New Jersey State Board of Public Accountants
New Jersey State Board of Architects
New Jersey State Board of Nursing
New Jersey State Board of Optometrists
State Board of Professional Engineers and Land Surveyors
State Board of Medical Examiners
State Board of Veterinary Medical Examiners
State Board of Shorthand Reporting
State Board of Registration and Examination in Dentistry
State Board of Mortuary Science of New Jersey *
Board of Pharmacy of the State of New Jersey

A twelfth board—the State Board of Examiners of Ophthalmic Dispensers and Ophthalmic Technicians—was created in 1952 and placed in the division.

As of mid-1954 little had been done to coordinate the work of the twelve boards in the Department of Law and Public Safety. Each continued to operate independently of the others and without departmental direction. The professional division has never had a director. However, late in 1954 the department initiated a program designed gradually to supply centralized supervision and control.

At the time of the 1948 reorganization, four formerly independent agencies were placed in other departments. The State Board of Barber Examiners and the Board of Beauty Culture Control were assigned to the Department of Health; the New Jersey Real Estate Commission was given divisional status in the Department of Banking and Insurance; and the New Jersey Racing Commission was placed under the jurisdiction of the Department of the Treasury.

In addition to the licensing activity of the formerly independent boards, a number of the departments issue occupational licenses. For example, detectives are licensed by the State Police, and health officers, inspectors, laboratory technicians, and sewage and water plant operators by the Department of Health. Admission to the practice of law is under the jurisdiction of the Supreme Court.

---

* In 1952 the Board of Embalmers and Funeral Directors of the State of New Jersey was changed to the State Board of Mortuary Science of New Jersey.

Composition

The composition of license-issuing boards varies. Accountants have a boards of three members, the barbers have four, the mortuary scientists five, the dentists eight, and the physicians eleven full members and two qualified members—a chiropodist and a bio-analytical laboratory director. In most instances, members of a board must be practitioners of the occupation they represent. Rarely are board members appointed to represent the public; the beauticians are an exception, one of six may not be identified with the business of beauty culture. Appointments are made by the governor although for each member to be appointed the governor's choice is often limited to one of a list of three submitted by a society of the members. In general, board members may be removed by the governor, for cause, upon notice and opportunity to be heard.

The fact that board membership in New Jersey is restricted exclusively to members of the occupation selected by their trade associations is not unique. This is the normal pattern throughout the country. The practice is defended on the grounds that politics is kept at a minimum, competent individuals are chosen, and the cooperation of the regulated group is more easily secured. Opponents of the practice argue that the public interest can not properly be served by board members who have an economic stake in the regulations they issue and in the actions they take.[3] There is no easy solution to this dilemma. The reconciliation of the public interest with that of the occupational group would seem to require some lay representation on the boards. The list of three unduly restricts the governor's choice in an occupational group numbering in the hundreds or thousands. Centralized administration of the boards would tend also to reduce the opportunity for arbitrary action on the part of any licensing group.

Powers and Duties

Occupational boards have as their principal functions the making of rules in accordance with legislative direction, the examination of persons desiring licenses, and to some degree the policing of the occupation. Licensing requirements are usually spelled out in considerable detail in the statutes.

Holders of occupational licenses are required to comply with regulations established by administrative rule. These rules must be in accordance with legislative standards. They must not enlarge upon the statute: "administrative implementation cannot deviate from the principle and policy of the statute."[4] Nor may the rules be arbitrary, oppressive, or unreasonable.[5]

Financing

When eleven of the professional boards were transferred to the Department of Law and Public Safety in 1948, they were required to prepare an annual budget for submission to the attorney general.[6] The object of the law was to apply the same budgetary procedures to the professional boards as were applicable to other agencies. The law also required that moneys received from licenses, registrations, fines, and other sources be deposited in the State Treasury to the credit of the boards. Expenditures were to be made upon the basis of appropriations. Vouchers required the warrant of the director of the Division of Budget and Accounting and the certification of the presiding officer of the board.

The new law was a sharp contrast with the old. Formerly the boards retained all income in their own treasuries. They were required simply to pay all expenses, and their accounts were subject to audit. Notwithstanding the 1948 law, the new procedures were adopted slowly. In actual practice the operations of the boards have been governed largely by the amounts available from fees. The budget procedures have amounted to little since the general appropriation act permitted the boards to spend up to the amounts they received. Thus a proposed expenditure which had been deleted by a budget examiner could be made by the agency on the basis of the authorization in the appropriation act.

LICENSING REQUIREMENTS

Qualifications

Citizenship, good moral character, and a designated minimum age are customary qualifications for an occupational license. Over the years there has been an increasing emphasis upon experience and training as a prerequisite to examination and licensing. For example, in 1877 the New Jersey Pharmaceutical Association obtained a law which required prospective pharmacists to pass an examination by the then newly created Board of Pharmacy. In 1886 a four-year experience requirement was added. Training and experience were combined in 1901 with the provision that two years of college could be substituted for two years of experience. From time to time additional educational requirements were added. Since 1932 a prospective pharmacist must have been graduated, or met the requirements for graduation, from a four-year school or college of pharmacy approved by the board. After completion of the required course work, the applicant must pass written examinations in four subjects. He is then qualified to enter the program of "Pharmacy Interneship" in an "Approved Training Pharmacy." After a minimum of one year as an interne and the passage of an examination in practical pharmacy and laboratory work, the applicant is entitled to a certificate of registration as a pharmacist.[7]

Examination

In most instances the agency in charge of licensing for a given occupation prepares and administers the examination. For example, the Board of Bar Examiners prepares, administers, and grades the examination for prospective members of the New Jersey bar. However, there are exceptions to this practice. Accountants are given an examination, which is uniform for the country as a whole, prepared by the American Institute of Accountants. National associations administer uniform examinations for dentists and doctors. An applicant for admission to the practice of medicine in New Jersey may be exempt from the examination by the State Board of Medical Examiners providing he passes the examination of the National Board of Medical Examiners. The state board in 1953 examined sixty-three applicants for a license to practice medicine and surgery. Of this number, forty-nine passed and were licensed. However, 163 applicants were licensed on the basis of credentials from the National Board of Medical Examiners.[8] Other applicants, numbering 156, presented acceptable credentials from other states. While the 156 doctors were moving into New Jersey from other areas of the country, seventy-eight New Jersey doctors applied for endorsement of their licenses to other states.

Apprenticeship

Apprenticeships are frequently required prior to licensing. A pharmacy graduate, for example, is required to obtain a minimum of one calendar year of practical experience. The rules of the Board of Pharmacy provide that a registered pharmacist in an "Approved Training Pharmacy" may become the "Pharmacy Interne Preceptor" for a "Pharmacy Interne." No pharmacy will be approved which has an annual volume of prescriptions under 5,000.

The prospective attorney must serve an apprenticeship of nine months with a preceptor who is a counsellor of law. The clerk is required to be in attendance daily in the counsellor's office for six hours a day. He must visit the courts on sixteen occasions of one day each. He must visit the legislature. He is required also to keep a log of his activities.

The apprenticeship period varies considerably. For barbers it is eighteen months, for architects, three years, for mortuary scientists, two or three years depending upon the amount of formal training, and for real estate brokers, two years. However, the apprenticeship period is waived for disabled veterans who have completed their formal training and passed the examination for real estate broker or real estate salesman.

The value of the apprenticeship depends upon the amount of attention given the beginner and the technical nature of the occupation. In some instances a period of apprenticeship would seem to afford an opportunity for exceedingly valuable training. In others, the question may well be raised whether the principal purpose of the apprenticeship is to train new people or to discourage prospective entrants.

LICENSING PROBLEMS

Interstate Reciprocity

Interstate reciprocity presents problems. Should an individual who passes an examination in another state be permitted to practice in New Jersey? Or should an individual who has engaged in an occupation in one state for a number of years be permitted, without restriction, to practice in New Jersey?

The licensing agencies have different approaches to these questions. The Board of Pharmacy in 1953 had arrangements with the boards of all except three states which do not engage in reciprocity, namely, California, Florida, and New York. Registration as a pharmacist on the basis of an examination in another state was approved by the board, providing the standards in the other state equaled the standards in New Jersey. Of 24 certificates of registration granted by reciprocity in 1953, 10 applicants were required to pass the examination in practical pharmacy and laboratory work.

The Board of Nursing has no agreement with any state or school. Each applicant is considered on an individual basis. The board takes into account the requirements of New Jersey law at the time the applicant was graduated from nursing school. In 1953, 854 licenses were issued by endorsement from other states. During the same period 553 nurses were endorsed to other states.[9]

Attorneys in other states who apply for admission to the bar in New Jersey receive no concessions. They are required to meet the educational and other qualifications established for beginners. The requirements include not only an examination but a nine-months clerkship in the office of a counsellor-at-law who acts as a preceptor. The lack of any reciprocity is declared to be justified on the basis of the differences in the law and legal procedures among the states. A member of the bar would argue that a doctor can diagnose the ills of a patient equally as well in Atlantic City as in Los Angeles, whereas an attorney who had practiced in Los Angeles would be greatly handicapped in Atlantic City until he had mastered New Jersey law and legal procedures.

A dentist who has been licensed in another state for ten years may take a special examination given once each year. This examination excludes the three days of writing required of other applicants. All candidates for dental licenses must be citizens of the United States.

Investigation and Discipline

Disciplinary action against the holder of a license is not uncommon. The origin of the action may have been a complaint to the board. For example, the State Police Narcotic Drug Squad investigates irregularities such as the improper labeling of a narcotic drug prescription or the acceptance of a telephoned prescription for narcotic drugs. The regular procedure of the Board of Pharmacy would be to hold a hearing at which the officer making the investigation would present evidence of the alleged offense. The pharmacist involved would be given an opportunity, with counsel, to plead his case. The board would then take appropriate disciplinary action, such as censuring or fining the offender or suspending or revoking his license.

Some of the boards have staff personnel who look for violations on the part of licensed members or persons practicing in the field. In 1953 the staff of the Board of Medical Examiners made 380 visits, some of which included receiving treatments. Of 145 cases under investigation, seventy-eight involved suspicion of practicing chiropractic without a license, and twenty involved allegations of druggists practicing medicine.

Board members themselves may initiate or conduct investigations and present complaints. The Superior Court overruled the action of the State Board of Optometrists in 1952 when one of the board members took too active a part in a license suspension proceeding. He had persuaded one of his own patients to act as an investigator. With funds supplied by the board member, the investigator had obtained an eye examination and glasses for $11.90. The glasses were turned over to the board member and action was brought on the grounds that the optometrist concerned was incompetent since he had supplied improper lenses. He was accused also of obtaining a fee by fraud and of misleading advertising. The board suspended the optometrist's license for ninety days. The court held that there was insufficient evidence to sustain this action. The court pointed out the fact that the board member initiating the investigation had previously sold glasses to his patient-investigator costing $45. The court declared:

Under all the disclosed circumstances [the board member] should have disqualified himself. It may well be that his entire participation was motivated by zeal in the discharge of a highly important public duty, which zeal does not disqualify, but where the investigation, prosecution and judicial functions repose in the same board, its members must be zealous in the recognition and preservation of the right to hearing by impartial triers of the facts and the courts must impose a most careful supervision of that element of the hearing.[10]

Licensing boards are empowered by law to refuse an application for a license or to suspend or revoke a license. For example, the Board of

Pharmacy may take such action if it determines that a certificate of registration had been obtained by misrepresentation or fraud. Chronic inebriety, drug addiction, conviction for the violation of state or Federal narcotic laws or of a crime involving moral turpitude—for these and other statutory reasons, a license may be refused, suspended, or revoked. The law requires that the accused person be furnished with a copy of the complaint and that he be afforded a hearing. He may obtain a review of the action of the board by an appeal to the appellate division of the Superior Court. The board may also levy fines. These must be sued for in the courts unless the person accused settles out of court. The latter is the common practice. A jail sentence may be imposed by the court for refusal to pay the amount of the court judgment.

LOCAL LICENSING

Occupational licensing is not confined to the state level. The municipalities have wide powers to license persons engaging in a variety of businesses. For example, municipalities are authorized by ordinance to license the owners and drivers of vehicles used for the transportation of passengers, baggage, and merchandise. The licensing power extends not only to a particular business but to the person operating the business such as the proprietors of hotels, rooming houses, trailer camps, garages, bathhouses, and swimming pools. In general the courts have held that so long as the licensing power has been authorized by the legislature and is not used in a manner which is unreasonable, arbitrary, or discriminatory the municipality's action will not be curbed. For example, it may distinguish between certain classes of businesses; a license may be required to sell used cars from vacant lots although no license may be required to sell used cars from a garage.[11] However, to require that the used car dealer on a vacant lot be also an authorized new car dealer was held to be an unreasonable interference with the conduct of business.[12]

The character and degree of public acceptance of a particular business has much to do with the licensing process. In 1857 the courts held that an ordinance requiring the payment of a five cent fee by any person selling hay within the City of Paterson was unreasonable and illegal and not in the interest of "peace and good order." [13] But a license fee of $500 a month for an itinerant vender selling bankrupt stocks by handbill methods was held by the courts not to be unreasonable or prohibitive.[14]

County governments play only a small part in the field of occupational licensing. However, honorably discharged war veterans and exempt firemen may obtain a license from the county clerk which entitles them to the privilege of peddling anywhere within the state.

NOTES

1 N.J. State Employment Service, *Directory and Handbook of Occupations and Professions Licensed by New Jersey State Boards and Commissions 1947* (mimeographed).

2 *Occupational Licensing Legislation in the States* (Chicago: The Council of State Governments, 1952), Table I, pp. 78-80.

3 *Occupational Licensing Legislation in the States, op. cit.*, p. 38.

4 *Abelson's Inc.* v *N.J. State Board of Optometrists,* 5 N.J. 412, 424 (1950).

5 *Labash* v *Bd. of Embalmers, etc., State of N.J.* 12 N.J. Super. 334 (1951).

6 L., 1948, ch. 439, p. 1707.

7 N.J. Board of Pharmacy, *Pharmacy Laws and Regulations* (Trenton: 1954). For early developments in the licensing requirements, see David L. Cowen, "The New Jersey Pharmaceutical Association 1870-1945, An Historical Review," *The New Jersey Journal of Pharmacy,* XVIII (Dec., 1945), 16-36.

8 N.J. *Sixty-third Annual Report of the State Board of Medical Examiners,* 1953.

9 N.J. *Annual Report of the New Jersey Board of Nursing for the Fiscal Year July 1, 1952, to June 30, 1953* (Newark), p. 5.

10 N.J. *State Board of Optometrists* v *Nemitz* 21 N.J.Super. 18, 36-37 (1952).

11 *Chaiet* v *East Orange,* 136 N.J.L. 375 (1948).

12 *Segnore* v *Rizzolo* 9 N.J.Super. 539 (1950).

13 *Kip* v *The City of Paterson* 26 N.J.L. 298 (1857).

14 *Levin* v *Asbury Park* 9 N.J. Misc. 515 (1931).

CHAPTER 24

Municipal Government

THE MUNICIPALITIES of New Jersey follow no single pattern either in their origin or in their form of government. In the late 1600's communities were established at Newark, Woodbridge, and Elizabeth by groups of persons migrating from New England and accustomed to the town organization. Perth Amboy was populated as a result of the encouragement of the colonial proprietors. New Brunswick became a community, it is reported, because "its members dropped in one by one." [1]

In both East Jersey and West Jersey, the proprietors delegated the power of incorporation to the Assembly. Burlington, for example, was incorporated by the Assembly of West Jersey in 1693. During the period 1718-1746, after the end of the proprietary period, royal charters were issued establishing the cities of Perth Amboy, New Brunswick, Burlington, Elizabeth, and Trenton.

THE CHARTER

Early charters were based upon English models. The charter usually stated the object of incorporation, outlined the reasons for the founding of the city, designated the original holders of the city's offices, and established the judicial powers and administrative functions to be exercised. [2] The motivating force for incorporation was usually economic in character. The New Brunswick charter of 1730 declared that the town stood "near the head of a fine Navigable River and being the Most Convenient Place for Shipping off the produce of a large and plentifull Country Lying on the back thereof is a place of very Considerable trade and Commerce. . . ." The charter petitioners promised "to promote trade Industry rule and good order amongst all our loving Subjects. . . ." [3] The first officials were to be a mayor and clerk of the market, recorder, six aldermen, six assistants, clerk, treasurer, coroner, sheriff and water bailiff, marshal, over-seers of the poor, and constables. The 1730 charter was the first of seven for New Brunswick.

During the nineteenth and early twentieth centuries, the legislature granted charters whenever the inhabitants of a local area wanted to es-tablish themselves as a body politic. However, many of these charters have relatively little meaning today since they have been superseded by general laws. For example, the borough law of 1897 superseded the spe-cial charters of the state's approximately 250 boroughs. Also during the nineteenth century, municipalities were occasionally operated under the direct supervision of the legislature. Legislative commissions were ap-pointed with full power to exercise control over all municipal functions. For example, in 1871 the legislature provided a new charter for Jersey City by which the members of the Board of Works, the Police Board, the Fire Board, and the Finance Board were to be appointed by the legislature in joint meeting.[4]

Constitutional status was given to the various types of local governments by an amendment in 1875; cities, towns, townships, boroughs, and villages were specifically mentioned. Another amendment in the same year pro-hibited the enactment of special or local laws. Only general laws could be passed. The passage of this amendment resulted in the classification of cities according to their population and their geographical location. There are four classes of cities. First-class cities have a population exceeding 150,000; second-class, from 12,000 to 150,000; third-class, less than 12,000; and fourth-class, all those bordering upon the Atlantic Ocean. The 1875 amendment also led to the frequent passage of laws which were general in form but which often applied to one municipality and sometimes to one individual within a municipality.

TYPES OF GOVERNMENTAL UNITS

Throughout the United States local governments are usually classified under one of three general forms, mayor-council, commission, and council-manager. There are many variations of each of these forms. For ex-ample, the mayor-council form is classified as weak mayor or strong mayor, depending principally upon the appointive and fiscal powers of the chief executive.

In 1949 a special Commission on Municipal Government, established to study the structure of local government, reported that it was virtually im-possible to classify New Jersey's municipalities in accordance with recog-nized forms because of the "duplication, overlapping and specialized requirements" of existing law.[5]   The commission reported that there were about twenty different types of municipal governments operating at that time.

The five categories of municipalities established by law—cities, towns, townships, boroughs, and villages—have few identifying characteristics. For example, most people think of a city as being a densely populated area, and a township as being sparsely populated.   Yet Corbin City in Atlantic County had a population of 238 in 1950, while Teaneck Township in Bergen County had 33,372 inhabitants.   The commission observed that the township plan was in reality a commission plan, that the borough on paper was similar to the mayor-council plan, but operated in a manner similar to the commission plan.   The picture was still further confused, the commission pointed out, by laws governing special classes of municipalities and by an extensive amount of mandatory and permissive legislation.

The results of a recent analysis of municipal types of government in New Jersey made by Dr. Stanley H. Friedelbaum of the Bureau of Government Research, at the State University, are given in Table 27.   The analysis was based upon the reports of the Division of Local Government, the *Legislative Manual,* and correspondence with a number of municipalities.

TABLE 27

MUNICIPAL TYPES AND PLANS IN NEW JERSEY

Municipalities Types of	Com- mission Plan	Council- Manager Plan	Mayor- Council Plan	Borough Plan	Township Plan	Village Plan	Total
First-class cities	1	0	1	0	0	0	2
Second-class cities	9	2	14	0	0	0	25
Third-class cities	2	0	13	0	0	0	15
Fourth-class cities	8	1	2	0	0	0	11
Towns	7	0	14	0	0	0	21
Boroughs	21	4	0	232	0	0	257
Townships	10	3	0	0	222	0	235
Villages	0	0	0	0	0	1	1
TOTAL	58	10	44	232	222	1	567

Source: Stanley H. Friedelbaum, *Municipal Government in New Jersey* (New Brunswick: Rutgers University Press, 1954), p. 17.

MUNICIPAL ORGANIZATION

Mayor-Council Government

The oldest and most commonly used form of municipal government is that of mayor and council.   Table 27 indicates that in 1954 there were only forty-three municipalities operating under the mayor-council plan.

However, in actual practice the 232 boroughs shown in the table under the borough plan were in effect operating under the mayor-council form. For example, the borough plan provides for an elected mayor and six elected councilmen. Although the mayor is elected independently of the council, he has little authority in such important fields as the control of fiscal matters and the appointment and supervision of administrative officials.

Except for those municipalities which have recently adopted one of the mayor-council plans under the optional municipal charter law described below, most municipalities have weak mayor government. Paterson, the third largest municipality, has operated since 1907 under a mayor-council form that differs markedly from the normal pattern in New Jersey. The mayor appoints boards of finance, of public works, and of police and fire. The boards are primarily responsible to the mayor rather than to the council.

Commission Government

Commission government came to New Jersey in 1911 with the passage of the Walsh Act.[6] At the time, the commission form was considered an improvement over existing mayor-council forms. The commision form may be adopted by popular referendum. Three commissioners in municipalities of less than 10,000 population and five in those over 10,000 are elected from the municipality as a whole at four-year intervals in what legally is a non-partisan election. The members of the commission exercise all legislative and administrative functions. They are the only elected municipal officials. All others are appointed by the commission. Each commissioner heads one of the following departments:

> Department of Public Affairs
> Department of Revenue and Finance
> Department of Public Safety
> Department of Public Works
> Department of Parks and Public Property

The specific municipal activities to be assigned each of the departments is determined by the commission.

The members of the commission elect one of their number as mayor. Custom dictates that the commissioner receiving the highest number of votes be elected mayor. However, this practice is by no means universal. Although the mayor is the titular head of the municipality, his authority from a legal standpoint is coordinate with that of his colleagues.

When the Commission on Municipal Government reported in 1949 proposing a number of optional charters, the commission form was not among them. Instead commission government was sharply attacked. The report declared:

> . . . it has inherent weaknesses, which, in the judgment of the Commission, are responsible for many of the municipal difficulties in commission governed cities that we face today. These weaknesses include the placing of both legislative authority and administrative authority in the same hands—namely, in the elected commission. This condition fosters "log-rolling," delay and "personal politics" within the governing body.
>
> The commission plan offers no opportunity for sound budgetary practices—there is no practical way to co-ordinate a planned expenditure program as among five independent administrative authorities. There is no single responsible executive in the commission plan—this makes impossible a unified public policy as well as a known and effective responsibility.[7]

In recent years, the commission form has seldom been adopted. In 1953 the largest city of the state, Newark, abandoned the form in favor of one of the new mayor-council optional forms.

Council-Manager Plan

In contrast with the initial wave of adoptions of the commission plan, the council-manager movement in New Jersey had little success. The plan provided for the election of a small council on an at-large basis, and the selection by the council of a specialist in municipal management who would supervise the administration of municipal services. Legislation authorizing municipalities to adopt the manager form was passed in 1923.[8] However, at the time of the passage of the new optional forms in 1950 only eight of 567 municipalities were operating under the plan. The reasons for its lack of popularity are difficult to determine in view of the manager government's outstanding successes in a number of states. A general disillusionment with reform proposals, the tendency of labor groups to view the plan with suspicion, and particularly the opposition of county and municipal political leaders—all were factors contributing to the small number of adoptions.

The Optional Municipal Charter Law

In 1950, following the report of the Commission on Municipal Government, the legislature enacted the optional municipal charter law. The law provided for the establishment of a charter commission, and made available a series of optional charters under the mayor-council plan, the council-manager plan, and the small municipalities plan. Any of the options were available also by direct petition and referendum without the use of a charter commission.

Charter Commission. By petition and referendum the people of a municipality may set up a charter commission of five members. Candidates for the commission may be nominated at the same time the people ballot on the desirability of a commission. The commission is required to study the government of the municipality, to hold public hearings, and to report its findings and recommendations to the people. It may recommend that (1) one of the optional forms be adopted, (2) a special charter be enacted, (3) the form of the existing government be retained, and (4) "such other action as it may deem advisable consistent with its functions. . . ." [9]

Mayor-Council Plans A-F. Fundamentally, the six mayor-council plans provided for in the optional municipal charter law are the same. However, they differ in such matters as partisan or non-partisan elections, ward or at-large elections, and the election of all councilmen at once or on an overlapping term basis. For example, Plan A calls for the non-partisan election of five councilmen who are elected on an at-large basis, all at the same time. On the other hand, Plan F provides for the partisan election of five, seven, or nine council members who are elected both from wards and on an at-large basis, and who serve overlapping terms.

All six plans give the mayor extensive powers. He has administrative supervision over department heads, of whom there may not be more than ten. He appoints department heads with the consent of the council. He is responsible for budget preparation, and he may veto ordinances. However, his veto may be overridden by a two-thirds vote. The plans call for a business administrator, appointed by the mayor, with the consent of council, to assist him in budget, purchasing, and personnel matters.*

Council-Manager Plans A-E. The council-manager plans provide for the election of a council of from five to nine members with the optional features described above. The council elects one of their own members as mayor. He presides over the council, votes in council, executes contracts, and fills certain vacancies. The council selects and may remove the manager who is the chief executive and administrative official of the municipality.

Small Municipality Plans A-D. Municipalities of under 12,000 population may adopt one of four options. The over-all purpose of the plans is to place the chief executive in a position of greater leadership and responsibility than he exercised under the old borough, town, or township plans. For example, he presides over and votes in the council. He appoints other municipal officers with the consent of the council. He is charged with the preparation of the budget, and with the enforcement of all laws and ordinances.

Popularity of Optional Charters. For three years the optional charter law was little used. But in 1952 a charter commission was elected in Newark. The work of that commission, its report, and the campaign for

* In first-class cities the administrator's supervisory powers extend to all departments. L., 1954, ch. 68, p. 420.

adoption of one of the mayor-council options aroused state-wide interest.[10] A number of other municipalities have since taken action to reexamine and in several instances to change their forms of government.

MUNICIPAL POWERS

Municipalities derive their powers from the state. The people of a municipality have no inherent right of self-government. This doctrine was confirmed by the United States Supreme Court in a case involving the city of Trenton: "In the absence of state constitutional provisions safeguarding it to them, municipalities have no inherent right of self government which is beyond the legislative control of the state." Drawing upon an earlier case the court observed:

The state, therefore, at its pleasure, may modify or withdraw all such powers, may take without compensation such property, hold it itself, or vest it in other agencies, expand or contract the territorial area, unite the whole or a part of it with another municipality, repeal the charter, and destroy the corporation. All this may be done, conditionally or unconditionally, with or without the consent of the citizens, or even against their protest. In all these respects the state is supreme; and its legislative body, conforming its action to the state constitution, may do as it will, unrestrained by any provision of the Constitution of the United States.[11]

About twenty states have what is called constitutional home rule. Municipalities may frame and adopt charters of their own choosing. Thus they may set up their own structure of government and amend it in accordance with changing needs.

New Jersey is not among the states having constitutional home rule. A constitutional amendment in 1875 prohibited local legislation, but the amendment was not particularly effective. Following the recommendations of a Home Rule Commission, a Home Rule Act was passed in 1917 conferring a number of powers upon municipalities. Additional powers stem from general laws applicable to all municipalities or laws applying to certain classes and types of municipalities.

Home rule was not extended to municipalities in the Constitution of 1947. Provision was made for special laws upon petition of the governing body. The constitution also called upon the courts to construe liberally the laws concerning municipalities and counties:

The provisions of this constitution and of any law concerning municipal corporations formed for local government, or concerning counties shall be liberally construed in their favor. The powers of counties and such municipal corporations shall include not only those granted in express terms but also those of necessary or fair implication, or incident to the powers expressly conferred, or essential thereto, and not inconsistent with or prohibited by this constitution or by law.[12]

From the standpoint of structure, the optional municipal charter law offers municipalities a considerable choice of forms of government. A charter commission which prefers to draft its own charter, as distinguished from taking one of the options, may do so. However, without the cooperation of the municipal governing body the process is a tortuous one.[13]

FISCAL ADMINISTRATION

State Administrative Supervision

Following an unhappy experience in the depression when large numbers of municipalities were in serious financial condition, the state has maintained reasonably close supervision over certain aspects of fiscal administration. As long ago as 1917, a Department of Municipal Accounts was established to administer the laws relating to the annual audits of counties and municipalities, and to require standards for the operation of sinking funds.[14] However, the degree of actual control was limited. A substantial amount of state supervision came in 1938 with the establishment of a state department of local government. It was given divisional status when the state Department of Taxation and Finance was established in 1944 and was continued in that position in 1948 when the Department of the Treasury was reorganized.[15] Within the division is a local government board consisting of the division director as chairman and four members, all appointed by the governor with Senate consent. Rules governing municipal and county financial practices are prepared and promulgated by the board.

An indication of the vast amount of state authority in the financial field may be obtained from the law setting forth the board's powers to prescribe "systems of financial administration."

Systems of financial administration shall include:
1. Definite procedures for the receipt, custody, control and disbursement of public funds.
2. Forms for receipts, requisitions, disbursements, purchase orders and other necessary documents.
3. The exercise of a comptroller function by a designated local officer.
4. Definitions of the respective powers and duties of the several local officers engaged in financial administration.
5. Instructions, rules and regulations for the proper procedures and practices of financial administration.[16]

In addition, by law and by regulation, the state prescribes detailed procedures for the preparation of the municipal budget, the issuance of bonds, the installation of accounting systems, and the form and content of the audit report. Under special circumstances, the director of the division may require that an audit be made only by a member of his staff.

Special restraints may be imposed upon municipalities in an unsound financial condition; for example, if a municipality defaults in the payment of interest or principal upon its bonded indebtedness, or if it fails for two years to pay amounts owing to the school district or county, the degree of financial supervision may be increased. In extreme cases the Local Government Board may appoint a local administrator of finance. In the late 1930's these special financial controls were applied to 60 municipalities.[17] None received special supervision in 1956.

State financial supervision does not extend to exercising a veto over a municipal appropriation. So long as the governing body meets the regulations prescribing the form of the budget, and so long as the appropriation is for a legal purpose, the determination of how the money is to be expended is fully within local jurisdiction. State control is concerned primarily with assuring financial solvency.

Cash Basis

Municipalities are required to operate on a cash basis system. The expression "cash basis" has a specialized meaning under New Jersey statutes. It is a system designed to assure the collection of sufficient revenues to meet the estimated needs. The system involves applying the preceding year's rate of collections to the present year's tax requirements and adding an "overlay" to the levy. Assume, for example, that the budget calls for an expenditure of $100 and that revenues other than taxes amount to $40. There remains $60 to be raised by taxation. Assume also, that last year's collection rate was 80 per cent. The amount to be raised, $60, times the collection rate, 80 per cent, would yield only $48. At this point the governing body "overlays" the levy. It assumes that $60 equals 80 per cent of the collections. Then 100 per cent would amount to $75. This sum becomes the final tax levy. At a collection rate of 80 per cent, $60 would be obtained.[18]

The objectives of the system are said to be twofold. It provides the necessary funds and, by improving the municipalities' credit position, reduces interest costs on loans for capital expenditures. The principal objection to the plan is that the overlay is an additional tax extracted from those who do meet their municipal obligations. In practice the overlay is not as large as it might appear from the above illustrations since in the following year revenues from delinquent taxes would offset the first year's additional burden. That the overlay might indeed be greater is illustrated from the experience of the depression period. At the end of 1933, 40.40 per cent of all taxes levied in New Jersey's municipalities were uncollected. At the end of a second year 17.94 per cent of the 1933 levy remained out-

standing. By contrast, in 1951 only 5.06 per cent of total taxes levied
were uncollected at the end of the year. A year later the percentage of
1951 taxes outstanding had fallen to 0.69 per cent.[19]

Municipal Revenues

Municipal revenues in New Jersey are classified under four headings:
(1) surplus revenue, (2) miscellaneous revenues, (3) delinquent taxes and
liens, and (4) current taxes.

By surplus revenue is meant the free cash available, that is, monies not
committed in any form. The term "surplus revenue" is to be distinguished
from "cash balance." Existing law does not require a municipality to include a statement of its free cash at the time of the publication of its budget.
Nor is it required to appropriate its entire surplus in the following year's
budget.[20] Governing bodies sometimes build up their surplus revenues
over a period of years. Then, in election year, simply by drawing on this
source, they are able to effect a sizable decrease in the tax rate. This
practice is contrary to the original purpose of the fund, which was to provide a cushion enabling the tax rate to remain relatively stable.

Miscellaneous revenues include the income from state aid, licenses, fees
and permits, fines and penalties, interest and costs incident to the collection of delinquent taxes, and franchise, gross receipts, and bus receipts
taxes.* For most New Jersey municipalities, miscellaneous revenues, aside
from state aid, arise from regulatory measures as distinguished from the
practice in certain states of developing the miscellaneous revenue source
as a means of relieving the burden on real estate. The municipality may
not without state permission anticipate a greater sum from any of the miscellaneous revenues than was realized the preceding year.

In determining the income from delinquent taxes and the sale of tax
liens, a similar rule applies. That is, the municipality may not anticipate
an amount larger than the percentage of collections received the preceding
year. These regulations are designed to prevent over-optimistic budget
estimates on the part of the governing body.

Property taxes constitute approximately 80 per cent of municipal revenues. For example, the total current revenues of the city of Newark in
1951 amounted to $57,000,000. Property taxes accounted for $46,-
000,000, or 81 per cent.[21]

Property is assessed on October 1 for the next calendar year. The
property owner receives but one bill, payable in four installments, to cover
municipal, school district, and county taxes. Payments by the municipality to the school district and the county are mandatory. What is left is
available to the municipality. Of the total taxes collected, the municipality has jurisdiction only over what is referred to as the local purpose

* For an explanation of the franchise, gross receipts, and bus receipts taxes, see
pages 131-32, 138.

levy. For example, in Newark the 1954 total tax levy amounted to $60,500,000. The city was required to pay $23,000,000 to the schools and $8,100,000 to the county. The remaining $29,300,000 constituted the local purpose levy available for municipal services. To obtain the total tax levy, a tax rate was established of $8.55 per $100 of assessed valuation. The three components making up this rate were the local school tax rate of $3.27, the county tax rate of $1.15, and the local purpose tax rate of $4.13.[22]

Municipal Expenditures

An expenditure, as defined by the Division of Local Government, "includes not only cash disbursements, but in addition, amounts reserved to meet unpaid claims of the current fiscal year." [23]   Thus, in reporting the amount expended for a given fiscal year—which in all counties and municipalities is the calendar year—municipal officials are required to count as an expenditure not only all sums paid out but all actual commitments. As indicated above, the total sum expended by a municipality includes required payments for local school taxes, county taxes, and any special district taxes. For example, in 1955 the grand total of the budget for New Brunswick was $4,961,862. But the governing body of the municipality was responsible for the expenditure of only $2,197,563, or 44 per cent of the total. All municipal services were paid from the 44 per cent available to the governing body.

The state requires municipal governing bodies to report their expenditures in a uniform manner. Table 28 lists the functions performed and the amounts expended in 1955 for the city of New Brunswick. Similar data for each municipality are published annually by the Division of Local Government.

Operating expenses of all municipalities in the state amounted to $229,355,350 in 1953. This figure represented an increase of 72 per cent over the $133,091,270 expended in 1946.[24]   However, during the same period total income payments in New Jersey increased 64 per cent, from $6,188,000,000 in 1946 to $10,153,000,000 in 1953.[25]   Translated into a percentage of the total income payments to individuals spent for municipal services, the figure increased from 2.15 per cent in 1946 to 2.25 per cent in 1953.

Comparisons of the burden of government from one year to the next are realistic only when the number and quality of the services performed are also compared. The slight increase in the expenditures for municipal government relative to total income payments to individuals assumes no change in the number or character of services performed. Obviously this assumption is not valid. Increasing urbanization has required and will continue to require many municipalities to supply services on a regular and continuing basis which previously were supplied irregularly, if at all. The

TABLE 28

EXPENDITURES FOR MUNICIPAL FUNCTIONS,
NEW BRUNSWICK, 1955

Function	Amount
General Government	
Administrative and executive	$ 215,154
Assessment and collection of taxes	69,300
Finance department	—
Protection to persons and property	
Fire	373,000
Police	464,210
Other	—
Streets and Roads	
Repairs and maintenance	126,400
Street lighting	60,358
Sanitation	
Street cleaning	38,750
Garbage and ash removal	274,300
Sewers	173,500
Health and Charities	
Health service	69,200
Welfare (public assistance)	67,000
Hospitals (aid and maintenance)	15,000
Other	—
Recreation	
Beaches and boardwalks	—
Parks and playgrounds	168,775
Other	—
Educational (exclusive of school districts)	72,500
Unclassified purposes (including contingent)	10,115
TOTAL	$2,197,562

Source: N.J. *Eighteenth Annual Report of the Division of Local Government, 1955,* p. 339.

percentage of income payments necessary for police and fire protection, streets, health services, parks and playgrounds, and other municipal functions will almost inevitably increase during the next decade.

MUNICIPAL SERVICES

The services performed by New Jersey's 567 municipalities are legion. The kinds and quality of services differ enormously depending upon a variety of factors such as geographical location of the municipality and its area, the size and density of its population, the economic status of its inhabitants, and their willingness or unwillingness to increase municipal functions. From a legal standpoint, a municipality may provide only those services authorized by state law.

Public Safety

Police. The maintenance of law and order is fundamental. Every municipality may provide for police protection. Throughout the United States major crimes are on the increase, and in 1953 reached a new high. Nationally, crime outstripped population growth by a ratio of four to one.[26] Comparative data sent to the FBI by New Jersey police departments for the periods 1943 and 1953 are indicated in Table 29. In 1943, 125 cities were included; the number submitting data in 1953 was 136.

TABLE 29

NUMBER OF OFFENSES, NEW JERSEY, PER 100,000 INHABITANTS

	1943	*1953*	*Per Cent Increase*
Murder, non-negligent manslaughter	2.17	2.7	24
Robbery	24.1	38.1	58
Aggravated assault	44.3	54.6	23
Burglary—breaking or entering	259.8	346.8	33
Larceny—theft	436.4	607.9	39
Auto theft	140.7	131.9	−6

Source: *Uniform Crime Reports, Annual Bulletin, 1943,* XIV, 68; *1953,* XXIV, 89.

How many full time police there are in New Jersey municipalities is difficult to determine. For years many areas had no police protection. The lack of an organized force in many rural municipalities was a major factor in the establishment of the State Police in 1921. The rapid increase in motor transportation has made traffic regulation one of the principal responsibilities for the police in the larger municipalities and has forced many smaller areas to supply police protection. Table 30 indicates the

TABLE 30

POLICE DEPARTMENT EMPLOYEES (INCLUDING CIVILIANS), 1943-1953
(New Jersey cities over 100,000)

	Population, 1950 [a]	*No. of Employees*	
		1943	*1953*
Newark	438,776	1,177	1,371
Jersey City	299,017	928	1,010
Paterson	139,336	255	266
Trenton	128,009	238	269
Camden	124,555	215	285
Elizabeth	112,817	220	256

Source of Police Data: *Uniform Crime Reports, 1943,* XIV, 24; *1953,* XXIV, 26.

[a] The population in New Jersey's six largest cities remained stable between 1940 and 1950; in no case was the increase as much as 10 per cent. *Uniform Crime Reports* cautions against making comparisons among police departments solely on the basis of size.

number of police department employees in New Jersey municipalities with a 1950 population of 100,000 or above.

Fire. Most municipalities have protection against fire. In the larger areas, fire protection is a definite governmental function. Paid fire departments are as completely accepted as paid police departments. In smaller municipalities, fire protection is recognized as a service to be provided by the governing body, but the department may have only a small paid staff. The remaining members of the department serve on a volunteer basis. In rural areas the township committee may provide protection through a fire department, or it may supply funds to a volunteer company. Fire districts may also be established. These are corporate entities governed by elected fire commissioners who have authority to levy a fire district tax.

In 1954 there were about 510 fire departments in the state. Only thirty-eight of these were fully paid. There were fifty departments in which at least one person was paid. The remaining 422 were volunteer.[27]

TABLE 31

FIRE DEPARTMENT DATA, NEW JERSEY MUNICIPALITIES OVER 50,000

	No. of Full-time Paid Employees	Building Fires per 1,000 Population	Fire Loss per Building Fire, 1955
Atlantic City	215	6.4	$2,688
Bayonne	174	1.9	—
Camden	210	—	—
Clifton	93	1.5	2,868
East Orange	155	3.7	529
Elizabeth	225	1.7	1,903
Hoboken	155	5.7	689
Irvington	129	3.7	273
Jersey City	589	4.0	2,587
Newark	887	6.1	1,396
Passaic	110	5.3	1,727
Paterson	243	—	—
Trenton	238	3.9	744
Union City	117	4.3	1,641

Source: *The Municipal Year Book, 1956,* pp. 372-78.

Public Works

Streets. One of the oldest municipal functions is the construction and maintenance of roads and sidewalks. As explained in Chapter 20, state grants-in-aid and some Federal funds are now available for municipal as distinguished from state or county highways. However, the major street costs are borne by the municipality.

Water and Other Utilities. In 1955 there were 190 municipalities which supplied water to their residents. The municipality may have its own water supply. Newark, for example, obtains most of its water from a city-owned sixty-three square mile area in the Pequannock watershed in the northern part of the state. Or water may be obtained on a contract basis from a neighboring municipality or from a private company. In many communities, private water corporations sell directly to the consumer. For example, the Hackensack Water Company supplies water to the people of a number of municipalities in the northern part of the state. City-owned wells constitute the principal source of water in several municipalities.

Three municipalities—Madison, South River, and Vineland—operate electric utilities having operating revenues in excess of $250,000.[28] Several municipalities operate sewer utilities and a few operate a joint water and sewer utility. Millville and Morristown operate airports. Utilities are required to maintain separate sets of accounts. Operating deficits are met from general taxation. An operating profit may be used to reduce taxes.

Refuse Collection and Sewerage. In most of the larger municipalities, expenditures for street cleaning, garbage removal, and sewers are regularly accepted items in the budget. But there is no uniformity. The municipality may operate its own sewerage system, it may contract with a private agency, or it may join with other municipalities. For example, Newark has direct responsibility for certain sewers. At the same time it is a member of the Passaic Valley Sewerage Commission which services a number of municipalities in the Newark area. The provision of an adequate sewerage system has become an acute problem in many municipalities which have experienced sudden growth in the last decade.

Garbage collection and disposal is a function of the city in many municipalities. In others the municipality contracts with a private firm. In still others, the governing body takes no action.

Education, Health, and Welfare. The largest single function of municipal government is that of providing an educational system. Chapter 15 describes the educational system in some detail. Municipalities also are required to establish a board of health. Local health services are described briefly in Chapter 16. Municipal responsibility for welfare is limited chiefly to the field of general assistance (see Chapter 17). Hospitals may be established by municipalities although the legislative grant of authority is limited in regard to the type of municipality or to the type of hospital.[29] Jersey City, Newark, and Irvington are the only cities having municipally owned general hospitals.

Other Municipal Services. In addition to the functions previously mentioned, municipalities operate parks, playgrounds and recreational areas, control the planting and care of shade trees, and operate libraries, museums, airports, and public baths. No one municipality performs all of these functions. But taken collectively, municipalities have obtained authority from the legislature, either by general law or by legislation more limited in character, to perform these and a variety of other services.

NOTES

1 William H. Benedict, *New Brunswick in History* (New Brunswick: Published by author, 1925), p. 34.

2 Austin Scott, "The Early Cities of New Jersey," *Proceedings of the New Jersey Historical Society, Second Series*, IX (1897), 151-73.

3 John P. Wall, *The Chronicles of New Brunswick, New Jersey, 1667-1931* (New Brunswick: Thatcher Anderson Company, 1931), p. 19.

4 William Edgar Sackett, *Modern Battles of Trenton, Being a History of New Jersey's Politics and Legislation from the Year 1868 to the Year 1894* (Trenton: John L. Murphy, Printer, 1895), pp. 86-95.

5 N.J. *Local Self-Government in New Jersey: A Proposed Optional Charter Plan, Report of the Commission on Municipal Government* (Trenton, 1949), p. 3.

6 L., 1911, ch. 221, p. 462.

7 *Local Self-Government in New Jersey . . . , op. cit.*, p. 20.

8 L., 1923, ch. 113, p. 217.

9 L., 1950, ch. 210, p. 464. For an explanation of the optional plans and an analysis of the work of a charter commission, see Benjamin Baker, *Municipal Charter Revision in New Jersey* (New Brunswick: Rutgers University Press, 1953).

10 *Final Report of the Charter Commission of the City of Newark* (Newark, 1953).

11 *Trenton v New Jersey*, 262 U.S. 182, 186-87 (1923).

12 Art. IV, sec. VII, par. 11. See Henry W. Connor, "Home Rule," N.J. *Constitutional Convention of 1947*, II, 1728-45.

13 L., 1948, ch. 199, p. 995.

14 L., 1917, ch. 154, p. 472. The department was merged with the office of state auditor in 1933. L., 1933, ch. 295, p. 793.

15 L., 1938, ch. 158, p. 324; L., 1944, ch. 112, p. 287; L., 1948, ch. 92, p. 511.

16 L., 1947, ch. 151, p. 656.

17 For a review of early practice see John H. Marion, "State Supervision in New Jersey over Municipalities in Unsound Financial Condition," *The American Political Science Review*, XXXVI (1942), 502-8.

18 N.J. *Fifteenth Annual Report of the Division of Local Government, 1952* (Trenton: Department of the Treasury, 1953), p. xiii.

19 *Ibid.*, p. xv.

20 *In re City Affairs Committee of Jersey City* 129 N.J.L. 589 (1943).

21 *Financial Review, A Guidebook to Newark Municipal Finance* (Newark: Bureau of Municipal Research, Inc., 1953), p. 11.

22 *Seventeenth Annual Report of the Division of Local Government, 1954* (Trenton: Department of the Treasury, 1955), p. 338.

23 N.J. *Sixteenth Annual Report of the Division of Local Government, 1953*, p. iii.

24 New Jersey Taxpayers Association, *Financial Statistics of New Jersey Local Government, 1954* (Trenton, 1954), p. 41.

25 U.S. Department of Commerce, *Survey of Current Business*, XXXIII (August, 1953), 12; XXXIV (August, 1954), 15.

26 *Uniform Crime Reports, (1953)*, XXIV, No. 2 (Washington: Federal Bureau of Investigation, 1954), p. 67.

27 Friedelbaum, *op. cit.*, p. 21.

28 *Statistics of Electric Utilities in the United States, 1952* (Washington: Federal Power Commission, 1954), p. vii.

29 Friedelbaum, *op. cit.*, pp. 27-28.

CHAPTER 25

County Government

THE COUNTY in New Jersey is an important unit of government, much more so than most people realize.[1] The functions it performs have increased dramatically in the last two decades. Some of the increased county services have resulted from the action of the Federal government in establishing programs in cooperation with the states. Others have been added to meet local needs. At the same time, traditional functions have been retained. The net result has been a considerable stepping up of the number of services performed and, in part at least, a change in the character of county government.

GOVERNMENTAL ORGANIZATION

The county derives all of its authority from the state. In this respect it is no different from a municipality. But the municipality usually has been given a greater freedom of action. For example, optional laws permit municipalities to establish one of several forms of government. Under the most recent legislation of this character, the municipality may, through a charter commission, prepare its own charter. The county has virtually no discretion of this kind. It has always been considered an arm of the state.

Early municipalities were given charters and were classified as true corporations. The county, on the other hand, had no charter. It was considered a quasi-corporation since only a few of the privileges of a corporate body, such as owning property and making contracts, were applicable. In recent years the legal distinctions between counties and municipalities have been less pronounced. Legislation which pertains to one is frequently made applicable to the other. However, with respect to the structure of government, the county operates within rigid limitations.

Counties are classified by the legislature according to population and location. The several classifications follow:

BASES FOR CLASSIFYING COUNTIES [2]

Class	Population	Bordering the Atlantic Ocean	Not Bordering the Atlantic Ocean
First	More than 600,000		x
Second	200,000 to 600,000		x
Third	50,000 to 200,000		x
Fourth	Under 50,000		x
Fifth	More than 50,000	x	
Sixth	Under 50,000	x	

Board of Chosen Freeholders

New Jersey is the only state in which the county governing body is called the Board of Chosen Freeholders. The words "chosen freeholders" sound strange when compared to the titles of other public offices. The expression probably arose in an effort to express clearly and simply the political facts of the time. Just as the term "selectmen" in the New England town referred to those men of the community selected by the voters to hold office, so the "chosen freeholders" were the owners of property chosen to govern the early counties.

The basic law establishing the boards of freeholders was passed in 1798.[3] It provided for representation on the board from each municipality. The structure of the governing body remained unchanged until 1912 when the legislature authorized the election of a small board representing the county at large.[4] This action was made contingent upon public acceptance of the new form by means of a referendum. Seventeen of the twenty-one counties now are governed by small boards, ranging from three to nine freeholders each. Of the four counties operating under the early form, Atlantic County has the largest board, with thirty-four members.

The freeholders are elected on a staggered basis for three years. Any qualified voter is eligible to run for the office. In actual practice, candidates are selected by the party organization, and the direct primary is simply an endorsement of their action. Since the election in the small board counties is on an at-large basis, the members of the board usually all belong to the same party. New Jersey has no requirement, as does Pennsylvania, for example, of bi-partisan representation on the board.

The board of freeholders is fundamentally a commission form of government. The members are at one and the same time legislators and administrators. The same group which determines policy is responsible also for the execution of that policy. One freeholder is elected by the members as director of the board.

In most small board counties the board operates by means of a series of committees appointed by the director. Each member is usually chairman of one committee and a member of several others. On the committee of which he is chairman, the member's voice may overrule that of his colleagues, not because he has any more legal authority, but because his colleagues expect to dominate the committees which they head.

The first-class counties, Hudson and Essex, have a slightly different form of organization. In 1900 the legislature authorized the election, by the people, of a county supervisor in addition to the boards of freeholders. The supervisor's term of office is three years, but the practice in both Hudson and Essex counties has been to return the incumbent to office term after term so long as his party retained its majority in the year of his election. The supervisor is the chief administrative officer in these counties. However, his authority is extremely limited. He has no power of appointment, no staff to assist him in supervision, and no control of the preparation or the execution of the budget. He has a limited veto of board resolutions. The supervisor usually attends the meetings of the board and may serve as an ex officio member of all committees.

Perhaps the most striking organizational feature of county government in New Jersey is the existence of the two types of boards. Atlantic, Cumberland, Gloucester, and Salem counties have held to the large board. The number of freeholders varies with the classification of the county, and the type and population of the municipality. For example, counties with a population of from 75,000 to 200,000 have boards consisting of a representative from each city ward, two representatives from every town, one from every township, and one from each borough having a population of at least 2,300. One result of the large board type of representation is the inequality among communities of different sizes. For example, in Atlantic County, in 1950, Corbin City with 238 inhabitants was entitled to elect two members of the board, or one member per 119 persons. At the other extreme, Atlantic City with a population of 61,657 was entitled to only four freeholders, or one member per 15,414 persons.

County Officials

The principal legislative and executive authority in county government is the Board of Chosen Freeholders. But it is by no means the sole agency charged with county administration. On the contrary, there are several elective and state-appointed officials who share in the administration of county functions.

Three constitutional offices are filled by election in each county—sheriff, clerk, and surrogate. Elected for a term of three years, the sheriff's principal functions are in connection with the operations of the courts. Although he retains the powers of a peace officer, the sheriff's law enforcement duties are secondary to his role as a court official. The county clerk and the surrogate serve five-year terms, the functions of the clerk ranging over the whole gamut of county government, while the surrogate is limited largely to such matters as the settlement of estates. Several counties have an elected registrar of deeds and mortgages. This office may be established by referendum in counties with a population of over 250,000. As indicated above, the first-class counties of Essex and Hudson elect a county supervisor. Some counties continue to elect coroners. In others—with appointive county physicians—the position of coroner is not filled. The office no longer has constitutional status.

In addition to the Board of Chosen Freeholders and other elective officials, each county has a number of state appointed administrative officers. These include the county prosecutor, the judges of the county courts, the board of taxation, and the superintendent of schools.

COUNTY FINANCES

In most states the county levies taxes directly upon the individuals within the county. New Jersey counties in common with those in some of the New England states, such as Massachusetts and Connecticut, collect from the municipalities. This procedure, which was begun early in the colonial period, has the advantage of simplicity. The property owner pays one tax bill—to the municipality. The collection process for the county is an easy one since the record keeping operation involves a few municipalities rather than many thousands of individuals. However, the plan has distinct disadvantages. Individuals pay nothing directly to the counties. As a consequence, the degree of citizen interest is less. Surprisingly few people know much about their county government. This lack of interest and knowledge is always harmful. Furthermore, the absence of any county tax consciousness on the part of the public tends to encourage more carefree spending on the part of those holding public office.

In the field of tax assessments, the county board of taxation acts as an appeals agency. It is, in reality, a state agency. Three members—five in first-class counties—are appointed by the governor with Senate consent. The salaries of the members are paid by the state. A property owner dissatisfied with the municipal assessment on his property may appeal to the county board of taxation. In recent years much emphasis has been placed upon "equalization," that is, the problem of assuring that different taxing districts in the same county assess properties at relatively the same percentage of true value.

The principal sources of county revenues are property taxes, payments by the state, and fees and other revenues. In 1951 property taxes constituted 74.2 per cent of total county revenues. State payments accounted for 14.6 per cent, and fees and other revenues for 11.2 per cent. The counties having the highest and lowest revenues from each of the three sources, together with the state-wide average, are shown below:

SOURCES OF REVENUE [5]

(in per cent)

State Average		High		Low	
Property Taxes	74.2	Hudson	83.6	Hunterdon }	49.1
State Payments	14.6	Hunterdon	39.5	Cumberland }	49.1
Fees and others	11.2	Sussex	21.9	Union	8.4
				Warren	7.4

On a per capita basis in 1954 revenues ranged from $47.58 in Sussex County to $16.83 in Somerset. The state-wide average was $26.70. Total county revenues in 1954 amounted to $129,111,452.

The principal payments to the counties by the state are in the form of grants-in-aid. The largest single grant-in-aid is for highway construction and maintenance. Welfare programs, particularly those financed in part by the Federal government, constitute the second largest grant-in-aid.

County expenditures in 1954 amounted to $131,774,909. Per capita expenditures ranged from $47.89 in Ocean County to $17.51 in Somerset. The state-wide average was $27.25. The largest single area of expenditure was for charitable, correctional, and penal functions. The construction and maintenance of roads and bridges came second.[6]

Certain phases of county fiscal administration are regulated in detail by law and by the regulations of the Division of Local Government, Department of the Treasury. For example, the form of the budget is prescribed, and appropriations must be classified under "operations," "debt service," and other specified headings. The proposed budget must be approved by the Board of Chosen Freeholders and later by the Division of Local Government. The budget must be published at least once in a local newspaper, and a public hearing held some time during a prescribed three-week period before final adoption.

State laws and regulations are not designed to limit the amount of money which the county governing body may spend. For any function which the county is authorized by law to perform, it may spend as much or as little as the board of freeholders may determine. Approval of the budget by the Division of Local Government signifies that the county is operating on the cash basis system prescribed by law. In effect this means that the county has taken the necessary steps to obtain revenues in an amount sufficient to cover its proposed expenditures. State approval is in no sense a judgment upon the wisdom of these expenditures.

In order to spread the burden of expenditures over a period of years, the county governing body may issue bonds rather than make substantial increases in the levies upon the municipalities. However, state law places a limit of 4 per cent of assessed valuations on the amount which may be borrowed. That counties have not made a practice of borrowing to capacity is evidenced by a state-wide net debt percentage of 1.86 in 1954.

The range was from 3.65 in Camden to 0.0 in Hunterdon, Gloucester, and Salem counties.*

COUNTY SERVICES

The twenty-one counties vary markedly in the number and scope of the services they provide.[7]   All counties are required by law to perform certain functions; others are of an optional character.

Courts and Law Enforcement

Perhaps the oldest and most widely recognized functions are those related to the courts and law enforcement.   The county acts as an arm of the state to preserve law and order.   Not only in connection with breaches of the criminal law but also in relation to civil disputes the county has always been a center for the administration of justice.

The judicial system of the state is described in Chapter 13.   Suffice it to say here that at the county level there exist county courts, district courts, juvenile and domestic relations courts, and surrogate's courts.   The county court is a constitutional court; in subject matter, though not in area, its jurisdiction is largely concurrent with that of the Superior Court.

The principal law enforcement officer is the county prosecutor.†   The authority of the county governing body over the prosecutor is limited. They may request his replacement, but this is an unusual step.   His staff consists chiefly of detectives and investigators.‡   The maximum size of the staff depends upon the classification of the county.   Not until the prosecutor desires to exceed the number of employees permitted by law is the board of freeholders required to grant approval.   Even the budgetary authority of the freeholders is limited since the prosecutor may exceed the amounts appropriated for his office, providing he has the approval of the assignment judge of the superior court for that county.

Other county law enforcement or regulatory activities include the operation by the sheriff of county jails to house those who are awaiting trial or are serving relatively short sentences.   A few counties maintain workhouses for persons convicted of law violations.   The counties operate offices to assist and supervise persons released by the court on probation. The county coroner, physician, or medical examiner is concerned with the investigation of sudden or suspicious death.

Education

The principal role of the county in the field of education is that of super-

* The debt limit is inoperative under certain emergency conditions.
† See page 193.
‡ In 1951, detectives were included in the classified civil service.   Investigators, however, serve at the pleasure of the prosecutor.

vision and service through the office of the county superintendent. As explained in Chapter 15, the superintendent of schools is a state officer representing the commissioner of education. The county superintendent is required to approve school transportation contracts and routes. He assists the Department of Education in the processing of teachers' certificates. Helping teachers appointed by the commissioner of education to aid teachers in the schools of two or more districts, supervisors of child study, and attendance officers are paid upon the order of the superintendent. In addition, the superintendent's office serves as a source of information and advice for boards of education, schools, and individuals and groups concerned with the educational system.

Several counties operate vocational schools. In 1952, for example, Bergen County completed construction of a vocational and technical high school designed to accommodate 700 students. In addition to basic courses of a broad educational nature, students are given specific occupational training. Supervision of a county vocational school is the responsibility of a five-member board, one of whom is the county superintendent.

Health, Welfare, and Institutions

Welfare services are administered in each county by a welfare board of five citizens, two freeholders, and in most instances, the county adjuster. At least two members must be women. The board is responsible, through an executive director, for operating three of the categorical aid programs: old age assistance, aid to dependent children, and aid to the permanently and totally disabled. The fourth categorical aid program—aid to the blind —is administered principally by the state although the welfare board makes a preliminary investigation and the county contributes financially. The county also assists financially in the program of foster home care for children and in the treatment of crippled children.

The counties maintain a number of different kinds of institutions. There are hospitals for the chronically ill, the mentally diseased, the tubercular, and those with communicable diseases. For example, Hudson has a hospital primarily for maternity cases, Middlesex one primarily for polio cases. Many of the counties operate almshouses and welfare houses, principally for the aged who require constant care. The counties pay the state for indigent persons in state institutions.

Roads

A traditional function of counties is the construction and maintenance of roads. In terms of total road mileage in New Jersey about 23 per cent falls within the jurisdiction of the boards of freeholders. The board has extensive powers to acquire property for road purposes by purchase, gift, or condemnation and to maintain, improve, beautify, or vacate any road under its control. The board may issue bonds to pay for improvements up to 4 per cent of assessed valuations.* The construction and maintenance of bridges are also county functions. However, a special legislative act is required to erect a bridge over a navigable stream.

Other Services

Counties may, by referendum, establish free libraries. These are financed by a special tax levied and collected by the freeholders from those municipalities which do not themselves maintain public libraries. However, a municipality which operates its own library may be admitted, upon request, to the county library system. In 1950 legislation was enacted requiring that plans for the support of new county libraries be approved by the head of the state bureau of public and school library services.[8]

The counties have traditionally played a major role in the election process. In first-class counties, a superintendent of elections is responsible for the operation of the election machinery. In most counties four-member bipartisan boards of elections selected by the parties supervise the election process. The county clerk distributes election supplies and transmits the results of elections.

The counties also act as a center for the recording of documents. For example, records of real estate transactions, veterans' discharges, and other matters may be traced through the county clerk's office or in some counties through the office of the registrar of deeds. The surrogate is responsible for filing certain records such as those concerning the settlement of estates.

The counties exercise other functions. They inspect weighing and measuring devices. Some conduct limited health activities such as mosquito extermination, or the maintenance of various types of health clinics. The freeholders may establish sewerage authorities. Agricultural and home demonstration agents provide extension services in all counties except Hudson. At least nine counties maintain park systems, some of which offer extensive recreational facilities. Counties are authorized to establish planning boards. Their functions embrace subjects such as land use and development, highway construction, water supply, and stream pollution.

ADMINISTRATIVE REORGANIZATION

Administrative reorganization at the county level is a subject which has received little attention in New Jersey, and, indeed, in most states. In great contrast to the emphasis upon improving administration at the state level, the counties have been content to operate as they always have. Nor has the state government taken the lead in urging modernization.

The structure of county government has many of the defects ascribed to the state prior to the adoption of the new constitution. For example, there is no responsible executive head to supervise and coordinate the operations

* L., 1935, ch. 77, p. 191. This limitation is general in character and does not apply solely to funds for roads.

of the county.   Nor does the governing body have any substantial authority over many county activities.   The freeholders are required to appropriate funds for the courts, the prosecutor, and the sheriff.   Yet the governing
body has no real control over these offices.   The sheriff and the county
clerk continue to be popularly elected, a factor which precludes effective
administrative integration.

Modern management controls are lacking among most counties.   For
example, little has been done to establish effective procedures in budget
preparation and execution.   The same criticism may be made with respect
to personnel matters.

County governments operate as commission governments do; that is,
supervision of the operating departments is divided among the members
of the legislative body.   In recent years commission government has been
subjected to continuous criticism on the municipal level.   Yet rarely is
there any criticism of the same system at the county level.   In 1950 the
state enacted legislation which would permit the municipalities to adopt
optional charters, basically the strong mayor–council plan or the council–
manager plan.   Legislation designed to permit an improved structure of
county government is also highly desirable.

The importance of county government increases daily.   The growth of
the state has created problems which can be solved only by governmental
units larger than the municipalities.   The county is the natural agency to
be given additional responsibilities.   However, before that is done the basic
structure of county government needs revision.

NOTES

[1] A more detailed presentation of the functions of county government may be
found in James M. Collier, *County Government in New Jersey* (New Brunswick:
Rutgers University Press, 1952).   This sixty-four-page booklet has served as the
basis for much of the material contained in this chapter.   In recent years, principally through the action of the governing body or units of the League of Women
Voters, a number of descriptive pamphlets have been published concerning the
functions of individual counties.

[2] Collier, *op. cit.,* p. 7.

[3] L., 1798, ch. DCXC, p. 270.

[4] L., 1912, ch. 158, p. 228.

[5] Adapted from New Jersey Taxpayers Association, *County Finances, A fiscal
background for the study of County Government in New Jersey, 1952 edition*
(Trenton, 1952).

[6] New Jersey Taxpayers Association, *Financial Statistics of New Jersey Local
Government* (Trenton, 1955), p. 53.   For expenditures by function, see N.J. *Seventeenth Annual Report of the Division of Local Government, 1954* (Trenton, 1955),
p. c45.

[7] For a description of the functions performed by the fifty-two offices and agencies
of the county government of Essex, see Walter S. Gray, *County Government in
Essex, New Jersey, An Outline of Its Origin, Its History and Its Functions Today*
(Newark: Essex County Board of Chosen Freeholders, 1953), 108 pp.

[8] L., 1950, ch. 189, p. 423.

CHAPTER 26

Intergovernmental Relations

THE PEOPLE of New Jersey live under several layers of government. For example, a family in Newark—and indeed every person in the state—is subject to the jurisdiction of four governments: the United States, the state, the county, and the municipality. The school district constitutes a fifth unit. But the family in Newark may be affected by other governments as well. For example, disposal facilities may be connected with the system of the Passaic Valley Sewerage Commission; the water supply comes in part from the North Jersey Water Supply Commission. The functions performed by each unit of government change with an ever-changing social, economic, and political climate. Furthermore, each unit has an impact upon every other unit.

RELATIONS WITH THE FEDERAL GOVERNMENT

Constitutional Framework

The several layers of government operating upon each individual do so within the framework of the Constitution and laws of the United States and the constitution and laws of the state of New Jersey. The general theory of the separation of powers between Federal and state governments was described briefly in Chapter 6. Suffice it to say here that in addition to those areas where the two governments function independently, or where one government is prohibited from functioning at all, there are areas where the Constitution requires both to work closely together. For example, the states act as electoral units for the selection of the President, Vice President, and members of Congress. Aside from the specific limitations in the Fifteenth and Nineteenth amendments, the Constitution places upon the states full responsibility for determining who shall vote for Federal elective officers.   The executive authority of a state is charged with taking the initiative in filling a vacancy in Congress, either by making a temporary appointment to the Senate or by issuing a writ of election for a vacancy in the House of Representatives.   The states share also in the constitutional amending process.

The Federal Constitution prohibits the states from performing a number of functions such as coining money, or, without the consent of Congress, keeping troops in time of peace.   But, in contrast to these and other prohibitions, the United States is required to help the states by guaranteeing to each state a republican form of government, and by protecting each state against invasion and, when requested, against domestic violence.

It is beyond the purpose of this chapter to delineate in detail the Federal-state relationships stemming from specific provisions of the United States Constitution.   Nor is it possible to describe the vast series of complicated interrelationships arising out of the administrative services performed by the Federal government.   However, as the demands have grown for additional governmental services at all levels, one phase of intergovernmental relationships has become increasingly important to the people of New Jersey.   The field of intergovernmental fiscal relationships presents one of the most challenging problems in the entire governmental spectrum.

Fiscal Relationships

Tax Problem.   New Jersey is a part of a federal system.   This means that at least two major governments must obtain their support from the same economy.   Both the state and the Federal governments have large taxing powers.   What might appear to New Jerseyites to be a logical division of that taxing power might not seem so logical to New Yorkers whose tax pattern has developed differently.

For example, in recent years the argument has frequently been made that the Federal government should relinquish any claim to gasoline taxes and that alcoholic beverage and other excise taxes should be reduced.   In return for this concession the states should relinquish their claim to other taxes, such as the income tax.   This solution would be a happy one for New Jersey which has had no income tax.   The suggestion would not be well received in the thirty-odd states which rely upon the income tax as a principal source of revenue.   Nor would it be favorably received by the Federal government which has needed every revenue source at its disposal.

The states and the Federal government are concerned with obtaining sufficient revenues to finance the services each provides.   Partly as a consequence of this competition for the tax dollar "Federal-State relations have been marked by coolness, distance, suspicion, and jealousy." [1]   Over a decade ago a Federal study commission observed that the solution to the problems of overlapping and multiple taxation lay in "coordination and cooperation rather than subordination and coercion": [2]

. . . the seeds of solid achievement lie in the scantily tilled field of inter-governmental cooperation and coordination. Progress in this field requires some willingness to compromise, to surrender vested interests, to forget jealousies on the part of both the Federal Government and the States.[3]

A number of coordination techniques have been devised to ease inter-governmental fiscal problems. These include separation of sources, joint administration, tax sharing, mutual deductibility, tax credits, uniformity of tax bases and methods of computation, tax supplements, auditing coopera-tion, and others.[4]

The problem of obtaining coordination and cooperation in fiscal matters applies to relations between the states as well as to relations between the national and state governments. Taxation of the same source by two or more states has been a matter of considerable concern, particularly with respect to personal and corporate income, railroad, death, and capital stock taxes. One of the arguments most frequently heard against a personal income tax in New Jersey is that a resident of the state working in New York would pay an income tax to both governments. However, reciprocal legislation could solve this problem by granting credit to non-residents for taxes paid to their state of residence.

One student of the problem has observed that because of the widespread adoption of the income tax, those states not having the tax are penalizing themselves unduly:

It does not seem sensible that they should continue to deny to themselves this highly productive source of revenue and make a gift of it partly to the federal treasury and partly to their neighboring income-tax-levying states. The federal treasury gains thereby a part of the revenue which would have been collected by the state since there is no deduction to be allowed by the treasury in this case from the amount of its tax. The neighboring income-tax-levying states gain, as they collect from the residents of the non-income tax states who are employed within their jurisdiction, the taxes which otherwise might have gone to these other states. If these states, therefore, continue to suffer from an inability to take care adequately of their fiscal needs, they have only themselves to blame for it.[5]

But coordination and cooperation between the Federal government and the states and among the states themselves are not enough. The necessity of obtaining sufficient revenues to provide governmental services is a serious problem also for municipal governments. Although the state has authority to give or to take away municipal taxing powers, in actual practice New Jersey has moved very slowly in providing a system of taxation which is adequate and equitable.

Federal Grants-in-Aid.   The Congress has used the grant-in-aid as a device to advance programs which it considers to be in the national interest.   The first Hoover Commission declared that the grant-in-aid was a "term used to define a method of operation whereby funds derived from a tax levied and collected by one level of government are made available for expenditure and administration by another level, usually upon a matching basis, for some particular activity, and in accordance with definite and specific standards and requirements." [6]

Opponents of the device contend that the grant programs are uncoordinated, that they have developed haphazardly, that they have transferred policy-making powers from the state governments to the national government, and that the states have initiated programs in order to qualify for Federal funds while neglecting other needed services.   On the other hand, those who favor the grant-in-aid device argue that it has raised the level of state services, not only those which receive aid but others as well.   They contend also that the grant-in-aid decreases inequalities among the states, increases state resources, and stimulates the development of services which are desirable in the public interest. [7]

The Federal government operates approximately forty grant-in-aid programs.   In most of these, the money is channeled directly to the state government.   According to the Bureau of the Census, cash revenues amounting to $37,645,000 were received by New Jersey from the Federal government in the fiscal year 1955. [8]   In addition, grants are made under some programs directly to the municipalities.   Total grants in 1955 amounted to $52,377,981.   Table 32 lists the programs in which New Jersey participated and the amounts received.

TABLE 32

FEDERAL GRANTS-IN-AID TO NEW JERSEY, FISCAL YEAR 1955

Department and Basis of Grant	Amount
Agriculture	
Experiment station	$ 272,006
Cooperative agriculture extension work	274,687
National school lunch program	1,554,281
Cooperative projects in marketing	28,408
State and private forestry cooperation	120,263
Distribution of surplus agricultural commodities	1,994,545
Special school milk program	544,659
Commerce	
Federal airport program	313,737
Highway construction	6,579,681
Interior	
Wildlife restoration	107,316
Payments from receipts under migratory conservation Act and	
Alaska Game Law and Migratory Bird Conservation Act	45

TABLE 32 (*Continued*)

Department and Basis of Grant	Amount
Health, Education, and Welfare	
White House Conference on Education	20,731
American Printig House for the Blind	6,962
Vocational rehabilitation	496,840
Colleges for agricultural and mechanic arts	118,233
Cooperative vocational education	580,067
School construction and survey	1,464,102
Maintenance and operation of schools	1,325,837
Venereal disease control	6,950
Tuberculosis control	129,115
General health assistance	238,034
Mental health	65,971
Cancer control	68,343
Heart disease	26,971
Hospital construction, survey and planning	1,308,237
Old age assistance	8,206,664
Aid to permanently and totally disabled	1,331,106
Aid to dependent children	3,959,473
Aid to the blind	372,474
Maternal and child health services	169,250
Services for crippled children	162,409
Child welfare services	82,050
Construction of community facilities	75,130
Housing and Home Finance Agency	
Defense community facilities and services	13,588
Public Housing Administration	4,416,107
Urban renewal fund	4,919,052
Federal Civil Defense Administration	
Federal contributions	420,213
Veterans Administration	
State and territorial homes for disabled soldiers and sailors	110,619
Supervision of on-the-job training	4,374
Labor	
Unemployment compensation and employment service administration	10,489,451
TOTAL GRANT PAYMENTS	$52,377,981

Source: *Annual Report of the Secretary of the Treasury on the State of the Finances, for the Fiscal Year Ended June 30, 1955,* Treasury Department, Document No. 3187 (Washington, 1956), pp. 626-33.

INTERSTATE RELATIONS

The boundary lines of the states remain stable, but the people within the states have become increasingly mobile. A criminal crossing the Delaware into Pennsylvania at Easton creates an interstate problem, as may a tourist from Iowa who has an automobile accident within New Jersey. Increasingly, the state government is required to work with the governments of sister states in the solution of mutual problems.

Article IV of the Constitution of the United States is concerned with relations between the states. Each state is required to give "full faith and credit to the public acts, records and judicial proceedings of every other state." Particularly in the field of divorce, this clause has undergone varying interpretations among the states. The New Jersey courts have held that the full faith and credit clause "does not protect a divorce decree not based upon a bona fide domicile of one of the spouses when such decree is later attacked in another state." [9] The "decree may be impeached by showing that neither of the parties had acquired a bona fide domicile in the granting state, contrary to the findings of the court of that state." [10] Nor do the courts look kindly upon a divorce granted in another state when one of the parties was not present or represented by counsel. However, if both parties participated and the jurisdiction of the court was fully established, the decree is entitled to full faith and credit though the "proceedings may have been nothing more than mere shadow play, the court formalities an empty show of the judicial proprieties . . . ." [11]

Other provisions of Article IV are designed to prevent discrimination against citizens of other states, to provide for the delivery of fugitives from justice, and to govern the admission of new states. However, these are not the only constitutional provisions affecting interstate relations. For example, there are two of considerable importance to New Jersey in Article I, section 10. The first, which prohibits import duties without the consent of Congress, was designed to prevent the erection of interstate trade barriers; the second authorizes interstate compacts.

Varying state interpretations of these constitutional provisions have resulted in a movement for the adoption of uniform state laws. For example, the Federal Constitution declares that a person charged with a crime who flees to another state "shall on demand of the executive authority of the state from which he fled, be delivered up to be removed to the state having jurisdiction of the crime." There has been much litigation in the courts of New Jersey and in other states concerning the meaning of this clause. In addition to the central question whether the governor may be compelled to surrender a fugitive—and the courts have held that he may not—there are problems relating to the nature of the warrant of arrest, the rights of the person arrested, bail, and other matters. These are simplified by the Uniform Criminal Extradition Act, adopted by New Jersey in 1936. [12] Forty-one states were operating in accordance with the act in 1955.

The movement for uniform state laws and model acts has been led by the National Conference of Commissioners on Uniform State Laws and the Council of State Governments. As of 1955 New Jersey had adopted twenty-four uniform or model acts.

INTERSTATE SPECIAL DISTRICTS

A large part of New Jersey is surrounded by water. This fact, coupled with the strategic location and high population density of the state, has had widespread economic implications. One of these is the state's inability alone to develop adequately, and to protect, its port and transportation facilities, and its marine industries. The fact also that the populous northwestern area is a part of the metropolitan region of New York City has created special problems with respect to water supply, sewage disposal, recreational services, and other governmental functions. To overcome these difficulties the state has entered into a number of interstate compacts.[13]

In some instances agencies have been established which are essentially advisory in nature. For example, the Atlantic States Marine Fisheries Commission, organized by interstate compact in 1943, coordinates the efforts of member states in obtaining the maximum yield from the coastal marine fisheries. New Jersey has three members on the commission.

State cooperation has been achieved in some instances without the benefit of a formal compact. In 1936 New Jersey, New York, and Pennsylvania through their commissions on interstate cooperation established a joint advisory board called The Interstate Commission on the Delaware River Basin. The Commission, known as Incodel, has been active in the promotion of plans for the proper use and control of the resources of the basin, particularly in the field of stream pollution abatement. It was instrumental also in the passage of legislation by the three states in 1944-1945 concerning the diversion of the waters of the Delaware River. The commission's most ambitious project was the promotion of the Delaware River Basin Water Commission. This was a four-state water conservation development program which would have involved the construction of a series of dams, reservoirs, and tunnels.[14] New Jersey, New York, and Delaware signed the compact creating the new body, but in 1953 Pennsylvania rejected the plan as not adequately providing for that state's needs.[15] In mid-1956 the future status of the project was uncertain.

The interstate compact device has been used to establish a number of independent bi-state and tri-state operating and regulatory units of government. By far the largest and best known of these is the Port of New York Authority.

The Port of New York Authority

The Port of New York Authority was established by interstate compact in 1921. New York and New Jersey pledged "each to the other, faithful co-operation in the future planning and development of the port of New York . . . ." [16] The compact was a supplement to the agreement of 1834 in which the two states had determined their respective jurisdictions over the waters of the Hudson River and the New York bay areas. The compact created The Port of New York Authority and a Port of New York District, a region within a radius of approximately twenty-five miles of the lower end of Manhattan. The Authority was granted full power to "purchase, construct, lease and/or operate any terminal or transportation facility within said district." Congress gave its consent to the compact in 1922.

A comprehensive plan was adopted by the legislatures of both states in 1922. The early years of the authority were devoted principally to an effort to unify railroad terminal operations. However, the railroads were uncooperative and little progress was made. As a consequence, the authority engaged in other projects designed to develop the port area.[17] From time to time the legislatures authorized the creation of interstate bridges and tunnels, marine terminals, airports and other facilities. At the end of 1955 the authority operated seventeen facilities including six interstate bridges and tunnels, three marine terminals, two union motor truck terminals, a railroad freight station, a union bus terminal, and four airports.[18] The authority's physical properties in New Jersey amounted to approximately 40 per cent of the total investment.[19]

The port authority operates in what has been described as "a very narrow band of economic practicability." Heavy developmental costs are usually involved. These are usually so great that private management is not interested in a proposed undertaking. Since the authority has no taxing power, the projects it undertakes must have substantial revenue producing qualities; "if a necessary public project is so far to the other side of the financial spectrum as to present no prospect at all of ever becoming self supporting, the problem becomes one for the general taxpayers." [20]

Organization. The Port of New York Authority is an administrative agency exercising jurisdiction in two states. It is governed by a twelve-member board of commissioners, six representing each of the two states. New Jersey's representatives are appointed by the governor with the consent of the Senate, for terms of six years, or until a successor is appointed and qualified. Four of the members must live within the New Jersey portion of the port district. The position of commissioner carries no compensation.

The determination of the policies of the port authority is the responsibility of the board of commissioners. A majority of the members present from each state—and at least three from each state—must approve any proposed action. The members elect from their number a chairman and vice chairman. They select also an executive director who is the administrative head of the organization. All operations are grouped under three major departments—engineering, operations, and port development.[21] In addition, there are a number of staff and service departments responsible to the director.

The authority has complete control over the appointment of its staff. Personnel administration is entirely separate from the civil service agencies of New York and New Jersey. The port authority has no retirement plan of its own. Instead, members of the staff may join the New York State Retirement System. At the end of 1955, the staff numbered 3,972.

In theory, New Jersey has a number of controls over the authority. How effective they are is a matter of dispute. The first review of authority policy is by the legislatures of the two states. They must approve each new program. Then, too, the governor may exercise a measure of control over policy through his appointive power. Another control lies in the power—never used—to remove a member of the commission; charges must be preferred, and the commissioner must be given a hearing by the Senate. The minutes of all meetings must be transmitted to the governor, who may veto the action of any New Jersey commissioner.

The port authority is subject also to the jurisdiction of the courts. This control was exercised with startling suddenness in 1954 when the Supreme Court of New Jersey ruled that the $100,000,000 third tube of the Lincoln Tunnel was being constructed without legislative authorization.[22] The authority contended that it was merely constructing an addition to existing facilities. By a vote of 4-2 the court rejected this point of view. Work on the tube was stopped for a few days until a validating act was passed by each state.

Finally, there are a number of financial controls. For example, the books of the port authority are subject to examination by the director of the division of budget and accounting; the general reserve fund may not exceed 10 per cent of outstanding debt; surplus funds above those required to maintain the reserve fund may be used only as directed by the two states; and annual financial reports must be submitted to the legislatures of New York and New Jersey.[23]

Finance. The Port of New York Authority has no taxing power. Nor are its bonds secured by a pledge of credit of either state. The authority may issue bonds which are payable from the income of its revenue producing facilities.

The financial status of the port authority in its early years was precarious. In 1923 the army would not accept 4 per cent bonds in payment for a government-owned spur railroad in Hoboken. Three years later, with state loans equal to 25 per cent of the cost, the authority was able to sell bonds for its initial program of bridge construction at an interest cost of 4.76 per cent. At first each issue was secured only by the revenues from the bridge which was to be constructed.

Later, the legislatures gave the Port of New York Authority greatly increased financial protection. Surplus earnings were permitted to be pooled in a general reserve fund established to support all bonds. Also the authority was given a monopoly position by the legislative requirement that all vehicular crossings in the port district be constructed and operated by the authority. Bonds now issued are secured not only by the revenues from a particular facility. They have additional backing through the General Reserve Fund. In contrast to the 4.76 interest cost in 1926, the authority was able to sell forty-year bonds two decades later at an interest cost of 1.36 per cent. "Affluence rather than penury" has been said to be the port authority's "potential financial hazard." [24]

Delaware River Joint Toll Bridge Commission

New Jersey and Pennsylvania agreed in 1934 to establish a commission to take over the operation of joint state-owned bridges north of the Pennsylvania Railroad Bridge at Trenton.[25] The commission was authorized also to construct additional bridges, to issue bonds, and to collect tolls for the redemption of the bonds. Congress gave its approval to the agreement in 1935. A supplemental agreement in 1947 enlarged the commission's jurisdiction to include the area as far south as the boundary line between Mercer County and Burlington County. The commission was authorized to replace existing bridges at such locations as it might determine and to construct necessary approach highways. A supplemental compact in 1953 authorized the commission to construct and operate port and terminal facilities north of the Philadelphia-Bucks County line.

In 1953 the toll bridge commission operated 21 bridges across the Delaware. Sixteen were toll free. They had been operated by the commission from appropriations of two states. Five were new toll bridges. Three of the old bridges were scheduled for destruction.

The commission is a ten-member body. The five New Jersey commissioners are appointed by the governor for terms of three years. Any action of the commission must be approved by a majority of the members from each state. Annual reports to the legislature and the governor are required.

The headquarters of the commission is in Morrisville, Pennsylvania, with maintenance offices in New Hope, Pennsylvania, and in Philipsburg and Belvedere, New Jersey. The maintenance force and the bridge police are responsible to the commission and have no relationship with the New Jersey Department of Civil Service. New employees are required to enroll in the retirement system of New Jersey or that of Pennsylvania.[26]

Delaware River Port Authority

New Jersey's most recent bi-state authority concerned with construction and development projects is the Delaware River Port Authority. The authority was created by compact in 1951 to replace The Delaware River Joint Commission.[27] Congress approved the compact in 1952 and authorized an additional river crossing.

The authority is charged with responsibility for operating the Philadelphia-Camden bridge, constructing new facilities across the river, establishing a rapid transit system within a thirty-five mile radius of Camden, and promoting and developing the port district.* Field offices for the solicitation of traffic are maintained in New York, Chicago, and Pittsburgh. The principal asset of the authority in 1956 was the Benjamin Franklin Bridge between Philadelphia and Camden. A high-speed rail transit line is operated on the bridge by the Philadelphia Transportation Company. The Walt Whitman Bridge was under construction, and scheduled for completion in 1957, connecting South Philadelphia with Gloucester City.[28]

The Delaware River Port Authority is governed by eight commissioners from each state. The New Jersey members are appointed by the governor, with the consent of the Senate, for terms of five years and until their successors are qualified. Annual reports must be made to the respective governors and legislatures.

Palisades Interstate Park Commission

Civic-minded individuals anxious to preserve the scenic beauty of the Palisades, overlooking the Hudson River, were responsible for legislation —in 1900—establishing the Palisades Interstate Park. By far the greater portion of the park lies in New York. Of a total acreage in 1952 of 51,673, only 1,822 acres were in New Jersey. Most of the land from the George Washington Bridge to the New York State line lying between U.S. Route 9W and the edge of the cliffs was acquired by John D. Rockefeller, Jr. In 1935 he donated the land to the governing body of the park.

New York and New Jersey entered into a compact in 1937 establishing a corporate body known as the Palisades Interstate Park Commission.[29] Provision was made for a governing body of ten persons, five from each state. Appointments were to be made by the governor with the consent of the Senate for terms of five years. The members of the commission annually select one of their number as president.

The appointment and removal of employees is within the jurisdiction of the commission. Those employed wholly or partly in New Jersey are eligible for membership in the state retirement system, and, with respect to the workmen's compensation act, are deemed to be employees of New Jersey.

The park commission is authorized to maintain its own police force. A "police court of the Palisades Interstate Park" may be held in the park or in any municipality of Bergen County in which a portion of the park may lie. Judges of the court are appointed by the governor with Senate consent.

The park not only has its own municipal court, it is a health district as well. The commission has all the powers of a local board of health.

The park commission is required to report to the legislature its annual

* The port district includes Philadelphia and Delaware counties in Pensylvania and Camden, Burlington, Gloucester, Salem, Cumberland, Cape May, Atlantic, and Ocean Counties in New Jersey.

receipts and expenditures. Lands taken by condemnation proceedings must also be reported. Operating expenses amount to approximately $400,000 annually. Over three-fourths of this amount is met by state appropriations; the balance is obtained from the operation of facilities such as boat basins, refreshment stands, gasoline service stations, and parking areas.[30]

Interstate Sanitation Commission

New Jersey, New York, and Connecticut entered into a tri-state compact in the mid-thirties for the purpose of abating the pollution of the waters in the New York harbor area. An Interstate Sanitation District was established extending in New Jersey from the northeastern corner of Bergen County, down the Hudson River, and along the eastern portions of Hudson, Essex, Union, Middlesex, and Monmouth counties to Sandy Hook Bay. An Interstate Sanitation Commission was created consisting of five persons from each state to be selected according to the laws of each state. The New Jersey commissioners are appointed by the governor with the consent of the Senate. Three members are required to be departmental officials; two are from the state at large.[31] The office of the commission is in New York City.

The sanitation commission maintains a professional and clerical staff of about one dozen persons to obtain information for pollution control purposes. For example, in 1953, ninety sewerage treatment plants were visited one or more times, and samples taken of influents and effluents. Laboratory analyses and other tests were made to determine the adequacy of the treatment plants. In addition, shore surveys were conducted in order to locate illegal sewage discharges.

The compact provides that the commission may require municipalities—after notice and hearing—to treat sewage in accordance with prescribed standards. In order to supplement this provision of the compact, New Jersey law authorizes the commission to seek the assistance of the courts. For example, the commission ordered the city of Elizabeth to prepare plans for a pollution control program by April 1, 1949, and to let contracts for necessary equipment, labor, and material by July 8, 1950. On September 1, 1950, the commission filed a complaint in the Superior Court alleging that the order had not been obeyed. The court entered judgment against the city, and set up a schedule for the completion of the pollution abatement program. The sanitation commission later instituted contempt proceedings but withdrew the action after the city had awarded construction contracts.[32]

The sanitation commission is supported by state appropriations. New York and New Jersey each pay 45 per cent and Connecticut pays 10 per cent of the annual costs. Annual reports are submitted to the governors and legislatures of the three states.

Waterfront Commission of New York Harbor

In order to stamp out the crime and corruption on the docks of New York and New Jersey, the two states established the Waterfront Commission of New York Harbor in 1953. Hearings before the New York State Crime Commission had revealed that thousands of dock workers were being subjected to discriminatory hiring practices through the "shape-up," a system whereby the longshoremen formed a circle at each dock every morning and waited for a hiring boss to select the "gangs" or individuals who were to work during the day. The operation of the piers was conducted in such a manner that a second set of workers called "public loaders" were hired to load and unload trucks. Racketeers extorted money and special favors from workers and steamship executives alike.[33]

Following the revelations of the crime commission, New York and New Jersey entered into a compact which was approved by Congress in August, 1953. The Waterfront Commission of New York Harbor consists of two members, one chosen by the governor of each state with Senate consent for terms of three years. The commission is authorized to make and enforce rules concerning hiring and loading practices. Its powers of inspection extend not only to the piers and waterfront terminals but to all vessels in the port of New York district.

The law requires that employment information centers be substituted for the shape-up. Hiring agents, licensed by the commission, must obtain workers at the centers. The object of the law is to assure that the longshoreman, who must himself be registered with the commission, is no longer dependent upon one hiring boss. If not selected by an agent representing one pier, the worker may proceed to other hiring agents within the commission's employment center. By rules of the commission, the centers are used by the "casuals." Regular employees, that is those who work for a single employer report directly to the appropriate pier. The commission estimates that 25,000 men are sufficient to work the port. As of June 30, 1955, over 31,000 were qualified.

Other provisions of the agreement include the prohibition of public loading, the outlawry of the collection of union dues by an organization having convicted felons among its officers, and the requirement of licenses not only for hiring agents but for pier superintendents, port watchmen, and stevedoring concerns.[34]

The waterfront commission began its work with appropriations totaling $600,000 from New York and $300,000 from New Jersey. However, these funds were to be refunded and the commission financed from a tax on the stevedoring companies amounting to not more than 2 per cent of payroll.

The problems of the commission are not easy of solution. The passage of a law and the establishment of an administrative agency cannot quickly bring peace and order to an area long characterized by lawlessness and corruption. However, there is little doubt but that the commission has improved waterfront conditions and that respect for law and order has been substantially increased. The hiring problem, particularly favoritism by hiring agents, continues to be a center of controversy.[35]

INTRASTATE SPECIAL DISTRICTS

In addition to bi-state governmental units designed to operate in areas where the state is unable to act by itself alone, New Jersey has created a number of governmental units designed for limited functions. These special units operate in metropolitan regions where the people of several counties or several municipalities are served. Three of these state-created, single-function entities, are described briefly below.

South Jersey Port Commission

In 1926 the legislature established the South Jersey Port District as a public corporation embracing the counties of Mercer, Burlington, Camden, Gloucester, Salem, Cumberland, and Cape May.[36] In order to develop port facilities within the district, an operating agency, the South Jersey Port Commission, was established. The original act provided for a three-member body appointed by the governor with the consent of the Senate. In 1942 the commission was enlarged to seven members, one from each county, to be named by concurrent resolution of the legislature. Although there has been no legislation changing the 1942 act, following the adoption of the new constitution new members have been appointed by the governor with Senate consent. The term of office is five years.

The commission operates the Camden Marine Terminal, "the only publicly-owned and operated marine terminals on the New Jersey side of the Delaware River from Trenton to the sea, that are open to all on equal terms." [37] The terminals, which have been in operation since 1931, were constructed by the commission with funds obtained from a bond issue of $2,000,000. An agreement between the port district and the city of Camden obligated the city to raise by taxation the funds to support the bonds while the port district was obligated to return surplus funds to the city. By 1953 over $1,000,000 had been returned.

The board of commerce and navigation in the Department of Conservation and Economic Development is given general supervisory powers over the commission. An annual report to the legislature is required by law.

Passaic Valley Sewerage Commission

During the late 1890's and the early 1900's the Passaic River was transformed from a "pleasant waterway" into "an ugly, black, oily, and stinking drain." [38] To stem the pollution, a Passaic Valley District Sewerage Commission was established by the legislature in 1902.[39] The commission consists of five members appointed by the governor with Senate consent for terms of five years. In a suit brought by New York State to enjoin the discharge of sewage into New York Bay, the Supreme Court of the United States held the commission to be a state agency.[40]

The Passaic commission operates a 21.7-mile trunk sewer which was begun in 1912 and completed in 1924. The main intercepting sewer runs from the Great Falls in Paterson to the Newark Bay pumping station where suspended solids are removed. The remaining effluent flows through a tunnel to a diffusion area in New York Bay. Operation and maintenance costs are apportioned among the municipalities contracting with the commission. In 1953 the legislature authorized the commission to issue $10,000,000 in bonds for the improvement and enlargement of the sewerage system.

North Jersey District Water Supply Commission

The need of Newark, Paterson, and other municipalities for increased water supplies led to the creation in 1916 of the North Jersey District Water Supply Commission.[41] There are five members on the commission, appointed by the governor with Senate consent for terms of four years. No more than three members may belong to the same political party.

The commission operates the Wanaque Water Supply System. A twenty-one-mile aqueduct was completed in 1930 which carries water from the Wanaque Reservoir in Passaic County to Newark, Paterson, Kearny, Passaic, and other municipalities. The costs of the project are apportioned among the participating municipalities on the basis of the water consumed.

State-Authorized Units

Under New Jersey law several kinds of special districts may be established. Some are designed to permit two counties to unite in performing a function of interest to both; for example, a joint county bridge commission, or a regional housing authority. Two or more municipalities may also unite for certain purposes such as the creation of a housing authority, the acquisition of a waterworks, or the establishment of a sewerage district. Individual townships may establish fire districts with elected boards authorized to issue bonds and levy taxes. There are other kinds of special districts. Some meet the essential characteristics of a governmental unit as determined by the Bureau of the Census, that is, existence as an organized entity, governmental character, and substantial autonomy. Others, such as county mosquito extermination commissions and municipal parking authorities, do not. However, all perform governmental services and all are ultimately responsible to the people.[42]

STATE-LOCAL RELATIONS

State Supervision of Local Services

The last half century has witnessed an ever-increasing degree of state supervision over the administrative services performed by government at the county and municipal levels. In some areas of governmental activity, such as finance, state control arose out of the inability of local governments to cope with the disastrous effects of an economic depression. State action at first was bitterly resented by local officials. However, in time, owing to a beneficent rather than a punitive approach, state officials charged with administering fiscal laws and regulations were able to obtain complete compliance and cooperation.

State supervision has increased also by virtue of Federal legislation which required conformity to certain standards. As a consequence of the state-county structural arrangement for the administration of the old age assistance and other categorical aid programs, some areas of county government operate under a reasonably close degree of state supervision. Some functions performed by officials at the county level are in fact state functions. The prosecutor, the tax board, the superintendent of schools— all are appointive state positions. In recent years there has been a very considerable increase in the degree of state supervision exercised over these officials.

The trend toward greater state control is most evident in connection with the judiciary. Both county judges and municipal magistrates are regulated to a degree seldom contemplated prior to the establishment of the new court system in 1948. This development has come about principally as a result of the rulemaking power of the supreme court rather than through legislation. The new rules regulating local judicial practice were in response to widespread public dissatisfaction with a system which previously was almost completely unregulated.

As local functions of government increase in complexity and in cost, the need increases for state technical assistance and for state financial help. The demands for increased school facilities, and problems such as water supply, sewerage, health, and a host of others no longer can be solved easily or adequately on a strictly local basis. Local communities and the state are literally forced into an ever-widening circle of interrelationships.

State Grants-in-Aid

The state also conducts a number of grant-in-aid programs. Some of these are related to the Federal programs. Others, particularly in the field of education, have no relation to Federal grants. In the fiscal year 1957 the state granted over $138,000,000 to the counties and municipalities.

This sum amounted to 43 per cent of total state expenditures of approximately $321,000,000.*

INTERGOVERNMENTAL COOPERATION

A growing number of the major public services require for their performance the cooperation of several levels of government. For example, old age assistance in New Jersey is a joint program of the Federal, state, and county governments. Other services require for their performance the participation of two or more units of government operating on the same level. For example, the municipality of New Brunswick supplies water to the municipality of Milltown. Seldom, indeed, does one level of government or one unit of government operate by itself alone. A given action by one official or by one governing body must take into account the jurisdiction and interests of other units of government. A high degree of administrative cooperation is required in order to accomplish the performance of governmental services with a minimum of friction.

The principal agency of semi-official cooperation is The Council of State Governments which was established in 1935. The council was responsible for the creation of a Commission on Interstate Cooperation in each state consisting of ten members of the legislature and five administrative officials. New Jersey was the first state to establish such a commission.[43] The council and the state commissions, together with organizations related to the council, have done much to unify state laws and to iron out interstate conflicts in a number of fields.†

Within the state the governing bodies of the counties are voluntarily bound together through the Association of Chosen Freeholders of New Jersey. Since 1942 the association has published the monthly magazine *New Jersey County Government*. Payment of annual dues to an organization composed exclusively of boards of freeholders was authorized in 1936.[44]

---

* New Jersey's interpretation of what constitutes a grant-in-aid differs considerably from the Hoover Commission's definition. For example, the state includes certain shared taxes and fees. Also included are the salaries of county superintendents of schools, members of county boards of taxation, and 40 per cent of the salaries of county judges. These officials are located in the counties but they are appointed by and responsible to the state. The sum of those items which are not strictly grants-in-aid constitutes a small percentage of the total.

† The Council of State Governments serves as the secretariat for the American Legislators Association, the Governor's Conference, the Conference of Chief Justices, the National Association of Attorneys General, the National Association of State Budget Officers, the Legislative Service Conference, the National Association of State Purchasing Officials, and the Parole and Probation Compact Administrators Association. The Council also cooperates with the National Conference of Commissioners on Uniform State Laws. The main office of the council is at 1313 East 60th Street, Chicago 37, Illinois. Branch offices are maintained in New York, San Francisco, and Washington, D.C.

At the local level, the New Jersey State League of Municipalities supplies professional research and advisory services to the member municipalities. Enabling legislation was enacted in 1915 authorizing municipalities to form an organization for joint action upon questions affecting their general welfare.[45] Fifteen organizations of municipal officials are allied with the League.* The league in turn is a member of the American Municipal Association, a federation of over forty state leagues. At the local level also, the New Jersey Association of Township Committeemen represents a number of the smaller municipalities.

NOTES

[1] U.S. *Federal, State, and Local Government Fiscal Relations,* Senate Document No. 69, 78th Cong., 1st sess. (Washington, 1943), p. 5.

[2] *Ibid.,* p. 1.

[3] *Ibid.,* p. 117.

[4] U.S. Treasury Department, *Federal-State-Local Tax Coordination* (Washington, 1952). For a recent discussion of these techniques see Tax Institute, *Federal-State-Local Tax Correlation* (Princeton: Tax Institute, Inc., 1954).

[5] Paul Studenski, "Alternative to Grants in Aid," Tax Institute, *op. cit.,* pp. 105-7.

[6] The Commission on Organization of the Executive Branch of the Government, *Federal-State Relations, Overseas Administration, Federal Research* (Washington, 1949), p. 29.

[7] *Ibid.,* pp. 30-32. See also *Federal Grants in Aid* (Chicago: The Council of State Governments, (1949), pp. 41-43, and U.S. *Intergovernmental Relationships between the United States and the States and Municipalities,* Senate Report No. 94, 82d Cong., 1st sess. (1951).

[8] U.S. Department of Commerce, Bureau of the Census, *Compendium of State Government Finances in 1953, State Finances: 1955 (G-SF55-No. 2)* (Washington, 1956), p. 14. Additional revenues of $1,031,000 were classified as other than fiscal aid.

[9] *Eberle* v *Somonek* 24 N.J.Super. 366, 373 (1953).

[10] *Judkins* v *Judkins* 22 N.J.Super. 516, 524 (1952).

[11] *Roskein* v *Roskein* 25 N.J.Super. 415, 424 (1953).

[12] L., 1936, ch. 42, p. 110.

[13] For an extended analysis of interstate compacts, see Frederick L. Zimmerman and Mitchell Wendell, *The Interstate Compact since 1925* (Chicago: The Council of State Governments, 1951). See also Vincent T. Thursby, *Interstate Cooperation, A Study of the Interstate Compact* (Washington: Public Affairs Press, 1953).

[14] For the engineering report see The Interstate Commission on the Delaware River Basin, *Report on the Utilization of the Waters of the Delaware River Basin* (1950).

[15] For the compact see L., 1951, ch 283, p. 978.

* The affiliated organizations are: Association of Municipal Assessors of New Jersey, New Jersey Institute of Municipal Attorneys, Building Officials Association of New Jersey, Municipal Clerks Association of New Jersey, Municipal Electrical Inspectors Association of New Jersey, New Jersey Association of Municipal Engineers, Municipal Finance Officers Association of New Jersey, New Jersey Health Officers Association, New Jersey Association of Housing Authorities, New Jersey Federation of Official Planning Boards, Municipal Receivers and Tax Collectors Association of New Jersey, Public Recreation Association of New Jersey, Municipal Welfare Association of New Jersey, the New Jersey State Plumbing Inspector's Association, and the New Jersey Municipal Managers' and Administrators' Association.

16 L., 1921, ch. 151, p. 413.

17 See Erwin Wilkie Bard, *The Port of New York Authority* (New York: Columbia University Press, 1942), pp. 160-69.

18 The Port of New York Authority, *35th Annual Report, 1955* (New York).

19 Billings Wilson, "The Port of New York Authority," *Proceedings of the New Jersey Historical Society,* LXXI, No. 3 (1953), 199.

20 Austin J. Tobin, *Authorities as a Governmental Technique* (The Port of New York Authority, 1953), p. 27.

21 See Frederick L. Bird, *A Study of The Port of New York Authority* (New York: Dun and Bradstreet, Inc., 1949).

22 L., 1954, ch. 11, p. 58. For the case, see *Port of New York Authority* v *Weehawken Tp.* 14 N.J. 570 (1954).

23 Tobin, *op. cit.,* pp. 4-5.

24 Bird, *op. cit.,* p. 186.

25 L., 1934, ch. 215, p. 498.

26 Delaware River Joint Toll Bridge Commission, *Annual Report, 1953* (Morrisville, 1954), p. 40.

27 L., 1951, ch. 288, p. 1044.

28 *Report of the Delaware River Port Authority to the Governors and Legislatures of the Commonwealth of Pennsylvania and the State of New Jersey, 1955* (Camden), p. 9.

29 L., 1937, ch. 148, p. 364.

30 Palisades Interstate Park Commission, *Fifty-third Annual Report of the Palisades Interstate Park in New Jersey,* (Bear Mountain, 1953), pp. 10-11.

31 L., 1935, ch. 322, p. 1054.

32 See the annual reports of the commission. For a list of the sewage treatment plants discharging into the interstate sanitation district waters, see *Interstate Sanitation Commission Report 1953* (New York, 1954), Appendix.

33 *Fourth Report of the New York State Crime Commission (Port of New York Waterfront) to the Governor, The Attorney General and The Legislature of the State of New York, May 20, 1953* (Albany, 1953), pp. 7-64.

34 L., 1953, ch. 202, p. 1511.

35 Waterfront Commission of New York Harbor, *Annual Report for the Year Ended June 30, 1955.*

36 L., 1926, ch. 336, p. 759.

37 *Twenty-ninth Annual Report of the South Jersey Port Commission to the Legislature of New Jersey for the Year 1954* (Camden, 1955), p. 2.

38 *Passaic Valley Sewerage Commissioners, 1924-1949.*

39 L., 1902, ch. 48, p. 190.

40 *People of State of New York* v *State of New Jersey,* 256 U.S. 296 (1920).

41 L., 1916, ch. 71, p. 129.

42 U.S. Department of Commerce, Bureau of the Census, *Local Government Structure in the United States,* State and Local Government Special Studies, Number 34 (Washington, 1954), pp. 55-58.

43 Hubert R. Gallagher, "Work of the Commissions on Interstate Cooperation," *The Annals,* CCVII (January, 1940), 103-10.

44 L., 1926, ch. 54, p. 93.

45 L., 1915, ch. 163, p. 321.

CHAPTER 27

A Look Ahead

THE CONSTITUTION of New Jersey adopted in 1844 declared that "government is instituted for the protection, security, and benefit of the people, and they have the right at all times to alter or reform the same, whenever the public good may require it." [1] That there was real meaning underlying this provision of the bill of rights was demonstrated in 1947 when the state's basic document was subjected to a major overhauling. New constitutional language made possible a whole series of developments, both large and small.

The establishment and operation of the new judicial system has received widespread acclaim as a remarkable demonstration of the manner in which important reforms can be effected given the proper constitutional structure and forceful leadership. While the reorganization of the executive agencies has been less spectacular, there has been a substantial record of accomplishment. The legislative branch also has taken a number of steps designed to improve its procedures and to provide a greater degree of public participation in its deliberations.

The large developments, such as constitutional revision and judicial reform, tend to obscure other changes less all-embracing in scope. In almost every agency new functions have been added or new methods developed for performing old functions. This continued striving on the part of public officials and employees to improve the character of the state's services is a healthy sign. It is in keeping with the philosophy expressed by Governor Robert B. Meyner that there is "need for continuous study and action" in the "endless campaign against smug self-approval." [2]

THE CONSTITUTION

The delegates to the constitutional convention of 1947 presented the people of New Jersey with a basic document second to none. Public approval of two amendments in 1953, however, demonstrated that the people did not consider it a perfect document, proof against change for all time. In general the constitution is remarkably concise and flexible. Nonetheless, there are provisions—or omissions—which in time may prove obstacles to the achievement of improved governmental structure and procedures. For example, one omission was a proposed provision for periodic constitutional revision. The proposal was considered and rejected by the delegates not so much on its merits but owing to the political pressures in the convention. Other provisions, such as that establishing county courts —the principal obstacle to a fully integrated judicial system—were included for the same reason.

When, at some future date, the legislature or the governor initiates a movement to modernize the structure of county government, the fact that so many county officers are named in the constitution—more particularly, the clerk, surrogate, and sheriff—will make the task of modernization more difficult. The cumbersome and political means of determining that a vacancy exists in the office of governor is another illustration of the fact that the new constitution, excellent though it may be, merits continued reexamination.

THE REPRESENTATIVE SYSTEM

The legislature was less directly affected by constitutional revision than either the executive or judicial branches. However, in recent years it, too, has been concerned with the process of self-evaluation.

A basic question concerns the degree to which the constitutional structure permits a representative legislature. In the constitutional convention of 1844 the lone dissenting vote against adoption was due to one delegate's unalterable opposition to the principle of Senate representation based upon boundary lines rather than upon people. In the century which followed, this issue became a highly emotional one. That the question of the representative character of the Senate has great political and emotional overtones was demonstrated anew in 1947. The constitutional convention was possible only after action was taken to bind the delegates to omit consideration of the subject. The likelihood of any constitutional change in the near future seems extremely remote.

However, the Senate is not as unresponsive to public opinion as is commonly supposed. Nor are the rural-urban differences at present so sharp as to prevent agreement upon most large issues. One of the principal political results of the increasing industrialization of New Jersey will be gradually to reduce the sharp divergences in viewpoint so prevalent in the past. The problems of adequate schools, highways, water supplies, and sewerage facilities will be common alike to the large and small counties.

The fact that the problems facing the members of the Senate will be increasingly common to all does not remove the inequity of the system. However, it does increase greatly the probability that proposed legislation will be in the interest of all the people of the state rather than of a particular section.

There is no constitutional issue in connection with the allocation of representatives in the General Assembly. The constitution requires an apportionment among the counties according to population following each Federal census. The problem is one of obtaining agreement concerning method. As of mid-1956 the legislature had resisted acceptance of either a modern mathematical approach or of an automatic apportionment device, both of which the Congress adopted a decade and a half ago.

A final problem concerning the representative structure relates to the method of electing members of the General Assembly. Court decisions in the late nineteenth and early twentieth centuries made unconstitutional the election of an assemblyman within a district of a county. Since that time assemblymen have been elected on an at-large basis. Governor Woodrow Wilson, in his annual message of 1912, called for a constitutional amendment requiring a return to a system of assembly districts. He declared that in a self-governed country there was an obligation upon the state to make "the representative body from which legislation proceeds in fact representative, as nearly as possible a mirror of the character and opinion of the communities of which the State is composed." [3]   Under the existing system, the minority, however large, is deprived of all representation in the General Assembly. A return to the system of district elections, under judicial or other safeguards, would seem to assure a more representative lower house.

In recent years the legislature has taken steps to improve its own internal operations. For example, the number of committees has been reduced, and their names and jurisdictions made identical for both houses. The next few years will be a testing period to determine whether the committee system is being used and whether through a greater use of public hearings and other means, the public is participating to a larger degree in the legislative process. The staff of the legislature has been increased in order to provide additional research and law revision services. These have always been in short supply. The legislature continues to be handicapped by the lack of adequate physical facilities such as offices and hearing rooms.

THE EXECUTIVE

The new constitution strengthened the position of the governor. A longer term, the opportunity for election to a second term, the conditional veto—these have served to increase the governor's participation in the legislative process. At the same time the virtual elimination of the pocket veto has forced the chief executive to declare himself on every issue. The constitutional language concerning the administrative structure has enabled the governor to exercise a greater degree of managerial leadership.

Despite the governor's new powers, he is still lacking in the basic authority commensurate with his position. The vast majority of his appointments require the confirmation of the Senate. This constitutional provision might be justified if the Senate were to use its power as a means of reviewing the qualifications of the persons selected by the governor. The provision has no justification if it serves merely as a lever by means of which an individual senator exerts pressure upon the governor to accept a proposed appointee or legislative measure.

The governor continues to lack authority also over some of the principal departments. The argument may seem plausible that in order to keep particularly sensitive functions of government out of politics they should be headed by boards whose members are appointed for long terms and are thus free from partisan influences. The worth of this argument deserves careful investigation. For example, has public welfare in New Jersey been neglected or has it enjoyed special public favor as a consequence of the removal of the Department of Institutions and Agencies from direct gubernatorial control? This question and other related questions are not simply academic. They are of vital importance to the 50,000 persons housed in the mental and correctional institutions of the state, and to additional thousands affected by the several welfare programs. But the questions have a broader significance. Other groups seek similar special consideration. Should other departments be given a status similar to that of institutions and agencies? Or should all department heads, regardless of function, be made directly responsible to the elected chief executive?

The structure of some departments could be improved by making direct the line of authority of the department head. At present that line is broken by the governor's appointment of many division directors. They are usually subject to Senate confirmation. This procedure may result in a higher priority being given the wishes of particular senators than the requirements of the department head. At present, the law in this regard is much more restrictive than the constitution requires.

Although the new constitution enabled the governor to exercise increased managerial control, lack of an adequate staff in his immediate office has prevented anything approaching a full realization of this objective. The political, ceremonial, and other facets of the office of governor do not permit room for the managerial facet unless he has several able assistants directly responsible to him.

The administrative structure of the executive branch has undergone a considerable change in the last decade. The series of actions beginning with the limited administrative reorganization of 1944-45 and particularly those following the adoption of the new constitution have resulted in what appears on an organization chart as a relatively simple structure. However, the simplification may have been overdone. Some expansion of the number of departments may be advisable in order to eliminate the placing under one roof of agencies performing unrelated functions. New departments may be necessary in order to focus public attention upon important functions which have not received proper emphasis owing to the pressing and immediate demands of other functions upon the time of the departmental supervisory staff.

Nor is the administrative structure so simple as it may appear. The act of transferring a formerly independent agency to a department is a step which cannot be accomplished merely by the passage of a law. Moreover, the integration of that agency into the department is a complex process. In a number of agencies genuine integration has yet to be achieved.

ADEQUACY OF STATE SERVICES

No two persons will have identical answers to a question concerning the number and adequacy of the services performed by New Jersey's state government. For some, the activities of the state are already vastly overextended. For others, the state has been guilty of neglect through failure to expand its services sufficiently. The views of most people probably lie at some point midway between these extremes depending upon their philosophies of the proper role of government in modern society. But philosophies may be altered by events.

Within the last decade, the state government has undergone striking change. In response to an insistent public demand, old functions have been enlarged in scope and new functions established. Nor is the end in sight. The rapid increases in population, in industrialization, and in urbanization have resulted in a multitude of new problems. Some can be solved at the municipal level, others at the county level. But more and more problems transcend local boundary lines. As a consequence, municipal and county governments must look to the state government for advice and leadership, for financial aid, and occasionally for assistance in actually carrying out some function.

The provision of an adequate water supply is a case in point. Originally, water supply was an individual problem. In time it became a municipal problem. In many areas private companies were formed to supply water—and still do. As the state developed, neither the municipalities alone nor the private water companies alone were able to meet the increased demands. Over a quarter century ago in North Jersey the problem was solved temporarily by the creation of the North Jersey Water Supply Commission, a separate governmental entity embracing a wide area. In recent years the widespread shortage of water in many parts of the state led to the question whether the state government should assume primary responsibility for obtaining, developing, and operating water facilities. Legislative recognition of this responsibility was highlighted in 1956 by an act authorizing the state to purchase Round Valley.

The struggle to provide an adequate education for the youth of New Jersey affords a second illustration of a problem which is beyond the resources of many individual communities. Here the principal solution is not one of state operation but rather of increased financial aid to local communities. This problem was met in part by legislation enacted in 1954 and in 1956. But the sharp increase in the number of births together with the industrial and residential development of New Jersey presage a school enrollment of an unprecedented character. Greatly increased school expenditures seem inevitable in order to obtain an adequate supply of qualified teachers and to provide the necessary classroom facilities.

Water and education are two of the most pressing problems. But there are many others. The completion of the New Jersey Turnpike and the Garden State Parkway—magnificent though these achievements may be—has in no sense solved the need for improved highway facilities. The State Highway Department has estimated that in order to modernize the highway system, an expenditure of $2,500,000,000 will be required within the next decade.

The state will be seriously handicapped in its efforts to meet public demands for increased services until new sources of revenue are made available. There are two aspects of this problem which deserve special attention. One is the necessity for obtaining sufficient revenues to meet operating, capital, and state aid needs. A second aspect concerns the desirability of introducing a greater degree of equity into the tax structure. No citizen of New Jersey can take pride in the knowledge that his state has one of the most inequitable systems of taxation among the forty-eight states.

The necessity for state action in the building of schools and highways and institutional facilities does not lessen the need for action of a different kind in other areas equally within the orbit of state government. The list of functions needing reappraisal is as long as the list of functions being performed. Almost every public official has suggestions for improving the services with which he is most closely connected. This is as it should be. For if government is to be dynamic and responsive, it must be ever changing.

NOTES

[1] Art. I, par. 2.
[2] *Inaugural Address, Robert B. Meyner, Governor of New Jersey to the Legislature, January 19, 1954*, p. 11.
[3] N.J. *Senate Journal* 1912, p. 15.

Appendix

CHRONOLOGY OF SIGNIFICANT EVENTS

1665 "Concessions and Agreements" issued by Lord John Berkeley and Sir George Cartaret to form basis of government in the province.

1668 First Assembly called by Governor Philip Cartaret to meet at Elizabethtown.

1676 Province divided into East New Jersey and West New Jersey by Quintipartite Deed.

1677 "Laws, Concessions and Agreements" issued by William Penn for West New Jersey.

1683 "Fundamental Constitutions" of East New Jersey drawn up.

1702 Proprietary system brought to an end.
New Jersey united with New York under Lord Cornbury, the first royal governor.

1738 Province made an independent royal colony.

1774 First Provincial Congress met at New Brunswick.

1776 First state constitution of New Jersey adopted.

1787 Federal Constitution ratified by New Jersey.

1790 Trenton selected as state capital.

1798 Basic county law enacted establishing boards of freeholders.

1844 Second state constitution adopted.

1848 State Hospital for the Mentally Ill established at Trenton through the efforts of Dorothea Dix.

1851 First child labor law enacted.

1852 Assembly districts created within the counties.

1864 Rutgers designated by legislature as Land Grant College of New Jersey.

1867 State Board of Education established.

1872 State Board of Agriculture established.

1877 State Board of Health established.

1878 Bureau of Statistics of Labor and Industries created.

1880 New Jersey Agricultural Experiment Station established.

1883 Council of Charities and Corrections established.

1884 First Civil Rights Law enacted.

1891 State aid provided for county roads.

1893 Assembly districts declared unconstitutional.

1894 Office of State Commissioner of Public Roads established.

1903 Direct Primary introduced.

1906 State regulation of motor vehicles undertaken.

1908 Civil Service Law enacted.

1911 Commission form of government (Walsh Act) authorized for municipalities.
The Geran Act passed to effect a reform of election procedures.
Employees Liability Law enacted.

1912 Election of small county boards of freeholders authorized.

1915 State public employment service established.

1917 Employers liability insurance law enacted.
Department of municipal accounts established.

1918 Workmen's Compensation Bureau established.
1921 Port of New York Authority created by compact between New Jersey and
      New York.
      Retirement System for State Employees established.
      State Police established.
1927 Zoning authorized by constitutional amendment.
1932 State program for old age assistance established.
1936 Legislation enacted supplementing Federal Social Security Act.
1941 New Jersey State Board of Mediation established.
1943 Permanent registration made applicable to all elections.
1945 Anti-discrimination law enacted.
      Migrant Labor Act passed.
      Rutgers designated the State University of New Jersey.
1947 Third state constitution adopted.
1948 New court system established by law in conformity with terms of new consti-
      tution.
1950 Optional Municipal Charter Law enacted.

STATE-WIDE ELECTION STATISTICS

County	For President, 1956 Republican	Democrat	For United States Senator, 1954 Republican	Democrat	For Governor, 1953 Republican	Democrat
Atlantic	44,698	21,668	33,936	20,315	35,452	19,481
Bergen	254,334	82,169	131,483	84,291	115,605	110,530
Burlington	38,145	24,258	21,039	25,321	20,043	23,236
Camden	85,067	75,152	46,117	63,095	41,867	68,183
Cape May	16,887	5,897	12,308	6,622	11,957	6,531
Cumberland	24,067	17,309	15,328	14,711	15,716	14,420
Essex	234,682	146,313	129,375	137,245	127,782	141,996
Gloucester	30,646	20,007	20,342	17,978	18,216	18,012
Hudson	183,919	107,098	74,830	143,503	89,501	160,425
Hunterdon	16,150	5,957	8,618	6,397	7,628	8,513
Mercer	56,029	52,684	28,944	50,306	28,351	50,624
Middlesex	100,071	64,538	44,474	65,128	40,685	72,592
Monmouth	83,828	32,329	46,259	35,232	43,046	38,615
Morris	76,571	19,503	44,087	19,988	36,100	26,899
Ocean	28,033	9,367	17,390	9,001	16,326	9,302
Passaic	101,182	61,859	57,674	58,782	60,599	65,852
Salem	14,091	9,276	8,599	8,319	7,694	9,919
Somerset	37,930	14,529	18,587	13,250	15,737	17,921
Sussex	15,867	3,756	8,768	4,756	7,566	6,727
Union	146,228	67,540	83,896	63,182	61,973	76,144
Warren	18,517	9,128	9,474	10,736	7,224	16,788
Total	1,606,942	850,337	861,528	858,158	809,068	962,710

Source: N.J. *Result of the General Election Held November 6, 1956* (Compiled under Direction of the Secretary of State); *Manual of the Legislature of New Jersey, 1955*, pp. 671, 673.

THE GOVERNORS OF NEW JERSEY [a]

Name	Political Party [b]	Date
ELECTED ANNUALLY BY STATE LEGISLATURE, 1776-1844		
William Livingston	F	1776-1790
William Paterson	F	1790-1792
Richard Howell	F	1792-1801
Joseph Bloomfield	JR	1801-1802
John Lambert, Acting	JR	1802-1803
Joseph Bloomfield	JR	1803-1812
Aaron Ogden	F	1812-1813
William S. Pennington	JR	1813-1815
Mahlon Dickerson	JR	1815-1817
Isaac H. Williamson	JR	1817-1829
Garret D. Wall	D	1829
Peter D. Vroom	D	1829-1832
Samuel L. Southard	W	1832-1833
Elias P. Seeley	W	1833
Peter D. Vroom	D	1833-1836
Philemon Dickerson	D	1836-1837
William Pennington	W	1837-1843
Daniel Haines	D	1843-1844
ELECTED BY VOTERS OF STATE		
Charles C. Stratton	W	1845-1848
Daniel Haines	D	1848-1851
George F. Fort	D	1851-1854
Rodman M. Price	D	1854-1857
William A. Newell	R	1857-1860
Charles S. Olden	R	1860-1863
Joel Parker	D	1863-1866
Marcus L. Ward	R	1866-1869
Theodore F. Randolph	D	1869-1872
Joel Parker	D	1872-1875
Joseph D. Bedle	D	1875-1878
George B. McClellan	D	1878-1881
George C. Ludlow	D	1881-1884
Leon Abbett	D	1884-1887
Robert S. Green	D	1887-1890
Leon Abbett	D	1890-1893

THE GOVERNORS OF NEW JERSEY [a] (Continued)

Name	Political Party [b]	Date
ELECTED BY VOTERS OF STATE		
George T. Werts	D	1893-1896
John W. Griggs	R	1896-1898
Foster M. Voorhees, Acting	R	1898
David O. Watkins, Acting	R	1898-1899
Foster M. Voorhees	R	1899-1902
Franklin Murphy	R	1902-1905
Edward C. Stokes	R	1905-1908
John Franklin Fort	R	1908-1911
Woodrow Wilson	D	1911-1913
James F. Fielder, Acting	D	1913
Leon R. Taylor, Acting	D	1913-1914
James F. Fielder	D	1914-1917
Walter E. Edge	R	1917-1919
William N. Runyon, Acting	R	1919-1920
Edward I. Edwards	D	1920-1923
George S. Silzer	D	1923-1926
A. Harry Moore	D	1926-1929
Morgan F. Larson	R	1929-1932
A. Harry Moore	D	1932-1935
Harold G. Hoffman	R	1935-1938
A. Harry Moore	D	1938-1941
Charles Edison	D	1941-1944
Walter E. Edge	R	1944-1947
Alfred E. Driscoll	R	1947-1954
Robert B. Meyner	D	1954 ——

Source: New Jersey History Committee, *Outline History of New Jersey* (New Brunswick: Rutgers University Press, 1950), pp. 364-65; N.J. *Manual of the Legislature of New Jersey, 1954* (Trenton: 1954), pp. 19-20. These volumes contain also the names of the governors prior to the English period, 1624-1664, during the proprietary government, 1664-1702, and during the period of royal government, 1703-1776.

[a] New Jersey has had approximately fifty presidents of the Senate or speakers of the Assembly who have served for brief periods as acting governor. Their names are listed in the *Legislative Manual.*

[b] F = Federalist; JR = Jeffersonian Republican; W = Whig; D = Democrat; R = Republican.

SUMMARY OF APPROPRIATIONS

APPROPRIATIONS RECOMMENDED BY THE GOVERNOR FOR THE YEAR
ENDING JUNE 30, 1958 [1]

GENERAL STATE OPERATIONS

Legislative Branch

The Legislature	$ 816,059.00
Law Revision and Legislative Services Commission	130,007.00
Legislative Budget and Finance Director	56,567.00
State Auditor's Department	375,166.00
Miscellaneous Legislative Commissions	131,065.00
Total Legislative Branch	$ 1,508,864.00

Executive Branch

Chief Executive Office	$ 184,900.00
Department of Law and Public Safety	15,948,683.00
Department of the Treasury	7,893,714.00
Department of State	360,070.00
Department of Civil Service	1,035,771.00
Department of Banking and Insurance	1,724,778.00
Department of Agriculture	1,397,946.00
Department of Defense	1,974,776.00
Department of Public Utilities	592,508.00
Department of Health	2,556,382.00
Department of Labor and Industry	4,574,185.00
Department of Conservation and Economic Development	7,161,895.00
Department of Education	22,220,691.00
Department of Highways	19,501,362.00
Department of Institutions and Agencies	56,594,044.00
Miscellaneous Executive Commissions	646,948.00
Total Executive Branch	$144,368,653.00

Judicial Branch

The Judiciary	$ 1,948,847.00

Inter- and Non-Departmental Items

Rents: Office and Building	$ 1,896,411.00
Pensions, Social Security Taxes and Contributions to State Pension System Funds	9,478,999.00
Emergency Fund	150,000.00
Salary Adjustments, Increments, Salary Range Revisions and Other Employee Benefits	4,500,000.00
Total Inter- and Non-Departmental Items	$ 16,025,410.00
Grand Total, General State Operations	$163,851,774.00

SUMMARY OF APPROPRIATIONS (Continued)

STATE AID

Executive Branch

Department of Law and Public Safety	$ 12,500.00
Department of the Treasury	5,458,892.24
Department of Health	200,000.00
Department of Conservation and Economic Development	1,435,000.00
Department of Education	107,655,324.00
Department of Highways	16,889,315.00
Department of Institutions and Agencies	18,425,550.00
Total Executive Branch	$150,076,581.24

Judicial Branch

The Judiciary	$ 759,167.00
Grand Total, State Aid	$150,835,748.24

CAPITAL CONSTRUCTION

Executive Branch

Department of Law and Public Safety	$ 335,000.00
Department of Conservation and Economic Development	135,000.00
Department of Education	2,500,000.00
Department of Highways	23,556,440.00
Department of Institutions and Agencies	1,250,000.00
Grand Total, Capital Construction	$ 27,776,440.00
GRAND TOTAL	$342,463,962.24

[1] *Budget Message of Robert B. Meyner, Governor of New Jersey, for the Fiscal Year Ending June 30, 1958* (Trenton: 1957), pp. 33b-39b.

Selected Bibliography

GENERAL WORKS

Andrews, Charles M., *The Colonial Period of American History, The Settlements III* (New Haven: Yale University Press, 1937).

Baisden, Richard N., *Charter for New Jersey, The New Jersey Constitutional Convention of 1947* (Trenton: N.J. Department of Education, Division of the State Library, Archives and History, 1952).

Baker, Benjamin, *Municipal Charter Revision in New Jersey* (New Brunswick: Rutgers University Press, 1953).

Bard, Erwin Wilkie, *The Port of New York Authority* (New York: Columbia University Press, 1942).

Bebout, John E., *Documents and Readings in New Jersey Government* (Ann Arbor: Edwards Brothers Inc., 1931).

————, *The Making of the New Jersey Constitution, Reprint of Introduction to the Proceedings of the New Jersey State Constitutional Convention of 1844. Together with a New Foreword* (Trenton: MacCrellish and Quigley Co., 1945).

Bird, Frederick L., *A Study of the Port of New York Authority* (New York: Dun and Bradstreet, Inc., 1949).

The Book of the States, 1956-57 (Chicago: The Council of State Governments, 1956).

Boots, Ralph Simpson, *The Direct Primary in New Jersey* (New York: Columbia University, 1917).

Brush, John E., *The Population of New Jersey* (New Brunswick: Rutgers University Press, 1956).

Buck, A. E., *The Reorganization of State Governments in the United States* (New York: Columbia University Press, 1938).

Bureau of Government Research, Rutgers University, *Handbook of New Jersey State Government* (New Brunswick: Rutgers University Press, 1952).

————, *Legislative Apportionment in New Jersey, A Survey of Modern Methods Available* (New Brunswick: Processed, 1952).

————, *Pension Legislation for Public Employees in New Jersey* (New Brunswick: Processed, 1950).

Cadman, John W., Jr., *The Corporation in New Jersey, Business and Politics 1791-1875* (Cambridge: Harvard University Press, 1949).

Carpenter, William Seal, *The Unfinished Business of Civil Service Reform* (Princeton: Princeton University Press, 1952).

Collier, James M., *County Government in New Jersey* (New Brunswick: Rutgers University Press, 1952).

Cunningham, John T., *This Is New Jersey* (New Brunswick: Rutgers University Press, 1953).

————, *Made in New Jersey* (New Brunswick: Rutgers University Press, 1954).

————, *Garden State* (New Brunswick: Rutgers University Press, 1955).

Edge, Walter Evans, *A Jerseyman's Journal* (Princeton: Princeton University Press, 1948).

Erdman, Charles R., Jr., *The New Jersey Constitution of 1776* (Princeton: Princeton University Press, 1929).

Final Report of the Charter Commission of the City of Newark (Newark, 1953).

Fisher, Edgar Jacob, *New Jersey as a Royal Province, 1738 to 1776* (New York: Columbia University, 1911).

France, Robert R., and Lester, Richard A., *Compulsory Arbitration of Utility Disputes in New Jersey and Pennsylvania* (Princeton: Industrial Relations Section, Department of Economics and Social Institutions, Princeton University, 1951).

Friedelbaum, Stanley H., *Municipal Government in New Jersey* (New Brunswick: Rutgers University Press, 1954).

Gray, Walter S., *County Government in Essex, New Jersey, An Outline of Its Origin, Its History and Its Functions Today* (Newark: Essex County Board of Chosen Freeholders, 1953).

Leech, Carl Graydom, *The Constitutional and Legal Basis of Education in New Jersey* (Norwood, Pa.: The Science Press Printing Co., 1932).

Lutz, Harley L., *The Taxation of Railroads in New Jersey* (Princeton: Princeton University Press, 1940).

McCormick, Richard P., *Experiment in Independence; New Jersey in the Critical Period, 1781-1789* (New Brunswick: Rutgers University Press, 1950).

——, *The History of Voting in New Jersey; A Study of the Development of Election Machinery 1664-1911* (New Brunswick: Rutgers University Press, 1953).

McKean, Dayton David, *Pressures on the Legislature of New Jersey* (New York: Columbia University Press, 1938).

New Jersey History Committee, *Outline History of New Jersey* (New Brunswick: Rutgers University Press, 1950).

National Institute of Public Administration, *Report on a Survey of the Organization and Administration of the State Government of New Jersey* (Trenton, 1930).

Newman, Philip Charles, *The Labor Legislation of New Jersey* (Washington: American Council on Public Affairs, 1943).

Our State Legislatures (rev. ed., Chicago: The Council of State Governments, 1948).

Rumney, Jay, and Murphy, Joseph P., *Probation and Social Adjustment* (New Brunswick: Rutgers University Press, 1952).

Sackett, William Edgar, *Modern Battles of Trenton, Being a History of New Jersey's Politics and Legislation from the Year 1868 to the Year 1894* (Trenton: John L. Murphy, Printer, 1895), Vol. I.

——, *Modern Battles of Trenton* (New York: The Neale Publishing Co., 1914), Vol. II.

Schaffter, Dorothy, *State Housing Agencies* (New York: Columbia University Press, 1942).

Silzer, George S., *The Government of a State* (Newark: Soney and Sage, 1933).

Stafford, Paul T., *Government and the Needy, A Study of Public Assistance in New Jersey* (Princeton: Princeton University Press, 1941).

Tanner, Edwin P., *The Province of New Jersey, 1664-1738* (New York: Columbia University, 1908).

Tippetts, Abbett, McCarthy, Stratton, *Survey of New Jersey Water Resources Development*, Legislative Commission on Water Supply, State of New Jersey (New York, 1955).

Waltersdorf, M. C., *Regulation of Public Utilities in New Jersey* (Baltimore: Waverly Press, Inc., 1936).

Weiss, Harry B., *History of the New Jersey State Board of Agriculture, 1872-1916* (Trenton: New Jersey Agricultural Society, 1949).

——, *The New Jersey Department of Agriculture, 1916-1949* (Trenton: New Jersey Agricultural Society, 1950).

DOCUMENTS AND SOURCE MATERIALS

Constitutional

Constitution of the State of New Jersey (Trenton: Department of State, 1947).
N.J. *Constitutional Convention of 1947,* I-V.
New Jersey Writers Project, *Proceedings of the New Jersey State Constitutional Convention of 1844* (Trenton: New Jersey State House Commission, 1942).
Proceedings Before New Jersey Joint Legislative Committee (Trenton: The Committee, 1942).

Executive

Annual Message of the Governor to the Legislature.
Budget Message of the Governor.

Legislative and Statutory

Acts of the Legislature of the State of New Jersey. Annually.
Journal of the Senate of the State of New Jersey. Annually.
Manual of the Legislature of New Jersey. Annually.
Minutes of the Votes and Proceedings of the General Assembly of the State of New Jersey. Annually.
New Jersey Statutes Annotated (cited as N.J.S.A.).   An unofficial compilation and codification of New Jersey statute law in force.
Revised Statutes of New Jersey: 1937 (cited as R.S.).   An official compilation of the public statutes effective December 20, 1937.

Judicial

New Jersey Equity Reports (cited as N.J.Eq.).   Record of cases under court system prior to 1948.
New Jersey Law Reports (cited as N.J.L. under court system prior to 1948).
New Jersey Miscellaneous Reports (cited as N.J.Misc. under court system prior to 1948).
New Jersey Reports (cited as N.J. under existing court system).
New Jersey Superior Court Reports (cited as N.J.Super. under existing court system).

MONOGRAPHS, REPORTS, AND SPECIAL STUDIES

Goldman, Sidney, and Graves, Thomas J., *The Organization and Administration of the New Jersey State Highway Department.*   Prepared for Roger Hinds, Governor's Examiner of the New Jersey State Highway Department (Trenton, 1942).
Lucas, Dorothy F., *Bibliography of New Jersey Official Reports 1925-1945* (Trenton: Archives and History, 1947).
Commission on State Tax Policy, *First Report* (Trenton, 1946).
———, *Second Report* (Trenton, 1947).
———, *Third Report, The Taxation of New Jersey Railroads* (Trenton, 1948).
———, *Fifth Report, Taxation and Public Policy in New Jersey* (Trenton, 1950).
———, *Sixth Report, The General Property Tax in New Jersey; A Century of Inequities* (Trenton, 1953).
———, *Seventh Report, Public School Financing in New Jersey* (Trenton, 1954).
Committee on Civil Liberties, *Civil Liberties in New Jersey, a Report Submitted to the Honorable Alfred E. Driscoll, Governor of New Jersey* (1948).

Constitutional Convention of 1947, I-V.

Department of Conservation and Economic Development, *Development Plan for New Jersey* (Trenton, 1950).

Department of Conservation and Development, *Forest Management in New Jersey*, prepared by E. B. Moore (Trenton, 1939).

Department of Institutions and Agencies, *Hospital and Public Health Resources in New Jersey* (Trenton, 1947).

Law Revision and Bill Drafting Commission, *Ten Years of Continuous Revision of Statutes in New Jersey, a Report on the Work of the New Jersey Law Revision and Bill Drafting Commission, January 9, 1940 to January 9, 1950, by Charles DeF. Besore.*

Local Self-Government in New Jersey: A Proposed Optional Charter Plan, Report of the Commission on Municipal Government (Trenton, 1949).

Mental Deficiency in New Jersey, A Report to Governor Robert B. Meyner and the Members of the Senate and General Assembly by the Commission to Study the Problems and Needs of Mentally Deficient Persons (Trenton, 1954).

Proceedings of the New Jersey State Constitutional Convention of 1844, compiled and edited by the New Jersey Writers Project of the Works Projects Administration with an Introduction by John Bebout. Sponsored by the New Jersey State House Commission, 1942.

Record of Proceedings Before the Joint Committee of the New Jersey Legislature to Ascertain the Sentiment of the People as to Change in the New Jersey Constitution, 1942.

Report of the Commission on Revision of the New Jersey Constitution, May 1942 (Trenton, 1942).

Report of the Commission on Taxation of Intangible Personal Property (Trenton, 1945).

Report of the Commission to Survey Public Education (1928).

Report of the Committee to Examine and Investigate the Prison and Parole Systems of New Jersey to His Excellency Alfred E. Driscoll, Governor of the State of New Jersey (1952).

Report to Governor Robert B. Meyner by the Governor's Committee on Legislation Relating to Public Utility Labor Disputes (Trenton, 1954).

Reports of the Joint Legislative Survey Committee of New Jersey (Trenton, 1925).

Rules Governing the Courts of the State of New Jersey (Newark: Soney and Sage Co., 1953).

State Employment Service, *Directory and Handbook of Occupations and Professions Licensed by New Jersey State Boards and Commissions 1947.*

State Police, *Scientific Laboratory Services of the State Bureau of Identification*, 1946.

SELECTED PERIODICALS

Legislative Index. Published weekly during the session of the Legislature by the State Service Bureau. The series summarizes and traces the development of bills and resolutions currently before the Legislature.

New Jersey Counties. Published monthly by the Association of Chosen Freeholders of New Jersey.

New Jersey Educational Review. Published monthly, except July and August, by the New Jersey Education Association.

New Jersey Law Journal. Published weekly by the New Jersey Law Journal Publishing Company.

New Jersey Municipalities. Published monthly, except July, August, and September, by the New Jersey State League of Municipalities.

New Jersey Session Law Service. Published periodically during the legislative session by Soney and Sage Company. The series provides the text and classification of laws currently enacted and a summary of legislative highlights.

Review of New Jersey Business. Published quarterly by the New Jersey State Department of Conservation and Economic Development and the School of Business Administration of Rutgers, The State University.

Rutgers Law Review. Published during the academic year by the School of Law of Rutgers, The State University.

ANNUAL REPORTS

Annual reports are prepared by the agencies listed below. Departments which prepare an over-all report for the units under their jurisdiction are indicated with an asterisk. Several subdivisions of departments prepare mimeographed reports, the distribution of which is extremely limited. As a consequence, the list below may be incomplete.

Administrative Office of the Courts
Department of Agriculture*
Department of Banking and Insurance
　Bureau of Banking
　Bureau of Insurance
　Bureau of Building and Loan Associations
　Division of the New Jersey Real Estate Commission
Department of Civil Service*
Department of Conservation and Economic Development
　Division of Veterans Services
　Division of Fish and Game
Department of Defense*
Department of Education
　Division of Business (Annual Financial Report)
　Division against Discrimination (Biennial)
　Vocational Division
Department of Health*
　Board of Barber Examiners
Department of Highways
　New Jersey Turnpike Authority
　New Jersey Highway Authority
Department of Institutions and Agencies
　Board of Child Welfare
　Some of the institutions publish annual reports
Department of Labor and Industry*
　Division of Employment Security
　Rehabilitation Commission
　Bureau of Migrant Labor

Department of Law and Public Safety
　Division of State Police
　Division of Motor Vehicles
　Bureau of Traffic Safety
　Division of Weights and Measures
　Board of Registration and Examination in Dentistry
　Board of Medical Examiners
　Board of Pharmacy
　Board of Shorthand Reporting
Department of Public Utilities*
Department of the Treasury
　Division of Taxation
　Division of Local Government
　Local Government Board
　Division of Investment
　Division of the New Jersey Racing Commission
　Police and Firemen's Retirement System of New Jersey
　State Employees' Retirement System of New Jersey

Commissions and Authorities

Beach Erosion Commission
Commission on Interstate Cooperation
Delaware River Joint Toll Bridge Commission
Delaware River Port Authority
Interstate Sanitation Commission
Law Enforcement Council
Palisades Interstate Park Commission
Port of New York Authority
South Jersey Port Commission
Waterfront Commission of New York Harbor

Index

95; organization, 350-54; planning and zoning, 278-79; police, 360; powers, 354-55; public works, 361; revenues, 357; services, 359-62; types of, 349
municipalities, number of, 2n
Museum, State, 217-18
Mutual Aid Compacts, 122

narcotics, 227
National Association of Attorneys General, 389
National Association of Insurance Commissioners, 325
National Association of State Budget Officers, 389
National Association of State Purchasing Officials, 389
National Conference of Commissioners on Uniform State Laws, 378, 389
National Guard, 115-17
National Institute of Public Administration, 105, 114, 144
natural resources, 8
Naval Militia, 117
navigation, 298
Negroes: in migrant labor force, 305; in population, 5
Newark College of Engineering, 214
Newark State Teachers College, 213
New Brunswick, budget of, 358-59
New Jersey Agricultural Experiment Station, 265
New Jersey Commission for Constitutional Convention, 20n
New Jersey Council, 267n
New Jersey County Government, 389
New Jersey Division of Veterans Service Bulletin, 119
New Jersey Education Association, 82
New Jersey Farm Bureau, 33
New Jersey Fish and Game Code, 276
New Jersey Highway Authority, 151, 294
New Jersey Home for Firemen, 238
New Jersey Law Journal, 74
New Jersey Memorial Home, 238
New Jersey Neuropsychiatric Institute, 238
New Jersey Pharmaceutical Association, 342
New Jersey Police Academy, 190
New Jersey Racing Commission, 336
New Jersey Real Estate Commission, 340
New Jersey Reformatory, 241
New Jersey Reformatory for Women, 241
New Jersey School for the Deaf, 199, 211
New Jersey State Board of Agriculture, 257
New Jersey State Board of Childrens Guardians, 253
New Jersey State Board of Mediation, 306-07
New Jersey State Board of Nursing, 340
New Jersey State Board of Optometrists, 340
New Jersey State Board of Public Accountants, 340
New Jersey State Chamber of Commerce, 82
New Jersey State Guard, 117
New Jersey State Housing Authority, 279
New Jersey State League of Municipalities, 31, 390
New Jersey State Museum, 217-18
New Jersey Taxpayers Association, 82
New Jersey Turnpike Authority, 110, 151, 292-94
New Jersey Veterans Employment Plan, 118
New Lisbon State Colony, 248
Nicolls, Richard, 11
North Jersey District Water Supply Commission, 387

North Jersey Training School, 248
nursery inspection, 261
Nursing, Inspection Board of, 344

oath legislation, 209-10
occupational licensing, see licensing
Office of Civilian Defense, 120-21
Office of Milk Industry, 263
old age asisstance, 250-52, 370
Opthalmic Dispensers and Technicians, State Board of, 340
Optional Municipal Charter Law, 352-54
Optometrists, State Board of, 340, 345
Outdoor Advertising Tax, 137

Palisades Interstate Park Commission, 383
Paraplegic Pension Law, 119
pardon, 95
pari-mutuel taxes, 138
Parker, Joel, 18, 70
parks, state, 270-71
parole, 95, 244-45
party organization, 37
Passaic Valley Flood Control Commission, 262n
Passaic Valley Sewerage Commission, 386-87
Paterson State Teachers College, 213
Penn, William, 11
Pennington, William, 14, 16
Performance Rating Appeals Committee, 162
Perth Amboy, early capital, 11
petition, nominating, 43
pharmacy, see Board of
planning, 278-80
pocket veto, 97
police: Consolidated Police and Firemen's Pension Fund, 165; municipal, 360; retirement system, 165
political organization, 37
population, 3-5
Port of New York Authority, 379-82
poultry industry, 260
predator controlmen, 276
Prerogative Court, 172
Presidential elections, 40, 43, 44
President's Commission on Migratory Labor, 306
pre-trial conference, 183
primary, direct, 44
printing, 148
Prison Farm, at Leesburg, 240; at Rahway, 240
prison reform, 242-43
probation, 243
procurement, 147-48
Professional Boards, Division of, 340
property management, 148
property tax, 125-28, 138-39, 357-58, 367
protector, 275
Provincial Congress, 10-13
Public Employees Retirement System, 164
Public Health Council, 222
public health nursing, 230
public schools, see education
Public Utility: Commissioners, Board of, 327; Governor's Committee on Legislation Relating to Disputes, 308
public utility regulation: control of security issues, 330; rate regulation, 330-31; report of governor's committee, 308; safety, 329-30; standards of service, 327-29
public utilities, taxes on, 131-32
Puerto Ricans, in migrant labor force, 305
Purchase and Property, Division of, 147
purchasing, 147-48